Speech and Language Therapy

THE DECISION-MAKING PROCESS WHEN WORKING WITH CHILDREN

EDITED BY

MYRA KERSNER
AND JANNET A. WRIGHT

 David Fulton Publishers

David Fulton Publishers Ltd
The Chiswick Centre, 414 Chiswick High Road, London W4 5TF

www.fultonpublishers.co.uk
www.onestopeducation.co.uk

First published in Great Britain by David Fulton Publishers 2001
Reprinted 2003, 2004, 2005
10 9 8 7 6 5 4

David Fulton Publishers is a division of Granada Learning Limited, part of ITV plc

British Library Cataloguing in Publication Data
A catalogue record for this book is available from the British Library.

ISBN 1 85346 668 9

Typeset by Book Production Services, London
Printed and bound in Great Britain.

Contents

Terminology and Abbreviations

Although this book relates to working with children with communication difficulties in relation to their families and relevant social and educational settings, the processes discussed may apply to working with any client group.

The term 'parent(s)' will be used to mean parent, carer, guardian, significant other – anyone who takes on the care and responsibility for a child. The terms 'treatment', 'therapy' and 'intervention' are used interchangeably throughout the book. The phrase 'learning disabilities' has been taken to imply that there is a cognitive deficit, whereas 'learning difficulties' is used to indicate a specific problem – as in 'specific learning difficulties' (see Chapter 18).

Throughout the book there will be conventions and abbreviations used. Although each is given in full at its first occurrence, they are all listed below for ease of reference.

AAC	alternative and augmentative communication
ABG	alveolar bone grafting
ADD	attention deficit disorder
ADHD	attention deficit hyperactivity disorder
ASLP	acquired speech and language problems
BCLP	bilateral cleft lip and palate
ASD	autistic spectrum disorders
BBCS	Bracken Basic Concept Scale
BPVS	British Picture Vocabulary Scale
BSL	British Sign Language
CAMHS	child and adolescent mental-health service
CC	community clinic
CCTV	closed-circuit television
CDC	child development centre
CELF	Clinical Evaluation of Language Fundamentals
CHIT	Children's Head Injury Trust
CLAPA	Cleft Lip and Palate Association

CPLOL	Prevention Commission of the Standing Liaison Committee of Speech and Language Therapists (in the European Union)
CSAG	Clinical Standards Advisory Group
DC	Demand Capacity (stammering model)
DES	Department of Education and Science
DfEE	Department for Education and Employment
DoH	Department of Health
EBD	emotional and behavioural disorders
EEG	electro-encephalogram
ENT	ear, nose and throat
FEES	fibre-optic endoscopic evaluation of swallowing
FOLKS	Friends of Landau–Kleffner Syndrome
GP	General Practitioner
IEP	individual education plans (for setting targets for children in schools)
IMLI	Interactive Model of Language Impairment
INSET	in-service training
IPA	International Phonetic Alphabet
IPR	individual performance review
IQ	Intelligence Quotient
LEA	Local Education Authority
LKS	Landau–Kleffner syndrome
LSA	learning support assistant
MAMG	multi-agency management group
NHS	National Health Service
NQT	newly qualified therapist
PCIT	parent–child interactive therapy
PCT	primary care team
PEG	percutaneous endoscopic gastrostomy
PLI	pragmatic language impairment
POSP	Paediatric Oral Skills Package
QCA	Qualifications and Curriculum Authority
RCSLT	The Royal College of Speech and Language Therapists – the professional body
RDLS	Reynell Developmental Language Scales
REEL	Receptive-Expressive Emergent Language
SLD	severe learning disabilities
SMCP	submucous cleft palate
STAP	South Tyneside Assessment of Phonology
Statement	Statement of special educational need
SENCO	Special educational needs coordinator
SLI	specific language impairment

SSLI	specific speech and language impairment
TACL	Test for Auditory Comprehension of Language
TOM	therapy outcome measure
TROG	Test for the Reception of Grammar
UCLP	unilateral cleft lip and palate
VOCA	voice output communication aid
VPD	velopharyngeal dysfunction
WHO	World Health Organisation

List of Figures

List of Tables

Contributors

Carolyn Anderson is a lecturer in the Department of Speech and Language Therapy, University of Strathclyde, Glasgow. She is a speech and language therapist and RCSLT advisor in feeding difficulties in children. She is the co-editor of *Teaching Children with Pragmatic Difficulties of Communication*.

Heather Anderson is the Head of the Children's Speech and Language Therapy Service in Hounslow and Spelthorne Community and Mental Health NHS Trust. She is a clinical supervisor for speech and language therapy students.

Sarah Beazley teaches in the field of deafness. She was a university lecturer; a Speech Therapy Advisor at the RNID, and tutor for the Advanced Clinical Studies course in Speech and Language Therapy with Deaf People. She is co-author of *Deaf Children, Their Families and Professionals: Dismantling Barriers*.

Anne Harding-Bell is a speech and language therapist specialising in cleft palate speech. She works at Addenbrookes Hospital, Cambridge, Lister East and North Herts Hospital as well as at DeMontfort University, Leicester.

Monica Bray is a Senior Lecturer in Speech and Language Pathology and Therapy at Leeds Metropolitan University. Her specialist areas include dysfluency, learning disabilities, and psychological issues in speech and language therapy. She is the co-author of *Speech and Language Clinical Process and Practice*.

Mike Clarke is a speech and language therapist working at the Ace Centre Advisory Trust in Oxford. He is conducting research related to the use of augmentative and alternative communication systems.

Keena Cummins is a clinical tutor at City University, London. She worked as a speech and language therapist in community clinics, mainstream schools, special schools, and nurseries. As a specialist therapist in parent–child interaction, she was manager of the Early Years service in Camden and Islington, London.

Ruth Frost is a speech and language therapist and freelance consultant specialising in working with deaf children. She was the co-ordinator for the Advanced Clinical Studies course in Speech and Language Therapy with Deaf People, City University, London. She worked on the Cochlear Implant Research Programme, University College Hospital, London.

Marie Gascoigne is a lecturer at City University, London, responsible for the development of the Centre for Clinical Education and Therapy. She is a speech and language therapist with specialist experience in working with children with specific language impairment in language units and mainstream schools.

Kim Grundy is a Principal Lecturer in Speech and Language Therapy in the Division of Psychology and Speech and Language Therapy at De Montfort University, Leicester. She is a speech and language therapist and is the editor of *Linguistics in Clinical Practice*.

Judy Halden is a speech and language therapist and teacher working with deaf children. She is a clinical tutor/lecturer at City University, London. She was a Speech Therapy Advisor at the RNID. She is an assessor and consultant for specialist services for deaf people in LEAs and health trusts.

Sarah Hulme is Principal Speech and Language Therapist for the Early Years service in Camden and Islington, London. She specialises in parent–child interaction therapy, and has extensive experience of developing and delivering training on this approach to speech and language therapy students.

Nicola Jolleff is the Lead Clinician for the Neurodisability Service. She is a senior specialist speech and language therapist at Great Ormond Street Hospital for Children NHS Trust, London.

Myra Kersner is a Senior Lecturer at University College London responsible for clinical and professional development on the Masters Programme. She is a speech and language therapist and dramatherapist. She has co-written several publications with Jannet Wright, including *How To Manage Communication Problems in Young Children*.

Janet Lees is an Honorary Research Fellow at the Institute of Child Health, London, and honorary lecturer at the University of Sheffield. She is an advisor to Friends of Landau–Kleffner Syndrome and a specialist advisor to RCSLT. She is the author of *Children with Acquired Aphasias*.

Carolyn Letts is a lecturer at the University of Newcastle. Her research and teaching interests are in bilingualism, child language disorder, and pragmatic impairment. She has also worked at a speech and language therapist in Wales. She is the co-author of *Children's Pragmatic Communication Difficulties*.

Ann Parker is a Senior Lecturer at University College London responsible for clinical and professional development. She has developed specialist courses for supervising clinicians which she has run nationally and internationally. As a speech and language therapist, she specialised in working with deaf people. She is the author of *PETAL*.

Aileen Patterson is a Senior Lecturer at the University of Ulster. She is the Coordinator: Academic Affairs (Communication) and the course director for the BSc (Hons) in Speech and Language Therapy. She has a Certificate in Education and is a speech and language therapist. She was a Councillor for Education for RCSLT.

Jill Popple is a speech and language therapist based at the Rowan School, Sheffield, which is a school for children with severe communication disorders. She has a special interest in working with children with specific speech and/or language impairments and collaborative working approaches between therapists and teachers.

Gaye Powell is a Senior Lecturer in the College of St Mark and St John, Plymouth. She is a speech and language therapist and was a manager of speech and language therapy services for learning disability in Bristol and Plymouth. Her research interests include children and adults with learning disabilities.

Katie Price is a Senior Specialist Speech and Language Therapist (Neurodisability) at Great Ormond Street Hospital for Children NHS Trust, London. She specialises in the area of augmentative and alternative communication systems.

Oonagh Reilly is a Senior Lecturer at the University of Central England in Birmingham and is director of the BSc (Hons) course in Speech and Language Therapy. She is a speech and language therapist and has an honorary contract with North Birmingham Community Trust Speech and Language Therapy Services.

Sue Roulstone is Clinical Research Director at the Speech and Language Therapy Research Unit, Frenchay Hospital, North Bristol NHS Trust, Bristol Institute of Child Health, University of Bristol.

Debbie Sell is Senior Specialist Speech and Language Therapist and Head of Department at Great Ormond Street Hospital for Children, NHS Trust, London. She is also an Honorary Senior Lecturer at The Institute of Child Health, London and De Montfort University, Leicester. She is co-editor of *Management of Cleft Lip and Palate*.

Jane Shields developed the National Autistic Society's EarlyBird Programme: an autism-specific early-intervention parent programme. As a speech and language therapist, she specialised in developmental language disorder before pursuing research that led to full-time involvement with autistic spectrum disorder.

Sarah Simpson is a clinical tutor at University College London. She is a speech and language therapist specialising in specific learning difficulties. She is also the course tutor for the OCR Certificate for those working with people with specific learning difficulties.

Wendy Wellington is a speech and language therapist based at the Rowan School, Sheffield, which is a school for children with severe communication disorders. She has a special interest in working with children with specific speech and/or language impairments and collaborative working approaches between therapists and teachers.

Alison Wintgens is a speech and language therapist in the Child and Adolescent Mental Health Service, St George's Hospital, London. She specialises in children who have both emotional/behavioural disorders and disorders of communication. She was a founder member and chair of the RCSLT's Special Interest Group in Emotional and Behavioural Disorders.

Janet Wood is a clinical tutor and Senior Research Fellow at University College London. As a speech and language therapist, she specialised in working with children with specific language difficulties in mainstream schools and was responsible for the speech and language therapy service to mainstream schools in a London borough.

Jannet Wright is a Senior Lecturer at University College London, and is responsible for admissions. She is the co-editor of the journal, *Child Language Teaching and Therapy*. She has co-written several publications with Myra Kersner, including *Supporting Children with Communication Problems: Sharing the Load*.

Louise Wright is a Senior Lecturer at Manchester Metropolitan University. She is a speech and language therapist specialising in stammering. She is an RCSLT regional specialist advisor and also Speech and Language Therapy Advisor to the British Stammering Association. She is co-author of the *Stuttering Self-rating Profile (WASSP)*.

Preface

This book will be relevant to speech and language therapy students and potential students, and also to therapists returning to the profession. Furthermore, it should be of interest to newly qualified therapists, specialist teachers, SENCOs and specialist teachers in training.

The focus of the book is on the decision-making process that underpins the management of children by speech and language therapists. The contributors all have expert knowledge in the subject on which they are writing. They have been drawn from speech and language therapy education establishments, specialist centres and specialist speech and language therapy services in the UK. Each author focuses on the decision-making process in relation to her or his given topic. The authors do not address specific aspects of intervention but refer the reader to relevant texts where appropriate.

The book is divided into four Parts. Each Part has a one-page introduction outlining the main focus of the chapters within the Part. Learning outcomes are given at the beginning of each chapter so that readers will know what to expect. As this book will not necessarily be read in chronological order, wherever relevant there is cross-referencing between the chapters to facilitate the reader in making links.

Chapter 1 provides a framework for the decision-making process. The skills required in order to make these decisions are discussed in Chapter 2, which also provides information about the knowledge and skills required to be a speech and language therapist and the learning process of the developing professional. Chapter 3 relates to job applications and newly qualified therapists in their first job.

How the decision-making process varies within different settings in which speech and language therapists may be employed is covered in Chapters 4–8. This includes health and education settings.

Chapters 9–11 are concerned with different types of decisions that may confront therapists when working with others. The training role of speech and language therapists in relation to working with professionals and parents is highlighted in Chapters 9 and 10. Indeed, speech and language therapists do not work in isolation and several chapters emphasise the importance of collaborating with others.

Chapters 12–24 include a wealth of information about a wide range of communication problems encountered in children, and some of the ways in which the decision-making process is made relevant to these specific client groups is considered.

Myra Kersner and Jannet A. Wright
August 2001

PART I

Learning how to be a professional

In this Part of the book, the decision-making process in the assessment and management of speech and language therapy is outlined and the skills that are required in order to work in professional practice are discussed.

It is recommend that Chapters 1 and 2 are read together. The reader is guided through the issues relating to professional development, the first job and the learning process of the developing speech and language therapist. In Chapter 3, a speech and language therapy manager highlights some important areas of consideration when applying for a first job.

CHAPTER 1

The decision-making process in speech and language therapy

Myra Kersner

Learning outcomes

By the end of this chapter, the reader should:

- be aware of the speech and language therapy decision-making process when working with children;
- be aware of the speech and language therapy process, from referral to review and discharge;
- be aware of the choices available and how speech and language therapists make decisions in their work.

Introduction

In this chapter the decision-making process in speech and language therapy will be outlined. When children are referred for speech and language therapy, the management process begins and therapists need to make decisions about how to proceed. Additional decisions will then be made at appropriate points throughout the process. Initial decisions will relate to the choice of assessment procedures; then, if required, decisions will follow about the choice of therapy approach. Later, options for review and ultimate discharge will have to be considered.

There are some decisions that need to be made irrespective of the specific problem. See the flowchart in Figure 1.1, where, despite the decisions shown in that figure appearing to be in linear order, the decision-making process is in fact a cyclical – or spiral – process. (See also Figure 2.1 in Chapter 2.) This means that the order in which the decisions need to be made is not always fixed. Some decisions in the chart may be bypassed; some may be made in a different sequence; others may need to be made simultaneously.

Specific decisions will need to be made in relation to specific disorders (see Chapters 12–24) or because of the nature of the setting in which the child is seen (see Chapters 4–8).

There are different ways in which the decision-making process may be represented – see, for example, Bray *et al.* 1999; Gerard and Carson 1990; Whitehurst and Fischel 1994; Yoder and Kent 1988; and Chapter 6. Figure 1.1 nevertheless offers a framework – one way in which the process may be considered. Within this chapter there will be a discussion of the types of decisions that need to be made within this framework, the choices available, and the ways in which speech and language therapists approach the process as a whole.

The hypothesis-testing approach

Normally, speech and language therapists begin the decision-making process by forming working hypotheses about children's difficulties. They then gather further information through their own observations and assessments and through the children's parents as well as through other professionals. They interpret the collated data in relation to their knowledge of accepted 'normal' patterns of development and begin therapy, often while continuing their investigation. This is discussed more fully in Chapter 2.

A process comprises a series of actions that, by definition, occur over time. Processes are organic, so that each aspect of a process affects, and is affected by, other aspects. Within a process there is a fluidity of movement, sometimes back and forth, until an agreed end point – and hopefully a desired outcome – is eventually achieved.

Thus, in any decision-making process in speech and language therapy each decision made will affect, and be affected by, other decisions as well as being influenced by the specific setting, the individual child, and the context. The questions that need to be asked and the decisions that need to be made within the framework shown in Figure 1.1 are outlined below.

The time period

There is no intrinsically specified length of time in which individual decisions have to be made regarding speech and language therapy; these are normally governed by the context and the setting. In some instances, all the assessment, case-history taking and decision-making regarding future management may occur at the initial meeting. In a Child Development Centre, for example, the focus may be on multidisciplinary assessment, so that the children are only seen once, or for a limited period, before they are referred on to other centres for therapy. In other settings, such as when working as part of a mainstream school team, information may be gathered over a longer period of time and assessment–therapy–reassessment may be part of an ongoing diagnostic therapy process. (See Chapter 2 for a discussion of diagnostic therapy).

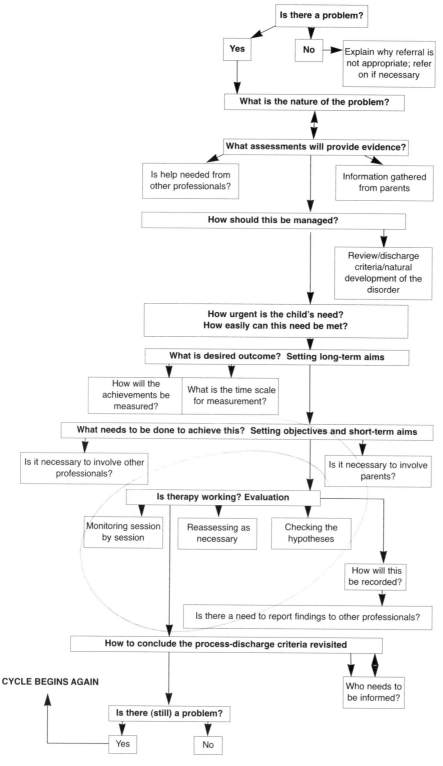

Figure 1.1 The decision-making process

The length of time required for improvement or change to occur in children with communication problems may vary greatly and, although some children achieve their goals within a specified period, others may require help and support over a more protracted time. In some settings, where intervention is indicated following assessment, there may be a fixed length of time set for a block of therapy. The decision will then need to be made about the number of therapy blocks required.

A child is referred

When a child is referred to a therapist for possible treatment, a large number of significant issues have to be weighed up in the process, as set out below.

Is there a problem? (*Decision: Yes/No*)

The management of a child by a speech and language therapist begins on receipt of the referral. The therapist forms an initial working hypothesis about whether or not a problem exists, what might be the nature of the problem and what to do about it.

For instance, a therapist might receive a referral letter about Mary, aged 3 years 2 months, who is described as having 'unintelligible speech'. From the time of receiving this referral, the therapist draws on professional knowledge to help identify the nature of the problem and possible contributing factors, and to establish whether the problem outlined on the referral note is one that may be dealt with appropriately by a speech and language therapist.

The first question to be asked is whether or not the problem actually exists. This may sound like an unnecessary question, but there are three reasons why it is important for it to be asked:

- a child may sometimes be referred by a concerned teacher, or a conscientious health visitor, although the parents may not consider that there is a problem;
- teachers or medical personnel may not agree;
- the child might once have had a problem, but might have made spontaneous improvement in the period between referral and assessment so that the problem no longer exists.

If observation and investigation indicate that speech and language therapy referral is inappropriate, it will be important to explain to the referrer that, whatever the *perceived* difficulty, it is not one that the therapist is able to address.

Sometimes it may not be easy to discern whether or not a problem exists. For example, at initial interview some children may be unwilling to speak. Children often perform differently when faced with an unknown adult than when interacting with a group of their peers. Some children have high-level language difficulties, which might not be apparent on first meeting. Or a child who has been referred because of a stammering difficulty may speak fluently when addressing the therapist.

In order to make the decision about whether a problem exists, as in the example case of Mary, supporting evidence must be gathered, for instance from focused observations of her play and interactions. These observations can then be compared with the norms for her age and developmental stage. Preliminary questions will be asked of her parents and additional information gathered from appropriate sources, such as her nursery teacher, as well as from any previous notes.

It may be that the decision is 'no, this is not a problem for the speech and language therapist'. Then it needs to be decided whether the problem described on the referral note may be more appropriately dealt with by someone else. For example, where a child is developing slowly in all areas, or a child has a literacy problem that would be better dealt with by colleagues in education, it may be preferable to refer the child back to the original referent; or on to another specialist, with an appropriate report.

If the decision is 'yes, a speech and language therapy problem exists', as is likely with Mary, then working hypotheses need to be developed and tested.

What is the nature of the problem? *(Decision/question: What are the working hypotheses?)*

In order to develop the working hypothesis to understand the nature of the problem, it will be necessary to gather a body of more detailed information. This will include recording and transcribing a detailed speech sample and/or a language sample and using appropriate assessment procedures (Lees and Urwin 1997). By using both formal and informal assessments and by asking appropriately targeted questions of the parents and other professionals such as teachers, details can be established about the child's communication in a variety of contexts and settings. As pieces of the puzzle are gathered, so new hypotheses will be formed and tested. Each will be accepted or rejected, until an accurate holistic picture of the child is achieved that indicates the most appropriate approach to therapy.

What assessments will provide appropriate evidence to support or refute the hypotheses? *(Decision/question: What are the criteria for choosing or rejecting assessments? What are the choices available?)*

It is not appropriate to subject a child routinely to a battery of tests without a clear rationale. For example, Mary is only 3 years and 2 months old and may well be upset by the use of too many formal tests. It is, therefore, important to decide which tests might provide the most detailed evidence to help support or refute the working hypotheses. Of course the specific tests chosen will vary greatly according to the apparent nature of the problem, and details of some assessments are referred to in relation to specific areas of difficulty in Chapters 12–24. However, when choosing any formal assessment it is important to consider the following aspects (Lees and Urwin 1997):

- It must be age appropriate.
- It should test what it purports to assess.
- It must be appropriate for the child socially and culturally.
- It must have been standardised on appropriate norms.
- The child must have adequate attention skills to be able to concentrate for the period of time required for testing.

Is help needed from other professionals to complement/aid assessment? (Decision/question: Yes/no? If yes, which professional?)

Speech and language therapists work alongside many different professionals – such as audiologists, psychologists and different medical specialists – all of whom may be involved in aspects of assessment of children with communication problems. There are many instances when additional input from professionals will help the therapist to confirm or refute a working hypothesis about the child's problems.

For example, it is always important for an audiologist to establish whether there are any hearing difficulties or to investigate whether there have been intermittent problems at a time that is critical to speech and language acquisition (Moorey and Mahon 1996). This would be particularly pertinent in the case of Mary. In some instances, the intervention of an educational psychologist may be helpful with regard to establishing cognitive functioning levels, particularly with children of school age or who are about to enter the school system. When working with children with a cleft palate, a physical disability, or children with severe learning disabilities, additional specialist input from members of a multidisciplinary team may be essential for a more accurate diagnosis of the problem in relation to speech and language therapy. (This is discussed in more detail in the relevant Chapters 12–24.)

How should the intervention with the child be managed? (Decision/question: What is the frequency of the intervention and where will it take place?)

The decision made at this point involves forming a contract with the parents in relation to the child's need for speech and language therapy. Parents should be informed about the therapist's intentions, particularly as to whether this involves further assessment, a therapy programme, or whether the child will be put 'on review' and be called back at a later date to check whether there has been any spontaneous improvement. The parents will also need to know where any therapy will take place – such as in the nursery, the school or the health centre – and how long each session is likely to last. This latter will be based on a variety of factors including the child's attention span and ability to concentrate, and the child's behaviour, as well as the amount of time the therapist is able to allocate to individual clients.

In order to make appropriate decisions, the therapist needs to have some understanding of the natural development of the problem. For example, when making decisions about the management of Mary (described above) therapy will continue over a longer period if it is found that she has a significant hearing loss than if she had no hearing loss.

Where a referral has been made by a teacher, and the parents have given their permission for the child to be seen initially in school, it is important that there is a follow-up discussion with the parents about how the therapist will proceed. Indeed, therapy cannot continue without agreement from the parents. Where face-to-face meetings are not possible, communication should be in writing or by telephone.

There are several options that are available at this stage regarding the management of any child:

- A 'wait and see' policy may be adopted. It may be agreed that the parents will make the next contact if they are still concerned. Or, it may be that the therapist will automatically send a review appointment in three or six months time. The reason for this approach is that the assessment results indicate that the child is about to make a considerable amount of spontaneous progress. Whether this has occurred or not would be checked out when the child attends for the review appointment.
- The therapist may wish to offer a period of therapy. This may be, for example, once a week for a period of six weeks, or it may be daily attendance at a language group for a set period of time. Or, if the child is attending a mainstream school, with the parents' permission an learning support assistant (LSA) may work with the child for a set period (say a term). If the child receives therapy in school, those involved will need to establish among themselves whether the child will be withdrawn from the classroom or seen in that setting, and whether the therapy will be individual or in a group. The therapist will need to decide about whether to use a published language programme, to put together a structured and pre-planned (but individual and non-published) language programme, or to devise session by session an individual programme.
- If a child has complex difficulties, further assessment may be required for a complete diagnosis to be made. A period of diagnostic therapy may be decided upon.

In order to make the management decisions outlined above, it is important to prioritise the needs of the child and the therapist's overall workload.

How urgent is the child's need? How easily can this need be met? (Decision/question: What priority should be given to the case?)

There are four aspects of prioritisation that in practice will affect this decision: one relates to the child; one relates to the therapist; one relates to local policies, professional standards and guidelines; and a fourth aspect involves consideration of no intervention being offered.

With regard to the child, it is important to establish the nature of the child's need in relation to his or her environment and to investigate the extent to which the problem is affecting the child's everyday functioning, both socially and educationally. Not only must the actual severity of the problem be considered but also the seeming severity in relation to the child's age.

In another case example, Matthew is 8 years old and has expressive language difficulties that are interfering with his progress in school, which he often refuses to attend. Ian is 3 years old and he also has expressive language difficulties. Ian has just started to attend a nursery and his nursery teacher is interested in working with him on his speech and language. If there was a need to prioritise between these two children, it might be more urgent to see Matthew first. It might be important to work directly with him to enable him to function more effectively in school. The therapist could work indirectly with Ian by asking the nursery teacher to work with him. The therapist would then review Ian's situation at a later date.

Prioritisation with regard to the therapist means that the size and nature of the caseload has to be taken into account, as well as the facilities available within an individual clinical setting to deal with the specific problem. Each child would need to be considered in relation to the others on the waiting list.

In relation to professional standards and local policies, all therapists need to be familiar with recommended guidelines and procedures regarding prioritisation of specific communication problems (RCSLT 1996). Some local authorities also specify the ages between which children may be seen.

While planning intervention, additional decisions need to be made.

What is the desired outcome? (Decision/question: What should have been achieved by the time the child is ready to be discharged?)

For each child the long-term aim – that is, the desired outcome at the point of discharge – has to be set realistically in relation to the specific problem. Thus, even at the start of an intervention phase, therapists need to consider the criteria for discharge. For example, with one child it may be appropriate for the long-term aim to be the achievement of speech and language that is age-appropriate and on a par with peers. For another child who has, for example, a global delay as well as physical disabilities, the long-term aim may be to reach maximum potential with regard to functional communication. (For further discussion of aims and objectives, see Chapter 2).

What needs to be done to achieve this outcome? (Decision/question: What is the approach required in order to help the child reach the desired outcome?)

In order to reach the desired outcome, therapists need to identify the interim stages of the therapy. This may be done by setting short-term aims to be achieved within a specific time period – for example, a school term or a six-week therapy block. It is also important to establish how long each session will last and to write specific objectives for each session.

There are several approaches to intervention that may be considered:

- The therapist may wish to work directly with the child, either on an individual basis or in a group situation (see Chapter 4). For example, a child with a specific speech and language difficulty may benefit from an intensive therapy programme of direct intervention. As stated above, a decision needs to be made about where the therapy will take place.
- The therapist may choose to work indirectly with children's problems by training someone else, such as a parent, teacher or care assistant, to work with the child. There are some parent–child interaction programmes, for example, that specialise in helping parents to work with their children (see Chapter 5).
- There are instances where it may be necessary to recommend a change in a child's environment in order for the outcomes to be achieved. For example, improvement may be achieved if a class teacher supports verbal instructions with gestures or British Sign Language (BSL) or Makaton signs.
- It may be necessary to involve other professionals. For example, specialist medical or orthodontic help and advice may be needed with a child with oro-facial abnormalities; or a psychologist may be able to offer help regarding children with behavioural problems.

Is the therapy working? (Decision/question: How is the work to be monitored and evaluated?)

Therapists carrying out intervention with children need to monitor their work at different levels, and reassessment in some form is a part of ongoing therapy. Of course, progress may occur as a result of natural development over a period of time; or, if there has been some illness or trauma involved, there may be some spontaneous recovery.

During therapy sessions, therapists constantly evaluate whether the tasks are appropriate for the child involved in terms of level of difficulty and interest; the child's motivation and attention, and whether the tasks are enabling the child to make progress. The therapist needs to be flexible so that adjustments to the activities can then be made in response to feedback while the session is in progress. (See Chapter 2 for evaluation.)

At the end of each session it is necessary to monitor and review whether the objectives for that session have been achieved – that is, to evaluate the effectiveness of the therapy. In order to provide evidence of what has been achieved, it will be necessary to keep records of progress.

When all of a block of sessions have been completed, the therapist needs to evaluate the child's progress so as to decide whether another period of therapy is required. This evaluation will take the form of re-testing, although with standardised tests there is usually a specified period that must elapse before the test can be re-administered.

How to conclude the process (Decision/question: whether to discharge, review, or continue therapy?)

When the originally negotiated contract has expired, the therapist needs to make further decisions regarding future management. The three major options available are:

- To discharge the child if the long term aims have been achieved. In this case it must be decided whether any other professionals need to be informed about the child's discharge. For example, it may be important for a report to be sent to the child's head teacher at school advising that therapy is complete, or for a report to be sent to the referring agent.
- To review the child's progress within a specified period if it is felt that a plateau has been reached. Further improvement may occur spontaneously, or it may be that a break is needed before therapy can be resumed in order to allow the child to consolidate newly acquired skills. The child's progress can then be reviewed at a later date.
- To continue with therapy if there is still a problem. If therapy is to be continued, the cycle of decisions begins again.

Summary

This chapter has outlined a framework within which decisions need to be made from the point of referral to discharge. At each decision point, examples have been given of issues that need to be considered. This framework provides a structure that can be applied to clinical practice and demonstrates the way in which speech and language therapists approach their work with children with communication problems.

CHAPTER 2

Developing as a speech and language therapist

Ann Parker and Myra Kersner

Learning outcomes

By the end of this chapter, the reader should be able to:

- recognise two different learning models relevant to speech and language therapy;
- understand the concept of working hypotheses in relation to the decision-making process;
- understand the speech and language therapist's role in facilitating change;
- be aware of the key skills that need to be developed in a therapist in order to be effective in the role;
- understand the relevance and importance of feedback in the learning process.

Introduction

This chapter is about the nature of the skills required to make the decisions described in Chapter 1; about hypothesis-testing investigation and the process of change; and about speech and language therapists' professional development. The importance of feedback for therapists and clients will also be discussed.

The learning process

The practice of speech and language therapy involves the use of skills and overt behaviours – relatively complex actions that need to be learned and developed throughout the therapist's working life. The most obvious aspect of the work involves action. A less obvious aspect involves the covert activities of understanding, supporting knowledge, attitudes, and how therapists think about their work. Mostly, overt and covert activities function simultaneously and often at great speed: the 'hot action' of real practice (Eraut 1994). It is important to understand the relationship between the two in the lifelong professional learning process of a therapist.

Theory and practice

The theory underpinning the practice of speech and language therapy is drawn from several disciplines, including psychology, linguistics and anatomy (Crystal and Varley 1998), as well as from working experience (Eastwood and Whitehouse 1993).

Experience does not necessarily derive only from practical work itself; it may come from course-based teaching and learning. Activities involving covert behaviours in everyday practice, such as thinking about decisions, may need to be developed through rehearsal in more overt ways, such as through presentation, or discussion with peers and supervisors.

The learning cycle

The process of professional learning has sometimes been depicted as a 'learning cycle' (Kolb 1984; see Figure 2.1), a concept that emphasises the value of input from different types of learning in relation to the 'real work' of a practising therapist. Learning can begin with any activity, so that neither 'theory' nor 'practice' are necessarily the first point in the process. Spirals of practice, reflection, theory and rehearsal then provide a developmental perspective for lifelong professional learning.

The concept of a lifelong learning cycle, or spiral, offers a simple representation of a complex process, which may be seen as reflecting the structure of the practice of speech and language therapy, where it is just as important for therapists to reflect on actions as they progress and are completed, as it is to plan the process beforehand. (See Schon 1987; Eraut 1994).

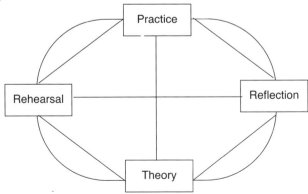

Figure 2.1 A professional learning circle (modified from Kolb 1984)

The Linear Technocratic Model

Some approaches to learning involve a linear structure, with a 'front loading' of theory (Eraut 1994). Sometimes, theory must precede practice; for example, it is necessary to understand the implications of a test's scoring system to explain to parents the significance of a child's scores. However, in the 'technocratic' model of professional learning (Bines and Watson 1992), there is an unchallenged assumption that theory must always be learned prior to practical application of that theory.

On speech and language therapy courses, students may experience a considerable amount of theoretical learning before starting clinical placements. The first placements are sometimes 'observation placements', in which students mainly watch the practice of the supervisor, beginning closely supervised clinical practice only towards the end of the course (see Figure 2.2).

Figure 2.2 A linear and technocratic model of professional learning

Advantages and disadvantages of the two approaches

There are many reasons why a linear structure may seem to be the most appropriate way for therapists to learn their skills. For example, it is often considered important to learn about 'normal' development before considering delayed or disordered development. However, in clinical practice, if the placement is the final stage of the process, this may tend to encourage dependency in students and the passive adoption of received routines.

Using a learning-cycle approach, action may be the first step – the process beginning with experience, which mirrors the work that is the ultimate goal, and observations perhaps occurring later when the learners have experience of practice on which to structure their observations. Through active involvement in the early stages of students' professional development, this may provide more opportunities for them to develop problem-solving skills, and the creativity and innovation that will be a necessary part of their professional practice.

The expectation of the development of theoretical understanding before practice also implies that speech and language therapy is solely concerned with 'correct' practice, or 'getting it right first time' (Collard 1993). Correct practice is sometimes a feature of the speech and language therapy decision-making process – as, for example, when completing the appropriate sections of a child's Statement. However, in many clinical situations, therapists often need to choose from a range of alternatives, to test hypotheses, or to change their approach, having recognised that a different solution might be more helpful than the one tried originally.

It may be difficult to develop confident, creative problem-solving skills and make decisions if there is a primary focus on the avoidance of error. Rather than constantly aiming for correctness, the concept of the 'aeroplane model' (adopted by Parker and Kersner 1998, after Emery 1978 and Jeffers 1987) uses the analogy of the constant adjustments to changing circumstances that are needed for successful aerial navigation – see Figure 2.3. Such adjustments are required in the professional learning process and in the practice of speech and language therapy, for neither need be error-free but rather should be seen as a process in which change is incorporated and managed. Within such a concept of practice and learning, every change of direction is prompted by an awareness of the need for change, and this is enabled by constant self-monitoring and the professional use of feedback.

Figure 2.3 The 'aeroplane model' (Parker and Kersner 1998)

Feedback needs to be received at a stage in the learning process – or in the therapy process – when there is still time to make appropriate adjustments (see the discussion below).

Using working hypotheses

'Working hypotheses' are used as a basis for understanding a child's speech and language development, and for making decisions about what should be done. Hypothesis-based investigation begins at referral, and means that the therapist is constantly forming and revising possible explanations for what is observed in a child's behaviour, and predicting and checking the outcomes of related decisions about intervention (see Bray *et al.* 1999). Initial working hypotheses are often related to the results of initial assessment of the child's communication skills and relevant factors in the communicative environment. Working hypotheses are always tentative and involve testing of the evidence for alternative interpretations.

A case example

A therapist received a referral about Hilary who is 3 years and 6 months old and 'not talking yet'. Clearly, there may be many possible initial working hypotheses. This includes the two extreme possibilities that Hilary has severely delayed language development in all modes; or that language and speech development are normal, and the referral is based on inaccurate observation.

If the referral is accurate, there still may be several explanations for the observed behaviour:

- a hearing loss may have affected Hilary's language acquisition;
- there may be a specific language difficulty;
- there may be a delay in one or more aspects of language or speech production.

The therapist's awareness of the range of possibilities will directly affect the next decision so that, for example, observations and assessment of Hilary's language will be planned and structured to find evidence to support or refute the various hypotheses. While the range of hypotheses needs to be tested, all possible sources of evidence need to be explored.

At this stage, therefore, a knowledge of the range of normal development will be an important component in the process of deciding the next stage of action, which will involve observation and information-gathering. Interpretation of the evidence will then form the basis for an initial decision about Hilary's development of language and communication. Since subsequent decisions will be concerned with the possible need for intervention, input from parents and professionals will be important at this stage.

The sequence of events in the early stages of contact with a child who has been referred to the speech and language therapist may involve:

- the formation of an initial set of hypotheses;
- structuring initial observations and assessments;
- gathering other relevant information;
- interpreting the information to develop more focused and specific hypotheses;
- testing these hypotheses and discussing further as the decision about the need for intervention is reached.

At this and every stage in the process, the therapist needs to keep an open mind so that a range of possible explanations may be considered. It is important that a therapist does not form only one hypothesis, then looks only for confirming evidence. The point of this process is to form *alternative* hypotheses and consider both confirming and refuting evidence for each. For example, when a child like Hilary is referred, one of the initial responsibilities for the therapist is to find out whether or not she has developed speech and language appropriate for her age. It would not be appropriate to assume that she has developmental language problems and then proceed to seek evidence to support this.

A crucial distinction must be made within this process between observation of behaviour and any interpretation of the observations. In attempting to test hypotheses about children's development, observations of behaviour need to describe what actually happens, and this needs to be kept distinct from interpretation or explanation of the meaning of what has been observed. This is because the behaviour itself is a matter of fact.

A case example

Tom, whose language is being assessed, is observed to produce only one- and two-word utterances. Descriptions of this behaviour when observed by two or more speech and language therapists would be expected to concur. However, there may be many interpretations of this observation.

- Tom may be unable to produce utterances of more than one or two words, and may also be unable to understand them.
- The conversation concerned may not have elicited longer utterances because of the nature of the subject, elicitation material, or structure of the questions.
- Two-word utterances may be the normal developmental stage for a child of Tom's age.
- Tom may use longer utterances in other situations but be inhibited by the assessment process.

It is therefore important that accurate observation of the behaviour comes first, because there are many different possibilities for interpretation. Once possible hypotheses have been formed, new observations need to be structured to test the different possibilities. If the adoption of a single interpretation, or a single hypothesis, precedes observation of events, then there is a danger that what is observed simply confirms the existing interpretation, because the observer is not attending to alternatives.

It is also important that the observer does not make value judgements, interpretations of events involving an attitude that is often negative, as these have no place in professional observation and assessment. In the case example above, it would be inappropriate to decide that Tom's limited output was because he was 'lazy' or 'shy'. Value judgements introduce a level of inappropriate certainty, which may preclude the therapist from developing alternative interpretations.

The time between the observation of events and their interpretation may vary, depending on the difficulty of the decisions that need to be made. The analysis and processing of the results of assessment may be time-consuming, involving for example a detailed linguistic analysis, as well as reflection on the implications of all the information gathered, in relation to initial and revised hypotheses. However, the time taken will be influenced by the experience of the therapist and his or her 'hot action' skills (Eraut 1994).

As an initial picture is obtained of the child's communication skills, a decision needs to be made about the necessity for intervention. The therapist will continue to develop working hypotheses as new evidence affecting the understanding of the child's communication emerges, even during the therapy process.

Assessment is usually part of the first stage of the speech and language therapy process, but it does not necessarily end when therapy begins. Often, the investigation continues as 'diagnostic therapy', with the therapist seeking supporting or refuting evidence for the working hypotheses that evolve. Reassessment is important at regular intervals during intervention to monitor the effectiveness of therapy. In this way, the work of the therapist can be seen as a cyclical process with much in common with the Kolb (1984) learning cycle, rather than being a linear referral–assessment–diagnosis–intervention sequence.

Facilitating change

Although assessment and intervention are often referred to as if they are two separate stages in the management process, in reality they overlap. The therapist will at some stage reach a decision about whether specific intervention is required to facilitate change in the child's communication – that is, to carry out 'treatment' or 'therapy'. With children who have not yet acquired normal speech and language, therapists will use their facilitative skills to help them improve and develop their communication skills. With children with acquired disorders, they may be teaching them to re-use skills they once had (see Chapter 22).

Change may be achieved using direct intervention, indirect intervention or through making changes in the child's communicative environment (see Chapter 1).

The nature of change

The expected level and rate of change that may occur as a result of intervention will vary for each child according to the nature of the difficulty, whether there are additional medical or cognitive factors, and the child's age. It is important to be realistic and to understand any possible limiting factors, although the therapist should not impose expectations that might limit a child's progress.

For example, children with a minimal speech and/or language delay may be expected to catch up with their peers following an 'episode of care', namely a period of intervention. For some children with a significant hearing loss, bilingual language development in BSL and English may be the aim (Parker and Kersner 1997). Some children with cerebral palsy may aim to achieve a functional level of communication using electronic aids (see Chapter 23), while for older children who have residual language problems it may be more appropriate for therapy to concentrate on the development of social skills and strategies for managing the problems (Miller and Roux 1997).

Setting aims and objectives

The general goals for therapy, namely realistic aims for a specified period and achievable objectives for each individual session, need careful consideration and discussion. One approach to objective setting is described by the acronym 'SMART' (Furnham 1997). Objectives must be:

S: specific, relating to children's individual needs and the communicative and social environment;

M: measurable;

A: achievable, given the time and help available;

R: realistic;

T: time-related, specifying a time within which they will be achieved.

Evaluating change

Monitoring, reflection and evaluation are part of an ongoing process for the speech and language therapist. Overall aims should be constantly reviewed and the effects of any external environmental factors should be monitored.

Monitoring needs to take place during, and at the end of, each session in order to decide whether adjustments need to be made. It is usually an indication that the therapy needs to be modified if children are, for example, failing, not being challenged by the task, losing interest, becoming frustrated or showing signs of uncharacteristically challenging behaviour. Therapists need to consider the following questions:

- Have the overall aims been set correctly in relation to the child and the environment?
- Are the specific objectives realistic and appropriate?
- Are the tasks and materials appropriate and at an appropriate level?
- Were the sessions enjoyable for the child?
- Is the communicative environment suitable?
- Is the input at the appropriate level?

At the end of a period of intervention, therapists need to evaluate therapy, to show whether or not the approach used was successful, to assess the extent of any change, and to make a decision about the next stage. Change in the child is not only evaluated from the therapist's point of view, but the parents' and teachers' and child's perceptions should also be checked.

While facilitating change in others, change also occurs in the therapist as part of the ongoing learning process. Through reflection and monitoring, therapists continue to hone, modify and develop their professional skills (Eastwood and Whitehouse 1993).

Supportive knowledge

To facilitate change in children, therapists need specific knowledge to enable them to make appropriate decisions and understand the available choices. For example, they need to know:

- about different therapy approaches and techniques;
- how to analyse the skills required at different levels of a task so that therapists can change the level during a session if required;
- how to interpret the results of assessment findings;
- how to set criteria for evaluating therapy;
- tasks, games and activities for children of all ages that will enable the process of change.

Therapists need to understand about the development of a therapeutic relationship and to have an awareness of self; to understand about their own reactions to change, and their own prejudices and attitudes if they are successfully to support change in others (Burnard 1992).

Key skills

To work effectively in speech and language therapy, key skills are needed that can be learned, improved upon and changed as students and therapists continue their professional development. These may be overt behaviours, such as interviewing skills, or covert behaviours such as paying attention when listening. Most student therapists have some level of key skills before they begin to study, but these then need to be developed for specialised application within the professional context.

Transferable skills

Many of these key skills, such as word processing or presentation skills, are transferable across different professions. Transferable skills are often used by different professionals in different ways. For example, listening skills are also used effectively by counsellors or school teachers. Speech and language therapists, however, need to develop their listening skills so that they not only comprehend and empathise, but can analyse the words and the interaction at the same time.

Profession-specific skills

The ability to transcribe and analyse communicative interactions is profession-specific to speech and language therapy. So is the way in which some 'everyday' skills are developed and managed, usually simultaneously, in the professional context. For example, therapists are often required to listen, observe, record and transcribe while structuring and maintaining an enjoyable and relaxed interaction with their clients; at the same time, they will be considering working hypotheses about the problems being observed, deciding areas of priority for assessment, as well as offering reassurance and appropriate explanations to parents.

Areas of necessary skill

There are five areas in which key skills apply. Each is discussed further below:

- interpersonal skills;
- information-gathering skills;
- therapy skills;
- problem-solving skills and decision-making;
- organisational skills.

Interpersonal skills

Interpersonal skills may be broadly classified into those needed so as to receive information (such as listening skills), those required for expression (whether spoken, non-vocal or written), and those that are required to work collaboratively with others. In practice, none of these skills is used in isolation. For example, when speaking there is normally a complex relationship between the overt behaviour of the speech and the covert activity of planning what to say, and meta-linguistic skills are needed to monitor what is heard and what is being said as part of the communication planning process (Hargie *et al.*1994).

Communication tactics

All therapists need to understand clients whose speech patterns differ from the norm. They also need to be able to modify their own communication according to the needs of individual clients. For example, when working with deaf children in spoken English, therapists need to ensure that their speech is lip-readable, and they also need to learn BSL.

Receptive skills – active listening

The process of listening involves paying attention to verbal and non-verbal signals, and therapists need to develop a more concentrated level of listening than is used in everyday conversation. They need to develop active listening skills – for example, when interviewing parents, so that they not only pay attention but also convey the level of that attention to the speaker. This enables an empathic rapport to be established, thereby encouraging fuller, honest and more open expression from the speaker. See Hargie *et al.* (1994), Burnard (1992).

Ground rules for active listening
- Provide speakers with a comfortable environment.
- Minimise external interruptions.
- Actively concentrate to a greater degree than in normal conversation.
- Be prepared to listen irrespective of personal feelings about the topic.
- Actively process the information heard.
- Provide opportunities for speakers to express themselves.
- Avoid interrupting unnecessarily.
- Overtly acknowledge that the speakers have been heard using verbal or non-verbal responses
- Reflect back to the speaker what they have said to confirm that their overt message is being received correctly.
- Be objective but also empathic. Avoid selective responses, which may be based on unsubstantiated pre-judgements.

Expressive skills

Receptive skills are also fundamental to the expressive process, for speakers need to listen to themselves to modify what they are saying and to listen to others to plan what to say next.

Within a professional context, therapists are often required to structure and manage interactions for a specific purpose – for example, when greeting clients in a way that encourages a rapport to be established. They often need to give clear explanations, such as describing activities; or provide information for parents or other professionals. Therapists may be asked to give a more formal presentation at a case review, or during a training session for parents or other professionals.

Expressive skills for professional practice include:

- oral skills used in everyday conversations adapted to suit a specific interactional purpose;
- specific oral skills, which may be required when presenting to a larger audience;
- written language skills;
- non-vocal, verbal communication skills such as sign language or Alternative and Augmentative Communication (AAC);
- non-verbal communication skills, such as facial expression and gesture.

Ground rules for explaining and presenting
- Explanations must be adapted to the needs of the listener and be compatible with the receiver's language.
- The language used should be clear and jargon should be avoided.
- Delivery should be well paced.
- Illustration by example is helpful, as well as highlighting the key facts.
- Check that listeners have understood the information given.
- Plan the structure, content and even specific words and phrases.
- Rehearsal may improve the clarity of an explanation.
- To hold their attention and interest when addressing a group, encourage members to participate.
- With larger groups, voice production and projection may be important.
- Audio-visual illustration and/or demonstration may be helpful when presenting to a large group.

When explanations, presentations, or reports need to be written, the language used must be appropriate for the receiver, with the key points summarised and highlighted. Legal and ethical issues need to be considered in written records. See RCSLT (1996) and Bray *et al.* (1999).

Collaborative skills
Speech and language therapists need to work together with different people in a range of settings, such as with parents, teachers, assistants and medical colleagues (Wright and Kersner 1998; see also Chapter 11).

Ground rules for collaborative working
- Arrange regular times to discuss the process.
- Find out about setting-specific conventions and procedures, which may differ between hospitals and schools, for example.
- Consider the larger context – such as inclusion issues when working in the educational system or the effects of legislation on speech and language therapy services in the UK's National Health Service (NHS).
- Clarify the nature of the therapist's role in relation to others.
- Be prepared to compromise and negotiate.

Information-gathering skills

Information-gathering skills are key to the decision-making process because they help to provide the evidence on which decisions are based. They are a complex set of skills involving simultaneous actions and covert planning, analysis and interpretation.

The subskills include:

- observation;
- technical skills;
- interviewing, questioning and researching;
- assessment;
- analysis and interpretation.

Observation

Observing is more active than looking. The purpose of specific observations needs to be clear, so that those observations may be appropriately structured and focused. Recordings of observations provide a basis for analysis. If a communicative interaction is being observed, a therapist may choose to remain outside or to be a part of the interaction. As discussed above, observation of events must be separated from interpretations and value judgements.

Therapists need to use accurate, focused observations to gather evidence that may support or refute their working hypotheses about a child's communication. Situations may be structured to facilitate observations, such as using specific toys to observe symbolic play. The time may be structured so that selective samples of behaviour are observed – for example, noting how many times specific signs are used in a short video sample.

Ground rules for observation
- Be clear about the purpose of the observation and the level of evidence needed to test a hypothesis.
- Decide the focus, the time frame and how to record the behaviour.
- Record whether the observer is detached or involved in the activity.
- Record the exact behaviour observed – without interpretation or value judgement.
- Record the context as well as the focus of the observation.

Technical skills

Three of the basic technical skills needed by speech and language therapists are:

- the ability to make a good audio recording (Parker 1999);
- the ability to make a good video recording;

- the ability to transcribe speech and language as required into its phonetic, linguistic and interactional components.

Additional technical skills may be required if therapists later specialise – for example, in using instrumentation related to voice work or dysphagia.

Interviewing, questioning and researching

To gain a complete and holistic picture of any child referred for therapy, information needs to be gathered from a variety of sources, such as: the child, parents, educational staff, medical professionals, as well as from existing records and reports.

When gathering information from parents, it is important to be sensitive to their perceptions and feelings about their child's difficulties and the speech and language therapy process; and to offer empathic non-judgmental communication that supports them in their role. Particular types of questions may be more or less effective. For example, closed questions may provide specific information but will not necessarily help parents to feel relaxed and may even prevent free-flowing conversation. It is important to consider how questions may be interpreted, because this may affect the response of those being interviewed (see Hargie *et al.* 1994). Answers cannot be hurried, and sometimes it will be important to leave a silence to allow reflection.

Ground rules for compiling case-history information

- Explain the purpose of the meeting when sending an appointment to attend.
- If parents do not use English, arrange for an interpreter to be present.
- Prepare the environment.
- Begin with an explanation of the process.
- Know why the information is needed, how it may be used, and make clear that it is related to the speech and language therapist's role.
- Ask questions that will help towards the acceptance or rejection of working hypotheses, or for clarification.
- Ask for relevant details regarding the social and educational context within which the child operates.
- Consider whether all questions need to be asked at once or could be asked over a period of time.
- Be sensitive to whether questions may appear intrusive and may harm the relationship being established.
- Be observant about signs of distress and be prepared to stop.
- Have empathy with parents' feelings.
- Close the session with explanations, information, advice, as relevant.
- Check that parents understand the process.

Assessment

During assessment, the primary focus is on managing the interaction and the materials while achieving the purpose of the assessment. At the same time, communication with the child and the parents need to be managed sensitively.

Ground rules for assessment
- Understand the different types of tests available and what the results might yield.
- Understand the implications of testing a working hypothesis and how alternative hypotheses may be tested.
- Become familiar with the administration details of formal assessment materials.
- Construct activities for the specific purpose of informal assessment.
- Continue noting informal observations even during formal testing sessions.
- Record speech and language samples using phonetic and orthographic transcription.
- Pay attention to the details of the child's responses, noting any verbal prompts given.
- Convey encouragement, not evaluation to the child.
- Help the child to feel positive about the assessment process.
- Remain objective.
- Control non-verbal clues such as eye pointing, intonation or gestures.

Analysis and interpretation

The information and data from all sources then need to be collated, analysed and checked against the working hypotheses. The implications of the results need to be considered so that decisions can be made regarding therapy and further management.

Therapy skills

The skills required for carrying out therapy are varied and complex and, as before, many will need to be employed simultaneously. They include being able to:

- work with individual clients;
- work with groups so that the therapy aims of individual children can be achieved as well as the group aims, while at the same time the children's behaviour is managed and their interest maintained (see Chapter 4);
- set appropriate aims and objectives;
- design and run appropriate activities in order to achieve the defined aims and objectives;
- monitor the appropriateness of the activities during the session and increase or decrease the levels of difficulty of the task;
- reflect on the overall therapy, evaluate its effectiveness, and measure outcomes.

Problem-solving and decision-making skills

Speech and language therapy is about problem-solving, from the formation of the first working hypothesis to the evaluation of the effectiveness of therapy. Once the problem has been identified, it may be helpful to consider a variety of possible solutions. These can then be reviewed for suitability, and possible actions can be selected and ranked in the order in which they might be tried. Decisions then need to be made about how these may be implemented.

There are decisions to be made at many different points during the management process and it is important to recognise that the decision-making process is in itself a skill.

Organisational skills

As students and as practising clinicians, speech and language therapists need organisational skills to manage themselves within the workplace. They need to manage:

- their time (Forster 2000);
- their overall workload;
- requisite administrative tasks;
- prioritisation;
- their caseload.

Feedback in the learning process

Feedback involves the reception of information that helps individuals to monitor performance and reflect on adjustments that may be needed. It also involves the capacity to make relevant adjustments and to assess their effect. Therapists need to receive and give feedback in relation to individual children, their families and other colleagues, and to use feedback to monitor and improve their own developing professional skills.

Direct and indirect feedback

It is important to distinguish between indirect feedback, such as feedback from the responses of clients and colleagues, and direct feedback, which is deliberately elicited – for example, through questionnaires or after observation of work by peers or senior colleagues. Both types of feedback are important for professional learning, and different levels of directness may be relevant at different stages.

For example, experienced therapists may make use of the continuous indirect feedback they receive about their professional effectiveness by monitoring the progress of the children and the reactions of families and colleagues. If attention is paid to this feedback, it may be used as a basis for considering change or for continuing what is working well. However, therapists might find that the demands of everyday practice may preclude the effective use of more formal, direct feedback for professional learning unless time is specifically arranged.

Within the workplace, direct feedback may be available for staff, for example, through an appraisal process, peer support groups, and individual peer support.

At earlier stages in their professional development, students and newly qualified therapists (NQTs) may need to learn how to transfer the emphasis from direct feedback processes, such as those given by clinical supervisors and tutors, to the more independent skills involved in indirect feedback. The structured emphasis on regular, formal feedback is important for students who benefit most from an overt, explicit system in the early stages of their professional learning process. However, the transition to professional working life must involve a development of the covert processing skills required for personal reflection and decision-making. Students must also develop the ability to use all sources of indirect feedback to ensure continual professional development.

It is important, therefore, that – even before qualification – developing therapists should begin to learn how to receive and utilise indirect, situational feedback in addition to direct and structured feedback. In the same way, practising therapists need to ensure that they have opportunities for direct feedback and reflection as it is a combination of both types of feedback that will be most beneficial.

Giving and receiving feedback

If receiving feedback is to be a positive experience, clear ground-rules about how to conduct the process need to be negotiated before a feedback session begins. For example, it is important to aim for balanced feedback and to counteract any tendency for givers or receivers to focus differentially on either positive or negative comments. It is also important to agree the level of confidentiality, so that participants can be clear about what will happen to any information that is exchanged.

Feedback does not have to include all the factors that have been observed and it will often be more useful if the session is focused on specific skills and behaviours. A written record helps to counteract the tendency to remember negative comments rather than positive ones, and such a record will provide evidence of progress over time.

Feedback needs to be specific – to state more than, 'That was good.' It may be more helpful to say, ' You achieved your aims during the first activity because you introduced it clearly and it was at the appropriate level.' Or, 'There are three ways in which that activity might be improved next time ….'

Ground rules for feedback
- Agree the ground rules and the confidentiality level beforehand.
- Agree roles beforehand.
- Agree the scope of the feedback.
- Agree the focus.
- Agree the circumstances for feedback, and the status of the feedback.
- Agree the structure of the feedback session – it is usually recommended that the 'learner' comments first on his or her own performance.
- Ensure inclusion of positive factors and suggestions for improvement.
- Include discussion about how the learner can check whether the improvements have taken place.
- Make a written record, as this can give a view of development over time.

Summary

This chapter has been about two approaches to speech and language therapists' learning and professional development. The skills that are needed by therapists to make some of their clinical decisions have been identified. A reflective model of practice has been discussed in order to highlight the importance of feedback in the learning process and in therapists' continuing professional development.

CHAPTER 3

The first job – bridging the gap

Heather Anderson

Learning outcomes

By the end of this chapter, the reader should:

- know some of the important aspects that need to be taken into account when applying for a first job;
- understand the importance of supervision and mentoring for the newly qualified therapist;
- understand the clinical governance agenda;
- understand the need for the organisation and management of self;
- understand the importance of administration, including reporting and note-keeping, and the collection of statistical data.

Starting out

The first decision for students who have graduated – or are about to graduate – relates to where they would like to work. This is usually followed by decisions about the type of clients they wish to work with and the setting that they would prefer if they are given a choice. The application form and, hopefully, the ensuing interview then offer newly qualified speech and language therapists the first opportunity to market themselves.

Le May (1999) offers some suggestions for when applying for a position, centring on obtaining information and supplying information. First, gather as much information as possible about the position on offer. Normally, a job description and a person specification outlining the skills, experience, knowledge and personal attributes desired for the advertised post will be sent with an application form. Phone calls, discussions with relevant people, literature and an excursion onto the Internet may provide additional information. Once an application form has been received and an applicant intends to proceed, the applicant should provide the requested details, outlining any special attributes that are relevant to the post, particularly in relation to the person specification and job description. The application form should be completed – legibly – according to any instructions provided, and all aspects of the submission should be proofread before they are submitted. A photocopy of the form should always be kept. Finally, the form should be returned before the deadline and attendance at interview confirmed as soon as possible.

The application form is normally a means of short-listing candidates for interview and provides a first impression, so it is important for it to be professional in terms of presentation and content. At interview, applicants have the opportunity to demonstrate their suitability for the post by making links between the questions asked and their relevant experiences. While answering the questions they should use every opportunity to discuss and promote their relevant skills, knowledge, expertise and experience.

First posts do not usually involve specialised roles, although they may include elements of more specialised caseloads within them. Most therapists start working with a mixed caseload. In a paediatric post, this usually means working within a community clinic or a schools' team. This in turn will mean that the children who are referred will have a wide range of difficulties. With some children, other professionals will also need to be involved – for example, if the children have a physical or a learning disability. Further specialised assessment or intervention may be provided in settings such as Child Development Centres.

NQTs are competent to work with adults and children as the remit for accredited speech and language therapy courses is to provide students with a general professional education. Thus, it is not until they are in their first job that therapists' special skills and interests, as suited to a specific client group or setting, can be more clearly identified. Other factors may be involved in deciding career direction. For example, some therapists might enjoy the detail of working directly with the clients themselves; others might enjoy training and facilitating other professionals to carry out therapy goals so that they may be well suited to working in schools, or working with parents in a health centre (see Chapter 5).

Some therapists may continue to develop their expertise by working with a general caseload; others will take on specific duties with particular types of clients, developing more specialised areas of responsibility and expertise. This aspect of career development will usually be discussed and acknowledged in therapists' annual individual performance review (IPR) as it relates to continuing professional development. However, it is important to remember that managers of speech and language therapy services have a duty to provide a service to meet the needs of all people with communication difficulties. This may involve some compromise and negotiation when a therapist's professional development is in conflict with the overall service needs.

The speech and language therapist who has just begun work as a qualified practitioner will function as a registered speech and language therapist while a member of the graduate register of the RCSLT. After approximately a year – although this may vary according to the individual situation – an upgrading interview will be undertaken with a view to transferring the therapist's name to the full practice register.

Starting work

When starting their first job, new graduates should be offered a period of induction. As suggested by the RCSLT in *Communicating Quality 2* (1996): 'It is important that newly qualified staff … be given a balanced induction to the employing authority's services, management structure and areas of specialist expertise.' That same document lists the activities and skills that NQTs should ideally experience during the early stages of their employment. These include the clinical orientation referred to above and aspects of administration such as writing case notes and sending in statistical returns.

The line manager – the person immediately senior within the management structure – might have a prepared induction programme, although it would also be helpful for new post-holders to reflect on what specific experiences or observations they would consider to be desirable or helpful. NQTs will bring from their education and training an understanding of different learning styles and appreciate the activities from which they are most able to learn. For example, some might prefer to observe and shadow others when first starting work, while others might find that they benefit more if they are able to learn through their own practical experience.

Once in post, new therapists need to read the service handbooks and the health and safety manuals so that they familiarise themselves with the standards of practice of their employing service.

Supervision

It is important that newly qualified staff should have regular supervision, usually by the line manager to whom they are accountable. In addition, it is helpful for a therapist to have access to a mentor, who may act in a specific supporting role enabling the NQT 'to reflect and learn and be guided through a particular stage of professional development' (Bray *et al.* 1999: 205).

Non-managerial supervision may also help NQTs to reflect and improve on their clinical work with the clients (Green 1995). Moreover, ongoing clinical supervision of this kind is crucial to the profession in ensuring that services provided are of the best quality and that competence and skills are continually developing throughout a speech and language therapist's career. Immediately after qualification, it is of particular importance to use clinical supervision to review practice systematically alongside a supervisor. Whitehead (1999) has confirmed the centrality of supervision in developing and retaining speech and language therapists when they first come into post.

If the therapist has close working contact with professional colleagues, it might be possible to develop a network – for example, of those who work in an associated area. Indeed, team meetings and support groups can provide helpful learning experiences and support at all stages of a therapist's career.

Continuing professional development

Students and NQTs are expected to take responsibility for their own learning, and to maximise all opportunities to develop as professionals (RCSLT 1996). Throughout a speech and language therapist's career, ongoing decisions need to be made in order to make the best use of any learning opportunities.

A working portfolio may function as a record of achievements and career highlights, but it can also be used to record thoughts, ideas, feelings and reflections on everyday practice (Stewart 1998). Richards (1993) also stresses the importance of keeping records relating to learning, and points out that these can help when preparing for the annual IPR. This can be done by utilising the record of continuing professional development activities (the 'log') that RCSLT requires all speech and language therapists to complete annually (Hamrouge 1998). Continuing professional development needs to be seen as a process, as opposed to a set of targets to be achieved, in order for ongoing development and learning to take place (Stewart 1998). While keeping a record of learning, it may in addition be helpful to keep a reflective and critical account of work undertaken.

Clinical governance

'Clinical governance' provides the framework within which therapists may review their practice, keep up to date, and assess and address pertinent issues. It has been defined (DoH 1998) as: 'A framework through which NHS organisations are accountable for continuously improving the quality of their services and safeguarding high standards of care by creating an environment in which excellence in clinical care will flourish.'

Clinical governance includes clinical audit, quality monitoring, and improvement; but it also includes a wide range of educational and professional development initiatives. It is relevant clinically to all those employed by the NHS. It is of particular importance to NQTs as this is the time when professional learning patterns begin to be developed that might influence long-term styles of working. It is important that an open learning style should be encouraged at the beginning of a therapist's career and that NQTs recognise the value of continuing professional development and self-analysis. A good clinical-governance strategy within a speech and language therapy service will include a well-organised system of clinical supervision.

Managing time

Managing time is a crucial skill in any job, and new graduates will need to learn how to manage their time efficiently and effectively. It will not happen automatically and it can take time to achieve the appropriate skills and experience to work efficiently in a first job. The demands of planning, working with clients, writing up the case notes and reports, liaising with other professionals, attending meetings and dealing with other administrative tasks are considerable for any therapist; and they are particularly demanding for the NQT. Thought needs to be given to the way in which time is managed, because many of these tasks will take longer for the NQT than for a more experienced clinician (Forster 2000).

It may be useful to allocate time so that all aspects of a case are dealt with within the allotted time-span and nothing is held over. In this way the client will be seen, and the case notes and relevant reports written within the period allowed. There will be a surprising number of calls on a new graduate's time, including meetings with managers and supervisors, locality or multidisciplinary team meetings, case conferences, and project and strategic developments. It is, therefore, important to try to avoid spending too much time on each individual task at the expense of others. Jobs must be prioritised and time-managed to ensure that no important task is omitted. By the achievement of a balanced approach, there is more possibility of job satisfaction. Richards (1993) suggests that no more than 80 per cent of time should be strictly allocated, leaving 20 per cent to be managed more flexibly according to need.

Support from peers and mentors may help NQTs in decision-making and prioritising in order to achieve effective management of their time (Bray *et al.*1999).

Record keeping

Objectives

When therapists are working with clients, helping them to achieve a new or enhanced skill, it may be helpful if they work towards SMART objectives (see Chapter 2). Clients' objectives should be understandable and accessible to others. This means, for example, that it is important that case records – known also as case notes – are written up clearly.

Moon-Meyer (1998) suggests that three components should be included when writing objectives: 'performance, condition and criterion'. This means that the objective should be written so that it describes what the client is going to do (perform) in order to show mastery of a new skill (for example, to greet another person); in what condition (for example, within the therapy session); and what the criterion for achievement will be (for example, achievement in 90 per cent of therapy sessions).

Report writing

Prior to qualification, students often write reports as part of their course work, but these will differ from those written as part of their clinical placement experience. Thus, as

NQTs, they may have had previous experience of report writing although this will have been related to specific settings. When writing a report in their first job, in order to make it informative, comprehensible and relevant, therapists need to be clear about the report's purpose and the audience who will be receiving it (Bray *et al.* 1999). Not only will the report need to show knowledge of the child, but it will need to communicate clearly what actions are required by the receiver. It is important to remember that parents may see the report. Positive statements about the child need to be included, strengths identified, and relevant information about therapy given.

Hegde and Davis (1992) stress the importance of the presentational aspects of report writing. Readability, neatness, accuracy, sequencing, grammar, spelling and punctuation all need to be considered. Technical terminology should be explained, with examples for those who do not have a good knowledge of speech and language therapy.

Reports may be written for medical staff, teaching staff and other professionals, as well as parents, and it is important that they are kept succinct. Usually it is advisable to include a brief summary of the presenting difficulty, the progress to date and, more importantly, an action plan of what is going to be offered to the child. Some reports may also include other practical recommendations and ideas.

Reports may be written for the local education authority (LEA) in the process of educational multiprofessional assessment – i.e. Statementing (DfEE 2000b). Reports contributing to a Statement should describe the child's presenting speech and language difficulty in a way that is understandable to the lay person and should show how this relates to the child's overall functioning. These reports then need to outline the impact of any speech and language difficulty on the child's educational needs and offer an action plan for speech and language therapy involvement. Many health trusts provide guidance for writing such reports, and it is important that initially they are checked with a line manager.

Reports may also be required to be used in a court of law – for example, in child protection or abuse cases, in educational tribunals or in cases of medical negligence. Usually, the manager of the service will need to be briefed immediately, along with other professionals such as a specialist nurse for child protection; or the health trust lawyer may need to be consulted. In such cases, it is vital for any therapist to discuss the draft of a report with the manager or other senior colleague before it is circulated more widely. It is important to ensure that the information in such reports can be backed up by hard evidence and that reports are factually based.

Case records

Before writing case records (case notes), it is important to read the current speech and language therapy professional standards and guidelines (RSCLT 1996) as well as any locally based standards. 'In Britain, since the Access to Health Records Act of 1990 clients have had a right to access all personal information held on both manual (written) and computerised health records' (Bray *et al.* 1999: 194). Case records can be read by parents on request, so care should be taken to avoid judgmental statements and ambiguity. Case records must be written contemporaneously, and certainly within 24 hours of the session.

Moon-Meyer (1998) makes the following suggestions when writing case records:

- make objectives explicit in every entry;
- use the information recorded as a guide for future therapeutic intervention;
- provide as much objective data as possible to back up case records;
- measure performance in terms of the client's achievements rather than the therapist's;
- proofread case-record entries.

If an error is made in the case records, a line should be put through it, but it should never be erased or covered with correction fluid. This is to protect the therapist from claims of dishonesty. If the erroneous entry can still be read, no claims beyond the factual information can be made about the content of the notes and ultimately the therapy.

Collection of statistical information

Information about the performance of a speech and language therapy service is required by the Department of Health (DoH). The data may be collected in different ways – for example, in terms of numbers of client contacts, care aims or care packages, and the data will be used to monitor contracts. Every speech and language therapist is required to collect information on every client seen. Although it is not always easy to see the relevance of the data collection to the clinical work undertaken, it is of importance that data are collected as they may provide the basis on which budgets for speech and language therapy are set each year. (See Bray et al.1999 for further details.)

Overview of the clinical process

It is important for the NQT to develop from the outset ways of seeing the 'larger picture' within his or her clinical work. A number of tools are available that can help in developing this, each of which are described further below:

- episodes of care;
- care aims;
- prognostic skills;
- cooperative working.

Episodes of care

Each episode of care must have a specified predicted time-span, which should include a review date where appropriate; an action plan with agreed input from all involved professionals, and an agreed overall approach; a care aim; specified and measurable goals that are agreed by the child, parents, and other professionals; and a specified objective-measurement evaluation for the achievement of those goals.

Care aims

Care aims are a useful tool for helping therapists define the purpose of their intervention. The care aims that apply to speech and language therapy might be:

- curative;
- enabling;
- rehabilitative;
- supporting;
- assessment;
- maintenance,
- anticipatory.

Care aims are helpful in guiding a therapist's decisions about why the therapy is being offered. Is it, for example, to support the parents? To enable changes in the child's environment, which might then facilitate change in the child? Or to help prevent any future difficulties arising?

A curative care aim, for example, refers to helping children develop their function and skills to within the average range. This, therefore, might apply to children with delayed speech and language. A rehabilitative care aim might be more appropriate for children with learning disabilities, as this aims to help them develop their existing skills so that they can function to the best of their ability. An enabling aim refers to facilitating change within the children's environment, which then allows them to maximise their skills, rather than aiming to change the children's skills; this approach might apply to children who stammer or to a child with selective mutism. A maintenance aim might involve offering coping strategies to help children sustain their optimal level of functioning.

Normally, only one care aim will relate to each episode of care but, for example, if a child has a feeding difficulty as well as a communication problem then there may be two different care aims, one relating to each of the areas of difficulty.

Therapists make a decision at the beginning of the episode of care about which care aim will be achieved, and estimate how long it will take. For instance, they may decide on a rehabilitation care aim, stating that they will aim for an improvement of functioning over a period of ten weeks.

The care aims model provides a framework for clinical decisionmaking in all settings. It would be appropriate for a therapist working in a mainstream school or a special school to provide supportive care to some children, while offering rehabilitative, enabling or even maintenance care to others.

Prognostic skills

The development of prognostic skills provides another way in which speech and language therapists gain a holistic picture of the child. Prognostic skills are high-level skills, which often take time to develop after qualification. Therapists need to understand how different types of child profiles develop and respond to therapy.

Working together

Another way of helping to build a holistic picture of a child may be through working with others. Shadowing other therapists or working jointly with them can be extremely useful. Learning from teachers and classroom assistants when working in educational settings or from other professionals within a multidisciplinary team (see Chapter 11), is also important. However, uncertainties about a child's problems can also be taken to clinical supervision or discussed with a line manager or senior colleague, to aid the decision-making process.

The organisational context

Speech and language therapists work within the context of larger organisations such as the health or education authorities. It is particularly important that NQTs begin to develop an understanding of the wider context within which they work, to understand the factors that might influence their working context, and to be in a position where they may take a proactive and positive approach to developments and change.

Summary

Professional development continues after graduation, and the NQT will learn much during the first year of professional practice. This will not necessarily all be related to intervention with clients. While employers should provide a range of supervision opportunities, NQTs need to take a proactive role in ensuring they receive support and advice. The newly graduated therapist may well be pleased to be qualified, but this is only the first stage in an ongoing professional journey.

PART II

Management in different settings

This Part of the book addresses the different ways in which speech and language therapy can be delivered, including how services might differ in specific settings such as health centres, child development centres, hospitals, and schools.

Chapter 6 includes details on the educational context within which speech and language therapists work; these also apply to Chapter 7, and so it is recommended that these two chapters are read together.

CHAPTER 4

Managing children individually and in groups

Oonagh Reilly

Learning outcomes

By the end of this chapter, the reader should be able to:

- appreciate the advantages and disadvantages of group and individual therapy, and understand the rationale for both;
- understand factors that have an impact upon the choice between group and individual therapy;
- consider the main issues in running groups effectively;
- be aware of sources of problems and conflict within groups, and identify possible solutions.

Introduction

In this chapter, the complex process of group therapy will be explored. However, the initial focus will be on the decisions surrounding whether children should be seen individually or in groups. This will be set within the context of a model of the speech and language therapy management process, which should make explicit the decision-making required, and the skills needed, in the management of children with communication needs.

The management process

As discussed in Chapters 1 and 2, the speech and language therapy management process may be seen as linear. However, it can also be helpful to consider it as cyclical (see Figure 4.1) as assessment is ongoing throughout intervention. The two major aspects of management, namely assessment and treatment, are discussed next.

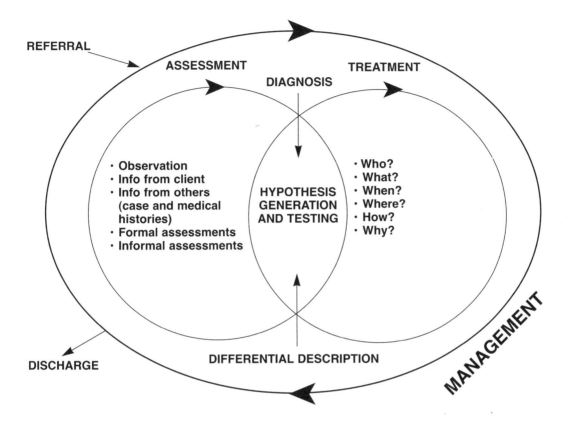

Figure 4.1 Model of the management process

Assessment

The starting point in the cycle is the clinician's acceptance of a referral, and this starts the first subprocess of intervention: the assessment process.

Initially, the clinician assesses the communication needs of a child through observation, formal and informal assessment, and discussion with parents and other professionals. Throughout the assessment process, the clinician is generating and testing hypotheses about the child's communication, profiling the child's strengths and needs. At any point in the process the clinician may make a differential diagnosis or provide a description of the child's needs, and this could be changed as the child's needs change or as further evidence is gathered.

Treatment

In Figure 4.1, treatment is shown as a separate subprocess. However, in reality, the clinician will move between assessment and treatment as necessary, and many clinicians use diagnostic therapy to help elucidate the underlying nature of a child's communication needs.

Features of the treatment process reflect the decisions to be made – the 'Who?', 'What?', 'When?', 'Where?', 'How?' and 'Why?' of therapy. Each decision interacts with others, and the question 'Why?' applies to every decision because it must be supported by a rationale.

The specific decisions surrounding group or individual therapy will now be considered. These primarily relate to whether treatment should be direct or indirect, and whether it should take place in a group or individually. With regard to the latter option, later in the chapter aspects of planning for group therapy and the group-leadership skills necessary to make it successful are considered.

Should treatment be direct or indirect?

Direct intervention, where the clinician works directly with the child, may be one-to-one or in a group, variably supported by parents (see Chapter 1). Alternatively, indirect intervention may be offered where the clinician works with the child's parents or other professionals such as teachers, assistants or nursery workers. The choice between direct or indirect therapy will depend on several factors, including the child's needs, the theoretical rationale behind the intervention, and the resources available. Some parents anticipate an 'expert' style of intervention (Cunningham and Davies 1985) and may be resistant to indirect intervention where they are asked to play a greater role.

However, direct and indirect treatment may be used together. Law (1999) suggests that a combination of child-only and parent-only groups may be more effective than if either of these is used alone. The decision to use direct or indirect intervention may change during the course of therapy, dependent upon the child's and parents' needs.

Indirect intervention

Indirect intervention may be appropriate for a child, for example, with 'normal non-fluency' (Van Riper 1973). The child may be seen only briefly by the clinician. Intervention will then take the form of prevention, working with the parents to ensure that the child's difficulties do not develop into a communication problem and that the environment is supportive of the child's communication development.

An indirect approach may also be effective if there is more than one child in the family requiring intervention, or if the focus of the intervention is on parent training – which can take place in groups, as in the Hanen Early Language Parent Programme (Girolametto et al. 1986) or similar parent–child interaction programmes (see Chapter 5). In the Hanen programme, groups of parents are trained to recognise their child's attempts at communication and to modify their own responses. This approach has been shown to be effective, for example in establishing turn-taking, increasing contingent feedback by parents, and encouraging longer conversational exchanges.

An important factor affecting the decision to choose direct or indirect intervention is the availability of support systems. For example, a class teacher, a special educational needs coordinator (SENCO) or a classroom assistant may each be able to integrate specific communication goals with other educational targets on a day-to-day basis. Children may then be seen within their normal classroom groupings, and intervention can take place in a more natural environment. Such a decision will be based on whether it is believed that the child would benefit as much from this indirect approach as from direct intervention.

Direct intervention

The nature of a child's difficulty is a factor to consider when choosing an approach. For example, a child with a phonological disorder may require direct intervention, and this would enable the therapist to monitor the child's progress and adjust the criteria of success throughout the session in order to change phonological goals and advise parents. Watson (1990) found that parents expected the therapist to be more active in phonological therapy groups than in language groups where they themselves expected to take a more active role.

Direct intervention, however, does not imply that the clinician works with the child in isolation. In order to take a holistic approach, the clinician must consider the parents so that intervention can take into account their involvement and consider their needs.

Group or individual therapy?

Rationale for individual therapy

In individual therapy, the dynamics between the clinician and child can ensure a focused response to the child's strengths and needs, so that the child is challenged enough to effect change and therefore gain success. The therapist can model appropriate techniques, encouraging parents to observe and try them with the child, with the support of the clinician, so that they may then be carried over into other settings.

When working one-to-one, distractions can be kept to a minimum, thus enabling children with attention difficulties to focus on the specific task. Individual therapy may be less intimidating than group therapy for children who are lacking in confidence.

However, as Urwin (1992: 13) states: 'Even the children who are most severely language impaired cannot exist in isolation and will have to learn coping strategies to deal with the wider communication environment, for which individual treatment does not always prepare them adequately,' and there are many instances when group therapy may be more appropriate.

Rationale for group therapy

Anderson-Wood and Smith (1997) see group therapy as providing a more naturalistic setting than individual therapy. Groups in classrooms can be used as a bridge towards whole-class activities, and natural and intermittent reinforcement is more likely to occur in groups. The dynamics of group communication may take the emphasis away from the 'form' of the communication, (Bloom and Lahey 1978) and help to establish and reinforce coping strategies.

Group therapy has the potential for a wider variety and greater number of adult-to-child interactions. It may also encourage child-to-child interactions such as turn-taking, sharing behaviours, clarification requests and repair strategies, as well as the development of self-monitoring behaviours through peer feedback.

Advantages and disadvantages of each

There are good reasons for both modes of intervention, but it is also worth considering the advantages and disadvantages of both ways of working, as well as the client's needs. These are shown in Table 4.1.

Two brief case examples

A 3 year-old girl has delayed symbolic development and delayed language development, and her parents are feeling isolated. This family may benefit from a preschool play and language group, in which parents are encouraged to meet each other as well as to observe and learn from the sessions.

A boy aged 4 years and 6 months with disordered phonology, who is aware of his difficulty in making himself understood, may benefit – at least initially – from individual therapy, which would provide a secure environment in which to experiment with new sound production.

A third case example

Oscar is 5 years and 3 months in age. He was referred for therapy just as he turned four. Since then, he has had two blocks of individual therapy for his phonological impairment. Progress has been slow, with little consolidation between the therapy blocks. Oscar continues to stop fricatives, reduce clusters and glide the liquid sounds. His hearing is within the normal range and there are no known causal factors that may account for his phonological impairment. He has been at school for 6 months in a class where there is a high ratio of children to adults and a large number of children with specific needs. Although Oscar is able to recognise whole words, he has poorly developed phoneme segmentation skills and his sound awareness is generally poor.

Decisions

The clinician has decided that Oscar needs further intervention because of his specific speech needs. The next decision that needs to be made is whether individual therapy

Table 4.1 Advantages and disadvantages of individual and group therapy

Advantages of individual therapy	Disadvantages of individual therapy
Child's individual needs can be targeted specifically.	It creates an artificial environment.
Therapy can be paced to match the child's needs.	Parents have reduced social contact with other parents who have children with communication needs.
A safe and secure environment is provided in which new skills can be practised.	Generalisation beyond the one-to-one therapy situation may not occur automatically.
All of the therapist's time is dedicated to the individual.	The process is more time-consuming for the therapist.
Appointments can be more flexible.	The total attention of one adult may be threatening or overwhelming for some children.
Explanations can be given to parents as necessary.	
It is easier to monitor progress and make notes.	
Therapy can be responsive to child's needs and changed as appropriate.	
Children with attention difficulties can be specifically catered for.	

Advantages of group therapy	Disadvantages of group therapy
It provides a natural communication environment.	Not all clients learn best this way – some might be too shy or inhibited.
It helps to encourage an awareness that others also have communication needs.	There will be less time focused on the individual compared with individual therapy.
Children can learn from each other as each has different strengths and resources.	There might be personality clashes within the group.
It offers a range of different communication models.	Children with disruptive behaviour might inhibit the group achieving its aims.
Competition can lead to greater motivation.	Some children's attention difficulties might be exacerbated by the group situation.
It increases the possible range of activities and the opportunities for interacting with others.	Children might learn bad habits from each other.

Table 4.1 (Continued)

Advantages of group therapy	Disadvantages of group therapy
It fosters the generalisation of skills taught in individual sessions.	Absence of some members might alter the group dynamics in a negative way.
It is more suitable for those who find the intensity and attention in individual therapy threatening.	The initial setting up of groups requires time for planning, organisation and other resources.
Multiple skills can be focused on.	Confidentiality might be more difficult to maintain.
It can provide a support network for parents.	It might be easier for children to opt out.
Through observation, parents can learn the facilitative techniques as modelled by the clinician.	Parents might be daunted by group involvement.
It provides a support network for children when groups are run in schools.	Parents might feel upset if their child is functioning at a lower level than others.
It can be part of the classroom activity and so might help the child not to feel singled-out for therapy.	
Group work can be a more economical use of the therapist's time.	

Source: based on the work of Weiss et al. 1987; Fawcus 1992; Anderson-Wood and Smith 1997; and Rustin and Kuhr 1999.

should be continued, or group therapy offered. Oscar needs therapy immediately, because he is learning to read, and he will need to improve his sound awareness skills before he can move on to the alphabetic stage of reading (Frith 1985). Because his spoken language is failing to develop normally, he is at risk of failing to develop appropriate written language skills (see Chapter 18).

Improved sound awareness skills should also bring about change in his speech. He needs to be able to increase the use of meaningful contrasts in his speech, and thus improve intelligibility. However, he has already had two periods of individual therapy in which progress has been slow and the therapist feels that he is no longer motivated.

The therapist decided that Oscar should be seen in a group because this would offer him a wider variety of activities and be more motivating for him. It would also offer greater opportunities for generalisation of skills. As there are other children on the therapist's caseload with similar therapy goals, it would be possible to form an appropriate group and the relevant resources are available.

Group planning

When planning any group, decisions must be made with regard to:

- the function and purpose of the group;
- criteria for entry and group composition;
- the specific aims of the group;
- learning opportunities and strategies for generalisation;
- the necessary structure of the sessions.

These are each briefly discussed further below.

Function and purpose

Goldberg (1997) suggests that speech and language therapy groups may have four functions:

- teaching of new behaviours;
- encouraging the generalisation of behaviours;
- gathering data by further assessment;
- being a discussion group for support or training.

In Oscar's case (see Case Example 3 above), the group will primarily have two functions, namely the teaching of new behaviours and the generalisation of those behaviours.

Criteria for entry and group composition

The more the members are matched in age, needs and interests, the more harmonious the group is likely to be (Goldberg 1997). However, the children do not have to be strictly matched. Some authors (Anderson-Wood and Smith 1997; Lees and Urwin 1997) recommend a mix of abilities so that children can learn from each other and provide different models. This is particularly important in social-skills groups.

Group sessions could become 'mini individual sessions' if care is not taken. However, limiting group size or running small, interactional groups within the larger group – perhaps in pairs – may help to prevent this occurring. Choosing activities that involve turn-taking, but in which everyone contributes in a different way, can also help.

Other factors to be considered in group composition are the gender and culture of group members. Smith and Inder (1993) found that groups of boys tended to be more boisterous than groups of girls, and that mixed groups functioned more like boys' groups than girls' groups. This has implications for the activities chosen.

Cultural considerations also need to be made. It may be culturally inappropriate for some children to speak without permission from an adult. Likewise, lack of eye contact may be considered a sign of respect. The clinician needs to be aware of these cultural differences and to avoid activities in which such cultural behaviours are challenged. It may be necessary to discuss some of the issues within the group if they are relevant to group members, such as in a social-skills group (see Chapter 16).

Finally, behavioural factors such as hyperactivity, impulsivity, inattention and sensitivity must be taken into account when considering group composition. One disruptive member might have a negative impact upon the group dynamics.

In the case of Oscar, it would be helpful if all children in the proposed group had a phonological impairment and age-appropriate comprehension. Although expressive language is likely to be delayed as a result of such phonological impairment, this should preferably not be a significant problem for any members of the group. The age range of the children would optimally be between 4 years 6 months and 5 years 9 months.

Specific aims

The specific aims of a therapy group are determined by the needs of the individuals in the group, and each group will have its own set of aims. In the case of Oscar, the aims for the group would be:

- to improve sound awareness skills;
- to eliminate the use of inappropriate phonological processes, namely fronting of velars and stopping of fricatives;
- to generalise the use of new sounds in short phrases, sentences and spontaneous speech;
- to provide homework for the children and give feedback to parents and teachers.

Within the group's aims there will also be aims for each of the individual members and specific objectives for what the children will be expected to achieve within each session.

Learning opportunities and strategies for generalisation

The learning opportunities and strategies for generalisation must be considered carefully when planning any group, so that the structure of the tasks is not just a list of activities. Rather, the teaching and learning methods must be considered so that each member's learning style can be accommodated and deeper learning can take place (Kolb 1984). This would involve giving members opportunities for reflective observation of their own and others' performance; abstract conceptualisation where they identify or describe patterns or rules, and active experimentation where they practise in a restricted way. Experience allows group members to practise new skills in a real-life situation, and this might there-fore involve trips outside the setting, if resources allow.

Structure

It is important to maintain the structure of each session in order to ensure that the aims are met and so that all members know what to expect. Different types of groups require different structures. A possible structure for Oscar's group during a 60-minute session is suggested as follows:

1. welcome/orientation;
2. introduce concept (e.g. semantic referents for sound class; rhyming);
3. listening activity involving the above concept and discussion;
4. production activity (no discussion required);
5. listening activity to include movement (reducing restlessness);
6. production and discussion (reflection) activity;
7. farewell, homework setting, and discussion with parents.

Group dynamics and process

In order to run a group effectively, clinicians should be aware of the group dynamics, namely what is happening within the group apart from the content. They also need to be aware of the group process or life-cycle and the skills required by group leaders to facilitate the group.

Group dynamics are dependent on group composition, but need to be considered in the context of the group process. Tuckman (1965) described a 'map' of the group process in adults as comprising of four phases: forming; storming; norming; and performing. These phases can also be applied to children's groups, although they are probably less overt in young children's groups and apply more to discussion groups such as social-skills groups for older children. However, it is helpful for clinicians to be aware of the life-cycle of groups.

During the first phase, 'forming', the group comes together for the first time and members start to discover their roles within the group as well as what will be expected of them. The second phase, 'storming', may be a time of conflict as members begin to stamp their personalities on the group. There may also be tensions between individuals' needs and the needs of the group. Out of this storming develops the 'norming' phase, when the members come to terms with the nature of the group and their role within it. By now, members know each other better, and usually a more secure and trusting atmosphere has begun to develop. The most productive phase in the group's life-cycle is the 'performing' phase, where the group has achieved a collective identity and the members work cohesively together.

It is important to establish ground rules at the start of any group. The number and type of rules will depend upon the purpose of the group, its composition, and the ability of the members to remember the rules. It is useful to encourage members to determine the rules themselves because then they are more likely to take ownership of them and respond to them. Such rules could be selected, for example, from those suggested by Anderson-Wood and Smith (1997) for groups focusing on meta-pragmatic skills:

- Be supportive of each other.
- No teasing or laughing at others.
- Take responsibility for yourself (no excuses or telling tales).
- Keep hands and legs under control (no poking or kicking).
- Listen to the person who is talking.
- Participate in role plays.
- Address positive feedback to the person who has done the role play, not necessarily to the clinician.
- Complete homework between meetings. If homework is not done, then it will be completed during the break periods when others are engaging in favourite activities.
- Allow others to have a turn at talking.
- Talk one at a time.

These rules could be adapted, depending on the type of group and the age and abilities of its members. Rules for pre-school groups are less likely to be negotiated with the members at the beginning but, instead, introduced in a simple way such as those used in the Social Use of Language programme: 'good listening', 'good looking' and 'good sitting' (Rinaldi 1992). Further detail on the group process and dynamics may be found in Burnard (1992), Fawcus (1992) and Pugach and Johnson (1995).

Group leadership skills

Group therapy is not the equivalent of simultaneous individual therapy with a larger number of clients. The clinician therefore needs specific skills to handle the group dynamics, to work with colleagues acting as helpers, and to ensure that the group and individual aims are being met.

Skills and qualities

The skills and qualities needed for successful group leadership are as follows (as adapted from Rustin and Kuhr 1999):

- flexibility to adapt to changes within the group and to alter targets as and when necessary;
- ability to develop strategies to maintain group cohesion and interest;
- ability to model techniques;
- ability to deal with behavioural problems quickly and effectively;

- ability to guide members so that all may participate equally;
- sensitivity to interpersonal issues;
- ability to train co-therapists or helpers;
- ability to deal with problems and conflict.

There are many sources of problems and conflict within group work, and a selection will now be considered together with some possible solutions (see also Rustin and Kuhr 1999 and Chapter 17).

One member does not participate

There may be many reasons for one member not participating. It is possible that the individual's abilities are different from those of the rest of the group members because the individual has been placed in the group inappropriately. In this case, if possible, it may be best to remove the individual and to try to find a group more suitable to that child's needs.

Assuming that the child has been placed appropriately and that the activities are at an appropriate level, there are several strategies that can be employed. First, the child should be encouraged to participate – for example, by choosing a topic or activity known to be of particular interest. Secondly, it may be possible to pair the child with another supportive group member, or with a helper. If the child has appropriate language skills, it may be helpful to talk outside of the group to try to discover the reasons for the behaviour.

One member constantly disrupts the group

Behaviour within the group should be clearly defined from the start, so that all members understand what is acceptable. Disruptive behaviour can occur if a child has been inappropriately placed. The tasks and activities of the group might not be at an appropriate level for each member's attention level and concentration span. It could also be that this child finds the work of the group to be challenging, exposing weaknesses, so that the behaviour is a form of sabotage. It may be necessary to ensure that tasks are chosen that highlight the individuals' strengths as well as their weaknesses. Possible strategies for dealing with the behaviour may include: strict reinforcement of the rules agreed for the group at the beginning, with temporary exclusion if necessary; open discussion within the group on the impact of the behaviour; encouragement of other members to become more active; an ignoring of the disruptive behaviour and praise appropriate behaviour; or, discussion of the problem outside the group with the individual(s) involved.

With younger children or those whose difficulties make reflection on behaviour impossible, it is important for the therapist to identify the triggers of the behaviour, with a view to avoiding them.

Two members consistently talk between themselves

There are times when talking in subgroups is to be encouraged, but this is not appropriate when the group as a whole come together to listen to other members or during a listening activity.

Burnard (1992) refers to two members consistently talking between themselves as 'pairing', and suggests that it can arise as a result of insecurity of one or of both of the pair, as a result of boredom or even as a means of testing the group leader. With older children, a possible solution could be to talk to each individual separately, explaining the disruptive nature of the behaviour and encouraging them to propose a solution. This may involve changing the pace of the sessions and ensuring their roles become more active. If a group member is having difficulty speaking in front of the whole group, preferring to talk to one other member, the leader – and possibly the other group members – will need to encourage that member to share comments with the rest of the group.

With pre-school children, subgroup distraction could be non-verbal and may be eliminated by changing the activities, enlisting the support of helpers, ensuring that the distractions within the room have been eliminated, and reminding all the group of the ground rules in order to keep them focused on the task.

Helper unintentionally sabotages the group

This may happen in many different ways, and it usually stems from the helper misunderstanding the aims for the group or individuals within it. These must be made explicit to the helper and any specific strategies must be demonstrated. For example, in the case of Oscar (see earlier in the chapter), the therapist might say to the helper, 'Oscar needs time to reflect – he may be slow to answer, but if given time will get there.' The helper should be advised to avoid jumping in and asking if anyone else knows the answer, as periods of silence are acceptable.

When working with a helper, it can take time to learn how to work well together and to appreciate each other's methods, strengths and weaknesses. Time set aside for note-taking and reflection after the session by the therapist and helper is, therefore, important and can speed up their process of learning how to work together efficiently for the good of the group.

Summary

The factors that need to be considered before deciding whether to offer group or individual therapy have been set in the context of a model of the speech and language therapy management process. The advantages and disadvantages of group and individual therapy have been discussed, and some of the skills necessary for effective leadership of a therapy group have been considered.

CHAPTER 5

Managing pre-school children in community clinics

Keena Cummins and Sarah Hulme

Learning outcomes

By the end of this chapter, the reader should be able to:

- identify who refers pre-school children to speech and language therapists;
- understand why it is important to intervene in the pre-school years;
- understand why certain children may be considered a priority;
- identify effective packages of care;
- understand why parent–child interaction intervention might be used.

Introduction

In this chapter, a model of service delivery is described that is being used increasingly in the United Kingdom. The focus is on pre-school children with speech, language and communication difficulties and the emphasis of the intervention approach is on parent–child interaction, which has a philosophy of 'care' rather than 'cure'.

A review carried out by Law *et al.* (1998) indicates that 5–10 per cent of three-year-old children have speech and language difficulties. Such problems are among the most common developmental difficulties in early childhood and may be predictive of increasing problems in later learning (Rescorla 1989; Stackhouse *et al.* 1999). Nevertheless, of those three-year-olds presenting with speech and language difficulties, approximately 60 per cent with expressive language delays improve spontaneously, as do 25 per cent of those presenting with receptive and expressive language delays.

The role of the speech and language therapist is to match the level of service delivery with the needs of the child. That is, the therapist should predict and identify those children whose difficulties are likely to resolve spontaneously or to resolve with support from other professionals such as nursery staff. Speech and language therapists can then focus on those children presenting with more entrenched and specific speech and language difficulties.

The referral process

Community Clinics (CCs) are usually geographically close to a child's home and part of a General Practice. Anyone may refer a child for therapy, with parental consent. The majority of the referrals of children in the pre-school years are from health visitors, Clinical Medical Officers, nursery staff and parents. Referrals often follow health surveillance checks carried out by GPs and health visitors at 6–9 months, 18–24 months and 3 years 6 months (Hall 1996). For example, a child aged 2 would be referred if there were parental concern, no recognisable words, lack of interest in toys and the child was not asking for things with gestures or words. A three-year-old child would be referred if there were parental concern, unclear speech, reduced interest in talking and communicating, and the child used only single words.

Not everyone is familiar with language and speech difficulties or with the remit of a speech and language therapist; many people would probably be more confident in identifying speech difficulties than in identifying language difficulties. It is, therefore, important for the speech and language therapist to become involved in the planning process of the local Health Surveillance programme (Bantock 2000) and to be involved in interdisciplinary preventative work through government initiatives such as the Sure Start programme (DfEE 1999d).

Children who are referred to the CC may have delayed or disordered language, which may be specific to language or be associated with a general delay in learning. These children are likely to have difficulties in one or all of the following areas:

- attention and listening skills;
- symbolic and social play;
- verbal comprehension;
- expressive language;
- speech development;
- pragmatics;
- fluency.

If a child is from a multi-cultural environment, the therapist will need to identify whether the child's difficulties relate to developing language itself or whether they are specific to learning English as an additional language (see Chapter 16).

Justification for early intervention

Rescorla (1989) suggests that language difficulties can be reliably identified from the age of two years. Key criteria that may be used to identify those children most at risk of ongoing language difficulties appear to be: reduced expression of communicative intent; severely reduced vocalisations (minimal speech sounds); and poor pragmatic skills (Whitehurst and Fischel 1994).

Smith (1998) indicates that intervention needs to begin early to prevent 'confrontational' interactive patterns developing, which may rapidly become entrenched if left unaddressed. Parent–child interaction and the modification of aspects of child management may be effective in helping to redress the interactive balance between parent and child, thus assisting the child in reaching its maximum potential.

Different types of parent–child interaction approaches

One model of intervention in which parents modify their interactions with their young children is The Interactive Model of Language Impairment (IMLI; Girolametto *et al.* 1999). In IMLI, it is suggested that parents have become involved in a negative communication cycle, not that they are responsible for causing the child's difficulty (Fey 1986). Using this model, different intervention packages have been developed that are used by speech and language therapists. One of these packages is described below.

Parent–Child Interaction Therapy (PCIT)

PCIT (Kelman and Schneider 1994) was developed in a speech and language therapy service in a health authority (HA) in London. It is from this model that the service described in this chapter has evolved. The basic philosophy of PCIT is partnership between the therapist and the parents, the parents providing the information about their child, and the therapist providing appropriate knowledge about language acquisition. Such collaboration combines parents' insight and experience with the therapist's knowledge and observations, enabling strategies to be developed that may increase the child's rate of language development.

Using the PCIT model, videos are made of the parent(s) playing with their child. The therapist and parents then watch the video, analysing the interaction and identifying communicative strengths and weaknesses of parent and child. The therapist enables the parents to identify when the interactions with their child have broken down and highlights successful strategies for communication repair. As the interaction improves and the child's communicative competence increases, the degree of detailed analysis reduces.

This model combines video analysis with parent workshops, and opportunities for parents to observe the speech and language therapist's strategies during group intervention sessions with the children.

Assessment

One of the ways of dealing with a high referral rate of pre-school children to speech and language therapy services is to operate a two-tier system for initial appointments. This may help to ensure that all children are seen within eight weeks of receipt of referral – that is, within the recommended time standard set out by the RCSLT (1996). An initial interview, lasting approximately ten minutes, may be offered within this period. A further appointment may then be arranged for a detailed assessment, should it be required. This system also provides a time-effective way of managing non-attendance at initial appointments. In addition, all speech and language therapy appointments should be preceded with written information about what to expect of the service and the assessment process. Similarly, all sessions should commence with a verbal description of what the session will entail and why.

The initial interview allows the therapist to meet and observe the child, to ascertain the parents' concerns, and to explain the assessment process. For the parents, the appointment provides an opportunity to meet the therapist and ask initial questions, while the child has the chance to become familiar with the environment of the clinic. A full assessment can then be arranged according to the child's needs so that, for example, an appointment may be made immediately for a child with a potential language disorder, while assessment of a child with a minor phonological delay may be scheduled several weeks later.

During the assessment process, the therapist will use formal and informal assessments to provide a profile of the child because there is no single screening tool that can be applied universally (Law *et al.* 1998). A detailed interview with the parents will enable the therapist to establish a rapport, to gather additional background information and to understand the parents' perceptions of their child's difficulties (see Chapter 2). Additional information regarding parental observations of the child's communicative strengths may be gleaned from an interview schedule (Dewart and Summers 1995). Information about any changes that may have occurred in the child's communication skills in the preceding weeks or months are a useful prognostic indicator. This is particularly relevant for children between the ages of 2 and 2 years 6 months as they are likely to make rapid spontaneous changes over short periods of time.

With children attending nursery/playgroup settings, particular note will be made of changes observed since their commencement. If a child is due to start in such a group subsequent to the assessment date, it is important to ascertain when, and to review the child two to three months after this. For many children, a nursery placement will rapidly increase their language development.

Children with language problems

Assessment of pre-school children usually commences informally. The therapist will observe the child on the way into the therapy room. Materials may then be presented in order to observe the child's responses. The toys chosen need to put the child at ease, and will have been specifically selected to provide the therapist with information relating to the child's symbolic play level and developmental stage (Lewis and Boucher 1997).

When using the PCIT approach, an assessment session may start with the parents and therapist talking while the child is at play; with the therapist and child playing, or with the parents and child playing together while the therapist observes the interaction through a video link. The use of a video link may put the child at ease and allow the therapist to make initial observations of the child's spontaneous use of language. It also provides information about the parent and child's current interaction strategies. An objective measure is immediately obtained.

Having observed the child's play, attention and concentration span, the therapist may join in the play to facilitate further investigation. Particular attention will be paid to the child's turn-taking abilities and responses as the therapist mirrors the child's actions and extends the child's play through non-verbal modelling. At this point there is no specific focus on talking.

If the child does not have the attention level required for formal assessment, an informal assessment based on The Derbyshire Language Scheme (Knowles and Masidlover 1982) may provide a baseline profile of the child's comprehension and expressive skills. This will complement the therapist's observations of the child's attention abilities and play skills, and may provide an elicited language sample to add to the spontaneous language already recorded on video. Observations of the child's non-verbal communication strategies are also made.

Having obtained an assessment profile of the child, parents are given specific strategies and recommendations for accelerating their child's progress. These need to be realistic and attainable and be devised so that they can be immediately implemented. The PCIT model ensures that parents are able to identify a strategy that works for them and to observe themselves, on video, implementing it within the session.

Case example

Philip's parents are advised to reduce the number of questions they ask him during play sessions. The play session is repeated and videoed. The parents reduce the number of questions and then watch themselves on video achieving their aim. The therapist highlights the positive effect on Philip's communication and the parents are encouraged to utilise this strategy at home (Kelman and Schneider 1994). Detailed records are kept of this discussion and the suggestions made. The severity of Philip's communication difficulty and the response to the parents' amended interaction forms the foundation for future intervention.

Children with speech problems

As speech generally matures following language development, the speech of a child who presents with a speech delay and language delay will not be assessed until later in the therapy process. Children who present with specific speech sound difficulties at initial appointment may be assessed using a variety of speech production assessments including a psycholinguistic approach (Stackhouse and Wells 1997).

The decision-making process

The therapist needs to draw together the information gained from parents, other professionals, observations, and the findings from the assessments in order to make decisions about possible intervention. In families where English is an additional language, knowledge about the child's culture must also be included.

When forming an initial opinion, the therapist will also note any changes that may have occurred in the child's communication as a result of the therapist's strategies or the parents' adaptations in the video session. While watching the video, the therapist will also have noted any characteristics within the child's profile that may be indicative of disordered language development.

Providing specific labels at an initial assessment is not necessarily appropriate, particularly with young children whose profile will change over time. A description of the child's strengths and weaknesses and any discrepancy between the child and his/her peers will provide a more relevant summary for the parents at this stage. A written report, which includes specific strategies, should be given to the parents before being distributed to the key professionals involved. Referrals may be made to other professionals, with parental consent – for example, to a psychologist for support with behaviour difficulties. Future sessions using the video link may then be arranged.

It is helpful if written information about language development is given to parents and nursery staff at this time. The therapist can then make reference to this when explaining the stage at which the child is currently functioning. Where a child's difficulties are of particular concern, close liaison with the nursery and key professionals will be necessary to ensure that the child accesses support within the Code of Practice (DfEE 2000b).

Throughout the process of intervention, review appointments are paramount. Due to the discrepancy in language development in children under the age of 2 years six months, those who have been identified as having language difficulties at initial assessment should return to the clinic within 3 months for re-assessment. At this point, in the authors' experience, it is possible to make a decision about the child's prognosis based on the amount of change seen in the child's language abilities, and in the parents' interaction style.

The child who has made large gains in language development with the help of the parents' adapted interaction style is likely to continue to make spontaneous progress and will be discharged from the service or reviewed again following a further consolidation period.

Therapy packages of care

It is important that within a speech and language therapy service there is a range of intervention packages available that can be matched to the wide range of individual children's needs. Thus a child with a more persistent, severe problem may be able to receive a more intensive package of care as swiftly as possible.

Children considered a priority are those who present with:

- disordered or severely delayed speech and language development, as distinct from marked phonological delay;
- difficulties that persist in the context of limited parental change;
- difficulties that persist, despite the parents having affected change in their own interaction style;
- excessive demands in relation to fluency (Matthews *et al.* 1997).

Language

Initial Video Interaction

The initial video interaction package (Cummins and Hulme 1997) provides a course of four individual weekly parent-and-child sessions and is offered after the initial assessment/review package. This course of therapy is provided once a child is 2 years and six months old, allowing for the large discrepancy among this peer group, but may be offered at two years if the presenting difficulty is severe and observable. A video is made of the child and parents at play and this video is watched by the therapist and parents. The parents are given feedback about the child's abilities and they are encouraged to evaluate themselves using a self-rating scale.

Using the PCIT model of parent–child interaction, the parents are given further strategies so that they may continue to adapt their interaction with the child. The therapist and parents identify realistic aims, which will enable the parents to work with the child to increase the child's rate of language development. Each session builds on the developments of the previous week.

In families where English is an additional language, the therapist needs to discuss with the parents the benefits of working with video. An interpreter or co-worker may help with this discussion.

The course of video sessions is preceded by a parent workshop, which focuses on play and the concept of a shared focus of attention. At the end of the four-week period, a child is offered a consolidation period. The parents are asked to continue working with the child at home during this six-week period, spending five minutes each day consolidating the new patterns of interaction. The parents and child then return for a review session with the speech and language therapist in order to evaluate any change.

The aim of this review is to gauge whether the child's language development has improved. The child's skills are therefore re-assessed and the new profile compared with the initial assessment profile. The therapist's decision about future intervention is based primarily on whether the discrepancy between the child and his/her peers is reducing and how quickly this may be occurring (Cummins and Hulme 1997).

If the parents have changed their style of interaction but the child's language has not improved and continues to contain characteristics of disordered development, such children will become a priority for further intervention. They may be referred to a local CC intensive group until a place is available within the parent–child six-week intensive course. Where there are serious concerns, they will also be referred to a pre-school language unit.

Where little parental change has been possible, CC intensive groups will be provided, followed by a review appointment to ascertain the rate of progress in response to direct therapy intervention. Many children's difficulties are likely to resolve within this context, particularly where there is good liaison between the therapist and the nursery.

Local community intensive language groups

Intensive language groups are offered to children with ongoing language difficulties. In the authors' health authority, intensive groups have been shown to be more effective for this group of children than weekly language groups. It is recommended that such groups last for two weeks and are run every two months at local health centres. Running such groups three or four times a week for two weeks on a rolling programme has been found to be an effective way of managing time, because children who are reaching the top of the waiting list can be slotted into the next group when a place is available.

After a two-week period of group therapy, there is a six-week consolidation period followed by a review. If necessary, children can be placed in the next group within the rolling programme. Each group is run by two therapists and each pair of therapists run three or four groups per day. There is a maximum of six children per group. Some children may need to attend further groups according to the nature of their difficulties.

Parents are expected to be involved in the language groups. They are provided with a plan of the group's aims and activities, and normally they are asked to observe the sessions, either through a viewing mirror or through a CCTV system. This provides an opportunity for the parents to discuss and observe the therapist using a variety of strategies. Parents may be involved in a more active way in parent-facilitated groups. The therapist organises the play materials, and the parents then follow the therapist's lead. In addition, workshops are run specifically for the parents involved. These workshops seek to combine parents' mutual support with information about the therapist's aims and objectives, general information about communication development and strategies for facilitating change.

If the child is attending a playgroup or nursery, the child's key worker or teacher is encouraged to observe one of the language group sessions. This provides an opportunity for the therapist to glean information and suggestions from key workers while demonstrating additional strategies with the child. Individual Education Plans (IEPs) can thus be drawn up collaboratively. Staff are often willing to carry out one of the group activities in the nursery on a daily basis. For the child, this provides a helpful carry-over into the nursery, while offering the staff pre-planned activities with specific targets. This may be helpful to other children with similar needs within the nursery.

Parent–child six-week intensive course

The parent–child six-week intensive course (Kelman and Schneider 1994) is offered following the child's attendance at a CC intensive course. It is offered to those children who present with disordered language development, and it consists of 18 sessions of therapy over a six-week period. The focus is on parental information as well as direct intervention.

Pre-school language unit

In the authors' authority, children with persistent difficulties are referred to a pre-school language unit after the families have attended a parent–child interaction course. This offers daily therapy and focuses on developing the child's skills within an educational context. The principles of PCIT are integrated into the unit.

Children with communication difficulties seem to benefit greatly if they are offered such intensive help prior to school entry and this may then preclude the necessity for additional support at school age.

Interaction packages for nursery staff

Where possible, the therapist will visit a child's nursery or playgroup in order to observe the child, discuss aspects of the child's communication with the staff, offer advice about relevant activities – possibly within the framework of a language programme – and model these suggestions. Three further packages of care may also be offered, which are aimed specifically at working with nursery staff or key workers who may be involved with the child.

The first is similar to the parent–child interaction package. In order to develop a child's abilities and the key worker's interaction with the child, a video course is offered to the key worker, who is invited to attend the local clinic with the child once a week for four weeks.

A second package is offered that aims to develop staff interaction skills generally. A group of nursery staff are invited to attend a four-session course at a central clinic. Each week, the staff bring a video of themselves interacting with a child, and they then analyse their interactions with the support of their peer group and the therapist. The therapist facilitates the session, guiding the group's observations, helping them to problem-solve, and suggesting modifications of their interactions. This enables the staff to discuss and understand in detail some of the difficulties the children are experiencing, and to generalise their observations to their own setting.

A third package has a pre-emptive function, focusing on children who are considered to be 'at risk' of having future difficulties with their language development. A four-week language-enrichment programme is offered by speech and language therapy students within the nursery setting (Parker and Cummins 1998).

Speech sound difficulties

Those children presenting with speech-sound immaturities should be provided with specific strategies within the initial assessment, followed by parent workshops, while their names are placed on a waiting list for therapy. Intensive CC speech groups may then be offered to those children presenting with more entrenched difficulties, followed by possible individual sessions for specific articulation work (Abba *et al.*1999). Key workers in nurseries are once again invited to participate.

Transfer

Many children will be discharged after attendance at a CC's intensive group. For a small minority, the speech and language therapist will need to contribute towards a Statement and will need to be involved in the child's transfer to a mainstream school or specialist educational setting. Feedback from therapists working in educational settings suggests that parents familiar with PCIT continue to be involved in their child's care to a greater degree than their peer group.

Summary

Although there are different ways of working with pre-school children with language problems, working on parent–child interaction has been shown to be a useful way of offering initial and ongoing help. In many instances no further intervention is needed.

CHAPTER 6

Managing children with communication problems in mainstream schools and units

Marie Gascoigne

Learning outcomes

By the end of this chapter, the reader should:

- have an understanding of the issues underlying the clinical decision-making process in mainstream schools and units;
- have an understanding of the educational legislation and national frameworks that have influenced educational provision;
- be aware of the context within which therapists working in mainstream schools and units function.

Introduction

Speech and language therapists working in mainstream schools and in units attached to mainstream schools need to have a clear understanding of the current political and legislative context for special educational provision as well as of the local management policy and practice.

Speech and language therapy services to mainstream schools exist at the interface between health and education services. Therefore, the clinical management decisions made by therapists will arguably be more closely driven by management policy decisions than is often the case in other clinical contexts. This highly sensitive, political, and increasingly legalistic environment has led to the evolution of management-led service models and systems of prioritisation (Topping *et al.* 1998; Luscombe and Shaw 1996).

Basic questions for which therapists need clear answers include:

- Who receives the speech and language therapy service within mainstream schools and language units? This will include: consideration of whether the children do or do not have a Statement; the severity of their problem; the type of difficulty and whether it is primarily a communication problem; the age range of the children; and the time they have been on a waiting list.
- What service is provided in this mainstream school or unit? This will include consideration of the frequency of visits; the size of the therapist's caseload; and the speech and language therapy time allocated.
- How is the service typically delivered? Factors for consideration here include whether there will be direct intervention from the therapist or indirect intervention through a Learning Support Assistant (LSA); whether there will be contributions to IEPs; whether individual or group therapy will be offered; and the level of intensity of the input.
- What degree of choice regarding therapeutic management do individual therapists have?

Unfortunately, there are currently no standard answers to these questions. Nor perhaps should there be. The answers in any given situation will be the product of a complex interaction between government policy, LEA policy and local health policy. This may be further complicated by individual differences at the level of school, classroom and professional colleagues. So, where to begin?

The inclusion–segregation continuum

Trends in education legislation have been away from segregated provision for children with special educational needs and towards inclusive education (DES 1988; DfEE 1994, 1996, 1997, 1998a, 1999c, 2000b). This inclusive agenda is not unique to England and Wales. The Salamanca Statement (UNESCO 1994), which resulted from a UNESCO conference involving 92 governments and 25 voluntary organisations, outlined the rights of every child to attend the school that they would have attended were they not disabled.

The philosophy underpinning the concept of inclusive education is broader than education itself. The World Health Organisation's categorisation of 'impairment, disability and handicap' (WHO 1980) has been influential in focusing the inclusion agenda. The ultimate goal is to achieve a fully inclusive society where the handicapping effects of disabilities and impairments are reduced by changes made to the fabric of society. Educational contexts offer a logical starting point for ensuring that children with disabilities are able to access the educational curriculum alongside their peers.

Despite this clear direction, endorsed internationally as well as by central government, there continues to be significant variability in the patterns of inclusion across LEAs (Norwich 1997). Some LEAs, such as Newham in London, have adopted active de-segregation policies (Roux 1996), while others retain relatively high levels of segregated provision. In practice, therefore, mainstream schools will vary considerably from one LEA to another, and even within an LEA, in terms of the number of children with special educational needs who are within a particular school, and the profile of their needs.

Many of the proposed advantages to mainstream education for all children lie in the social opportunities that are felt to exist in being part of a local community school. It has been suggested that children with disabilities benefit from role models and that these might not be available in specialist, segregated provision. Philosophically, the children in mainstream provision share experiences with their local community and develop strategies for dealing with the handicapping effects of their disabilities and impairments. This offers useful preparation for later life in wider society.

There is naturally some debate about the practicalities of successfully implementing inclusive education for all children. Much of the opposition comes from parents of children with disabilities, who feel that the specialist resources available in segregated provision cannot be adequately provided in the mainstream context (Simmons 1998). Resource issues are clearly paramount in implementing inclusive models with any degree of success, and both health and education services can always justify a need for additional resources.

Units attached to a mainstream school

The specialist unit attached to a mainstream school has evolved as a potential bridge on the continuum between segregated and mainstream provision. The now-familiar model of a language unit is of a separate classroom with a specialist teacher and LSA providing the curriculum for a group of six to eight children, with some input from a speech and language therapist. The therapist may be full-time or may only be in the unit for two or three days per week.

Children placed in such a unit may integrate with children from the host mainstream school for some classes or may simply share playground and mealtime facilities. However, some LEAs who strongly support the move towards inclusive education take a view that a unit as described above remains too segregated in philosophy. Consequently, inclusive resource bases are now emerging where a similar number of children are supported throughout the school by the same staffing levels and specialism, but the children are always based within their mainstream class of age peers.

The model of language unit provision will naturally influence the way in which the therapist supports the children within the setting. However, there will be core features of speech and language therapy input that will remain common across settings. For example, therapists working in either inclusive or segregated units will spend some of their time working with children individually, away from the main class group, and some of their time with the whole class. The principal difference in terms of opportunities for intervention will be found in the whole-class setting where, in an inclusive resource, this will be a larger group with a greater range of ability. If intervention is to be effective in this context, the therapist will need to plan carefully with the class teacher. This will help to avoid classroom-based intervention becoming little more than a speech and language therapy session happening in the corner of a classroom without reference to the class as a whole. An example of good practice in this setting might be a Literacy Hour session (DfEE 1998b), where the teacher and therapist are involved together in the story section and then work with small groups within the class, carrying out differentiated activities based on the same theme.

Children identified for places in a language unit, whatever its operational policy, are likely to conform to the 'specific language impairment' categorisation (Conti-Ramsden and Botting 1999). However, even then, the threshold of severity to warrant a place in a unit as opposed to a mainstream school or specialist segregated provision will vary across LEAs.

It would appear, then, that therapists in mainstream schools and units can make few assumptions about the precise nature of the provision where they will be working – or, indeed about the presenting profiles of the children they are to support. However, despite the infinite potential variations across services, the common frameworks provided by the National Curriculum and the Code of Practice for special educational needs provide some consistency.

The National Curriculum

The National Curriculum provides a common framework for all schools in terms of core subject areas and content, and access is an entitlement for all children. The explicit reference to speaking and listening skills as part of the core subject of English has played a part in highlighting the needs of children with communication difficulties. This has been further emphasised with the introduction of the National Literacy and Numeracy Strategies (DfEE 1998b, 1999b). The National Curriculum framework, therefore, provides the speech and language therapist and teaching colleagues with a common point of reference through which to discuss a child's communication skills.

The revised National Curriculum (QCA 1999) for Key Stages 1–3 is particularly interesting to speech and language therapists working in educational settings. Inclusive education is a prominent theme, as is the emphasis for all children on core skill areas of communication, application of number, information technology, working with others, improving own learning and performance, and problem-solving.

The relevance of these skills to the therapist supporting children with communication difficulties is both obvious and challenging. In order to provide effective speech and language therapy services within this context, these challenges need to be viewed as opportunities for developing the role of the therapist within all educational settings.

Opportunities presented by the revisions will include the increased level of awareness among all professionals of inclusion and access issues for pupils with communication difficulties.

Code of Practice for special educational needs

The Code of Practice for special educational needs (DfEE 1994) also provides a common framework across educational settings that can act as a point of reference for a child's special educational needs. This is helpful for the therapist who has to deal with the potential diversity of needs among children in the mainstream setting, giving an indication, from an educational perspective, as to the level of support required in order for a child to access the National Curriculum. The potential difficulties of relying on the Code of Practice as a guide to defining needs from a speech and language therapy perspective arise from the fundamental differences between education and health services in terms of function (McCartney 1999a). That is, education services exist for all, health services exist for a subgroup who have been identified as having a deficit.

The draft Revised Code of Practice (DfEE 2000b) outlines the proposed simplification of the school-based stages from three stages to two, which will be renamed 'School Support' and 'School Support Plus'. A therapist would typically be involved with a child receiving School Support Plus or a child with a Statement. The issue of speech and language therapy provision is specifically addressed in the foregoing consultation document, with an acknowledgement that speech and language therapy intervention can include:

'a variety of activities including classroom observation of the child to assess the effect of the child's language difficulties and monitor progress; liaison with the SENCO, class teacher or learning support assistant to discuss how programmes of therapy can best be delivered in the classroom and to agree targets and strategies; working individually or in a small group with the child for assessment or therapy; liaison with parents about how they can help to deliver the therapy programme at home; participating in IEP planning and reviews; attending annual reviews and providing in-service training to staff.' (DfEE 2000b)

This explicit recognition that speech and language therapy support can be more than one-to-one therapy is a significant step forward in reaching a shared understanding of how such therapy works.

Individual Education Plans

A key feature of the Code of Practice that has the potential for supporting collaborative practice between the speech and language therapist and other professionals involved in supporting a given child (see Chapter 11) is the IEP. McCartney (1999a) identifies the joint setting of IEP targets and strategies as one of the most successful areas of collaborative practice between therapists and teachers. The requirement for specific, measurable, time-limited targets to be set as part of an IEP, which in turn relates to broader objectives for the child, offers significant opportunities for therapists to ensure that their intervention is an integral part of the child's educational programme of support. However, the success of collaboration at this level will continue to be partly determined by the model of service delivery in which the therapist is working (Wright and Kersner 1998).

Models of service delivery

Speech and language therapy services within mainstream schools have evolved in parallel to the changes in special educational provision outlined above, and several have published their models of working within mainstream schools (Hoddell 1995; Lennox and Watkins 1998; Luscombe and Shaw 1996; New 1998; Topping *et al.* 1998). The services described demonstrate the different ways in which therapists have made decisions about the needs of children in mainstream schools in the light of varying LEAs' policies and procedures.

The concept of 'outreach' as described by Hoddell (1995) – where a therapist runs language groups with the purpose of training a member of a school's staff to continue groups without the therapist being present – features in several models described. Another prominent theme is that of using some form of rotational model, half termly or termly, to focus resources in a particular set of schools at any one time.

The DfEE together with the DoH and the National Assembly for Wales, commissioned a wide-ranging study (Law *et al.* 2000). The study, in three parts, provides:

- a profile of speech and language therapy services for school-age children in England and Wales;
- an analysis of the key factors that have been found to facilitate effective collaboration between health and education at management and practitioner levels;
- an evidence-based proposal as to how speech and language therapy services for school-age children might develop in the future.

Decision making

Decision making in speech and language therapy services to mainstream schools exists at two levels: clinical decisions and managerial decisions.

Clinical decision making involves judgements based on a therapist's interpretation of a series of observations. The challenges lie in making explicit the criteria on which any judgements are made and ensuring equity between practitioners in how they interpret these. Managerial decision making takes place at a service-planning level and is, therefore, rarely within the remit of an individual therapist. Although managerial decisions are made about all areas of speech and language therapy service delivery, the direct impact of this level of decision-making is perhaps felt more directly by therapists working in school settings.

Figure 6.1 provides a schematic diagram that represents the potential path of a child through a particular model of service delivery for mainstream schools. There will have been a number of management decisions in the evolution of such a model, which might not be immediately evident from Figure 6.1. However, as each clinical decision-making point in the process is expanded (Figures 6.2–6.4), the interface of clinical and managerial decisions will become apparent.

Clinical decision 1 following initial assessment

The first significant clinical decision that a therapist makes about a child follows assessment (Figure 6.2). This may be an initial assessment or a subsequent re-evaluation of the child's needs. The decision will be based on the therapist's observations of the child across a range of situations. These might include individual formal and/or informal assessment measures of language skill, but they should also encompass observation of the child's functional communication skills and ability to access the curriculum in respect of language demands. Information gathered from school staff, including copies of any IEPs, will provide invaluable information and a joint framework for discussion between the staff and a visiting therapist.

A concern of many school-based speech and language therapy services is the potential loss of contact with parents. A range of strategies might be employed to ensure adequate parental involvement. The school may prove an appropriate venue for the therapist to meet with the parents because a relationship may already exist between the school and the parents. Furthermore, removing the need for an additional journey to a health-based setting may increase the parents' access to the speech and language therapy service (Topping *et al.* 1998).

Following initial assessment, the therapist should have a comprehensive profile of the child's communication abilities. The first clinical judgement will be about the severity of the communication difficulties and of their impact on the child's ability to communicate functionally across a range of settings.

Enderby and John (1997) show how the WHO (1980) classification system of impairment–disability–handicap provides a useful structure in which to evaluate severity across different parameters. The Therapy Outcome Measures (TOMs; Enderby and John 1997) use this classification as a basis for identifying key indicators across different areas of speech and language therapy that can be used to measure objectively the outcomes for

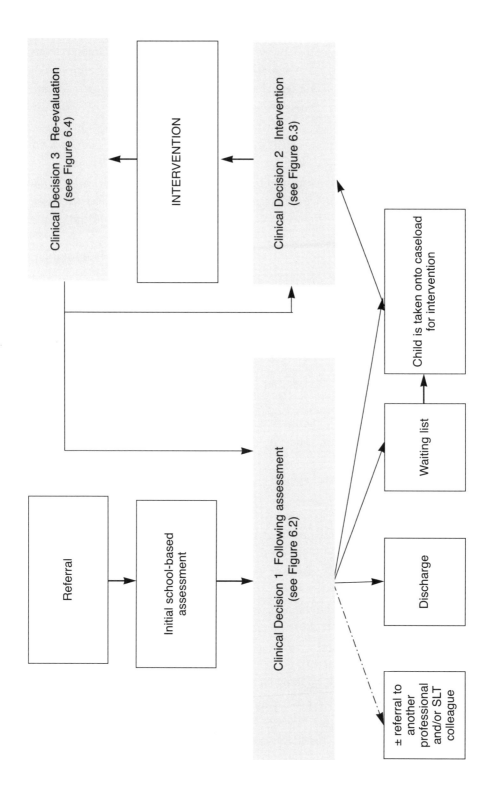

Figure 6.1 A simplified decision-making process for mainstream schools

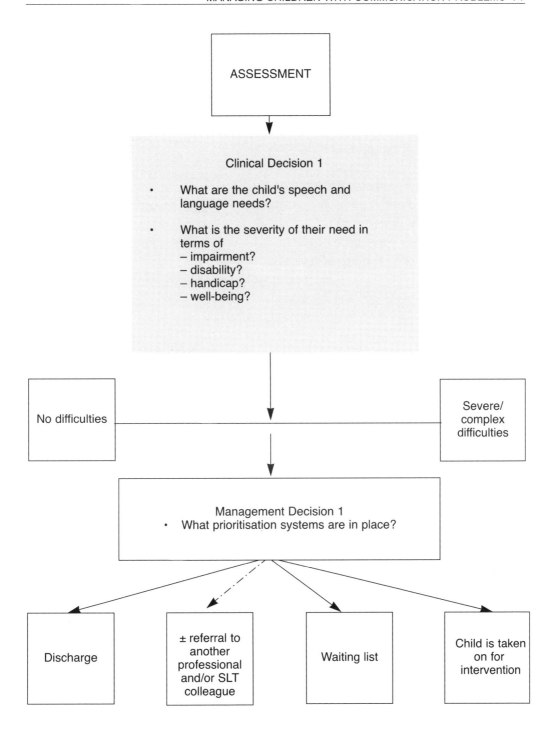

Figure 6.2 Clinical decision making following assessment

intervention. These TOMs can also be used as a starting point for clinical decision-making. TOMs provide scaled descriptors for severity across the parameters of impairment, disability and handicap. There is the additional parameter of well-being/distress (see Figure 6.2). The scaled descriptors provide reference outlines for the therapist for each of the points on the scale. For example, in the case of a child being profiled on the 'Child Speech Language Impairment' scale, the impairment descriptors include the following range (Enderby and John 1997):

- *0: Profound language impairment.* Profound problems evident in all areas; extremely limited language involving use, comprehension, expression, and phonology. Examples of standard test scores: at or below 55 on a standard score. First percentile: a lag of 2.5 years.
- *3: Moderate language impairment.* Moderate problems in some areas, and/or specific moderate problems in one area of language involving use, comprehension, expression, and phonology. Examples of standard test scores: at, or below 77 on a standard score. Seventh percentile: a lag of 1.6–2.0 years.
- *5: No impairment.* Age-appropriate language in all areas.

Using a tool such as TOMs will allow a structured classification of the information gathered at initial assessment so as to provide not only an evaluation of the degree of severity of a child's communication difficulties but also a baseline for measurement of efficacy of any intervention provided.

Case example

Jamie is six years old and attends his local community primary school. He is at Stage 5 of the Code of Practice and his school receives additional funds that equate to two hours per week with an individual support teacher or ten hours per week with an LSA.

He has the following profile of communication skills:

- comprehension scores on formal assessment – standard score 75 – are between one and two standard deviations below the norm, indicating a significant difficulty with understanding of spoken language;
- expressive scores show a similar delay;
- analysis of a language sample indicates a disorder of syntax;
- classroom observation shows that Jamie has some strategies for seeking clarification and makes good use of the support offered by the LSA when she is with him. He was observed to have difficulties following instructions in the whole class group without further explanation by an adult. Jamie was able to participate in a small-group activity such as painting a model that the group had previously built, taking turns and contributing non-verbally to the task. Peers were generally supportive of Jamie's contributions but appeared not to understand some of his verbal contributions. Jamie was observed to be reluctant to repeat verbal contributions when peers did not understand;

- playground observation showed Jamie engaged in solitary play on the climbing apparatus for much of the time, interspersed with periods of standing close to the teacher on duty.

Using TOMs to classify Jamie's communication yields the following results (and note that Enderby and John (1997) advocate the use of half increments where appropriate):

- *Impairment.* Jamie has delayed and disordered language skills for comprehension and expression of spoken language. Severity based on formal assessment falls in the 'moderate language impairment' category – Rating 3.
- *Disability.* Jamie is generally able to follow classroom routines but has difficulty following instructions in the whole-class group. He is also not understood on occasions by his peers. Severity based on observation in the classroom context – Rating 3.
- *Handicap.* Jamie appears isolated from his peers in social settings such as the playground. His active participation in more structured activities is partially dependent on an adult to facilitate his access. Jamie appears generally well included within the classroom and is welcomed, albeit as a relatively passive participant, by peers. Rating 3.5.
- *Well-being/distress.* Jamie appears more confident and participative in structured situations in the classroom than in the playground. In the social context, Jamie appears withdrawn. However, he is not exhibiting any outward signs of distress. His rating for this parameter could be 4.

The clinical decision will be, therefore, to identify where Jamie's overall profile fits best on the continuum of need. The position on the continuum will be influenced by the relative importance given to the parameters. If the therapists' philosophical approach is towards an impairment model of therapy, then the rating of the impairment scale may be weighted more heavily relative to the other scales. Conversely, if the philosophy is one of functional communication, the disability and handicap scales may be more influential. It is important that the influence of these different views on the decision-making process is explicit for those who interact with the service, especially parents and professional colleagues.

The action taken in relation to a child following an assessment will be influenced by the prioritisation system and the local management policy of the speech and language therapy service (see Management Decision 1 in Figure 6.2). For example, in the service in Islington LEA, London, a child whose clinical need was felt to be at the mild/moderate end of the severity continuum might be supported by a professional other than a speech and language therapist, such as a specialist teacher for language impairment (Topping *et al.* 1998).

Another option for Jamie is that he might be placed on a waiting list. Where speech and language therapy services to mainstream schools have a waiting list, it will be subject to some form of prioritisation. One of the ongoing tensions between speech and language therapy services and LEAs is what impact the presence or absence of a Statement has on the prioritisation system of that therapy's service. There appears to be an emerging consensus that 'severity' or 'clinical need' are primary factors for prioritisation (Topping *et al.* 1998; Luscombe and Shaw 1996).

Clinical Decision 2: Intervention

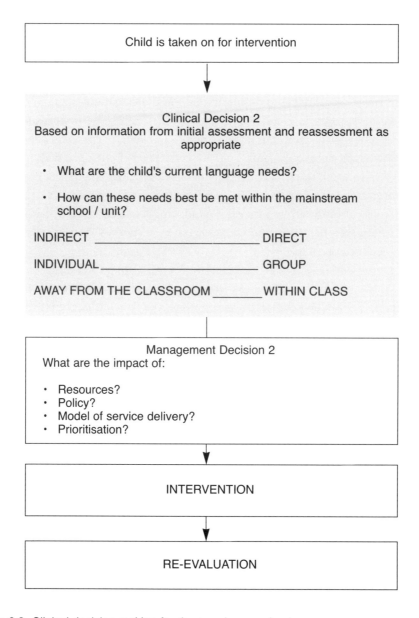

Figure 6.3 for the diagram structure is described in text below:

Child is taken on for intervention

Clinical Decision 2
Based on information from initial assessment and reassessment as appropriate

- What are the child's current language needs?

- How can these needs best be met within the mainstream school / unit?

INDIRECT _____ DIRECT

INDIVIDUAL_____ GROUP

AWAY FROM THE CLASSROOM _____ WITHIN CLASS

Management Decision 2
What are the impact of:

- Resources?
- Policy?
- Model of service delivery?
- Prioritisation?

INTERVENTION

RE-EVALUATION

Figure 6.3 Clinical decision making for the ongoing caseload

The TOMs framework used in interpreting the assessment data will prove useful in suggesting a focus for intervention. The nature of the intervention will vary across the parameters of direct/indirect; withdrawn from the class or within the class; individual or group intervention, and intensity/frequency of intervention.

Clearly, there will be times when various combinations of these options will be appropriate. However, therapists who are predisposed towards impairment-focused intervention may find it more appropriate to offer direct intervention on an individual basis away from the classroom. Therapists who aim to work functionally at the level of disability and handicap may prefer intervention to be indirect, group-based and within the classroom. In practice, different combinations across all these parameters will be appropriate according to the circumstances.

The most tangible difference between therapists in mainstream schools and therapists in units is the frequency and intensity of support. Therapists in units are likely to have a greater number of sessions available. However, more opportunity will not automatically suggest more direct, impairment-focused intervention.

The parameters will now be discussed in more detail:

- *Direct or indirect intervention?* There is little evidence as to whether direct or indirect work is more effective (Wood 1998). The key to successful indirect intervention lies in the effective development of skills in the person implementing that intervention (see Chapters 9 and 10).
- *Withdrawn from the classroom or within the classroom?* Working within the classroom requires the greatest level of collaboration between therapists and teachers. Careful planning and preparation is required in order to make this a positive experience (Wright and Kersner 1998).
- *Individual or group?* Group intervention has become an accepted pattern for speech and language therapy as there are benefits for interaction, and therapy targets can be made more interesting and accessible. However, there may still be times when it is more appropriate to work on an individual basis. A model of service delivery needs to be flexible, allowing either option (see Chapter 4).

Contributions to IEPs

Where therapists are more likely to be involved in some direct intervention, such as in units, the speech and language therapy aims would be best placed as targets within a child's IEP. However, in mainstream schools where the service offered may be primarily indirect intervention, a contribution of language targets to the IEP may be the only tangible evidence of speech and language therapy support for a child. It could be argued that the speech and language therapy aims for all children receiving support within a school setting should be an integral part of the IEP.

A well-written language target within an IEP, will specify the strategies for achieving that target and might propose a range of interventions – some to be delivered by the therapist, some by other staff. The monitoring mechanisms may include daily or weekly record keeping by school staff, as well as a less frequent review by the therapist. This involvement in the IEP target-setting would then encourage joint ownership of the target between the therapist and the teacher, which may provide a vehicle for effective collaborative working.

The continuing case example of 'Jamie'

A possible target for Jamie might be: 'Jamie will be able to show understanding and use of ten key items of science vocabulary.' This target could be relevant for many children being supported within mainstream classrooms or units. The achievement of this target could be approached in a number of different ways, and the parameters discussed above need to be borne in mind by the therapist as part of the clinical decision-making process.

One approach might be an impairment-based approach, which might involve the speech and language therapist working regularly with Jamie for 20–30 minutes in the school library with the aim of teaching him the items of science vocabulary. Here, the therapist will use direct therapy techniques, to develop Jamie's understanding and use of this vocabulary. At the same time, the therapist might also be able to gain insight into Jamie's language-processing system. As a result, the therapist may then develop a secondary aim of trying to influence his language processing system through the use of specific techniques. During the session, the therapist's clinical observations might lead to adaptations of the ways in which some of the tasks are presented.

Another approach to the same task might be a functional approach. This might involve an LSA running a vocabulary activity using materials associated with the topic, within the classroom, with a small group of children from the class, including Jamie. Here the target is also to develop Jamie's understanding and use of the science vocabulary and to develop his ability to use the newly acquired vocabulary appropriately in the classroom. That is, to take the specific task and make it a functional tool for learning.

It may be that a combination of both of these approaches is appropriate.

When making clinical decisions regarding intervention, the speech and language therapist needs to make explicit the link between a child's communication difficulties and the impact of these difficulties on the child's access to learning. Having made that link, the intervention needs to target the difficulties through the most effective medium. It is at this point that the therapist and the teacher may collaborate effectively.

Clinical Decision 3: Re-evaluation

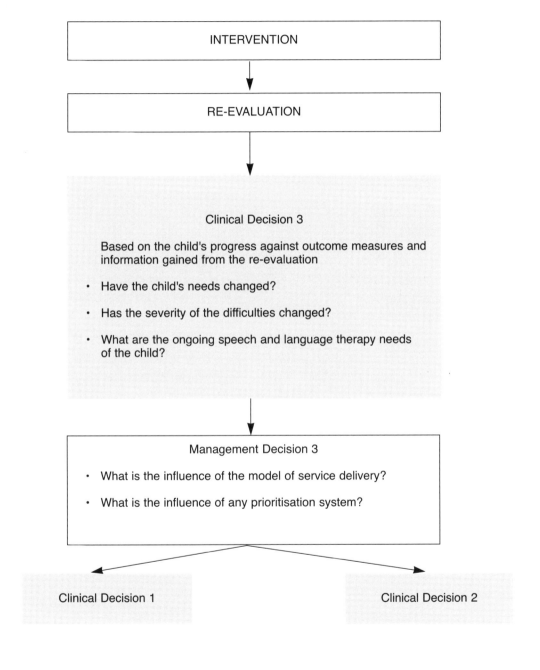

Figure 6.4 Clinical decision making on re-evaluation following intervention

This clinical decision follows a specified period of intervention, the 'episodes of care' or 'blocks of therapy'. Within schools, the term or half-term may offer a natural boundary for re-evaluation, which may occur in conjunction with a review of targets within the IEPs. Depending on the intervals between evaluation decisions, different measures of outcome will be appropriate.

Measuring outcome

The TOMs, as described above, provide one comprehensive set of scales to measure progress. However, evaluation at short intervals would not show measurable change on the TOMs. IEP targets, which are specific and measurable, can offer a highly relevant measure of outcome. Difficulties arise when targets have not been designed with sufficient detail that an 'achieved/not achieved' decision can be made.

The involvement of the speech and language therapist in IEP setting and review meetings is highly desirable and makes a significant contribution to effective support for a child in a school setting. This has been recognised in the Code of Practice (DfEE 2000b).

Where to go next

Whatever outcome measure is used for evaluation, the therapist has to assimilate this information and make a decision. This will depend on, first, whether the child's profile of needs has changed significantly and therefore a change of clinical management is required – or, secondly, whether the child's profile has *not* changed and further intervention is required.

It is appropriate to identify the clinical decision regarding re-evaluation as a discrete stage in the decision-making process to allow for varying rates of progress among the children. There is also a possible link with management decisions. Management Decision 3 (see Figure 6.4) might limit the number of periods of intervention that each child can receive in a given context. This can apply to mainstream schools and to units, because the criteria for placement in some unit settings may include a defined period of provision, for example two years.

Summary

There are considerable philosophical, political and theoretical issues that impinge upon the ways in which speech and language therapy services are delivered in mainstream settings. The reader should now have an understanding of how clinical decisions can be identified within this setting and how they have been influenced by the historical context.

CHAPTER 7

Managing children with communication problems in a special school

Jill Popple and Wendy Wellington

Learning outcomes

By the end of this chapter, the reader should be aware of:

- the role of the special school on the continuum of special educational needs provision;
- how speech and language therapy services may be delivered within a special school;
- ways in which speech and language therapists and teachers may work together in such a school.

Introduction

Although there is a thrust towards inclusive education (see Chapter 6), the need for a continuum of provision is recognised and there is still a place for some special schools. As the DfEE has stated (1997): 'The needs of individual children are paramount. Where these cannot currently be met in mainstream schools, specialist provision should be available.'

In contrast to the previous chapter, this chapter describes the speech and language therapist's role in one segregated special school for children with severe communication difficulties. The authors of this chapter are based in such a school in Sheffield. This school is funded by the LEA, although many similar schools for children with severe communication difficulties are run by voluntary organisations such as ICAN or the National Autistic Society.

Normally, in schools run by voluntary organisations all the staff are employed by the organisation. With LEA-funded schools, this may not be the case, as therapy staff may be employed by the health authority. Therapists in this situation may have split loyalties between the health authority's speech and language therapy team and the school. One way in which this may be addressed is to regard this post as a 'link', as has occurred in Sheffield. This has allowed a greater understanding of the different points of view between health and education.

The Sheffield school is for primary-school-aged children who have a Statement. The children's problems include specific speech and/or language impairments (SSLI) and/or autistic spectrum disorders. The school supports an inclusion policy and the ultimate aim is for children to return to their local mainstream schools wherever possible. This is in line with the view that 'it should not be assumed that all children requiring specialist provision at a particular time will do so permanently, or that the current capacity of mainstream schools to respond to their needs cannot be extended' (DfEE 1997).

Special schools follow the National Curriculum, the National Literacy Strategy (DfEE 1998b) and the National Numeracy Strategy (DfEE 1999b), with modifications as appropriate for each individual child. Each child has an IEP, which, in a school for communication impaired children, provides an opportunity for collaborative work between teaching staff and speech and language therapy staff (see Chapter 11).

Segregated, special schools usually have a smaller school population than most mainstream schools. The ratio of staff to children is usually higher within the classes. This could be as high as three staff to eight children, as in some classes in the Sheffield school. The staff usually comprises teachers, special support assistants, and speech and language therapists. Such schools are able to offer the children an intensive, integrated approach to speech and language therapy and small-group teaching.

Most children attending such schools are brought to school in taxis or minibuses, so that it might not be possible to maintain as regular face-to-face contact with parents as may be possible in some local, mainstream schools.

The role of the speech and language therapist

Although they do not form a homogeneous group, all the children in a special school of the kind described above have a communication problem, and this becomes part of the main focus of the work. Therefore, it is recognised that the role of the speech and language therapist in the segregated school may be different from that in other settings, such as health centres or mainstream schools. *Communicating Quality 2* states that 'a language unit/school placement is a unique acknowledgement by all parties of the child's speech and language therapy needs as being part of his/her education' (RCSLT 1996) .

Within such a school, the speech and language therapist is part of a consistent multi-disciplinary team that works collaboratively to develop the children's skills in all areas of curriculum and daily life skills (Popple and Wellington 1996). Often, the teachers have specialist skills and knowledge, which are developed through their working experience. This means that there needs to be 'a service which is committed to shared knowledge, skills, expertise and information between teaching staff and speech and language therapists' (RCSLT 1996).

Working with the staff

Working in a special school enables therapists and teachers to develop an in-depth knowledge about each others' disciplines and facilitates joint working for the benefit of the child. Collaborative working encourages the use of joint planning at curriculum level and also at an individual level for each child. Following assessment, joint goal-setting can be developed between teachers and therapists for each child's IEP (see Chapter 6), and the establishment of a joint IEP acts as a basis for developing and integrating the child's communication skills and learning. For example, groups run within the classroom, such as word-finding groups or concept groups, may be directly linked to curriculum activities.

'Where staff work together this will increase the opportunities for sharing knowledge and developing the understanding and nature of speech and language impairment (SLI). Sharing of knowledge and skills enhances the roles of the respective professions' (RCSLT 1996). Thus in special schools there may be opportunities for the development of training packages to be set up for teachers, therapists and support assistants – packages that are devised and implemented by a teacher/therapist team. As a result of this shared knowledge, work carried out by both disciplines can become more effective (see Chapter 10).

Collaborative working also allows and encourages the whole staff to use a common vocabulary and to minimise confusion created by the use of professional jargon. To integrate therapy and learning, the therapist and teacher need to use a 'common language' (Miller 1991). This enables the team to work together effectively and to develop a flexibility of approach. For example, for a child to be able to access the curriculum, particularly in such areas as science and maths, the therapist needs to make sure that certain concepts are in place or that they can be supported before language can be used effectively for learning.

Collaborative working may also enable a sharing of resources within the special school, and this sharing may take effect in different ways. For example:

- by the development of teaching and therapy equipment that can be shared by all staff within the school;
- by teachers and therapists developing and providing training packages for all staff;
- by taking part in parent support groups;
- by disseminating and discussing information about strategies, and teaching and therapy packages that have been found to be of particular help for the children.

Where LEAs make provision for children with communication problems within mainstream and special schools, it is also important that they 'find ways in which staff in special and mainstream schools can most effectively support each other', (DfEE 1997). Therefore the speech and language therapists – and teachers – from within the special schools need to find ways to disseminate to colleagues in mainstream education and to other agencies the knowledge and ideas about collaborative working that they have developed. It is important for them to share ideas and expertise, as well as to establish mutual support within their own school. This may be done in different ways – for example:

- by developing and disseminating joint working strategies with colleagues in mainstream schools;
- by developing and disseminating practical strategies for supporting children with specific speech and/or language difficulties and/or autistic spectrum difficulties in mainstream schools;
- by setting up jointly written and presented training courses for therapists, teachers and support assistants who are working with communication-impaired children in the mainstream school setting. Such a series of courses was set up by the Sheffield school and they continue to be repeated annually.

All these areas need to be continually evaluated and monitored in order to improve and update any provision that is required. Decisions will need to be made about how to identify the ways in which staff within the school work together, as well as the ways in which staff from special schools work with mainstream schools' staff.

In the school in Sheffield, the therapists and teachers have also had input into mainstream schools at three levels in relation to supporting specific children:

- At the point prior to admission. This enables communication and teaching strategies to be put into place before the child enters the segregated special school.
- At the point of part-time integration into mainstream school, following a period of full-time placement in the special school.
- When the child at the segregated school is ready for full-time re-integration into the mainstream school.

Visits between the schools involved were made by the speech and language therapist as well as the class teacher and/or the special support assistant, and time was taken to exchange information about each individual child and the methods used to support and enable that child to progress in both education and communication.

Thus, in order that children with severe speech and/or language disorders can maximise their full potential, speech and language therapists and education staff need to work together as a team. This includes using a common language, minimising jargon, and developing opportunities for joint training initiatives. Parents also need to be involved at all levels as closely as possible.

Working with the children

Therapists need to ascertain how a child's communication difficulties, as shown by the results of assessments, impact on communication for learning and social development. Appropriate therapy may then be devised so that it can be an integral part of the child's home and school life (see also Chapter 6). Therapists need to know about the child's speech and language development in terms of form, content and use of language (Bloom and Lahey 1978) in order to facilitate the use of newly acquired skills in different contexts.

Therapists working in any educational setting need to be flexible and take into account each of the children's strengths, weaknesses, and preferred ways of learning (Kolb 1984). They need to be aware of curriculum issues and to consider the topics being taught as well as any specific vocabulary that may be required. The results of any speech and language therapy assessments need to be shared and discussed with the educational staff and parents. Similarly, the educational staff need to share their assessment results not only with the parents but also with the therapists. If the parents find it difficult to attend school, then it can be helpful to use home–school books. Organising home visits and the setting-up of parents' evenings and parents' meetings during the day can also be effective in making them feel part of the team.

Within a special school, it is particularly important for the therapists to take a holistic approach when working with the children. Any support systems introduced for use with the children may then be consolidated and, ideally, used consistently throughout the school so that they become part of the child's day-to-day life. Such systems may include signing, symbols, Cued Articulation (Passey 1990a and 1990b) or Rebus symbols, which may be helpful in both literacy and therapy work. This holistic strategy, therefore, encourages a 'whole-school approach' and the therapist should be able to support this by ensuring that adequate training in the use of such systems is provided for the staff as well as for parents (see Chapters 9 and 10).

A senior management role

In the school cited above, the speech and language therapists are part of the senior management of the school and act as observers on the governing body. This role has allowed yet a further link to be established between the health and education authorities, enabling immediate and open discussion about any questions directly relating to the children's communication disorders and issues related to the speech and language therapy service. Through this arrangement, the staff of the speech and language therapy service have developed a better understanding of the school culture, and this has further encouraged a trusting and collaborative working climate to evolve.

Service delivery

It is important to remember that speech and language therapy must be part of a child's everyday life for it to be truly effective and useful for that child. Collaborative and open practice within schools provides opportunities for therapists to explore many possible ways of working with the children. One of the main decisions to be made when there is more than one therapist working in a special school is about the way in which the therapists should be deployed. Some of the possibilities and the advantages and disadvantages are outlined below.

First, each therapist could have responsibility for named children with differing disorders, across various classes. In this way, the therapist develops skills across all age levels and communication disorders, and the children and parents benefit from a continuity of approach as the children move through the school, helping to build up trust and confidence. It also allows the therapist to support the child and his or her teacher when the child moves to a new class. It allows the therapist and teaching staff to observe the development of each child longitudinally and to pass on information and knowledge about that child.

Secondly, there could be one therapist per class. In this way, each class teacher would only have to relate to one therapist. This can make joint classroom planning between teacher and therapist easier; however, it does not take into account the continuity of approach for the child and the family. There may be a heavier workload in one class than in another, as some children will require more intensive input than others and therefore need more speech and language therapy time.

A third approach is that there could be one therapist per disorder – for example, one therapist could specialise in autism, one in speech and phonological difficulties, and one in language disorders. In this way, each therapist would have responsibility for keeping up with specific research and becoming a specialist in that field. However, in practice children do not fit neatly into these discrete areas. It may be better for all therapists in the school to have a wider knowledge base to allow for the development and exchange of ideas.

Setting targets

In the Sheffield school mentioned above, decisions are made about the aims and objectives for each child's IEP in discussion with the teaching staff. The children's IEPs include direct communication aims. Following discussion, it is then determined who will take responsibility for delivering the child's communication programme. It could be the speech and language therapist, the teacher, or the special support assistant. Therefore, the speech and language therapy input for each child might be different, depending on the specific aims. This approach allows for a prioritisation of the speech and language therapist's time.

For some children with severe speech disorders, direct intervention by the speech and language therapist on an intensive basis may be appropriate. However, for some children with autism it is more likely that the communication aims need to be an integrated part of the school day in order to facilitate the development and generalisation of skills by utilising everyday situations. The agent of change in this case is likely to be the child's key worker, who may be any member of the team.

Delivering the therapy

Another decision to be made by the therapist is how the children receive their therapy within the school. The speech and language therapy could be offered away from the classroom, and this would involve the children being withdrawn from certain classroom activities. They could then work on an individual basis with the therapist on specific areas that have been jointly identified with the teacher and/or parents. Or, the therapist could take several children out of different classes to work as a group.

Alternatively, a jointly-planned communication programme could be delivered in the classroom directly by the speech and language therapist, by the speech and language therapy assistant, or by educational staff. In some instances, the therapist could work with the teacher to integrate speech and language therapy into the classroom situation – for example, by introducing phonology tasks into the Literacy Hour.

The therapist might work directly with the child in the classroom, doing individual work and facilitating the child's learning, or the therapist might take part in or lead whole-class groups. Groups may be particularly useful in helping to develop children's attention skills, use of language in social situations, vocabulary learning, word storage and accessing skills. Groups can also be used for the development of specific concepts that are needed for curriculum and topic work. Groups may be planned and run jointly by speech and language therapists together with members of the education staff. This enables the skills learnt in the group to be extended and practised in the classroom situation and so to be generalised (see Chapter 4). Furthermore, education staff working with the children might also be able to identify particular 'problem areas' that occur during the school day and put forward suggestions for these areas to be tackled more specifically in 'group time'.

It may be, in practice, that a combination of the approaches described above is used in order for therapy to be most effective. In addition, all these approaches would need to be reviewed and modified as necessary. Once the decision has been made about how therapy will be delivered, the process needs to be evaluated and monitored. To maximise the effectiveness, the decisions made will be influenced by continued evaluation of the child's progress and individual needs, as well as the child's home and school situation, in order to establish the kind of therapy that will be most suitable.

Therapy

Aims of therapy

The aim of the therapy is to 'maximise the child's potential to communicate'. Also, it is known that communication difficulties have 'an effect on family dynamics, interpersonal relationships and classroom performance' (RCSLT 1998). This, therefore, has a bearing on the way that therapy is planned within the school. In the Sheffield school, the aims are based on the Clinical Guidelines by Consensus for Speech and Language Therapists (RCSLT 1998). These broad aims constitute the main framework of all the planning and therapy that is devised for the children, and they comprise the following:

1. To raise awareness of the effects and range of difficulties that the children may encounter.
2. To look at the communicative environment in which the children work and live, and to advise those working with each child accordingly.
3. To produce a jointly planned set of short-term and long-term goals for the children, based on joint assessments.
4. To monitor, both objectively and subjectively, each child's progress and adjust the goals accordingly.
5. To work directly or indirectly with the children to develop the following areas of communication: speech production; receptive language; expressive language; verbal/augmentative communication – i.e. the range of ways that the children use their communication skills.
6. To review each of the children's performance through the annual review system.
7. To suggest strategies for helping each child to access the curriculum.
8. To facilitate the children's life skills and their ability to cope as independently as possible.

Meeting the aims

Once the information has been gathered from the therapy and education assessments, and the child's strengths and individual learning styles have been identified, decisions can then be made about how to meet the aims of therapy. The strengths in a child's profile are used to support the child's weaker areas. For example, a child with underlying phonological or auditory processing difficulties may benefit from using the psycholinguistic approach for assessment and therapy, as described by Stackhouse and Wells (1997). Ways in which this can be used in a school setting are described in Popple and Wellington (2001).

Evaluation of therapy

There needs to be 'an ongoing evaluation of the effectiveness of the intervention with modifications as appropriate', (RCSLT 1996). This is particularly important within a special school, not only to establish the effectiveness of therapy but also to ensure that the IEP aims have been met. In this special school, this requirement is met by the use of a variety of strategies and measurements, some of which are outlined below:

- *Regular meetings with the teaching staff.* This enables the monitoring of whether targets have been met and how the children are using strategies that have been taught in 'real' situations. Staff are then able to identify which teaching methods have been successful and which methods need re-appraising.
- *Meetings with parents* provide an opportunity to hear about the parents' evaluation of the child's progress. These meetings can take the form of parents' evenings, or less-formal contacts where the parents are able to look at the children's work and discuss any relevant issues.
- *Evaluation and recording of targets* can be achieved through the joint evaluation of IEPs between therapy and education staff.
- *The children are re-assessed at regular intervals*, both by education staff and by speech and language therapists.
- *Therapists may use specific outcome measures*, such as Therapy Outcome Measures (TOMs; Enderby and John 1997) to measure the effectiveness of speech and language therapy input in the areas of impairment, disability, handicap and distress.

Summary

Special schools provide speech and language therapists with different opportunities for service delivery. Generally speaking, there are more therapists and a lower staff-to-child ratio within such schools. Therapists may have more opportunity to take a 'whole-school approach' and to facilitate the generalisation of therapy into the classroom.

CHAPTER 8

The roles of speech and language therapists working in community clinics, child development centres, and hospitals

Sue Roulstone

Learning outcomes

By the end of the chapter, the reader should:

- be aware of the range of children seen in the three settings under consideration here;
- be aware of the unique aspects of the therapists' role in each setting;
- understand some of the key issues for speech and language therapists;
- be aware of strategies for evaluation.

Introduction

In this chapter the aim is to examine the work of speech and language therapists who are based in community health centres and clinics, in child development centres (CDCs) or who work with children in hospitals. Although there are commonalities shared by therapists across work settings, some aspects of the work are particular to a diagnostic group or to the specific function of that setting.

For example, the identification of risk is a common issue. In order to establish whether or not a child is at risk for long-term speech, language or communication difficulties, therapists must investigate features of a child's history as well as the presenting symptoms. A family history of speech difficulties or a history of birth trauma might alert a therapist to the potential for long-term difficulties for a child. Additionally, within each diagnostic or clinical setting, there will be particular clues to be found. For example, when working with children who have a cleft palate, resonance is of primary importance; when dealing with pervasive developmental disorders, aspects of joint attention will be crucial.

A therapist, therefore, needs to make decisions by continually integrating general diagnostic and therapeutic principles with those of relevance to a particular client group or setting and by applying them to the needs and difficulties of the individual child.

Community clinics

Background

Since 1974, when the NHS took on the responsibility for the employment of all speech and language therapists, community clinics and health centres have most commonly been the base from which they have operated. The importance of these clinics and centres as bases is likely to continue with the formation of Primary Care Groups and Health Trusts, which place an emphasis on locally determined care and require increasing collaboration with the Primary Care Team (PCT).

These centres are the focus of primary healthcare for local communities, and referrals to therapists working within such centres may cover the full range of speech and language difficulties. This may include simple developmental speech and language delays, specific language impairment and fluency disorders, as well as communication difficulties that are related to other developmental disorders such as learning difficulties and autism.

The range of speech and language difficulties seen in local health and community centres will depend on the availability of other specialist services, the structure of the speech and language therapy service, and the geographical location. For example, therapists working in rural areas may see children with a larger range of difficulties than therapists working within urban contexts where specialist clinics are available, or where initial assessments are dealt with on a centralised or specialised basis (Pickstone 1997).

Given that referrals of pre-school children come mostly from health visitors, therapists' ongoing contact with them in community clinics is invaluable for developing appropriate referrals and for accessing additional information and support. Parents, general practitioners, school nurses, and nursery and teaching staff will also refer children into the community clinic system.

The role of speech and language therapists in community clinics

Being based close to the primary health carers in this way puts the community speech and language therapist 'in the front line' – responding to concerns raised in the community by parents about children's speech, language and communication development. Depending on the location and size of the speech and language therapy service, the therapist may be part of a team of speech and language therapists serving a local area, or the only therapist for miles around. Whichever the case, the therapist's response to others' concerns should be part of an agreed role, structured as part of the speech and language therapy service response.

There are four key aspects to the speech and language therapist's role, and each is discussed further below. The four aspects are:

- health promotion and information giving;
- selection and prioritisation;
- onward referral;
- ongoing intervention.

Health promotion and information giving

An important role for therapists working 'at the coalface' is to provide information to parents and primary care workers, including nursery staff and school nurses, about normal language development and appropriate referral processes.

Current evidence about screening and early intervention for speech and language difficulties does not support the introduction of universal screening for these problems (Law *et al* 1998). However, health authorities specify the screening and surveillance package they require of primary care, which will set out the ages and stages at which the speech and language development of children is monitored. Hall (1996) recommends that this process should be embedded in an understanding of what is 'normal', give due consideration to families' needs and preferences, and be based on best evidence about the efficacy of intervention.

Speech and language therapy services can support the PCT in the implementation of this through the provision of training and supporting literature, as well as by making decisions about appropriate screening or surveillance packages and then negotiating their use.

Selection and prioritisation

As the first recipients of a referral into the service, speech and language therapists working in community clinics play a crucial part in making the decision about whether or not a child will gain access to the service. This is not simply about determining the presence or absence of difficulty, but it should also take into account the family's needs and wishes as well as the service's ability to deliver an effective package of care (see Chapter 1). Not all parents wish to bring their young child for a regular appointment; some might prefer to receive written information about the nature of their child's difficulties and an opportunity to make contact at a later date (Glogowska and Campbell 2000).

With younger children, there is the added complication of distinguishing between a long-term difficulty and a speech and language delay that is in the process of being resolved. There is some research to suggest that children with comprehension difficulties are particularly at risk for having ongoing problems and that the difficulties of those with purely expressive delays are more likely to resolve spontaneously (see Law *et al.* 1998 for a review).

There is a range of flowcharts available in the literature to support therapists through the initial assessment process (Gerard and Carson 1990; Roulstone 1997; Whitehurst and

Fischel 1994; Yoder and Kent 1988; see also Chapters 1 and 6). However, the application of these general principles to particular cases still requires professional judgement in making complex decisions, and it is important that the therapist allocates an appropriate amount of time for this. If an appointment is planned to cover initial selection and prioritisation, there needs to be time available: to provide opportunities for exploration of the difficulty with parents; for a discussion of options for intervention, and for writing up case notes and reports. At least one hour is likely to be needed.

A therapist's investigation must culminate in a decision that confirms whether or not the child's current communication context – the context currently provided by the child's family, and/or nursery – is sufficient for the child's level of need (Roulstone 1997). For example, a child with a relatively major delay may not require an intensive level of intervention if the family are relaxed and supportive, can handle the child's behaviour constructively, are able to adjust their own levels of communication, can provide appropriate activities, and there is access to nursery attendance. By comparison, a child with a mild to moderate delay may need a different level of intervention: if the parents are anxious and isolated; if they have few ideas about the most appropriate toys, games or activities for their child; and if they find the child's behaviour puzzling and difficult to manage. The first child might benefit from access to periodic advice spread over a long period; for the second, relatively short-term therapy, which is specifically targeted and intensive, may be preferable.

Finally, decisions about prioritisation have to be matched with action. If children are prioritised, do they get fast access? Do they receive more therapy? Or, do they have therapy for longer? Ideally, general principles for these decisions should be established at a service level in a manner that allows for interpretation for individual children.

Onward referral

A community therapist must also decide whether or not the child's problem is a relatively contained and manageable one, or whether further referral and investigation is appropriate. Decisions about when, and to whom, to refer a child will depend on the speech and language therapist's own expertise and on the range of specialist services available; so, community clinic therapists should always acquaint themselves with the structure of services in their locality.

The most common type of onward referral will be to the CDC for a multidisciplinary assessment for children who may have other developmental difficulties. Referral for hearing assessment may have been initiated already but, if not, this should always be considered. Other investigations might be appropriate for children who are observed with 'absences' that might be construed as epileptic in origin; a neurological investigation might be appropriate in this case. A referral to social services might be necessary if a family are in need of support. In some cases, it will be more appropriate for the referral to be made by the child's General Practitioner (GP), since the GP will be able to give a child's full medical history. However, a therapist's observations about the speech, language and communication, as well as other more general observations about the child's behaviour, will be invaluable to members of other disciplines and should be part of the onward referral.

Any further referral should, of course, always be discussed with the family first. This can be a difficult process where child protection issues are involved. Therapists working with children may be involved in child protection issues where the physical or emotional well-being and safety of a child are considered to be at risk. All NHS Trusts have standard procedures and training for their staff. Newly appointed staff who will be working with children are required to submit to a 'police check' whereby the local police investigate that member of staff to check whether they have been convicted of offences likely to endanger children.

There are two main ways that therapists become involved in child protection cases. First, a therapist may be asked to provide evidence – either at a case conference or in a court case – about a child's therapy attendance and about their difficulties and progress. The therapist may be asked for an opinion regarding the cause of the child's difficulties or rate of progress and, in particular, whether or not it is related to the care received from the child's family. Secondly, during a therapy session, a child may disclose information suggestive of harm or abuse, or the therapist may observe signs of abuse such as unusual or excessive bruising. How to recognise such signs and the subsequent action to take, including methods of recording and reporting, will be covered within local Trust procedures and training sessions. It is vital that therapists are clear about the procedures and how to access support from their manager to carry them through. In all cases, the safety of the child is paramount. It is good practice for therapists to inform parents of their concerns, their responsibilities to the child and their intentions.

Ongoing intervention

Decisions about the most appropriate therapy regime need to integrate existing knowledge from the literature about the efficacy of particular regimes and their effectiveness in clinical contexts with the speech and language therapist's knowledge of a particular child. It will often fall to a local community therapist to provide ongoing care for a child. Specialist assessments may take place, but regular intervention is usually needed as close to home as possible.

For unusual or complex cases, therapists will require support from their specialist colleagues and may need to set up joint sessions to access their expertise in areas such as acquired language problems (see Chapter 22).

Issues for the community clinic therapist

Large workloads and caseloads

There is no doubt that therapists working in community clinics face major issues relating to controlling their workload in order to remain effective. Therapists need to balance the number of children and the number of sites in order to maintain effective practice. There are no national guidelines for caseload size but therapists should seek guidance from their managers about accepted limits. Therapists responding to the pressures around them to see children need to remember to allocate time to complete reports and case notes, to plan therapy and prepare materials, and to think through cases thoroughly.

Working in children's contexts

Some therapists are fortunate enough to have a purpose-built base, designed to provide a child-centred environment. Often, therapists may still be working in less than ideal circumstances. They may be sharing a room with other professionals from other disciplines who may have different needs. For example, an examination couch is still a feature of many therapists' rooms. An important decision is whether or not to provide intervention in the clinic or whether to move to more child-friendly and familiar environments, such as nurseries, playgroups or indeed the child's home.

In practice, most therapists arrive at a decision that is a compromise between what is feasible and what is ideal. Where there are several children in one nursery, the establishment of good working relationships with nursery staff may provide the opportunity to have an impact on the child's broader communication environment and offer additional insights into a child's needs and difficulties.

Child development centres

Background

Children are referred to CDCs primarily for in-depth assessment and diagnosis, and management of complex and multiple disabilities. Referrals to the centres come from neonatal units, the PCT and locality teams, including speech and language therapists. Typical referrals would include children with cerebral palsy, with learning disabilities and with pervasive developmental disorders. Children are usually seen during their pre-school years but may be followed up throughout their childhood.

The speech and language therapist works as a member of a multidisciplinary team, which could include a paediatrician, psychologist, physiotherapist, occupational therapist and social worker (see Chapter 11). The team might also include play workers or nursery staff. Typically, speech and language therapists working in this context will have had approximately three years' experience (RCSLT 1996), particularly if they work alone.

The role of the CDC therapist

The therapist within a CDC has two particular roles: to make a detailed and coordinated assessment of children referred to the CDC; and to liaise with and support the other professionals involved. Each of these roles is discussed further below.

Detailed and coordinated assessment

Therapists in this context need to be able not only to collect detailed observations of a child's speech, language and communication behaviour but also to interpret them diagnostically in discussion with the team. For example, differences in a child's social communication and pragmatic skills can be instrumental in differentiating between autistic spectrum disorders and severe language delays.

As assessment information is acquired, a mechanism is needed whereby the therapist regularly feeds information into, and receives reports from, the rest of the team so that a coherent and inclusive picture develops. Changes needed to the assessment process will have to be negotiated as emerging data lead to new hypotheses about the child's needs and difficulties (see Chapter 2).

With so many professionals involved, there is the potential to 'flood' both children and parents with repetitive questioning and tasks. Having a collaborative plan for the assessment process is therefore vital for effective working. Ideally, this would be discussed with the family by a key worker who is a member of the team.

Liaison and support

As inclusive policies have become predominant in education (DfEE 1997, 1998a), it is becoming more usual for ongoing intervention to be provided by local therapists rather than continuing at the CDC (see Chapter 6). A management plan needs to be negotiated with the local therapist and should specify the level of support required. This might include joint sessions for demonstrating particular strategies, training for local nursery staff – for example, in the use of Makaton or the loan of particular equipment such as symbol boards (see Chapter 23).

As children return to the CDC for periodic monitoring, the CDC therapist will need to liaise with local speech and language therapists to obtain up-to-date information on each child's progress and on the current issues requiring investigation or support.

Issues for therapists working in CDCs

Dealing with parents' grief

For many families, the CDC assessment process will bring them to the point of diagnosis and – perhaps for the first time – they will be faced with the prospect of their child having a long-term disabling condition. The therapist may therefore have to work with families who are coming to terms with this knowledge, and to deal with their denial, their anger, and their distress. Knowing the typical stages of the grieving process (Kubler-Ross 1997) and being able to recognise one's own limitations in dealing with these is important. A therapist should be able to help the family in accessing other support mechanisms – through voluntary groups such as Afasic (a UK charity supporting families with children with speech and language difficulties), or through MENCAP (the main UK charity for people with learning disabilities), or through appropriate staff within the NHS and social services.

Working in hospitals

Background

Speech and language therapists working in hospitals are usually attached to medical specialities – for example, ENT (Ear, Nose and Throat), plastic surgery and neurology. Their role is a responsive one, attending to the communication and eating and swallowing difficulties that arise from medical conditions. For example, therapists may be working with children who have a tracheostomy, who have had head injuries, or children who have been admitted due to failure to thrive or with a history of nasogastric tube feeding (see Chapter 24). Referral of children with eating and swallowing difficulties, particularly in the neonatal period, has been increasing in recent years and now constitutes a significant demand on therapy services in hospitals.

As members of the multidisciplinary team, speech and language therapists' co-workers will include paediatricians, surgeons, physiotherapists, occupational therapists, clinical psychologists, social workers and, if the child is in hospital for a long time, the hospital teaching service provided by the LEA.

The role of the hospital therapist

Constraints imposed by medical and surgical interventions

Uniquely, the nature and organisation of speech and language therapists' interventions will be structured and constrained by the timing and location of the medical and surgical interventions. For example, when working with children presenting with a cleft palate, the therapist might meet the family soon after the child is born, and thereafter have recurring contact as the child undergoes surgery and follow-up until the child reaches adulthood. With the development of regional centres for cleft surgery, the specialist therapist has become the provider of ongoing assessment and of diagnostic or intensive therapy. Liaison with the child's local therapist will also be important since children will be seen in their home town for ongoing therapy (see Chapter 19).

On the other hand, for children who are recovering from a traumatic head injury which has affected their speech and language, short sessions on a daily basis for the period of their stay in hospital might be appropriate. The therapist's role would be to monitor their progress and, through ongoing assessment, to support the child, the family and the ward staff to establish effective and supportive communication strategies.

Informing medical and surgical interventions

Information about a child's orofacial functioning and progress in speech and language development can be crucial in determining the timing of medical and surgical interventions. For example, subtle changes, progress and deterioration in a child's speech or language noted by the speech and language therapist might be an important indicator of changes in a child's medical condition which might alert a doctor to the need for action.

In the same way, information about the safety of a child's swallow may enable a decision to be made about when the child could safely be discharged from hospital, and whether a nasogastric feeding tube needs to be inserted. If a therapist is to provide timely input to such decisions, regular involvement in medical rounds and specialist clinics will be an important feature of the therapist's working week.

Issues for the hospital therapist

Families in distress

Admission of children to hospital is, in most cases, in response either to an acute episode or to a serious medical problem. Families are, therefore, often in considerable distress. They will almost certainly be tired from the constant demands of supporting a child in hospital, from heightened levels of anxiety and, if they are staying in the hospital, from disturbed sleep. Speech and language therapists working in this context have to take account of this when discussing management strategies with families, considering, for example, the amount of new information provided at any one time, and the need for repetition and explanation.

Rapid change

While conditions such as cleft palate have quite a predictable history nowadays, many of the children seen in a hospital context will be in a period of rapid change and children can make progress that is at times quite astonishing. An ability to respond appropriately and flexibly to such changes is acquired through experience, although even the most experienced therapist can be surprised. Caution and good record keeping is vital in these circumstances.

Evaluation

Different aspects of a therapist's work will require different monitoring and evaluative approaches to ensure that the management and therapy offered to each child and family is appropriate and effective.

Evaluating training and the referral process

The effectiveness and appropriateness of any training offered and the appropriateness of referrals received from primary care may be evaluated using questionnaires such as those developed in the national audit project reported by van der Gaag *et al.* (1999). These provide ready-made tools for feedback on training, for examining referral processes and for the interpretation of the results of an audit.

Selection and prioritisation

The decisions about the selection of children for therapy and about prioritisation in relation to existing caseloads and waiting lists will be made by several different therapists in any health trust. It is important, therefore, to ensure that equity of access is maintained. Again, questionnaires may be used to collect data on this important aspect (van der Gaag *et al.* 1999).

In addition, periodic peer review is also useful. One way in which this might be used to discuss consensus within a department is thus:

- One speech and language therapist videotapes an initial assessment session (with the parents' permission).
- The therapist then watches the videotape and identifies key decision points – that is, where one activity was terminated by the therapist and another begun. For example, the therapist decides that enough case-history information has been collected and moves on to ask parents to engage in play with their child.
- The therapist selects approximately four decision sections to show to peers.
- The therapist provides referral information for peers, plus information gained during the session up to the first decision section to be shown.
- Peers and the therapist view the first decision section.
- At the end, peers are asked to write down their conclusions about the child's condition so far, and what they would do next.
- Peers and therapists then discuss the matter. Writing views down prior to the discussion helps to anchor views and provides evidence as to where and how their judgements coincide.

At the end of this process, the therapist may provide another piece of information and video section and the whole process may be repeated.

Onward referral

When evaluating the appropriateness of onward referral, there are various questions that need to be asked, for example about the relevance of the detail and complexity of any reports written by the therapist and whether the parents are happy with the process.

The process of peer review described above, together with feedback reports from specialist provision, can provide insight into whether each child has been referred on to the appropriate professional. It would also be good practice to confirm with parents at each stage that they understand and support the process.

Ongoing intervention

Even where programmes have proven efficacy through research trials, it is still imperative that therapists monitor the effect of that intervention as applied to an individual child.

If therapy is well structured and goal-related, then therapists can assess the child's progress against previously specified goals negotiated and agreed with a parent. For example, there may have been a specific and measurable objective set, such as: 'By the end of the episode of care, a child will be able to use two-word utterances.' At the end of the specified time, if the child has not achieved that goal, the reasons for this can be explored. It might have been, for example, that inappropriate tasks were set; or that there was insufficient input, or too high expectations; or that other underlying skills were insufficiently established.

Primary or secondary outcomes can be the focus of the evaluation. Primary outcomes will be those directly involved with changes in the child's communication – for example, their level of understanding or their intelligibility. Secondary outcomes are those that measure related aspects but not the communication behaviour of the child directly, such as the observed changes in the parents' interactions with the child (see Chapter 5).

The assessment process

It is important to establish whether the assessment process has been effective. Consensus among the team, parent satisfaction with the process and outcome, the provision of timely and complete reports and a clear management plan should all be part of such an evaluation. Multidisciplinary audits will be appropriate in this context and might include the use of parental questionnaires and the involvement of parents in user groups.

Team support structures

Speech and language therapists working in teams – for example, in a CDC as outlined above – can evaluate whether the support was structured in the most productive way, for instance by asking for feedback from local therapists. Although this could be done by questionnaire, periodic (perhaps annual) meetings to review the process might be more productive. Topics for discussion might include the effectiveness and efficiency of the joint sessions, the training offered, the reports provided and the resources available.

In well-established teams, children's progress in speech, language and communication and the therapist's input may be part of an ongoing clinical audit of the team's performances. Speech and language therapists in these contexts – for example, in a hospital – might be expected to suggest appropriate measures for the audit process and subsequently provide data for the team. These data would be used to evaluate the team as a whole, as well as the medical or surgical interventions.

Summary

For many years, newly qualified therapists have worked initially in community clinics before moving to what used to be considered more specialist environments. However, all three contexts considered here have their specialist aspects. Therapists working in community clinics, CDCs and hospitals will carry out many similar functions and share common skills, but the demands of each will enable the development of an expertise that is particular to the context.

PART III

Working with others

This Part of the book highlights the breadth of the role of speech and language therapists who increasingly work together with parents and other professionals. Information is provided about models of working, how approaches to training may change when working with different groups, and how to set up training courses.

CHAPTER 9

Working with parents

Monica Bray

Learning outcomes

By the end of the chapter, the reader should:

- understand the philosophy behind working with parents;
- understand that different approaches may apply in different contexts;
- be able to identify the strengths and weaknesses of different models of working with parents;
- be aware that there are a growing number of parent-based programmes available.

Introduction and underlying philosophy

Speech and language therapists are increasingly working in partnership with the people who are closest to children with developmental difficulties – those who are in daily contact with the children. They may be teachers or day-care staff, or the parents; this chapter focuses on working with the parents.

Consider the situation of a child of 3 years who is having difficulty in talking. Who is the most important person in this child's life? Is it the speech and language therapist or is it this child's parents? Parents are the most influential people in children's lives. The development of children's skills is often influenced by the parents' models, including the development of speech and language.

Most children who fail to develop language and speech do so because of some specific difficulty – which may be physical, sensory, neurological or cognitive. Some children have a language delay that does not have a definable cause. A few children have problems because they have suffered rejection, abuse or isolation. All such children probably require enhanced or better-than-normal parental input and parent–child interaction (Snow 1994), and parents therefore need to be involved in the speech and language therapy process whenever possible.

Case example

Tracey is four. She has been slow in developing language but her parents were not particularly worried because they had also been slow in their language development. Tracey is due to start school. She still has difficulty making others understand her, although her parents can interpret what she says.

The nursery that Tracey attended, with the parents' permission, referred her to a speech and language therapist, who found that Tracey has a delay in comprehension and expressive language and may need long-term help. Mrs F, Tracey's mother, is very upset as she had considered that Tracey would soon grow out of the speech difficulty. Mr F, her father is very angry; he feels that either the therapist is wrong or some other professional should have noticed this problem earlier. The parents cannot agree on what to do next. Mr F wants Tracey to have therapy daily if necessary to get Tracey's speech 'up to par' before she starts school. Mrs F is worrying that she did something wrong – she had had a feeling that Tracey was not developing her speech, but she put off doing anything or even thinking about it. Now she feels it is too late and she is to blame. She too wants Tracey to have therapy, but she also wants someone to talk to about how she feels.

If Tracey is seen for a half-hour weekly session with a therapist, will the family be satisfied? Possibly not: Mr F's anger and his unrealistic expectations of therapy, and Mrs F's guilt and desire to be helped and to be helpful, will both need to be addressed in some way in order for therapy to be successful.

Many parents, when faced with such a problem, will feel helpless and de-skilled. If a therapist then assumes the role of keeper of the knowledge, the parents will feel even less competent and may hand over responsibility for their child's progress to the professionals. Parents need to feel empowered – that is, to have the necessary information and knowledge to deal with the situation. They need to feel that they are partners in the ongoing process. They need to become effectively involved, sharing responsibility for their child's progress with the speech and language therapist.

Systems theory

The family is a system in the same way that a school and a community is a system. Each part of the system is dependent on the other parts, and in order to function effectively the whole system has to work cooperatively. A speech and language problem needs to be considered in relation to the effect it has not only on the child but also on the other members of that child's family. The behaviour of each member of the family has an effect on the other members.

So, for example, if John stammers, his mother may get upset and tense. This may annoy his father, which in turn makes John uncomfortable and may make him stammer even more. This is an example of what is called 'circular causality' in family systems theory (Barker 1998). Circular thinking is where A's behaviour affects B's behaviour, which affects C's behaviour, which in turn affects A's behaviour. This moves on from the simplistic linear model where A only affects B. It is a useful concept when considering the importance of involving parents in the process of therapy with children like Tracey or John.

Models of working

Over the years, approaches in speech and language therapy have shifted (Crystal and Varley 1998). At first, the profession focused on a medical framework but, since the emphasis has been placed more recently on communicative and conversational competence, the way of conceptualising clients' difficulties and approaches to treatment has shifted to a socially orientated model (Makin 1995).

The three models of professional practice, as described by Cunningham and Davis (1985) regarding professionals working with parents, encapsulate this change of focus. One of the decisions that therapists have to make is which model is best suited to the specific situation and to the individual needs of their clients.

Model 1: The expert model

This model fits with the medical concepts of diagnosis–treatment–cure, with the doctor as 'expert' dispensing treatment. In speech and language therapy, the therapist is the 'expert' who gives advice, ideas and practical tasks.

Does this work? Imagine a five-year-old child with a phonological problem. The speech and language therapist diagnoses the problem following observation and recording of the child's speech. The therapist then prescribes a period of therapy and defines the therapy tasks – which might, for example, consist of working on the contrasting of fricative and plosive sounds. The therapy is conducted weekly and the child learns to contrast the sounds. However, once the production of the sound is established, it also needs to be generalised to everyday situations. The therapist may give advice to the parents and request the completion of homework tasks. Regular practice is required outside of the therapy session.

This approach has some disadvantages:

- People do not take advice easily; indeed, they often reject it, fail to follow it or forget it. When a parent is asked to do homework with a child, this often does not get done, for a variety of reasons.
- When therapists acts as 'experts', they are setting themselves up to be seen as the one who carries out the therapy, and so the responsibility for the child's 'cure' is handed over from the parents to the therapist.

- An 'expert' may be seen as the only one who can 'do the job'. The parents will then depend upon the therapist to continue with therapy until the problem is resolved.

Model 2: The transplant model

The transplant model is useful for overcoming some of the problems indicated above, particularly those of practise and generalisation. Here the therapist – still seen as the 'expert' – models and teaches the parents the therapy tasks, involving them directly in the therapy. The therapist plans and makes decisions about therapy and the parents are placed in the role of 'teacher' in place of the therapist.

This is a commonly used model in speech and language therapy. It has proved to be useful with many families because it enhances the parents' skills and so develops their confidence to deal with the child's speech and language problems.

This model, too, has several disadvantages:

- It is difficult to be both parent and 'teacher' to a child. Children often reject the 'teacher-parent' role and refuse to comply with homework requests.
- Parents who try to be 'teachers' may become critical or demanding and may pressure an already vulnerable child.
- For many children with speech and language delay, the best approach to their remediation may be through a modified 'natural acquisition' approach, not through a teaching model. A more useful approach may be for the therapist to guide parents into modifying their behaviour, rather than giving specific homework tasks.

Model 3: The consumer model

The consumer model assumes that parents are able to make decisions and be involved in the planning of the therapy for their child. The therapist sets out the possibilities for therapy and discusses with the parents what is appropriate, not only for the child and his or her particular speech and language difficulty but also for the parents, their life-style, the needs of siblings, and other relevant factors.

In this model, parents bring their expertise about their child and their situation and the therapist brings expertise regarding speech and language development. Then, together, as equal partners, a plan for the child may be negotiated. This collaborative model in relation to children with speech and language difficulties has been shown to be an efficient use of therapist resources while fulfilling parental need (Iacono *et al.* 1998; Bowen and Cupples 1999).

As with the other two models, there are some disadvantages:

- The therapist must be prepared to give up the 'expert' role and must be able to negotiate what is best for the child.

- The parent must be engaged in the process and be willing to take responsibility. The therapist might need to work with some parents in order to achieve this.
- The process of negotiation and decision-making is time-consuming. It takes time to decide how the needs of parents as well as the needs of the child can best be met; to plan how and where therapy might be most productive; and to negotiate how much will be the responsibility of each of the therapist, the parents and the child. The therapist and his/her employer must support this approach and see the time commitment as a vital and integral part of the therapy.

Working within a particular philosophy

So, how do therapists decide on a particular orientation or approach? In considering what might be most useful for the child and the parents, therapists need to reflect from the basis of their own self-awareness, their sensitivity to the needs of others, and consideration of the influence of the context in which they work. Each of these three aspects is described further below.

Self-awareness

Competent therapists explore a range of information about people and their behaviour, know what they themselves believe, understand their own ways of looking at the world, and can translate this knowledge into a way of working with people that is comfortable and beneficial. As a result, not all therapists work the same way with parents, and decisions on the approach to take may be based on a particular philosophical stance. Examples of different perspectives from which therapists may work are thus:

- *A behaviourist perspective* sees the behaviour of parents or children as being shaped by the consequences of their actions. Parents can therefore be taught to modify their behaviour through a process of contingent reinforcement (Bandura 1969).
- *A client-centred perspective* means that the therapist takes the lead from the child or parent. It encourages open discussion and decision-making from the parent or child based on the belief that the individual is always striving towards improvement (Rogers 1951).
- *A cognitive perspective* is where the children's or parents' belief system and the ways in which they think about the problem is seen as influential in how they may deal with it. The therapist needs to challenge negative attitudes and engage with each parent and/or child in a joint exploration of the problem (Beck 1976).

Generally, those taking a behaviourist view are likely to be drawn to an expert model; those taking a person-centred perspective often relate to the consumer model; and the cognitive conceptualisation of behaviour fits comfortably with a transplant model of working. The way in which these ideas may direct therapy approaches can be explored further in Bray *et al.* (1999). See also Corey (1996) for an update on how some of these ideas have developed since they were first introduced.

Therapists also need to explore beyond these perspectives, especially in relation to clients from other cultures (see Chapter 16).

Sensitivity to the needs of others

Parents enter into the therapy process in different states of readiness to accept what is on offer. For example, a child may have been referred by someone else and the parents may be unsure why the referral has been made. There may be elements of anger or rejection related to therapy. These parents may need to be given information and knowledge from an 'expert' therapist before they can be engaged more collaboratively. Or, the child may have had therapy before, which the parents felt did not work; this could lead to an unwillingness to be engaged in therapy again, and the therapist will need to encourage the parents to say what they want and how they would like to see therapy develop.

From this consumer perspective, the therapist can help the parent regain trust in the therapy process. On the other hand, the parent may have been seeking therapy for a long time and may be desperate to receive help. Such parents can be involved immediately in sharing skills with the therapist and transplanting therapy ideas into the home environment. Parents may come from a different culture with different expectations of child rearing and development and here the therapist must be willing to watch and learn before offering advice and suggestions.

Each of these parents has different needs and, when children begin therapy, therapists must adapt their approaches accordingly.

Contextual issues

Therapy is about change (see Chapter 2). During therapy the child develops, the problem alters, the parents change, and so the needs of the child and/or parents change. Prochaska and Di Clemente (1986) put forward a model of change that defines different stages of readiness for therapy. These stages relate to the levels of awareness and preparedness to work on trying to change. For example, some parents may arrive at therapy generally unaware of the level of difficulty their child is experiencing, some may be there wanting to reflect in order to understand the child's needs, while others may want to be immediately active and involved.

All parents need to understand that change occurs in a series of steps, and that plateaux and regression of skills are part of the learning process. Of course, the parent and child may each be at a different stage. The parents may be ready to act while the child remains unaware of any need to change. As discussed above, if the therapist is sensitive to the stage that the parent and the child are at then the procedures of therapy can be matched to the expectations of both.

Therapy tasks and approaches must be flexible to accommodate any of the shifts in the child's and/or parents' needs. Also, during therapy the child will respond differently in different settings. For example, he or she may be talkative when in a play situation but more reticent in a face-to-face conversation. Many children are far more talkative at home than outside the home, which is why parents can be such effective agents of change. So, different approaches may be necessary at different times and in different settings. A therapist needs to be aware of the effect of all these factors.

Examples of working practice

Working with parents can take many forms, and different approaches may be used. An eclectic mix of two or more approaches at the same time is more likely to meet the needs of the clients. That is why it is important for therapists to have an understanding and knowledge of different philosophies, perspectives and models.

Example 1

A speech and language therapist may use a *behaviouristic* perspective with an *expert* or *transplant* model. As a result:

- the therapist might work directly with the child on the linguistic or communication difficulty and indirectly with the parent(s) by giving specific tasks for homework (behaviourist/expert);
- the therapist might work directly with the parent and indirectly with the child, by observing the child and giving advice or suggestions to the parent(s) on how the child's speech and language could be developed (behaviourist/transplant);
- the therapist might model to the parent(s) some ways of helping the child, and encourage the parent to try these out and report back, possibly using video feedback (behaviourist/transplant).

Case example

Mary is six years old and has Down's syndrome. Her parents want to help her develop more expressive language. The therapist has observed that Mary enjoys the game of hide-and-seek and suggests that the parents play a form of this with a set of ten objects that are interesting to Mary and that provide useful basic vocabulary. The parents are to name and sign each object as they hide it, and again when Mary finds it. They are asked to keep a chart of the number of times Mary names/signs the objects in order to measure change in her naming ability.

In order to use this approach, speech and language therapists need to understand the principles of behavioural training, especially task analysis and reinforcement, and to be able to offer to others clear and simple explanations and instructions.

Example 2

A therapist may use a *cognitive* and/or *social-interactionist* perspective and either a *transplant* model or a *consumer* model. As a result:

- the therapist might work with the family exploring issues of how the child's speech and language delay affects the family system and how the family can change to support the child. Tasks for the family to try at home will be negotiated and discussed at subsequent sessions (social-interactionist plus cognitive/consumer);
- the therapist might work with a parent and child together, encouraging a style and nature of interaction that will enhance the child's language learning capacities (social-interactionist/consumer);
- the therapist might work with a group of parents teaching skills and giving information without seeing the children at all (cognitive/transplant).

Case example

David is four and has been stammering since he was 2 years 10 months old. He is currently showing some struggle behaviour, closing his eyes and jerking his head. His parents are anxious and his brother, Peter, who is seven, is mimicking and making fun of David. The therapist decides to talk to the whole family about easy and hard speech. She asks them to think about how it feels to want to say something and find yourself stuck and speechless. From this, the parents and the therapist decide on some home-based approaches to help David – and Peter – feel more comfortable with the problems of David's stammer. The parents agree that they will give some special time to Peter, who may be feeling that he is not receiving as much attention as David. At the same time, the therapist arranges some sessions with David and his mother to work on ways in which his mother could make speaking a more relaxed and pleasurable activity for him (Van Riper 1973).

Therapists using this approach would need a clear understanding of the role of interaction in language acquisition and development, a knowledge of the role of belief and expectation in learning, and an awareness of systems theory and family therapy approaches (Barker 1998).

Example 3

Therapists may use a *client-centred* perspective and work with a *consumer* model. As a result:

- the therapist might work with the parent and child together, encouraging playful interaction and following the child's lead. This would act as a means of establishing a relationship between parent and child that might enable the child to use all his/her potential language ability;
- the therapist might work with groups of parents exploring the issues above, as well as relying on the supportive nature of the group to help parents to accept the problems they face and to move forward;

- the therapist might work with the parents alone, enabling them to help their child by talking about the difficulties they face and offering methods of coping with their child's speech and language problem. The therapist might also offer support to the parents while they come to an understanding and acceptance of the problems. In some instances, referral to another professional will be appropriate.

Case example

Two therapists ran a group for parents of children with speech and language delay who were approaching school age, because some of the parents expressed anxiety about their child starting school. The group ran for five sessions and ground rules were established about being open about feelings, respecting confidentiality, and the responsibility of all to be involved. The parents set the agenda with the therapists as facilitators. Following this group, the parents felt they understood the problems of their children better, they were more secure about what they would say to teachers when their children attended school, and some commented that they had gained skills from listening to ways in which other parents dealt with problems.

Therapists using this approach need to use the skills of listening, clarification and reflection as their main tools in order to allow the parents to take the lead.

Published material

A number of published assessment and intervention programmes reflect different approaches to working with parents, and these are outlined in this section.

WILSTAAR (Ward Infant Language Screening Test Assessment Acceleration Remediation; Ward 1992) was developed by a speech and language therapist who was concerned that young children were at risk of having developmental difficulties because of auditory inattention and poor listening skills. This was developed from a behavioural perspective. The environment is seen as causing the difficulty and the aim is to reduce the child's problems by changing the environment. Parents are given ideas to reduce background noise, such as turning off the television, and to improve the child's listening. The therapist identifies a difficulty following screening and further testing, and then offers advice either to the parent directly or to the health visitor who will follow up the programme with the parent.

The Hanen Early Language Parent Programme was developed in Canada and is based on a social-interactionist perspective (Girolametto *et al.* 1986). Parents are taught in groups about language development and the best ways to enhance this in their children. The group allows parents to learn from and support each other. A client-centred approach is taken so that the parents are encouraged to find for themselves the best ways of working with their children. The main therapy tool is video – the parents either video themselves at home with their child or they are videoed in a clinic. This video is then watched and discussed with the therapist, which enables the parents to see how a child-centred approach can be effective in encouraging language development. This also increases the parents' self-awareness, enabling them to change and gain skills in adapting to their child's needs.

Parent–Child Interaction Therapy, similar to Hanen, is based on a social-interactionist perspective. Originally, it was used with children with developmental language delay by Kelman and Schneider (1994) (See Chapter 5). Parents are encouraged to allocate a regular time each week where total parent attention is focused on their child and the parent follows the child's choice of activity. This is based on the idea that many parents do not attend and listen to their children nor do they respond in a semantically contingent way to the language of the children. Semantically contingent responses have been found to be a quality factor in the ability of a child to increase his or her language skill (Sokolov and Snow 1994). The task of the therapist is to encourage parents to set aside the time and to engage with their child. Parents are then asked to attend a regular appointment with the therapist to discuss their experiences, in order to begin the process of negotiating specific goals.

Parent-Based Interaction Programme (Gibbard 1998) is a training approach for groups of parents whose children have delayed language. Regular sessions are offered for the parents without children present. It introduces observation and recording skills and follows this up with ideas for parents to teach specific language skills to their children, such as discriminating between sounds or comprehension of verbs. Parents report back on progress at each meeting and are encouraged to problem-solve together and offer each other support and suggestions.

Parenting programmes

There are a number of different ways to provide parents with skills that are likely to help their children to develop positively (Einzig 1996). Many parents learn best by doing activities rather than listening to information, and such activities are offered in a programme such as 'Parentwise' (Cooper *et al.* 1994).

Active involvement in the therapy process, such as playing listening games with children or singing rhymes alongside regular daily activities – for example, dressing and bathing – may help the child to develop speech and language skills. This may apply to all, but especially to parents where English is not their mother tongue or parents who have difficulties processing information because of their own learning difficulties (Wills 1999).

A government-driven initiative, 'Sure Start' (Sheridan 1999), encourages professionals to work alongside parents in community settings in order to share skills of child rearing and to ensure the most beneficial early input to infants and young children from deprived areas.

Summary

There are many differing values and beliefs that lie behind parent work, and there are contrasting and overlapping models that may be applied. Therapists need to make a number of decisions when choosing a particular approach and when selecting a published parent-based programme.

CHAPTER 10

Training and educating colleagues

Aileen Patterson

Learning outcomes

By the end of this chapter, the reader should understand:

- how and why a therapist might be involved in educating and training colleagues;
- who the training is for;
- the purpose of the training;
- how to identify training needs;
- how the training will be delivered.

Introduction

Working in teams and contributing to colleagues' awareness of the speech and language therapist's role is not a new phenomenon. However, the expansion of knowledge, increasing specialisation, and use of speech and language therapy assistants and LSAs have led to an increasing need to share knowledge and skills effectively with colleagues. As the speech and language therapist's role continues to change, so it is important to educate others about these changes and to find new ways of working together.

Why therapists need to train colleagues

In educational settings, where the focus of practice is inclusion and excellence for all rather than segregation of those who have special needs (DfEE 2000b and 1997), there have been changes in the speech and language therapist's working practices. Now, the focus of intervention is often in the classroom, where therapists need to work not only with teachers but also with assistants.

For those therapists who work with school-aged children, local arrangements between health authorities and LEAs may influence the patterns of service delivery and therefore the nature of the contact between the therapists, teachers and support workers. This in turn will affect speech and language therapists' involvement in training. *Communicating Quality 2* states that, when working in education, 'intervention will normally include the provision of in-service training to all staff involved with the child, on both a formal and informal basis' (RCSLT 1996: 56). Similarly, in relation to language units it states that the speech and language therapist should 'seek to include in-service training of education staff as part of intervention' (RCSLT 1996: 63). The involvement of others will then assist therapists in delivering an effective service, and in using their specialist skills and resources, both human and fiscal, efficiently.

There have also been changes in healthcare, with the development of the Primary Care Team. *Health for All Children* (Hall 1996) underlines the importance of the role of speech and language therapists in training other professionals. The value of such training and the need to audit any training that is being undertaken is emphasised by van der Gaag *et al.* (1999).

The UK government's concept of lifelong learning has highlighted the need for professionals to develop and maintain knowledge, skills, competence and fitness to practise through continuing professional development (see Chapter 2). As registration for speech and language therapists includes an agreement to continue their professional development (RCSLT 1996), they should, as part of that process, learn how to share their knowledge, skills and goals effectively with others with whom they work, to facilitate good practice and teamwork.

Through the training of others there are benefits for the therapists themselves. Murray and O'Neill (2000) found, for example, that involvement in training was beneficial to the speech and language therapists who were acting as assessors, as well as to the assistants who were undergoing the training. Positive outcomes from such activities included a clearer understanding of skill mix, as well as delegation and evaluation of practice.

The speech and language therapist may be training a variety of other professionals, including teachers, assistants or others within the educational team; or they may be training members of a multidisciplinary healthcare team. Sometimes therapists and teachers might jointly train assistants. In their early-years training package, for example, Wood *et al.* (2000) focus on multidisciplinary training in relation to language and literacy. On other occasions, a speech and language therapist may contribute to an interdisciplinary training package as a member of a larger training team.

The purpose of training

One of the first and most important decisions to be made by the therapist when considering organising training is to answer the question: 'What is the purpose of the training?'

There are several reasons why training may take place, and different levels of training and different approaches will be required according to the underlying purpose.

Training may be needed to raise awareness; to prevent communication problems developing; to provide knowledge and information relating to children who have communication problems; and to enable others to continue therapy and integrate it into the classroom.

Raising awareness

When children are having problems with their speech and language development, therapists may help others who have limited knowledge of communication to understand the nature of these problems. It may be helpful for all those who come into contact with such children – including teachers, assistants, care staff and drivers of the school transport – to be more aware of different types of communication problems, and to understand why the children in their care may not always respond appropriately. Through training, therapists may then be able to help all those who work with such children to tailor their own responses appropriately, so helping to broaden a child's communicative environment.

Prevention of communication problems

In healthcare, there has been a general shift of emphasis from the concept of treating illness to one of prevention – an approach that promotes health and well-being. This naturally has important implications for speech and language therapists when considering training needs.

If therapists are able to provide training at appropriate times, it may be possible to prevent some children from developing more severe communication problems. For example, some young children may be 'at risk' of developing a severe stammer, yet with appropriate early intervention with the parents it may be possible to prevent this occurring (see Chapter 20). Another example would be training in the parent–child interaction programme as described in Chapter 5. Here parents learn how to change their interaction patterns when communicating with the child in order to help improve the child's speech and language and prevent further difficulties arising during development.

The definition of prevention drawn up by the World Health Organisation – as long ago as 1948 – identifies three successive stages in prevention: primary, secondary and tertiary prevention.

The Prevention Commission of the Standing Liaison Committee of Speech and Language Therapists of the European Union (CPLOL) has examined this definition in relation to prevention of communication disorders and has concluded that primary prevention in speech and language therapy 'mainly covers information and health education of a population, as well as training all those who have a role to play with the population in question'. CPLOL concluded that secondary prevention 'mainly concerns identification and early screening', while tertiary prevention in speech and language therapy 'relates to care provided, i.e. therapy, various rehabilitation techniques and intervention designed to assist the patient to return to educational, family, professional, social and cultural life' (CPLOL 1999: 69–70). Furthermore, the report states (p. 69) that [a policy of prevention] 'is cost-effective in the long term because episodes of care are shorter, less frequent and more effective – not to mention the incalculable improvement in well-being for the children and their families'.

Providing knowledge and information

Sometimes therapists need to provide training that offers specific information and knowledge about communication problems. For example, it may be beneficial for all the staff in the school to have some knowledge of a signing system that a particular child is using, so that the child will have a wider range of people with whom to communicate.

Through training, therapists may be able to provide other professionals, such as nursery teachers or health visitors, with specific knowledge about communication problems in order to assist early detection. This, in turn, should facilitate the referral system to speech and language therapy. Through training, therapists may also be able to demystify some of the speech and language therapy 'jargon', so making reports more accessible to other professionals.

Some professionals may already have knowledge about communication problems but, through training, therapists may be able to extend that knowledge in relation to particular children. They may be able to highlight recent research findings, such as genetic influences on a particular child's difficulties; or they may be able to interpret the results of a hearing test and explain the implications for a child's speech and language development.

Continuation of therapy

Speech and language therapists are responsible for the identification and assessment of children's communication problems. The therapist therefore accepts the overall responsibility for the 'duty of care' (RCSLT 1996). However, programmes of intervention often need to be jointly planned and carried out with other professionals. The actual therapy may be given by those who are in daily contact with the children – for example, by a classroom assistant, an LSA or the class teacher. Furthermore, within an educational framework it may be possible for speech and language therapy objectives to be integrated within the child's IEP. The therapist and teacher will need to ensure that these objectives can be met within the classroom.

Sometimes a therapist may work indirectly with a child. That is, the actual therapy is carried out, at least some of the time, by another professional. This might involve others working on a programme that has been set up by the therapist, or on a jointly planned programme. Or, it may be that the therapist's work is followed up by others within the classroom. This may encourage generalisation of specific speech and language work across different environments. The therapist should then offer appropriate training to those professionals to help them to carry out the specific tasks with the child.

Thus it can be seen that speech and language therapists need to be involved in educating others about communication problems in children, enabling other professionals to further their skills and knowledge. By working together, they may be able to optimise each child's ability to communicate effectively, and help the child to gain access to appropriate education and social inclusion.

Whom therapists train

Another decision point for the therapist as trainer is to answer the question: 'Who needs to be trained?' This will largely depend on the purpose of the training as discussed above.

Where therapists are working in healthcare settings, training may well be needed for any of the members of the multidisciplinary team as well as for speech and language therapy assistants, residential staff and care workers. Therapists working in an educational setting may need to train a range of school staff, who will have a variety of knowledge and skills, and different perspectives and goals: SENCOs, teachers and assistants, co-workers working with bilingual children, and any other learning support staff. For training more specifically relating to working with parents, see Chapter 9.

Speech and language therapy assistants

Speech and language therapy assistants are becoming increasingly incorporated into the workforce. They are employed by the speech and language therapy services where relevant training occurs, are responsible to the therapy manager, and may work in either education or health settings. Speech and language therapists' involvement in their formal training programme helps to ensure that the nature of that programme is appropriate to demands of the job.

Additional informal training occurs in the workplace and may be provided by their colleagues on the speech and language therapy team who are able to relate theoretical issues to relevant client groups and contexts. Richards (1999) advocates that such 'on-the-job' training should be at the core of any training programme.

Learning support assistants

LSAs work with children who have a range of special educational needs, including communication problems. The DfEE (1999a) found that, where assistants had clearly defined roles as a result of planning lessons with teachers, they were able to help pupils become independent learners. The effective use of LSAs is stated as being able to 'do an enormous amount to support teaching and learning in the classroom, motivate pupils and raise educational standards for all' (DfEE 1999a: 2).

Such assistants are often able to work effectively with specific children in relation to developing speech, language and communication skills. As they are part of the school team, they may be able to access formal training and achieve educational qualifications. However, if the LSAs are working with children who have communication problems, it is helpful if speech and language therapists are involved in this specific aspect of their training (Wood 1998).

Identification of training needs

Whoever is to receive training, the next decision involves answering the question: 'What do they need to know?' Naturally, this has to be linked to the purpose of the training, and a needs analysis should be undertaken prior to training so as to identify the specific needs of the trainees. If the training is to take place through a course, then the intending participants may be asked to complete pre-course questionnaires to facilitate the planning of the course. This can provide the trainers with details of the participants' prior experience and knowledge, their reasons for attending, as well as what they think they need to learn. This information will influence the course objectives and content, the choice of teaching–learning strategies, and the allocation of time.

Before undertaking training, it is also important to find out what the trainees' managers expect them to learn from such training and – even more importantly – what type of training they would be willing to support. This relates to financial support as well as allowing staff time off to attend a course, because this usually involves arranging cover. For example, when running a course, consultation with the managers should help the therapists take account of resources, constraints on numbers, and the feasibility of when a course can be offered. Consultation with prospective participants should also assist in the course design in terms of the level of the content and the nature of materials used.

Developing the training

This section focuses on the process of developing training once the trainees and their training needs have been identified and relevant managers have been consulted.

Types of training

Training may occur in many different ways: in one-to-one situations; through discussion with a professional colleague, or in more formalised groups such as at a staff or team meeting. It can be provided in work-based settings, or it may be accessed at different venues. In educational settings, therapists may provide single sessions for staff after school or offer sessions as part of teachers' INSET (in-service training) programmes.

Training can take the form of a course that may run for half a day or be spread over several days or weeks. Longer courses may be part-time, full-time or involve day release. Some courses may be award-bearing, and the achievement of such an award is often perceived as a strong motivator. One method of delivering courses, which allows people from a wide geographical area to access the same material, is distance learning. Contact with course tutors and colleagues may then be through telephone, e-mail and video links, and participants are generally able to access course materials and interactive learning packages using computerised technology. When embarking on such training, tutors' and participants' access to the resources must be taken into consideration.

Factors affecting planning

When planning training, there are other factors that must be considered, such as the importance of informal learning; the type of setting that the trainees work in; the available resources; the amount of contact that the trainees have with speech and language therapists; and whether the trainees are willing volunteers or have been 'volunteered' by their managers.

While trainees will learn from the formal teaching that takes place, for example, when delivering a course, Dale and Bell (1999) have found that informal learning in the workplace can result in the development of skills and knowledge. They suggest that many different activities can aid informal learning. These include instruction and demonstration, shadowing and role-modelling, and practice followed by constructive feedback. Other factors that can influence the climate in which such learning may flourish include openness, a readiness to listen, and acknowledgement of achievement.

Informal learning does not replace formal learning; it complements it. However, there are difficulties in accrediting and recognising informal learning. Also, such learning may be confined to superficial skills or non-transferable skills (Dale and Bell 1999). For example, in the speech and language therapy context this could be that the assistant/trainee learns informally how best to position the microphone to record Sally's speech in the classroom, or that Johnny can imitate the 's' sound at the beginning of 'see' but not at the beginning of 'straw'. The assistant may have the skills to make excellent recordings of Sally, or help Johnny to say 'see' perfectly. However, without some formal instruction in how to use a tape recorder effectively, or some teaching about normal speech sound acquisition, the assistant is less likely to develop a flexibility of approach so as to be able to respond to Sally and Johnny in changing situations or to apply these principles when working with other children.

If the trainees work in educational settings, it will be important to identify the type of school in which they are working, because there may need to be a different emphasis in the training. For instance, for some teachers working in mainstream schools the idea of joint goal-setting with speech and language therapists might be a new concept, and this will need to be developed; whereas for teachers working in language units, where they may be working alongside full time therapists, joint goal-setting may already be common practice.

It will be important to consider the frequency of contact that trainees have with children with communication problems. For example, in mainstream schools there may only be one or two children per class with a communication problem, so that teachers have limited opportunities for gaining experience of working with such children. The nature and frequency of contact between the trainee and the therapist also needs to be considered. This will depend on the frequency of visits that the therapist makes to the school, as well as the time the two professionals are able to spend together.

With regard to the organisation and resources available for running courses for training, it may be possible for personnel within the management structure in both the health and education services to assist with funding, budgeting, accommodation and other planning. Once the decision has been made about the purpose of the training, therapists should be able to design appropriate programmes.

Designing a course

Although training programmes may take many different forms, as discussed above, this section focuses on developing and designing a course. From the training needs analysis, the aims and objectives will be developed and this will facilitate the decisions that need to be made about course content as well as enabling eventual evaluation of the effectiveness of the course. Before the course begins, it will be important to make clear to the participants, through an induction, what the course aims to achieve, who it is designed for and, where relevant, how learning will be assessed. Introductory sessions focusing on team building and working together may be helpful and, particularly on longer courses, such sessions are often successful when facilitated by someone other than the tutor.

The topics included in the content of a course and the teaching–learning strategies used should meet the goals and learning styles of participants. On longer courses, these may change and develop over time. There should be flexibility in responding to the range of experience, knowledge and needs of the learners as identified by pre-course questionnaires. Possible course content in different contexts is suggested below.

Courses for teachers

These could include:

- how language develops;
- the nature of communication difficulties;
- how communication difficulties affect learning;

- the relationship between spoken and written language difficulties;
- joint goal-setting;
- encouraging collaborative working practices;
- how to help individual children with communication problems in the classroom setting;
- developing practical and efficient classroom strategies;
- the teacher's role in the early detection of difficulties;
- referral procedures for speech and language therapy;
- speech and language therapy, principles and practices;
- how adult language in the classroom can facilitate a child's language learning.

It may be appropriate to include information about facilitative techniques such as remodelling and expanding a child's utterances, and how to move towards a less directive, more conversational style – possibly using videotaped examples of the different approach.

Courses for speech and language therapy assistants

These could include:

- the specific application to the speech and language therapy context of any general staff in-service training – including topics such as health and safety, safe handling, back care, record keeping and administrative procedures, ethics, confidentiality and time management;
- presentation and interpersonal communication skills;
- language development and communication problems in children;
- the use of specific approaches, including AAC;
- information regarding specific client groups;
- making and using appropriate materials.

Delivering a course

Having decided on the length and type of course to be offered, the next decision relates to how it will be delivered. A variety of approaches can be used to encourage learning, from traditional lectures to individualised work-based activities. It may be possible to take a problem-based approach using a case example. Formal structured learning, such as lectures, demonstrations and modelling, may be complemented by work-based experience. Participants can be encouraged to bring to the course videotaped recordings that they have made in the workplace; these will be discussed and the participants given constructive feedback. The importance of feedback in relation to such learning cannot be overemphasised (see Chapter 2).

Course designers need to consider how technology can facilitate teaching, learning and feedback because use of the Internet and such rapidly advancing technologies are increasingly supporting all aspects of education. Also, developments in technology often allow live video link-up from the speech and language therapist to children in schools, or even in their own homes. This would help to consolidate work-based learning enabling the therapist to have additional contact with the teacher or assistant.

Evaluating a course

Training of colleagues is about learning together. There is much to be gained by all those involved, whether in the trainer or trainee role. For the trainers, receiving feedback can be a valuable way of ensuring that the next course offered is even better than the last. For the trainees, feedback is important in order to help them to maximise their learning. It is therefore invaluable to provide opportunities for formal and informal feedback throughout a course as well as at its end.

Course providers might wish to devise their own feedback methods, which might range from informal discussion to more formal evaluative rating scales. However, for examples of audit procedures and forms that might be used to evaluate training programmes, see van der Gaag *et al.* (1999).

Summary

There are many different reasons why speech and language therapists need to be involved in training their colleagues and thus why they need to develop their skills as educators and trainers. Training will not only benefit the children referred to them and enhance their work and those of their colleagues, but it will give an added dimension to job satisfaction and career development.

CHAPTER 11

Working with other professionals

Jannet A. Wright

Learning outcomes

By the end of this chapter, the reader should know:

- which professionals a speech and language therapist might work with;
- why it is important for therapists to work with these professionals;
- what may be gained by working together;
- what problems can occur when working with other professionals;
- ways in which people may work together.

Introduction

The UK government and the professional body have encouraged speech and language therapists to work with other professionals to support children with communication problems (DfEE 2000b, 1997; RCSLT 1996).

Students on pre-registration courses need to acquire the knowledge and skills that will enable them to work effectively with other professionals. This knowledge will be acquired via lectures, while on placements and during tutorials. However, when starting their first job, newly qualified therapists need management support to continue to develop collaborative working practices (Roux 1996).

Children with communication problems are at risk of falling behind at school, and therapists who work with children of school age need to be familiar with both the academic and the social demands of educational establishments. Therapists also need to be aware of the roles of the professionals who work within educational settings (see Chapters 6 and 7).

The focus of this chapter is on the professionals with whom speech and language therapists work, the ways in which they may work together, and the benefits that may result.

The other professionals

As has been noted in other chapters in this volume, speech and language therapists work with a range of different professionals including:

- health visitor
- school nurse
- GP/paediatrician
- staff-grade doctor
- audiologist
- clinical psychologist
- physiotherapist
- occupational therapist
- educational psychologist
- teacher/SENCO
- nursery teacher/nursery nurse
- Portage worker
- pre-school worker
- classroom assistant
- learning support assistant
- specialist teacher
- interpreter/co-worker
- social worker
- AAC technician

Prior to school entry, therapists are likely to be involved with health visitors, who are often the first people to make a referral to the speech and language therapy service. If a child whom the therapist is seeing has a recognised medical condition that has an impact on communication, then the therapist might be in regular contact with members of a specific medical team. In this case, the speech and language therapist may be a member of a child development team, based in a child development centre (Chapter 8), or a member of a specialist team as discussed in Chapter 19.

Once children enter the education system, therapists will normally liaise with those professionals who have contact with the children on a regular basis, such as the pre-school workers – including playgroup leaders, nursery nurses and nursery teachers – and the teaching and support staff for the older children. Although therapists might work closely with staff in schools, they will often be employed by the local health authority; and they are likely to be based either in a health centre where they will work closely with other health professionals, or be a member of the service to mainstream schools (Chapter 6) where they work with a learning support team.

If the children being seen by the speech and language therapist attend special schools or a unit attached to a mainstream school, the therapist may be a visitor to that school or may be a member of the school staff. When children have a communication problem with a medical basis, such as cleft palate, feeding difficulties (Chapter 24) or a hearing problem (Chapter 15), the therapist needs to liaise with the medical team or, indeed, be part of a specialist multidisciplinary team that continues to see the children as they grow up. If children have emotional behaviour problems, the therapist may need to liaise with the Child and Adolescent Mental Health Service – or in some cases be part of that team as it seeks to offer a specialist service (Chapter 17).

A team might be informally structured or have a formal structure with a designated coordinator and regularly timetabled meetings. Teamwork has been described by Lacey and Lomas (1993) as individuals working together to accomplish more than they could do alone. They further believe that 'effective teamwork can lead to better service provision, increased energy and greater job satisfaction' (p. 142). Having said that, the primary task of the team will influence its composition and its size. However, therapists face similar issues when working with other professionals in any context – decisions have to be made, for instance, about the definition of roles, the agreed aims and a clearly defined approach to the task in hand.

Topping *et al.* (1998) describe two different styles of operation for speech and language therapy teams providing a service to education. In one case, each school within an LEA has a named therapist and the team allocates a number of sessions to each school; the school then decides how to use those sessions. In another LEA, which has a multi-agency management group (MAMG) where health, education and social services work together, all referrals are discussed by the MAMG, it decides what action should be taken, and one professional is identified as the lead professional.

Sometimes, the contact between the therapist and the other professionals will be brief and specific, such as when further information or assessment is needed – for example, when a decision has been taken to refer a child to an audiologist to obtain information about the child's hearing, or if a child has been referred to a psychologist for an assessment.

The importance of working together

Professionals in health, education and social services need to work together in the management of children with communication problems because of the pervasive nature of language difficulties. The majority do so for the benefit of the children. By working together, professionals can aim for continuity of approach and try to ensure that the children and their parents receive a consistent message. This will also help to ensure that speech and language therapy is carried over into everyday situations. In some nurseries or schools, consistency of approach can be facilitated by a key worker with whom everyone can liaise. Such an approach can also help to provide all those involved with a holistic picture of the child.

Language is central to the curriculum and, for children in school, language is not only the content of the curriculum but also the medium of instruction. This means that children with communication problems are at risk of failing to access the curriculum as well as failing to understand the social demands of education. If therapists and education staff can work together, they may well be able to support these children, enabling them to fulfil their educational potential; and they may help them to reduce their chances of developing problems with reading and spelling (Snowling and Stackhouse 1996; Catts 1996).

What speech and language therapists gain

Working with other professionals can offer speech and language therapists different interpretations of children's behaviour, providing new insights that might at some stage influence management strategies. In a study reported by Wright (1996), therapists commented specifically on the new knowledge and information that they had gained from working with teachers. This acquisition of knowledge can contribute to continuing professional development (see Chapter 2).

Therapists might need additional information from other professionals about the children with whom they work. Teachers, for example, can report on children's academic progress. Health visitors, school nurses and clinical medical officers will be able to provide relevant details of associated medical problems and can suggest how they might be contributing to the speech and language problems. Information from the physiotherapist about mobility and the limitation of limb and head movements might be helpful when assessing children who have physical disabilities. Interpreters or co-workers are essential when gathering information about children for whom English is an additional language (see Chapter 16).

Therapists need to understand the wider context within which individual children function, so that they may be able to identify the communication skills that the children require in each of these situations. This includes an awareness of the attitudes and values that are held by parents and family members as well as those held by other professionals. Therapists need to know how these relate to the family's view of communication problems and of speech and language therapy. By gaining an understanding of the broader social aspects of the children's environment a therapist should be in a better position to identify realistic goals for the children when making therapy decisions.

What other professionals gain

Graham (1995) found that when professionals worked together they acquired more realistic expectations of one another. In this way, some of the mystery that surrounds speech and language therapy could be eliminated, so that colleagues did not tend so much to think that therapists can 'cure' all communication problems.

Teachers who work with therapists acknowledge that working together offers the opportunity to share concerns, give personal and professional support to one another, and reduce stress (Kersner and Wright 1996). When progress is achieved, joint working provides an opportunity to celebrate success with individual children and their families.

Factors affecting working together

A number of factors have been identified that can prevent people working together effectively. One of these is that professionals may have different employers. Individuals need to make explicit their different contractual obligations, in order to avoid misunderstandings; for example, some teachers may not be aware that therapists are able to take leave during term time (Wright and Kersner 1998). Therapists, on the other hand, need to appreciate the implications of such initiatives as the National Literacy and Numeracy Strategies (DfEE 1998b and 1999b).

Whether working in a team, in a small group or in just a pairing, there may be differences in priorities between the professional groups; and the professionals must balance the needs of an individual child against the competing needs of others (McCartney 1999b). For example, a teacher's main priority is to educate all children, whereas speech and language therapists work with specific children when a need arises.

In some instances, there may also be a lack of clarity of roles, and overlap can occur. For instance, in teams where speech and language therapists and occupational therapists are working together they may both focus on communication; similarly, in schools, therapists and teachers are both concerned with language. In these situations a detailed analysis of the children's needs is required. Decisions will then be made about the area on which each of the professionals will concentrate, and about the ways in which each can most effectively use their specific knowledge and skills.

When professionals are working together, it is not uncommon for them to feel professionally vulnerable, and they may even begin to feel de-skilled. When experienced classroom teachers take on specialist advisory roles without additional training, for example, they might feel that they do not have as much specialist knowledge about speech and language as the therapists. It is important for both professionals to have opportunities to discuss these concerns, so that they can acknowledge the specific aspects of their skills that each brings to the collaborative relationship.

When professionals are based in the same location, there will be more opportunities for collaborative working than if they are on different sites. However, even when they work on the same site there may be limited opportunities for meeting. This may also be true for members of a large multidisciplinary team. More frequent informal meetings and regular, timetabled meetings may help to alleviate potential problems.

Ways in which professionals can work together

Speech and language therapists can work with other professionals in a number of different ways. The case example following illustrates some of these ways.

Case example

Anne is eight years old. She has a specific language impairment and attends a mainstream school. Her class teacher and her speech and language therapist have jointly made decisions about some of the targets in her IEP. One of these targets is to encourage Anne to ask for help with her class work.

The two professionals then identify the ways in which they will work with Anne to achieve this target. This does not mean that they will necessarily have to carry out the work jointly. For example, they may decide that the therapist will need to do some individual work with Anne initially to help her formulate appropriate language when asking for help. They may then decide that during craft sessions the teacher will structure the activities so that Anne has to ask for specific materials that have not been automatically provided.

Further considerations

When children need to work on social skills, teachers and therapists can share the work in a different way. The teacher might run a social-skills group in the classroom while the therapist works with individual children in another room. The therapist will work on specific aspects of social skills so that each of these children will ultimately be able to join the classroom group. Sometimes, therapists and teachers may actually work together: for example, they may jointly run assessment sessions or run a group together in the classroom.

There are different models described in the literature for joint working. Idol and West (1991) describe cooperation as people with separate programmes working together to make them more successful. Such a situation can arise in a school where the teacher and therapist agree to work together to ensure that there is no conflict in the overall aims of their respective programmes. Alternatively, they may work in a collaborative way where both professionals have their own specialist knowledge, which they share during the process of working together. The term 'collaboration' can be interpreted in many different ways, which range from describing loose networking to intensive joint working practice (Reid *et al.* 1996).

When working collaboratively, the professionals who work together need to identify what they can realistically offer to a particular child. When a school-aged child has been referred by a teacher, the teacher and therapist need to listen to each other's point of view, agree their expectations of each other and negotiate a realistic working pattern. This process will necessarily involve some level of compromise in order for them to work together successfully.

Sometimes, therapists find that it is appropriate to work in a consultative role with other professionals. The joint DoH/DfEE working group (DfEE 2000a) suggested that increasingly therapists should work indirectly with children, particularly with those who have a less serious communication impairment. Therapists are encouraged to set up programmes that will be implemented by LSAs, under the supervision of the therapist.

When any professionals work together, decisions need to be made about the systems used for sharing information and record keeping. It will be necessary, too, to keep other team members informed of actions and outcomes of therapy. (For further reading, see Wright and Kersner 1998.)

The skills needed to work together

The two most important skills needed when working with other professionals are the abilities to compromise and to negotiate (see Chapter 2). Although therapists will need to be assertive and to enable others to understand their role – and sometimes even the nature of their work with the children – they will need to be realistic about what can be achieved. In order to be sensitive and empathic when working with professional colleagues, it is helpful to have an understanding of the settings in which they work. For example when working in schools, an understanding of the broader issues currently affecting those working within the educational system will enable therapists to work more sensitively with all staff.

Therapists also need to negotiate with the head teacher and with individual staff members about the way in which the service will be delivered within that school. Therapists need to be flexible – for example, when arranging meetings. Furthermore, in the light of ever-developing government initiatives in health and education, therapists will need to continue being responsive and creative.

Summary

By now, it should be clear that it is important for speech and language therapists to work together with other professionals, not only for the benefits of the children but as part of their own continuing professional development.

PART IV

Assessing and managing children with communication problems

In this Part, the chapters focus on a wide range of communication problems, demonstrating the decision-making process involved in assessment and management. The chapters are discrete and may be read in any order, and the titles reflect the client groups discussed. Although details regarding intervention are not included, the authors offer suggestions for further reading.

CHAPTER 12

Working with children with unclear speech: differentiating sub-groups of intelligibility impairment

Kim Grundy

Learning outcomes

By the end of this chapter, the reader should be able to:

- define intelligibility impairment;
- differentiate between speech production disorders and phonological disorders;
- define subgroups of speech production disorder;
- define subgroups of phonological disorder;
- outline the process of management for children with intelligibility impairment.

Introduction

In this chapter a conceptual understanding is presented that has gradually developed through practice and teaching over the last several years. It is the author's belief that the distinction between phonological disorders and speech production disorders has been confused from the point at which the linguistic term 'phonological disorder' was introduced to clinical practice in the late 1970s/early 1980s.

In the mid-1980s, before there had been adequate opportunity for full appreciation of the meaning and implications of 'phonological disorder', another new term emerged – 'semantic-pragmatic disorder' – which diverted the focus of attention for paediatric speech and language therapists and the opportunity for understanding was lost.

Given the above view, the reader may wonder why this chapter introduces yet another new term, 'intelligibility impairment'. The first aim of the chapter, therefore, is to explain what this term means and why it is suggested as useful for practising clinicians.

Why use the term 'intelligibility impairment'?

Both speech production impairments and phonological impairments are manifested through the medium of speech. Indeed, children who have either, or both, impairments present in clinic with the lay description of 'unclear speech'. If this term is adopted, then the diagnostic process begins from a point of potential confusion. In order to arrive at an accurate diagnosis, it is necessary to differentiate between 'speech production' and 'phonological system', and yet the initial label includes the term 'speech'.

Another way of saying 'unclear speech' is to say that the child's intelligibility is impaired. The advantage of referring to intelligibility is that it removes the term 'speech' from the initial description of the child's presenting symptoms and thus leaves open the possibility of considering – separately – speech production and phonology.

The purpose of differentiating between speech impairments and phonological impairments is to ensure that each child receives the most appropriate and effective therapy. Children who have speech production impairments will benefit from traditional articulation therapy, and those who have phonological impairments will benefit from phonological therapy. Children with mixed impairments will benefit from techniques used in both types of therapy (Grundy and Harding 1995).

There has been much discussion about therapeutic packages that have implied by their title that they are phonological therapies (Metaphon Clinical Forum 1995; PACT Clinical Forum 1999). Debate has arisen regarding whether or not Metaphon, for example, is truly a phonological therapy, because it includes techniques and strategies that relate specifically to speech production. By adopting the term 'intelligibility impairment' and approaching these packages as offering strategies for the remediation of intelligibility impairments, the debate becomes spurious and the value of the package can be properly evaluated.

Speech versus phonology

Having stated that intelligibility impairments can arise through either speech production impairment or phonological impairment, the next aim is to differentiate between speech and phonology.

Speech

The production of speech involves physiological processes. That is, when an individual is speaking, neurones are firing such that muscles are innervated and articulator movement occurs, resulting in speech sounds.

Phonetics is the discipline that studies the production of speech sounds. It has identified all of the speech sounds known to be produced by speakers of all the world's languages and has described how each sound is produced. This information is compactly represented through the International Phonetic Alphabet (IPA) chart. Speech sounds are grouped according to their place of articulation; manner of articulation; and voicing. Each speech sound has a written symbol, enabling transcription of any language whether known to the transcriber or not.

In their study of articulatory phonetics, speech and language therapy students learn the articulatory positions and movements involved in producing the majority of the world's speech sounds. They also learn to recognise and produce those sounds alongside learning the written symbols for each. This valuable knowledge enables students and clinicians to identify precisely those speech sounds that result in 'unclear speech' and can be used by them to help children modify their production of those sounds so as to improve intelligibility. The difficulties experienced by many students in learning to produce non-native speech sounds provides an opportunity to develop empathy for the difficulties experienced by children attempting to change aspects of their speech production.

Phonology

Phonology is a level of language. Linguists, in analysing language, have identified that it can be broken down into five different parts, which can be organised hierarchically into levels from the smallest unit to the largest unit – phonology, morphology, syntax, semantics and pragmatics (see Grundy 1995). The linguistic field of phonology studies the smallest units in language that signal meaning differences – phonemes.

Language is an abstract, psychological phenomenon. That is, unlike speech, language has no substance, no physical reality. Speech can be said to have physical reality because speech produces physical sound waves that can be transmitted and recorded. Language exists in the brains of individuals and is transmitted between people through the media of speech, writing, manual signing or symbolisation.

As phonology is a level of language and, as such, is an abstract, psychological phenomenon, phonemes do not exist in a concrete, physical way. Phonemes only exist in the brains of individuals. An individual cannot 'say' a phoneme because a phoneme is simply a category; an individual can only say a speech sound. To differentiate between phonemes and speech sounds, phonemes are written in slant brackets /t/ and speech sounds are written in square brackets [tʰ]. For example, in English phonology, the symbol /t/ represents all the physical speech sounds that can be produced as acceptable realisations (referred to as allophones) of the /t/ phoneme such as [tʰ] [t̚] [t'] [tˢ] [ʔ]. The voiced alveolar implosive[ɗ] and the alveolar click [!] would not be acceptable realisations of the /t/ phoneme in English.

In order for languages to convey meaning, they do not need to use the whole range of speech sounds that the human vocal apparatus can produce. In English, for example, no use is made of implosives, clicks, uvular or pharyngeal sounds. Each language conveys meaning through a limited range of the world supply of speech sounds – its phonology. The phonology can be said to comprise the phonological system (the set of phonemes identified as conveying meaning contrasts) and the phonotactic rules (the rules governing the ways in which the set of phonemes may or may not be combined).

To identify the phonemes of a language, that is the categories of speech sounds that convey meaning difference, linguists work with native speakers of the language and perform phoneme tests. So, if there was no recorded phonology for English, a linguist might ask a native speaker whether, for example, [batʰ] and [batˡ] have different meanings; to which the reply would be 'no'. The linguist might then ask whether [batʰ] and [bat˺] have different meanings – again, 'no'. But if they asked whether [batʰ] and [bak'] have different meanings, the reply would be 'yes'. The linguist would then conclude that the speech sounds [tʰ], [tˡ] and [t'] are allophones of the same phoneme (which they decide to represent as /t/) but that [tʰ] and [k'] are allophones of different phonemes. Having identified the phonological system of English, the linguist would then seek to establish the ways in which these phonemes can legitimately be combined – the phonotactic rules of English. Questions might include 'Do words in English start with/finish with /p/ /r/ /j/'; and 'Can /nj/ /mp/ /str/ be combined at the beginnings and ends of words?' Such tests would continue until the phonology of English was fully established.

Having discussed the theoretical distinction between speech sounds and phonemes, speech production and phonology, it is important to appreciate how these distinctions apply to the clinical population.

Speech production impairments

Where there is a speech production impairment, there is possibly some breakdown in the physiological production of speech. There are two main categories of speech production impairment: neuromuscular and articulation impairments.

Neuromuscular impairment refers to an impairment in the transmission of neural impulses to the muscles used for speech, and there are two main categories: dysarthria and dyspraxia. Dysarthria refers to an impairment of movement and coordination of the muscles required for speech, due to abnormal muscle tone. Muscle tone can be spastic or flaccid and thus subgroups of dysarthria have been identified within these broad parameters. As Milloy and Morgan-Barry have stated (1990: 109): '[Developmental dysarthrias] occur with varying degrees of severity and are most frequently linked with a general motor disability (cerebral palsy).'

In contrast, 'Dyspraxia refers to a disorder of the performance of an action' (Ozanne 1995). The clinical existence of dyspraxia in children has been disputed and widely debated, and clinicians tend to refer to children as exhibiting 'dyspraxic characteristics' rather than 'having dyspraxia'. The main characteristic of dyspraxia is an inability voluntarily to perform movements that can be performed involuntarily. So, for example, a child may struggle when asked 'Stick out your tongue' but be perfectly capable of licking an ice-cream. Characteristics of dyspraxia include: groping for articulatory precision;

inconsistency of articulatory production; difficulty in sequencing segments, syllables, words, phrases or sentences, and difficulty in imitating the same. See Milloy and Morgan-Barry (1990) and Milloy (1991) for more detailed discussions.

There are two main recognised categories of articulation disorder: structural impairment and learned misarticulation. 'Structural impairment' refers to any malformations in the physical structures involved in speech production – for example, cleft palate, submucous cleft palate, incompetent velopharyngeal closure, tongue tie, or dental anomalies. 'Learned misarticulation' is applied in situations where children appear to have no structural abnormality nor any neuromuscular impairment, yet they do not produce one or more sounds of their language with an acceptable native pronunciation. The assumption is made that they have simply mislearned the articulation of the speech sound. The most common example of learned misarticulation is a lisp where the target /s/ is produced as the [ɬ] or [s̪].

Phonological impairments

There are a number of phonological impairments that might apply. The rest of this section discusses some relevant aspects.

Pure articulation disorder versus pure phonological disorder

To understand the distinction between speech production impairment (see previous section) and phonological impairment, it is useful to differentiate between pure articulation disorder and pure phonological disorder.

Pure articulation disorder
In pure articulation disorder, a child is observed to replace one or more of the native speech sounds with a non-native speech sound. So, for example, a child who produces /s/ as [ɬ] will do so wherever the target phoneme /s/ occurs in the language. Although this may make the child's speech unintelligible on first meeting, once the listener has 'tuned in' to the child's substitution, there will be no loss of meaning contrast. That is, [ɬɛl] will be distinct from sounds such as [ʃɛl], [tɛl], [wɛl], [bɛl].

If a child with a pure articulation disorder is asked to produce the target sound in isolation, then an instruction, to 'Say the Sammy Snake sound' will yield the [ɬ] sound instead.

Pure phonological disorder
Children are said to have phonological impairments when the speech sounds they use reduce their ability to signal meaning contrasts. For example, a child might produce target /t/ and target /s/ as [tʰ], resulting in loss of contrast between words like /ti/ and /si/, and between /təʊ/ and /səʊ/, which will be produced as [tʰi] and [tʰəʊ] respectively.

If a child with a pure phonological disorder is asked to make the 'Sammy Snake' sound, he or she will say [s:]. The child with a pure phonological impairment does not have an articulation impairment and can produce all the native speech sounds in isolation. This child has not yet learned the full phonemic system of the language; what needs to be learned is that the speech sound [s] can function as a phonemic contrast to all allophones of the /t/ phoneme.

Description versus explanation

It is important to recognise that phonological impairment is a descriptive term and not an explanatory label. The identification of phonological impairment has arisen from the linguistic practice of analysing and describing language. In the same way that a phonologist will describe the phonology of a language but not attempt to explain why the language has evolved to that particular phonology, clinical analysis of a child's phonology simply describes it but does not attempt to explain it. This is another difference between articulation impairment and phonological impairment. In an attempt to explain articulation impairment, a child's oral structures and movements are examined to conclude that for example, the child cannot physiologically produce voiceless plosives because his or her velopharyngeal closure is inadequate. Or, when all structures and movements appear adequate to produce speech, it may be concluded that misarticulations are due to faulty learning.

Descriptions of phonological impairment involve identification of patterns, referred to as 'processes', in the child's expression of phonology. These relate to both system and phonotactic possibilities. In the system, for example, it is common in normal development for children's speech sounds to exclude [k], and target /k/ is realised by allophones of the /t/ phoneme. This pattern of realising target /t/ and /k/ with [t] allophones is labelled as the process of 'fronting of velar consonants'. A phonotactic pattern common in normal development is the process of 'cluster reduction', where target clusters are realised as single consonants, for example target /snæp/ may be realised as [næp].

Categories of phonological disorder

As might perhaps be expected, the clinical population of children with phonological impairment is not homogenous and various subgroups of phonological disorder have been identified. Grundy and Harding (1995) suggest that the following descriptive diagnostic categories could be clinically helpful:

* *delayed phonological development*: where children appear to be following the normal pattern of development, but development is at a slower rate than would normally be expected for their chronological age;

- *uneven phonological development:* where processes from one stage in development are seen to coexist with processes in a later stage – for example, a child may be observed to be fronting velar consonants (normally not evident after age two-and-a-half) when clusters are well developed (normally emerging from age three);
- *deviant consistent phonological development:* where some processes evident in a child's speech are unusual or idiosyncratic, but production of speech sounds is consistent;
- *deviant inconsistent phonological development:* in the absence of any characteristics of dyspraxia, which would indicate an articulation disorder, no observable error pattern is evident in the child's use of deviant speech sounds.

Complex intelligibility impairments

It is rare to have a child who presents with a pure articulation impairment or a pure phonological impairment, and this is where a differential diagnosis can appear confusing. Nevertheless, if a clear differentiation between speech and phonology is established, it becomes relatively easy to tease out the components of more complex impairments.

A phonological impairment exists where the speech sounds produced by the child result in a reduction in their ability to signal meaning differences. In the previous example of a pure articulation impairment, there is a one-to-one correspondence between the target phoneme /s/ and the physical realisation[ɬ], and there is no loss of meaning contrast. However, there are cases where children's speech production irregularities reduce their ability to signal meaning differences. A simple example of this might be where a child realises the phonemes /s/ and /ʃ/ as [ɬ]. In this case, there will be a loss of contrast between words such as 'sell' and 'shell'; 'she' and 'see'. A more complex example might be where a child with a cleft palate, who is unable to achieve adequate intra-oral air pressure to produce voiceless plosives, realises the three phonemes /p/, /t/ and /k/ as [h] instead. In both of these cases, where there is a clear aetiology of articulation impairment but phonological contrast is lost, the child could be described as having an articulation disorder with phonological consequences.

In other cases, it may be observed that a child has a clear articulation impairment, which affects production of specific sounds – for instance, /s/ and /ʃ/ are realised as [ɬ] – but, in addition, phonological processes are evident in the child's speech – for example, fronting of velars, cluster reduction and final-consonant deletion. Here, it may be preferable to describe the child as having a mixed articulation and phonological disorder.

The diagram in Figure 12.1 summarises the diagnostic distinctions discussed above.

Assessment as the first step to differential diagnosis

When a child presents with 'unclear speech', the clinician will want to take a case history and assess the child's output in order to make the relevant decisions. Some clinicians might

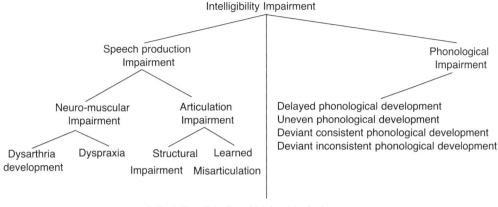

Figure 12.1 Summary of subgroups of intelligibility impairment

prefer to assess the child's output first, so that they can discuss it with the parent when taking case details; others prefer to take the case details first so that this background information can inform their assessments.

Assessment of a child's output

The purpose of intelligibility assessment is to obtain a sample of speech that can be transcribed and analysed. With a good knowledge of English phonetics and phonology, and the normal process of phonological acquisition, it does not really matter which assessment is used. What is needed is some means of eliciting from the child their productions of all target English phonemes in all possible phonotactic combinations. The key to diagnosis is accurate transcription that allows identification of non-English speech sounds and phonological processes.

A commonly used assessment is the STAP (South Tyneside Assessment of Phonology) (Armstrong and Ainley 1988), which provides pictures for elicitation, and analysis sheets. The STAP is portable, simple to administer, and a system where analysis can be completed by an experienced clinician in approximately 20 minutes. The STAP stimuli do not elicit the full range of target phonemes in all their phonotactic possibilities, but they provide enough data for differential diagnosis of the majority of intelligibility impairments.

Another published assessment is PACSTOYS (Grunwell and Harding 1995). The stimuli are toys, which are perhaps more appealing than pictures to very young or distractible children. PACSTOYS elicits all target phonemes in all possible word positions and combinations. The analysis sheets are comprehensive; a developmental profile is included, and there are also means for establishing articulatory maturity.

Having gained a speech sample for analysis, clinicians will want to examine the child's oral structures, assess the range and speed of movement of the articulators, and identify the child's ability to produce speech sounds in isolation and in sequences. Oral examination will reveal any structural abnormalities. To assess the range and speed of movement of articulators, the child is normally asked to copy the clinician's tongue and lip movements. Checking sound sequencing normally requires that the child is asked to produce [p t k] and [b d g] as many times and as fast as possible.

Taking the sounds out of a linguistic context and assigning a non-linguistic meaning to each sound is advisable when checking sounds in isolation. For example, the child might be asked: 'Can you make the sound that we use when we want people to be quiet?' and [ʃ] will be demonstrated. Or, the therapist might ask for, 'the dripping tap sound' demonstrating [tʰ tʰ tʰ]. The reason for doing this is to try to avoid interference from the child's phonological system. What is important to establish is whether the child can physiologically produce the sound. If the therapist inadvertently causes the child to associate the speech sound with that child's phonology, phoneme realisation might be produced that gives the erroneous impression that the child is unable to articulate the sound.

A holistic approach

To ensure that the management of a child is appropriate, it is essential to consider all possible factors that may contribute to his or her intelligibility impairment or may affect it in any way. Thus, birth history, development of feeding, current eating habits, early speech development, habitual use of a dummy or thumb-sucking, and hearing, need careful investigation in these cases.

Management decisions

Grunwell (1982) provides a developmental profile (included in PACSTOYS) against which a child's development of speech sounds and phonology can be evaluated. This enables the clinician to decide how far each child is from the norms of expected development. In cases of developmental delay, when a child is less than 2 years and 4 months in age, a clinician may decide to provide the parents with strategies to facilitate further development, and then to put the child on review. Where intelligibility is seriously affected, it is likely that therapy will be offered, either in a group or individually (see Chapter 4).

If a child is approaching school age, the clinician will be concerned to ensure that measures are taken to minimise the effects of intelligibility impairment on educational progress. It has long been recognised that children who have intelligibility problems at the age of five, and a family history of dyslexia, are more at risk of having difficulties with literacy development (Snowling and Stackhouse 1996). In these cases, the clinician may suggest the instigation of a Statementing procedure for the child in an effort to ensure that support is provided when the child enters school.

Referral to an audiologist might be necessary if the clinician suspects undiagnosed hearing impairment. A referral to an ENT specialist or to an orthodontist might be appropriate when structural anomalies are identified or suspected.

Intervention

It has already been stated that the purpose of differential diagnosis is to ensure suitable therapy. For a more detailed discussion of intervention, see Grundy and Harding (1995) for an overview.

In the remediation of intelligibility impairment, it is the author's belief that the most useful and effective approach is described by Lancaster and Pope (1989). These clinicians give a comprehensive account of the nature of intelligibility impairment and offer a wealth of techniques to remedy both articulation impairment and phonological impairment. A second publication (Flynn and Lancaster 1996) offers further suggestions and materials for working with these children and, in addition, contains an extremely useful and photocopiable chapter offering information and advice for parents and teachers.

Articulation therapy cannot address the difficulties that children with phonological impairments experience. If a child is not signalling a phonological contrast – for example, is stopping fricative /s/ to [t] – then what the child needs to learn is that [s] contrasts with [t]. Children will not learn this through learning to articulate [s] in isolation but will come to appreciate it if presented with minimal pairs, which are used to demonstrate that the contrast is essential in order to communicate meaning.

Summary

It has been demonstrated that the term 'intelligibility impairment' indicates that speech production and phonology can be different causes of the same outcome. Appropriate management of children with intelligibility impairments will encompass a holistic approach, an awareness of the possible sequelae for literacy development, and the use of a wide range of intervention techniques.

Acknowledgements

I offer my thanks to all my current and past students for the gift of your questions. I especially thank Karen Byrne for assertively appraising the first draft of this chapter.

CHAPTER 13

Working with children with comprehension difficulties

Jane Shields

Learning outcomes

By the end of this chapter, the reader should:

- be aware that difficulties in understanding may result from a number of different disorders;
- understand that children with specific language impairment do not form a homogeneous group;
- appreciate that both assessment and differential diagnosis are necessary to plan appropriate intervention;
- appreciate the decisions involved in the assessment and management of comprehension difficulties.

Introduction

Communication is a two-way process, involving the exchange of messages between minds. Verbal communication depends on both encoding – by the speaker or writer – and decoding – by the listener or reader – for the successful sharing of coded messages that aim to convey ideas, thoughts, information, requests or feelings.

Most normally developing children come to understand the nature of the communication process without help, and they learn the language(s) of the environment and culture in which they are reared. Their brains appear to be 'pre-programmed' to develop spoken language and, in normal development, their verbal comprehension develops a little in advance of their expressive use of language. In adulthood, receptive vocabulary exceeds expressive vocabulary and people function as efficient mind-readers, able to decode not only the surface linguistic meaning of spoken messages but also the underlying communicative intent of speakers. Such understanding requires the integration of linguistic information – both verbal and non-verbal – with social and cultural information, as people make sense of each other and of the world.

This chapter considers disorders in children that involve comprehension: the understanding of communication. Receptive difficulties may be restricted to the understanding of verbal communication or may also encompass the comprehension of non-verbal communication. They may be primarily linguistic in nature, or secondary to an underlying socio-cognitive deficit. They may form part of an overall delay in acquiring language, which might perhaps be part of a global developmental delay or might result from a specific language impairment (SLI).

Receptive difficulties are frequently accompanied by delayed or disordered expressive language, but can also be found in some children whose speech is apparently well formed yet is used inappropriately in conversation. The management of receptive difficulties will depend not only on assessment of the factors underlying verbal comprehension but also on differential diagnosis of the conditions that interfere with the development of comprehension.

Factors underlying comprehension

The response of one person to a message communicated by another depends on many underlying factors. It can be helpful to consider the various 'levels' of the process by which the brain decodes and responds to a verbal message.

If a 'bottom-up' approach is adopted, then the first level to consider is that of sensation: can the person receiving the message hear the speech or see the writing? If these sensory pathways are intact, is the person attending to the incoming sensory stimuli – that is, listening to the speaker or looking at the written words? Assuming that sensation is intact and that attention is appropriate, can the person perceive the vital details of the incoming sensation, discriminating the sounds of speech or the letters of writing? If perceptual processes are adequate, does the person have prior experience and understanding of the vocabulary and concepts referred to, that is, has the word meaning been encoded? Since speech, and writing, rarely convey messages in single words, can the person's working memory hold the sequence of words and decode the syntax that binds further meaning within phrase, sentence, discourse or text?

The process described so far has allowed for the decoding of the 'surface', linguistic meaning. But what of the speaker's intent? Can the person also decode the accompanying intonation and body language, which allow differentiation between literal and non-literal comprehension – between compliment and sarcasm; between yes/no questions and polite request. Can the person 'mind-read' (Baron-Cohen 1995), appreciating and guessing another person's knowledge, feelings and wishes so as to deduce the speaker's intent? Can the person use inferencing and the principle of relevance (Sperber and Wilson 1995) in allowing for the effects of context that may involve both speaker and situational factors (Leinonen and Kerbel 1999)? Communication occurs in social settings, and pragmatic comprehension impairments may result from socio-cognitive dysfunction.

Assessment of comprehension

The assessment of a child's comprehension of language must take into account not only what is spoken to the child but also the situation in which it is spoken, and the child's prior knowledge of the world. For example, a pre-school boy has a dirty nappy. His mother enters the room holding a nappy and says 'Come here and lie down for me to change your nappy.' The child approaches and lies down.

What can we assume about comprehension? Did the boy respond to the words, or to the sight of the nappy, or to the feel of a dirty nappy and his memory of the nappy-changing routine? Further investigation could clarify whether the words, or simply the situation were understood. The mother could try using the same words without holding the nappy, or choose a time when the boy does not have a dirty nappy, to test the same instruction.

Later, the boy might be told: 'Get your coat on, we're going to the shop to buy some biscuits', but he does not get his coat; instead, he goes to the kitchen cupboard where biscuits are kept – having understood only the key word 'biscuits'. That evening, the father might tell the child: 'Peter, turn the television off.' There is no response. The father says: 'Television – off.' Peter does not comply. His father walks over to the television, points to the switch and repeats: 'Television – off'. Peter complies – having understood the accompanying visual prompt. This example illustrates the need to look closely at the context in which spoken language is possibly understood by young children, and to tease out whether it is, in fact, the words that are being comprehended.

A full case history will be essential and should include details of the child's development, usually gathered from parents. Traditionally, speech and language therapy was considered by many parents to be concerned with encouraging speech, concentrating on the child's expressive use of language. Therapists should be cautious in accepting parental reports such as 'he/she understands every word I say' when taking the case history of a child with obvious expressive difficulties: parents are rarely aware of the effect of the accompanying clues that enable their child to respond – perhaps to a familiar situation, gesture or keyword – rather than to the parent's spoken sentence. It will also be essential to gather information about the child's hearing, either from previous health visitor screening or by requesting an opinion from professionals in an ENT department. The child's level of attention development can be assessed informally and by observation in home or school surroundings.

Formal assessments will also be necessary and should be selected according to the age and developmental level of the individual child. Some formal assessments measure, and permit comparison of, both receptive and expressive language. Such as:

- RDLS III (Reynell Developmental Language Scales III; Edwards *et al.* 1997). Age range: from 18 months to 7 years.
- Pre-school Language Scale (a UK adaptation by Boucher and Lewis 1997). Age range: from birth to 6 years.
- REEL (Receptive-Expressive Emergent Language Scale; Bzoch and League 1971). Age range: from 0 to 3 years.
- CELF – Preschool[UK] (Clinical Evaluation of Language Fundamentals Preschool UK Edition; Wiig *et al.* 2000). Age range: from 3 years to 6 years 11 months.
- CELF – 3[UK] (Clinical Evaluation of Language Fundamentals, Third Edition UK; Semel *et al.* 2000). Age range: from 6 to 21 years.

All of these tests provide developmental norms – some standardised on UK children – that are useful when considering the possibility of delayed language development.

Other formal measures assess and provide developmental norms for a particular aspect of understanding. For instance:

- Boehm Test of Basic Concepts, 3rd edition (Boehm 2000). Age range: from 5 to 7 years.
- Boehm – 3 Preschool (Boehm 2001). Age range: from 3 years to 5 years 11 months.
- BBCS–R (Bracken Basic Concept Scale – Revised; Bracken 1998). Age range: from 2 years 6 months to 8 years.
- BPVS (The British Picture Vocabulary Scale II; Dunn *et al.* 1997), which examines a child's understanding of spoken vocabulary. Age range: from 2 years 6 months to 18 years.
- TROG (Test of the Reception of Grammar; Bishop 1989), which examines a child's comprehension of syntactic structures. Age range: from 4 to 12 years.

Some tests measure several aspects of comprehension. For example:

- TACL (Test for Auditory Comprehension of Language; Carrow-Woolfolk 1998), which measures receptive spoken vocabulary, grammar and syntax. Age range: from 3 to 9 years.
- Understanding Ambiguity (Rinaldi 1996), which targets the understanding of pragmatic meaning. Age range 8 to 13 years.

The choice of assessments will depend on the child's chronological age, concentration span, and major presenting difficulties. It will also be essential to investigate the child's understanding in familiar surroundings, and to compare understanding in different environments, such as home and nursery. Observation in naturalistic settings is ideal, but demanding of a therapist's time. A compromise might be the use of checklists, which can be completed by adults in the child's familiar environments: a parent at home, and a teacher or nursery nurse at school. A useful tool is that produced by Dewart and Summers (1995), which includes a specially structured interview for parents and teachers of children in the age range 9 months to 10 years, and which elicits information about both the understanding and the expressive use of pragmatic aspects of communication.

It will be important to compare with results from formal tests a child's understanding of conversation in less structured, real-life situations. Examples of literal understanding should be noted and, for the older child, the understanding of sarcasm, metaphor, idiom and humour can be examined (Rinaldi 1996). It may also be necessary to look more closely at a child's development of social understanding. Informal procedures to examine aspects such as the child's understanding of facial expressions, emotions and beliefs, and pretence may be used (Howlin *et al.* 1999).

Decisions concerning diagnosis

When considering a child who may have difficulty with verbal comprehension, the process of diagnosis will involve a sequences of decisions.

Is this primarily a language problem?

If a sensory impairment such as hearing loss has been identified, then such a primary causative factor will be the first priority rather than diagnosing a specific language impairment. If the child's attention skills appear to be the major factor, then an appropriate diagnosis may prove to be that of attention deficit disorder. In either event, the child will need the care of a paediatric team in addition to that of a speech and language therapist.

Is verbal comprehension involved?

From assessment results, it will be essential to decide whether receptive deficits are present. If so, then are expressive abilities similarly involved? Some children with SLI show expressive deficits in the presence of relatively intact comprehension, although the majority of children with SLI have both expressive and receptive language involvement (Conti-Ramsden and Botting 1999).

Is language development delayed?

If comprehension deficits are present, is there a pattern of delay? Comparison with the child's chronological age will establish whether receptive skills are delayed. Are the comprehension difficulties accompanied by expressive deficits, and is there a similar pattern of delay in these two areas of communication? Delayed development of language frequently involves both expressive and receptive aspects, which may show similar equivalent age or standard scores on assessment batteries that provide developmental norms, such as RDLS III, CELF^{UK} or REEL (see above).

Is this delay confined to language?

Comparisons with a child's mental age will establish whether any delay in the development of language is part of a more generalised developmental delay. Receptive and expressive scores can be compared with non-verbal scores on tests, such as Raven's Matrices (Raven 1986), that give an indication of mental age, in the absence of more detailed psychological test information. Where language scores are delayed relative to chronological age, but are appropriate to the child's mental age, then a diagnosis of learning disability, rather than that of SLI, would be likely.

Which aspects of comprehension are impaired?

Where a diagnosis of SLI is indicated, an analytical approach to the nature of the verbal comprehension deficit will be appropriate, and assessments should look at the development of the component abilities of verbal comprehension – for instance, comparing scores for vocabulary (on BPVS) with those for grammar (on TROG). Such assessments produce quantitative results, including a comparison with developmental norms, but the qualitative information that they yield may inform differential diagnosis and can also aid the planning of appropriate intervention.

Could the receptive difficulties be caused by an aetiology other than SLI?

As mentioned earlier, difficulties with verbal comprehension can occur as the secondary consequence of hearing loss, or in association with general developmental delay. They are also found in other disorders, whose differential diagnosis will require careful observation of a number of aspects of the child's development and behaviour. Some of these are given below.

Landau–Kleffner syndrome (LKS)

Children with this rare syndrome typically show regression in language development, in association with the onset of seizure disorder (see Chapter 22). The onset of LKS is most commonly between the ages of three and eight years, and it can be either sudden or gradual. After a period of normal language development, a child with LKS develops severe receptive language difficulties and deafness is often suspected. Audiometry reveals normal peripheral hearing but electro-encephalogram (EEG) testing shows an abnormal pattern, with spike activity in one or both temporal lobes, which may or may not give rise to overt seizures.

Some children eventually lose their speech completely, and many become unable to recognise spoken words or environmental sounds. Some may have episodes of autistic-like behaviour. The prognosis is variable but the seizures, behaviour disorder and any additional neurological problems often settle down by adolescence. Some children then recover their language but many are left with a language disability. The long-term prognosis for language varies with the child's age at the onset of LKS, the worst long-term outcomes being associated with an early age of onset (Bishop 1985).

Autistic spectrum disorders (ASD)

Autism is a pervasive developmental disorder that is diagnosed by identifying the presence of a 'triad' of behavioural impairments in: social interaction, social communication, and imagination. The triad is usually accompanied by repetitive patterns of activity and a resistance to change in routine. The concept of the 'autistic spectrum' reflects how autism may, rarely, occur in isolation – for example, high-functioning autism, or Asperger syndrome, but often occurs in combination with learning disabilities.

More boys than girls have ASD: for classic 'Kanner' autism (Kanner 1943) the ratio is four males to one female; for Asperger syndrome it is nine males to one female. People with Asperger syndrome tend to have average or above average intelligence and show fewer problems with language, although they are likely to experience difficulty with social communication.

Many children with ASD have delayed language development, and some never acquire functional speech. A number of children with ASD develop some early language skills, which are then lost around the age of 18 months to 2 years. In those children who do develop language, comprehension difficulties are common, but these may not be immediately obvious in the verbal child who presents with fluent, well-articulated expressive language.

Unlike children with SLI, those with ASD may have the memory capacity to learn and imitate 'chunks' of language form, with only limited understanding of the appropriate use or meaning of these structures. Results of formal testing may then reveal scores of expressive abilities higher than receptive abilities. A similar pattern occurs as 'hyperlexia', where tests of reading show relatively high scores for word recognition, accompanied by depressed scores for reading comprehension.

Comprehension difficulties are often increased by adults using over-long and complex utterances, which overload the processing capacity of children with ASD. They may perform relatively well on structured tests such as BPVS and TROG, yet show receptive limitations in real-life situations, when their underlying social deficits give rise to literal understanding and pragmatic confusions.

The effects of 'mind-blindness' (Baron-Cohen 1995) leave even the able, verbal person with ASD with continuing difficulties in making sense of the social world and in understanding the subtleties of everyday conversation. Over-literal understanding is common because poor mind-readers lack the ability to 'think about thoughts' or to make sense of other people's behaviour in terms of mental states. Without such a 'theory of mind', the world can be an unpredictable place, which explains the person with ASD's preference for routine and tendency to anxiety, which further restricts his or her verbal comprehension in stressful situations.

Pragmatic Language Impairment (PLI)

Leinonen and Kerbel (1999) show how relevance theory (Sperber and Wilson 1995) can be used to demonstrate that difficulties once considered to be semantic – for example, with ambiguity, ellipsis or pronouns – do in fact fall within the domain of pragmatics. They encourage a move away from a mere description of surface behaviours to an understanding of the underlying cause(s) of a particular communication difficulty. Thus, a child might have difficulty in understanding pragmatic meaning for a variety of reasons: lack of world knowledge; difficulty in making inferences; difficulty in determining what is contextually salient; or difficulty in judging what another person knows or finds most relevant. Leinonen and Kerbel (1999) suggest a close connection between pragmatic impairments and socio-cognitive deficits, noting that Shields *et al.* (1996) had found very similar socio-cognitive deficits in groups of children with diagnoses of both semantic–pragmatic disorder and high-functioning autism.

Conti-Ramsden and Botting (1999), in their survey of seven-year-old children attending UK language units, found 9 per cent of children who did not fit into either of their categories relating to SLI, 'expressive SLI' or 'expressive-receptive SLI'. These children all had scores on the TROG that were lower than their scores on a battery of tests of expressive language. Professionals working with the children described their problems as having to do with the social use of language, social interaction with others, and understanding social situations – areas of deficit that are typified by the triad of ASD. Teachers were using the term 'semantic–pragmatic syndrome' to refer to this group of children.

In the UK, the descriptive term 'pragmatic language impairment' has replaced the earlier diagnosis of 'semantic–pragmatic disorder'. Conti-Ramsden and Botting (1999) recommend the use of the term PLI as a 'working' term, since some confusion remains at clinical level as to whether these children fall within the autistic spectrum. Professionals working with people who have ASD may use the term PLI to describe the nature of the communication impairments associated with the spectrum, rather than as a diagnosis. SLI can, of course, produce pragmatic impairments in communication, and some people with ASD have accompanying language difficulties. However, the communication difficulties found in verbal people with ASD appear to result from their underlying socio-cognitive deficits rather than being primarily linguistic in origin.

Decisions concerning management

The management of children with comprehension difficulties will differ according to the underlying causation of the receptive difficulties and will further depend on whether these reflect a pattern of delay or of disorder. It will be important to establish whether the receptive difficulties are primarily linguistic in nature; and whether they form part of a broader picture, such as developmental delay, or ASD. Both prognosis and appropriate intervention will vary with differential diagnosis, which must be based on a thorough assessment that examines a child's behaviour in both clinical and more naturalistic surroundings.

The decisions concerning management may include a number of questions.

Therapeutic intervention or remedial education?

The management of developmental difficulties may involve funding from health, education and social-services sources. Resources are finite and prioritising is necessary. Speech and language therapy services, in common with other parts of the NHS, must consider the effectiveness of interventions and balance their efficacy against the resultant costs. Many of the disorders associated with difficulties in verbal comprehension have a relatively poor prognosis, and these children will require help over a number of years. Such cases do not fit easily with concepts such as 'completed episode of care', and the decisions about when to intervene, and for how long, will not be easy. In general, early intervention is beneficial and can help to prevent secondary complications, such as behavioural problems, that may result from frustration.

If a child's comprehension difficulties result from SLI, then speech and language therapy will form a core part of help for that child and should begin as soon as the language impairment is identified, continuing as necessary after the child enters school. If the SLI is severe, the child may receive a Statement, and therapy can be incorporated into the appropriate educational package.

Where receptive difficulties form part of a more general developmental delay, speech and language therapy intervention is likely to be delivered as part of the local provision of services for children with learning disability. Group work and/or classroom-based intervention may be most appropriate, and the therapist may design programmes to be delivered by a speech and language therapy assistant or classroom support assistant.

Children with ASD require intervention that focuses on communication, rather than just language. In addition, they will require ongoing help in learning to compensate for their poor 'mind-reading' skills, so as to make sense of everyday communication in social settings. Since they have difficulty in generalising skills between environments, they are unlikely to benefit from short, isolated sessions of specific language work and will need specialist help that can be incorporated into their daily routines, both at school and at home.

What is the appropriate advice for parents?

The diagnosis of some of the conditions giving rise to comprehension difficulties will involve multidisciplinary cooperation. Where an underlying condition such as deafness is diagnosed, it will be vital to explain to parents the cause of their child's difficulties, as well as the prognosis and the proposed treatment. Similarly, should LKS be diagnosed, then parents will need to be informed of the associated seizure disorder and of the prognosis. It will usually be the role of a paediatrician to give such advice.

The detection of generalised developmental delay in a child may involve a psychologist, perhaps as part of a child development centre team (see Chapter 8). The child's parents will need to be told of the child's learning disability and of the most suitable educational placement. Usually, the speech and language therapist forms part of the team and may advise the parents about the child's communication development and how this can best be encouraged.

Where SLI is diagnosed, the speech and language therapist may have a lead role in management and will be expected to give the parents an explanation of the nature of the language impairment and of how they can best help their child. Evans and MacWhinney (1999) found that seven-year-old children with expressive-receptive (rather than expressive) difficulties relied on semantic cues rather than word order as their predominant processing strategy. These children may have impairments in auditory working memory that prevent them from attending to word-order cues. For such children, intervention needs to focus on developing comprehension strategies that use word order as opposed to whole-world knowledge.

Autistic spectrum disorders are best diagnosed by a multidisciplinary team and it will not usually be the therapist's role to give a diagnosis of ASD. However, in some cases, parents have been given a diagnosis of PLI and led to expect that their child's social difficulties will resolve with further language development. This can be both confusing and frustrating for parents if their child's difficulties prove to be more pervasive than a language impairment and if they are not then given appropriate help to understand the nature of the underlying socio-cognitive deficit. For instance, they might be encouraged to stimulate their child's language development by using enriched language themselves – which in certain circumstances could prove to exacerbate their child's processing limitations and comprehension difficulties.

Decisions concerning education

Although decisions concerning appropriate educational provision are not made by the speech and language therapist, he or she might well be involved in the decision-making process, contributing reports to the LEA that may form part of the Statementing procedure. Within that process, a variety of different questions will need to be asked and decisions made.

Statements

The system of provision of help for children with special educational needs has undergone several changes since the 1980s, and the number of children receiving a Statement has given rise for concern (see Chapter 6). Certain diagnoses carry a 'weighting' in the Statementing process, and some (e.g. ASD) qualify a child to receive state benefits. Whatever the percentage of children to be identified in the local setting, it will remain the job of the speech and language therapist to identify children with receptive communication difficulties and to contribute appropriate advice on the nature of their needs.

Mainstream or specialist provision: for SLI or ASD?

Wherever possible, children with special educational needs are now educated within mainstream settings. Speech and language therapy should be available to children with receptive communication difficulties and might be delivered within the classroom, possibly funded by the LEA, if the child has a Statement. Some authorities provide specialist resourced units (e.g. for SLI, or for ASD) within mainstream schools (see Chapter 6); others use special schools, run either by the LEA or by an independent body such as ICAN or the National Autistic Society.

Children whose communication deficit involves pragmatic abilities may be best placed in provisions for SLI, provided that the staff have experience and understanding of the possible underlying socio-cognitive difficulties. Such children are likely to be visual learners and may be helped by visual structure, together with specific teaching of social communication skills.

Summary

Difficulties in understanding verbal communication can result from a number of disorders. In managing the needs of children with receptive difficulties, assessment and differential diagnosis will be vital in planning appropriate intervention and education for children whose difficulties may not be primarily linguistic, and who are likely to have long-term needs.

CHAPTER 14

Working with children with language delay and specific language impairment (SLI)

Janet Wood

Learning outcomes

By the end of this chapter, the reader should:

- be able to describe different subgroups of children with specific language impairment;
- be able to form and evaluate hypotheses regarding differential diagnosis;
- know which factors should be taken into account in planning an assessment for a language-impaired child;
- be able to develop long- and short-term therapy aims, based on assessment findings;
- know which factors should be taken into account in making decisions about the form of intervention.

Introduction

Children may fail to develop language normally for a variety of reasons. In some cases, the cause is attributable to other developmental difficulties such as hearing impairment or learning disability, while in others the difficulties are specific to language development. This chapter will focus on the latter of these groups. A number of labels are used to describe children for whom language is the primary area of concern. These include: language delay, primary language delay, SLI, developmental language disorder, and specific language disorder.

Defining language delay and SLI

The array of terms in relation to problems with language development can be confusing, especially as each is used inconsistently within the literature. For example, a distinction is sometimes made between language disorder (where language development is not following a typical pattern) and language delay (where language is developing typically, but more slowly than expected). However, the term 'language disorder' has also been used as an umbrella term for all children with language difficulties (Adams *et al.* 1997), and some authors have questioned whether there is a real distinction between delay and disorder (Curtiss *et al.* 1992). In light of this, the more neutral term 'impairment' is now commonly used to avoid making a distinction between delay and disorder. Additionally, the terms 'primary' and 'specific' are used to denote cases where language impairment is the only, or the main, area of developmental difficulty.

SLI can be broadly defined as a significant language difficulty that cannot be attributed to sensory impairment, general learning disability, neurological or emotional disorder or environmental deprivation. However, a range of criteria is used in relation to the severity and specificity of the language impairment, and this issue will be discussed below.

Children with SLI often have persistent difficulties, and those who still have a significant impairment at 5 and a half years of age are at risk of continuing difficulties throughout childhood and into adolescence (Stothard *et al.* 1998). For some children, however, language development does catch up in early childhood and it seems more appropriate to use the label 'language delay' to describe them. However, even where language difficulties appear to have resolved early, there may continue to be subtle underlying processing difficulties. These often become apparent at a later stage, in relation to literacy development (Stothard *et al.* 1998).

Initial hypotheses: making a differential diagnosis

Having received a referral for a language-impaired child, the speech and language therapist will form initial hypotheses. These might well cover some of the following options:

* the child does have a language impairment, or does not have a language impairment;
* all aspects of language are affected, or only some aspects of language are affected;
* the language impairment is mild/moderate/severe;
* the language impairment is developmental, or acquired;
* the language impairment is specific, or associated with other developmental difficulties;
* the language impairment is transient, or persistent;
* the language impairment is caused by some combination of: defective genes, environment, sensory impairment, neurological damage, physical impairment and impaired development in other social and cognitive domains.

In order to start evaluating these hypotheses, the therapist will need to collect evidence from a range of sources: information provided by parents and other professionals, observation of the child, and informal and formal assessment. Some of the hypotheses may be accepted or rejected within moments of meeting the child, while others may take weeks, months or even years to evaluate. Throughout this period, the therapist will continually monitor the evidence and use it to plan appropriate intervention.

Referral information

Case example

A referral from a health visitor for a boy aged 2 years and 6 months stated:

> Matthew failed his 18-month developmental check in relation to language development and is still not linking words together. All other aspects of development appear fine.

On receiving this referral, the speech and language therapist may believe that there is enough information to accept the hypothesis that Matthew has a language impairment, especially as referrals from this health visitor are generally reliable. The therapist also knows that the child has expressive language difficulties, but needs to investigate further to find out if receptive language is also affected. It appears likely that this is a developmental, rather than an acquired, disorder, because there is no indication of an initial period of normal language development. The fact that the health visitor reports normal development in areas other than language indicates that it is a primary language impairment, but more specific information would be needed to further evaluate this hypothesis.

It would be useful if the therapist could tell whether Matthew's language impairment was likely to be transient or persistent, as this could influence management decisions. Unfortunately, there is no recognised set of accurate predictors (Ellis Weismer 2000), but it is possible to identify children who are most at risk of persisting difficulties. Olswang *et al.* (1998) suggest a number of at-risk factors, including:

* limited use of verbs;
* few spontaneous imitations;
* poor comprehension;
* limited range of consonants;
* a family history of persistent language impairment.

These factors should, therefore, be investigated during the initial assessment. In general, children with receptive difficulties are more at risk for a persisting language impairment than those who have expressive difficulties alone. Up to 60 per cent of children with circumscribed expressive language difficulties at 2 years have age-appropriate language skills by the age of 3 (see Law *et al.* 1998 for a review).

The information gleaned from a referral will vary depending on the referring agent and the age of the child. In all cases, however, referral information is invaluable in forming an initial concept of the nature of a child's difficulties.

The case history

The initial hypotheses can be further evaluated with regard to case history information.

Case example

Information taken from the case history of a six-year-old girl who was referred to a mainstream school speech and language therapy service included the following details:

> Katie was a 'late talker' and she is still sometimes difficult to understand. Her mother is concerned because Katie's school has reported that she has poor listening skills and has difficulty following instructions and learning topic words. She passed all the motor and self-help milestones at around the expected ages. She is good at drawing and enjoys looking at books, but she is not yet reading. Katie has been healthy, apart from a few coughs and colds and there have never been any concerns about her hearing. There is no evidence of epilepsy or neurological damage. She is the second of three children: her older sister has no problems with language development, but her brother, aged three years, is only just beginning to link words together.

On the basis of this information, Katie's speech and language therapist can accept the hypothesis that she has a developmental language impairment: there is no evidence to suggest that this is an acquired problem, and Katie seems to have had difficulties from the outset of language development. The therapist is not yet in a position to state which areas of language are affected, but there are several pieces of relevant information relating to this hypothesis. This will be used in planning the informal and formal assessment.

As Katie is continuing to have significant difficulties at six years old, it seems inappropriate to label her difficulties as 'language delay'. It is possible that her language impairment is specific, because there is no indication of other difficulties such as hearing impairment or neurological damage. More information regarding her general cognitive level is required in order to rule out language impairment related to general learning disability. However, the fact that she passed all her motor and self-help milestones at appropriate ages is of interest. There appears to be a family history of language impairment, and so the therapist might hypothesise that genetics are contributing to the aetiology. There is now a significant body of evidence to suggest that SLI is highly heritable (Plomin and Dale 2000; Tomblin and Buckwalter 1994) and therefore a positive family history should be noted carefully.

Informal assessment

It is generally advisable to begin the assessment process with observation of the child. This not only allows the child to become familiar with the therapist before being asked to demonstrate specific behaviours, but also enables the therapist to make some informed decisions regarding which aspects of language to assess in more detail. In a home or clinic situation, the child could be observed playing with the parent, while in a nursery or school setting the observation should occur within a normal class activity. At this time, the therapist will be noting attention control, social-interaction skills, speech output, expressive language, and the response to questions and instructions. It is also useful to record a language sample for analysis of phonology, syntax and discourse.

Observation of other areas such as fine and gross motor control, play, problem-solving and cognitive skills are also important, because this will help in evaluating hypotheses regarding the aetiology of the disorder. If the child is observed playing with the parent, the therapist will probably note the manner of parent–child interaction, especially if this is likely to form the basis of intervention (see Chapter 5).

It is also possible to ask parents and pre-school/school staff to complete checklists to provide specific information. A number of published checklists are available. The MacArthur Communicative Development Inventories (Fenson *et al.* 1993) is designed for use by parents, while others, such as The Early Language Skills Checklist (Boyle and McLellan 1998) and Teaching Talking (Locke and Beech 1991), are designed for nursery or school settings. Checklists help to provide a holistic view of a child's functioning and compensate for the fact that the child may not be performing at his or her best in a clinic.

Following a period of silent observation, the therapist may begin to interact with the child, continuing with the activity that the child was already involved in, probing for specific types of response, or introducing new materials. These could include pictures or objects for the child to describe, categorise or identify; story cards for sequencing; or toys with which the child is asked to perform specific actions. For a detailed account of informal assessment procedures, see Lees and Urwin (1997). The choice of materials will be guided by the information obtained from the referral and the case history, with an aim of confirming suspected areas of difficulty and screening for any additional problems.

Information obtained from informal assessment will provide further evidence for accepting or rejecting the hypotheses regarding differential diagnosis and will help the therapist to decide whether or not formal assessment is required.

Case example

Ben, aged 4 years and 3 months, was seen in his nursery for informal assessment. The following observations were made:

Ben initiated interaction with adults and peers and demonstrated appropriate eye contact and turn-taking. He appeared to understand questions and instructions within a game, but when instructions were given to the whole group he seemed to follow the lead of other children. Ben's phonological development appeared appropriate for his age, but his expressive language was significantly delayed. He used many non-specific words, such as 'thing' and 'doing' and his utterances were short and telegrammatic. Ben was observed to complete a 12-piece interlocking jigsaw without assistance and he demonstrated that he could count objects up to ten. No clumsiness was noted in gross or fine motor skills.

The observation of Ben indicates that pragmatics and phonology do not require further assessment, but that word knowledge and syntax for both receptive and expressive language should be investigated in more detail. His expressive language is definitely impaired, with evidence of a reduced expressive vocabulary and delayed syntactic development. Receptive language appears to be less affected, although there is some indication that he has difficulty following complex instructions. His difficulties appear to fit the description of lexical-syntactic deficit, one of the six clinical language subtypes described by Rapin and Allen (1983). These are:

- verbal auditory agnosia (an inability to comprehend spoken language with intact understanding of gestures);
- semantic-pragmatic deficit (fluent, well-formed utterances that are often echolalic or stereotypical; over-literal comprehension and poor understanding and use of social communication);
- lexical-syntactic deficit (severe word-retrieval difficulty and difficulty formulating sentences; some problems with comprehension of complex or abstract language);
- phonological-syntactic deficit (a predominantly expressive difficulty, with particular problems in speech production and use of morphology and syntax);
- phonological programming deficit (adequate comprehension and fluent long utterances, but significant problems with speech processing, resulting in poor intelligibility);
- verbal dyspraxia (adequate comprehension but severely impaired production of speech, resulting in short, often unintelligible utterances; evidence of a motor planning deficit).

Rapin and Allen's (1983) system of classification continues to be quoted within the literature, as does a similar system proposed by Bishop and Rosenbloom (1987). A more recent survey of 242 seven-year-old children with SLI indicated that this group of children broadly fitted into Rapin and Allen's six categories (Conti-Ramsden *et al.* 1997), hence proving their validity for research purposes. In practice, however, clinicians may find it difficult to categorise all children, and some terms are beginning to fall out of use. For example, Bishop (2000) now uses the term 'pragmatic language impairment' in preference to 'semantic pragmatic disorder/deficit' (see Chapter 13).

Returning to the case example of Ben, the description indicates that his difficulties are specific to language. The completion of the jigsaw puzzle indicates potentially good non-verbal cognitive skills, and counting objects up to ten in number indicates an ability to learn that is commensurate with his peers. Assuming that he does not have a hearing impairment, it would be reasonable at this stage to hypothesise that he has SLI. However, standardised assessment of both verbal and performance skills by a psychologist will be required to confirm whether or not there is a discrepancy in his learning ability in these two domains.

At this point, it would seem useful to discuss the exclusionary criteria that are generally applied to a definition of SLI. Traditionally, it is diagnosed in cases where the child has no sensory, neurological, physical, emotional or general cognitive difficulties. However, some clinicians would diagnose SLI in the presence of one or more of these difficulties, as long as the language impairment could not be wholly attributed to them (Lees and Urwin 1997). In terms of general cognitive or learning ability, the diagnostic criteria for developmental language disorder in the tenth revision of the International Classification of Diseases (ICD-10) (World Health Organisation 1993) requires that language skills are at least two standard deviations below the level expected for the child's age, and at least one standard deviation above non-verbal, or performance, IQ. Leonard (1998), however, applies slightly different criteria, namely that language test scores should be at least 1.25 standard deviations below the mean and that performance IQ should be at least 85 (i.e. no more than one standard deviation below the mean).

The validity of verbal/performance discrepancy criteria have been questioned (see Bishop1997, Fey *et al.* 1994 and Leonard 1998 for discussion of this point). The problems that are cited with using discrepancy criteria include the following:

- The cut-off point is partly arbitrary, considering that both verbal and performance tests will be liable to some measurement error.
- It would be expected that the language deficit seen in SLI would occur across the population, including children with low IQ.
- There is evidence that children with SLI also perform badly on some non-linguistic tasks.

In some cases, the level of performance IQ will be unimportant in the speech and language therapist's decision-making process. However, it may be important in relation to educational placement because, in most LEAs, strict discrepancy criteria will be adhered to in allocating language unit provision.

Formal assessment

Formal assessments fall into two categories, namely criterion-referenced tests (where the child's performance is measured against set skills) and norm-referenced, or standardised, tests (where the child's performance is measured against norms that are standardised for chronological age). Where formal assessment is used, the therapist must be clear about the reasons for doing this. These could be:

- to confirm whether difficulties noted during informal assessment are due to language impairment;
- to test hypotheses regarding the underlying cause of the language impairment, in terms of specific psycholinguistic processes;
- to determine the severity of the language impairment;
- to compare the severity of deficits across different aspects of language;
- to enable planning and prioritisation of speech and language therapy goals.

In relation to the case example of Ben, the therapist will want to investigate the level and severity of any receptive difficulty and confirm the exact level of breakdown in expressive language. As it has been hypothesised that Ben has SLI, the therapist might want to conduct a norm-referenced test. This would be useful for comparing language ability to other cognitive skills and for providing evidence of special educational need. Ben is aged 4 years and 3 months, and is suspected of functioning at a level beneath that of his chronological age. Any formal assessments selected should, therefore, be sensitive to stages of language development prior to age 4.

As the therapist wants to investigate a broad range of receptive and expressive skills, it may be useful to pick an assessment method that enables this, such as the Reynell Developmental Language Scales III (RDLS III) (Edwards *et al.* 1997), or the CELF – Preschool[UK] (Wiig *et al.* 2000).

The CELF – Preschool[UK] assessment may be particularly useful for Ben in that it contains a 'formulating labels' subtest to assess expressive vocabulary. This assessment also contains a word structure subtest, designed to assess production of morphology, but it does not investigate syntax more widely, other than in imitated sentences. RDLS III, on the other hand, investigates a wider range of syntactic abilities, including production of grammatical inflections, clausal elements, and questions. Both of these assessments have been standardised on UK populations and the test items should all be familiar to British children. The therapist might also consider using the Renfrew Word Finding Vocabulary Test (Renfrew 1988) as an alternative means of obtaining a norm-referenced score for expressive vocabulary, and the Renfrew Action Picture Test (Renfrew 1997) to obtain further information on sentence production. The receptive sections of either the RDLS III or the CELF – Preschool[UK] would provide information that could be used to confirm whether Ben has additional receptive language difficulties, and to indicate where the level of breakdown might be occurring.

Information from others

Up to this point in the assessment process, it would appear that the therapist has been working almost in isolation. In reality, however, this is not the case. At each stage, the therapist will collect additional information from others. Parents and pre-school or school staff, for example, will be able to provide detailed information regarding the way in which a child's language impairment affects the ability to communicate.

Two children with similar language profiles will present differently if, for example, one has developed strategies to overcome communication problems and the other has not. Additionally, one child may be better able to communicate in some settings than in others, as a result of factors such as group size. It is useful to know which strategies, if any, help a particular child: in a school setting, for example, the teacher might have discovered that the child is able to follow long instructions if those instructions are divided into shorter chunks. This type of information does not help in evaluating hypotheses about differential diagnosis, but it is of great importance for the next stage of management, planning intervention.

People who spend time with a child on a daily basis will also be able to provide information regarding the language skills that would be most functional for the child to develop. If they are going to be involved in carrying out or supporting intervention, they will need to feel that they have been consulted in the selection of targets, and so an exchange of views and findings should occur once some assessment has been conducted.

Additionally, the therapist will collate any information available from other professionals who have seen the child, such as an audiologist, paediatrician or psychologist. Each of these people may be able to shed light on the aetiology of the language impairment or, for example, any discrepancy between language and other areas of development.

Interpreting test findings and planning long- and short-term aims

Following the period of initial assessment, the speech and language therapist will have a clear idea about which areas of language ability are impaired, and the extent of the impairment. The therapist will have some understanding of the aetiology of the impairment and might be able to assign a label of either language delay or SLI, as appropriate. With this knowledge, the therapist will then be able to form a hypothesis regarding the child's prognosis, and this will be used to determine long-term aims. Of course, the therapist will continue to form and evaluate hypotheses throughout the period of intervention, and the long-term aims set at this early stage might need to be revised in the light of the child's rate of progress.

At this time, the therapist will also have an idea about how the language impairment affects the child's ability to communicate within the environment, and will know which aspects of the impairment are causing greatest concern to others.

Case example

Dipak, aged 8, has SLI and fits the description of Rapin and Allen's (1983) lexical-syntactic deficit. He attends a language resource integrated into a mainstream school. His speech and language therapist has identified that his word-finding difficulties are partially caused by under-specified phonological and semantic representations, and his class teacher has identified the word-finding difficulty as being a major influence on his ability to express himself in class. His poor phonological representations are also affecting his literacy development. Dipak has made good progress with syntactic development but continues to have difficulty in formulating complex sentences at the level that would be expected for his age. This is holding him back in his ability to express fictional narratives, but he seems to be making some spontaneous progress in this area and it is not a major area of concern at this time. On standardised assessment, Dipak performs at around 1.5 standard deviations below the mean for understanding of vocabulary and grammar, and he is reported to have difficulty in following a fast-moving class discussion.

In planning short-term aims for a given period of intervention, a therapist needs to consider:

- the child's current communication needs, as determined by the home or school environment;
- the language profile – areas of strength and weakness;
- factors underlying the impairment;
- the predicted rate of progress.

In relation to planning short-term aims for Dipak, it seems apparent that work on updating his lexical representations is a priority. This is the underlying cause of an area of particular weakness in his language profile, namely his word-finding difficulty, and it is having a significant effect on his ability to participate fully in the classroom. It is also affecting his literacy development, which will have far-reaching educational implications. It seems sensible to work on the lexical representations for current vocabulary being used in the classroom because this will be most functional for Dipak and it is more likely to lead to a generalisation of skills. It would be necessary to ascertain how many new words he would be likely to use in, say, half a term, in order to set an achievable target.

Work on complex sentence formulation does not seem to be a priority at the moment, and this may be left for the time being. Dipak's understanding of vocabulary and grammar are within 1.5 standard deviations from the mean. His difficulties in this area would, therefore, be described as being in the 'mild' range, and specific intervention for them may not be warranted. Mildly impaired development of receptive vocabulary and grammar is unlikely to be the main reason for Dipak's difficulty in following class discussion; thus, further assessment of his understanding of narrative would be appropriate as this might uncover higher-level receptive language difficulties.

Planning intervention

During the assessment process, the therapist will be deciding which format of intervention, if any, should be offered. This decision will be based on the therapist's evaluation of the effectiveness of different forms of intervention for that child. For example, would it be most effective to provide intervention now or later? Should the therapist work directly with the child, either on a one-to-one basis or in a group? Or should the therapist's involvement be indirect, via a parent or member of the school staff? How often should the child be seen? Which type of therapy approach would be most beneficial?

Law *et al.* (1998) provide a review of the outcomes of intervention for primary language delay, a category that includes language delay and SLI. They conclude that, while intervention is effective, further research is needed relating to the relative effectiveness of different formats. There is, however, some evidence that can be taken into account in selecting a format for intervention, and this is described below.

Timing of intervention

There is general acceptance that early intervention is beneficial for language-impaired children, due to the educational and emotional consequences of persisting difficulties. On the other hand, it is also known that some language-delayed children are just late talkers, who would anyway catch up naturally without intervention (Law *et al.* 1998). The provision of intervention for all late talkers would increase already stretched resources and deny help to those who need it most; it might also cause unnecessary anxiety for parents. On balance, it is preferable to ensure that young children with language delays have a supportive environment for language development and to monitor their progress carefully, looking out for signs of a persisting impairment. The children who are more at risk for persisting difficulties include those with both receptive and expressive difficulties and those with a positive family history (Olswang *et al.* 1998). Early intervention would be appropriate for such children.

Direct versus indirect approaches

Indirect approaches, where the therapist works in helping the parent to facilitate the child's language development in natural situations, are commonly used, especially for pre-school children with language delays (Chapter 5). In school settings, a collaborative approach between the teacher and the speech and language therapist is also common (see Chapter 11). In their review of the literature, Law *et al.* (1998) found that indirect approaches are at least as effective as direct approaches for children with receptive and expressive language impairments, but are less effective for children with phonological delays. For children with more persistent difficulties, however, it seems likely that some direct intervention will be required, especially if a parent–child interaction approach has not resulted in significant improvement.

Individual versus group intervention

Where the therapist is working directly with the child, the decision to work with the child on an individual or group basis will depend largely on the nature of the short-term aims, and the availability of other children to form a cohesive group (see Chapter 4).

Frequency of intervention

In general practice, the most intensive level of intervention that is available is provided for those with the most severe and specific difficulties. For example, a pre-school child with a mild delay in one area of language development may be put 'on review', to be monitored in three months' time. However, a young child with a severe impairment affecting several aspects of language functioning may be placed in a specialist pre-school language nursery, where language development is worked on daily. For school-aged children the patterns are similar, although many speech and language therapy services do not have the resources to provide frequent intervention for them, unless they are placed within a specialist resource such as a language unit (Chapter 6).

Choice of therapy approach

There are many therapy approaches available, such as:

- *focused stimulation*, where target structures are presented frequently in unambiguous contexts (Fey *et al.* 1993);
- *conversational recasting*, where the adult 'recasts' the child's utterance by including a target structure within it (Nelson *et al.* 1996);
- *cognitive therapy*, where the child is asked to reflect on specific linguistic structures and to make judgements about them;
- *active listening*, where the child is taught to request clarification of ambiguous or misunderstood instructions (Dollaghan and Kaston 1986).

Leonard (1998) points out that no one approach is likely to be suitable for all children, and Adams *et al.* (1997) suggest that it is most important not to select the wrong approach. Treatment approaches should be matched to the nature of the language aim and to the learning style of the child.

Summary

It will be clear that a hypothesis-testing approach should guide the therapist at each stage of the management process. Initial assessment will be based on what is already known about the child and will serve both to confirm suspected difficulties and to screen for any others. Decisions about the prioritisation of therapy goals will take into account each child's linguistic strengths and needs, and also the social and educational needs.

CHAPTER 15

Working with deaf children

Sarah Beazley, Ruth Frost and Judy Halden

Learning outcomes

By the end of this chapter, the reader should:

- recognise possible barriers to the development of effective communication for deaf children;
- have considered the therapist's role in decreasing these barriers;
- become aware of how a range of areas may impact on the decision-making process;
- understand the processes involved in deciding whether to see a deaf child for therapy;
- understand the processes involved in planning therapy.

Introduction

In this chapter, the decision-making process that a speech and language therapist employs in working with deaf children is examined. It is based on the social model of disability (Barnes 1990; Oliver 1996), which looks at the barriers that society places round a person with an impairment, which exclude and disable them. This is in contrast to the traditional way of viewing deaf children through the medical model, an approach that has encouraged people to label any difficulties as due to 'deficits' within the child.

The decision-making process will be broken down into two main aspects. First, the focus is on the environmental factors that might create barriers to inclusion for deaf children. These factors influence the speech and language therapist in making decisions about the need for therapy, its timing and location, and the people to involve. Secondly, the focus relates to the communication processes surrounding deaf children and how these influence planning decisions.

Throughout the chapter, the term 'deaf' is used to include all children who have the diversity of experience of not hearing, whether this is from birth or at some later stage; permanently or temporarily; to a lesser or greater degree; or through middle- or inner-ear impairment (Corker 1998; Lane 1995). The term 'impairment' refers to physical difference and 'disablement' to the barriers placed around someone by others in society (Oliver 1996).

The influence of environmental factors on the decision-making process

When a referral to see a deaf child reaches a speech and language therapist, the therapist has firstly to consider whether therapy is appropriate and if so how it is best delivered, by whom, where and when. The influences on the initial decision-making process are outlined in Figure 15.1.

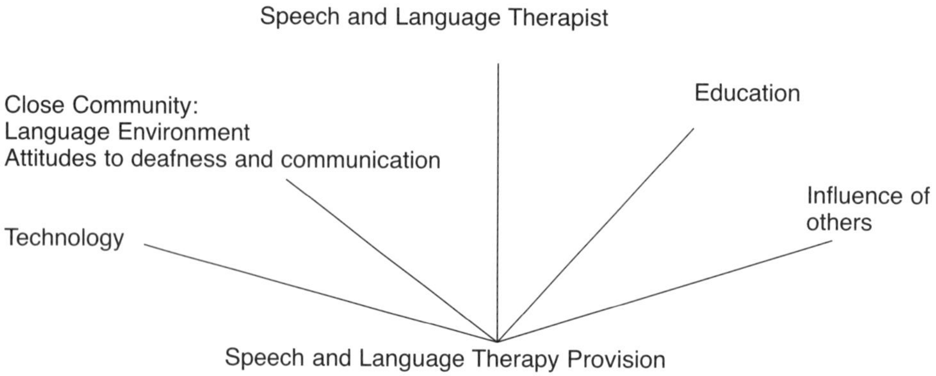

Speech and Language Therapist

Close Community:
Language Environment
Attitudes to deafness and communication

Education

Technology

Influence of
others

Speech and Language Therapy Provision

Figure 15.1 The influences on the initial decision-making process

Influences of a deaf child's close community

Language environment
The home language might be the dominant spoken language of the country, or a minority spoken language. Alternatively, it is possible – particularly if the parents are deaf – that the home language is a sign language (Bergman 1994) such as BSL. There may be a mixture of all or any combination of these in the home, school and other contexts. The

child and family might find it easy to use a language other than the home language, or they might not. Such information will influence how the therapist assesses communication and whether a co-worker who is a skilled user of another language is needed (see Chapter 16).

Children need to discover their own preferred language, spoken or signed, majority or minority (Pickersgill and Gregory 1998); and those involved with the child, such as teachers and therapists, need to consider the language that is going to provide the greatest likelihood of equal access to information.

Questions that need to be asked in the first stages of the decision-making process:

- What spoken and signed languages are used in the child's environment?
- What is the preferred language of significant family members?
- What is the child's preferred language?
- How effectively are the spoken and/or signed languages used by significant family members?
- What spoken and signed languages are used in the child's other surroundings, e.g. school?
- Are parents involved in sign-language classes and/or a deaf club?

Attitudes of family and of others to different languages and communication approaches

The choice of whether to use only spoken language, a signed language or both with a deaf child has been an ongoing and heated debate for over a hundred years (Lane 1995; Lynas 1994). It is important that the therapist is aware of the controversy and considers how it might influence decisions.

For example, others in the child's environment might have negative attitudes towards sign language. Families might be fearful that their child would be excluded by using BSL as a result of attitudes of the wider society. Others – family members or professionals – may feel anxious about the use of speech as the only medium for a deaf child. Local deaf adults may have bad memories of oral approaches and wish to sway families in a particular direction. The communication policies of the LEA will reflect a certain attitude. These mixed influences can be difficult for families to deal with (Beazley and Moore 1995), and the therapist will need to reflect and consider them when making decisions.

Gaining an understanding of the family's goals will be significant. For example, for many parents the burning issue in the early years is 'Will my child talk?' The therapist might spend some time talking with the family and introducing them to other families or to deaf adults, and this might be the priority rather than direct therapy with the child.

Questions that need to be asked at this stage in the decision-making process:

- What are the attitudes of family members towards signed or spoken languages?
- What are the family's goals for their child?
- Are they anxious for the child to talk?
- Have they met other deaf children and their families?
- Have the family met deaf adults?
- What are the attitudes of others in the child's life towards signed or spoken language, including the therapist's own attitude?

The speech and language therapist

As speech and language therapy students graduate and move into the work context, each therapist develops differently in terms of attitude, knowledge, skills and experience. A therapist hoping to work more with deaf children may need to train and read further to meet the specific needs of the child, whereas a therapist who rarely meets a deaf child would perhaps refer to a clinical specialist for support. In either case, the issues raised in this subsection can be applied individually to each therapist in his or her current context.

Attitude toward deafness and deaf people

All those working in the 'caring professions' can benefit from examining their motivations for their chosen career. Disabled people are increasingly querying the role of non-disabled people in their lives (Stone and Priestly 1996), and others have alerted professionals to issues connected with the politics of 'helping' (Davis 1993; Van der Klift and Kunc 1994). This chapter, for example, is written by people who are not deaf, and readers and authors might reflect upon the reasons for the absence of the voice of deaf people in such a text, and the inherent weaknesses this bestows upon it (Barnes 1990; Beazley 2000).

Speech and language therapists need to recognise that there are power imbalances between the professionals and the deaf children and their families for whom the service is provided. These are complex issues for each individual, the profession and society at large to address. Further reading is suggested (Corker and French 1999; Oliver 1990; Vlachou 1997). Clearly, however, each therapist's attitude toward deafness, disablement, the place of spoken language, signed language, and technology will have a strong bearing on decision-making. Homogenous attitudes are neither likely nor necessarily desirable, but it is helpful for therapists to examine their own feelings and, in some contexts, explain their position to others – particularly families with a deaf child.

Therapists need to ask themselves:

* What are my feelings about the place of spoken and sign language in society?
* How might that influence my decision-making about therapy for a deaf child?
* Have I ever met a deaf person?
* Why did I decide to become a therapist?
* Where can I discuss my feelings further?
* How would I talk to families about my attitudes?

Knowledge for working with deaf children

Therapists can draw effectively on existing understanding of language and communication for making decisions, especially if referring to other professionals for specialist support. However, for more informed and independent decision making, therapists need to acquire knowledge about the following areas:

* the historical context for speech and language therapists working with deaf children (Parker and Wirz 1986);
* how the role overlaps with other professionals (Mogford-Bevan and Sadler 1993);
* language development of deaf children (Galloway and Woll 1994; McAnally *et al.* 1987);
* current research in the area of deafness, from journals such as: *British Journal of Audiology*; *Deafness and Education International*; *Journal of Deaf Studies and Deaf Education*; and *SIGNPOST*, the newsletter of the International Sign Linguistics Association;
* the debates relating to communication policies, including bilingualism, total communication and the oral/aural debate (Gregory *et al.* 1998; Lynas 1994; Pickersgill and Gregory 1998);
* the range of amplification devices available, including contemporary hearing aids and cochlear implants (McCormick *et al.* 1994).

Therapists need to consider all their areas of knowledge, how these might help their decision making with a deaf child and how to fill gaps they have identified. If at any stage there is uncertainty concerning a client, a therapist should seek advice from a specialist.

Skills for working with deaf people

The degree to which therapists can become involved directly with a deaf child will depend upon their level of abilities and skills; they will need to question themselves about these, with the aim of:

- adapting the environment to improve communication conditions for a deaf child (Kaplan *et al.* 1987);
- adjusting the language level and mode of communication, whether signed or spoken (Wood *et al.* 1986);
- altering their communication to make it fully accessible to the client; to consider signing, lip readability and lip-reading skills, levels of language and conversational control;
- transcribing a child's speech, including vowels and non-segmental features (Parker 1999);
- applying acoustic phonetics in the development of comprehensive auditory training programmes (Ladefoged 1974);
- using technological aids, including visual displays and text phones;
- checking that hearing aids function and knowing what to do or whom to ask if it is not working.

Educational Influences

As soon as children are diagnosed as having a significant hearing loss, they are usually referred to a teacher of deaf children whose role is to oversee the audiological management. This includes: initial testing if hearing loss is suspected, and onward referral; the establishment and acceptance of personal and educational hearing aids; the efficient use and maintenance of these aids; and overseeing the development of listening skills. All of these aspects of management are carried out with the family and other related professionals. In addition, the teacher will monitor and have an active role in the development of speech and language skills, and advise parents on the methods of communication and hearing devices. The teacher will have an influential role in any Statementing process and the educational provision for the child. For pre-school children, teachers will often make regular home visits, and there is a significant overlap of roles between them and speech and language therapists. Thus, inter-professional negotiations are needed early in a child's management.

It is important that deaf children and their families are not swamped by different professionals giving conflicting advice, but that they can meet all the relevant people and receive the – often controversial – advice in a clear and supportive way (RCSLT 1996). If discrepancies are obvious, then further advice needs to be sought from the health and education line managers, or second opinions gathered from specialist speech and language therapists in the field of deafness.

Once a child reaches school age, the often complex decisions concerning appropriate placement become foremost. The choice of school will depend upon a range of factors, including the LEA's stance on placements, on communication approaches (Gregory *et al.* 1998), on educational options such as inclusion, and on resourcing. These factors will affect the location, frequency and nature of therapy, and careful consideration needs to be given about whether adequate speech and language therapy can be provided.

A child with a less significant and perhaps fluctuating hearing loss (Moorey and Mahon 1996) might not be supported by a teacher of deaf children, and the therapist may decide to involve a specialist teacher and/or work closely with the class and head teacher.

Questions that need to be asked at this stage in the decision-making process:

- Is a specialist teacher involved with the child and the family and what is her/his role?
- What type of provision does the therapist and others (including the family) believe may be needed once the child reaches school age?
- What is the LEA's policy on communication for deaf children?
- Does this policy agree with the communication mode/method that the parents, specialist teacher and therapist believe to be most appropriate for the child?
- Is there a discrepancy between the professionals and/or parents concerning the communication mode/method believed to be suitable for this child?
- If so, whom should the therapist consult so that the child's communication needs in education are met? This may be, for example, a speech and language therapy manager, or a specialist speech and language therapist for a second opinion.

The influence of others

There are often many other professionals involved with deaf children and their families, and so the speech and language therapist needs to work as part of a multidisciplinary team. It is worth noting that there is a general under-representation of deaf people within the support services for deaf children, despite efforts by some authorities and/or individual deaf adults. The team could include:

- A specialist speech and language therapist for deaf people;
- A health visitor;
- audiological services: an ENT/audiological consultant, a paediatrician, an audiological technician or an audiological scientist;
- members of cochlear implant teams;
- social services;
- a deaf support co-worker;
- a communicator;
- a medical officer.

It is worth identifying how the team works, particularly its success at interdisciplinary communication, so that the professionals do not create barriers for the deaf child and family. Equally, the skills, knowledge and attitudes of individual team members will influence the nature of support available. The therapist should establish what the lines of communication are and how effective they are.

The influence of technology

There have been huge technological developments over recent decades, and therapists need to be aware of the range of devices available for deaf children. Many of these aim to improve access to the auditory world. For example: high-powered hearing aids that are getting ever smaller and making deafness less visible; aids that transpose sounds from frequencies that individuals cannot hear to frequencies that they can; cochlear implants that provide electrical stimulation of the auditory nerve from a device within the ear; and assistive listening devices, which give children better access to their teachers in noisy classrooms – and to television.

However, such technology can become oppressive if it is seen as a 'cure' for the individual person. It is interesting to observe that deaf children and adults are themselves choosing to use the increasing number of technological advances designed for contact through the visual, rather than the auditory, medium: fax machines, e-mail, the Internet, videophones and text phones.

Information about the availability of technology will help the therapist to decide whether it is appropriate for use in therapy and the ways in which it may be used with a particular child.

Questions that need to be asked at this stage in the decision-making process:

- What listening devices is the client using?
- Is the client using it well/consistently? If not, why is that?
- Would the client benefit from the use of other assistive listening or visual devices, such as radio aids, telephone amplification, text phone, loop/electromagnetic field systems?
- How confident is the therapist in using technological aids such as visual displays and assistive listening devices? If not, how easy is it to get support with these?
- How accessible are these aids for the therapist and for the child?

The communication process and therapy planning

Once it has been decided that speech and language therapy should be provided, further decisions need to be made about the type of support that will be given. Here, the different areas shown in Figure 15.2 need consideration and are used to influence therapy planning.

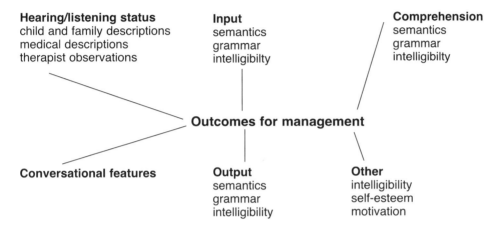

Hearing/listening status
child and family descriptions
medical descriptions
therapist observations

Input
semantics
grammar
intelligibilty

Comprehension
semantics
grammar
intelligibilty

Outcomes for management

Conversational features

Output
semantics
grammar
intelligibility

Other
intelligibility
self-esteem
motivation

Figure 15.2 The areas influencing therapy planning

There are particular issues for consideration when assessing communication with deaf children, and the choice and interpretation of procedures will influence planning. Some of the broad concepts that show the decisions that need to be made are discussed below.

The assessment process needs to examine barriers and enablers to communication, rather than being deficit-based. It is important to remember that most assessments used by therapists are not standardised on deaf children and are generally based on a medical model. Most are English-based and not transferable to another language such as BSL, or to a different modality, such as signing (see Chapter 16). Where a child is using more than one language, such as sign and spoken language, all the languages in a child's repertoire will need to be assessed separately – although overall multilingual communicative competence also needs to be considered (Cummins 1984; Woll 1998). This would mean employing the assistance of native BSL users.

The environment can reduce a deaf child's performance significantly – especially poor acoustic conditions or distracting visual backgrounds – and this needs to be taken into account. Speech assessment needs to cover non-segmental as well as segmental features (Parker 1999), and assessment checklists aimed at working with deaf people can also be helpful in looking at all aspects of language.

An exploration of the strategies that the child and family are already using is also important in decision-making. This is in line with the therapeutic thinking that aims to be solution-focused rather than problem-focused (Burns 1999; de Shazer 1985; George *et al.*

1990). Careful initial and ongoing recordings through video (Tait *et al.* 2001) and/or high-quality audio recording, the setting of clear targets, continuous monitoring, and follow-on assessments should together allow for precise measures of efficacy and effectiveness to be made. These can then be linked to NHS procedures for auditing.

Hearing/listening status

Child and family description

It is helpful for the speech and language therapist to decide about the family's perceptions of the child's hearing status and whether these match the views of the child and/or others. It is important to explore different areas, such as the family's experience of deafness and what the child feels he/she can hear. For example, perhaps the child is able to respond when called loudly or to describe awareness of some environmental sounds that may help to warn of dangers. A child with conductive loss might find it most difficult to hear speech when there is considerable background noise, such as in the classroom or at home when the television is on; and this, together with fluctuations, may have a significant bearing on listening and attention skills.

It is important to establish what the parents believe the child can hear, and the possible implications of this. For example, if it is difficult to attract a child's attention at a distance, this might have implications for the child's safety. The therapist also needs to ask what the child and family understand about the nature of the hearing loss and its consequences. For example, many people believe that, once children are fitted with a hearing device, they will be able to hear again as normal.

The therapist therefore needs to establish:

- Under what circumstances does the child feel it is easy/difficult to hear?
- Is there any family history or experience of deafness?
- Do the family and/or child notice that listening and attention skills fluctuate with hearing levels, or not?
- What do the child and family understand about the nature of the hearing loss and what it means?
- What do the child and family feel the child can hear?

Medical descriptions

Most therapists will be familiar with the types and degrees of recognised hearing loss (see Katz 1994; Northern and Downs 1991; Moorey and Mahon 1996). Nevertheless, it is important to remind readers of the several points:

- Conductive losses affect the middle ear and reduce the overall volume of input with no distortion to the speech signal.
- Sensori-neural losses distort the speech signal, and some speech sounds might be inaccessible.
- The amount of difficulty caused to a child depends on many external and internal factors. Some of these are difficult to define but relate to resources that the child can develop into functional strategies.
- Children with similar audiograms may have different listening and communication skills.
- Additional factors, such as learning disabilities, may have a significant influence on a child's overall functioning.
- The age of onset of hearing loss may have a bearing upon the prognosis for the development of spoken language.
- Audiological records need to be accessed, noted and carefully monitored by the therapist, including audiograms and information about amplification provision.

The therapist needs to establish a child's medical history and decide what bearing this might have on his or her functioning. The degree of hearing loss needs to be described, its history outlined, and how it is currently being dealt with by the audiological services described. Questions must be asked about whether the onset of hearing loss was from birth, pre-lingual or after language had started to become established, and whether any amplification systems are being used.

Therapist's observations

The range of skills observed include listening – in any context where the child is seen. This will help decisions to be made about how to grade the listening environment – for example, progressively adding noise so that the child builds on strategies already used to distinguish speech signal from noise with increasing effectiveness.

Such information will help a therapist decide how communication and hearing are influencing each other, what the acoustic considerations are for any listening work, and the way that current amplification might be working.

The therapist also needs to know how and when a child responds to sounds/speech and whether this varies with social, sound and/or linguistic conditions.

Conversational features

It is useful to consider what happens in one-to-one and group conversations with a child. These will vary considerably, depending upon a range of factors such as the acoustic environment, whether conversational partners are hearing or deaf, and whether or not they are using the same modality (Harris 2000).

Such information allows the therapist to determine whether support is needed in this area and, if so, how to help conversational partners and the child extend approaches to recognising and dealing with breakdown. For example, conversation may be helped by improving environmental aspects such as lighting or reverberation; or the therapist may help the teacher to monitor conversational opportunities in the classroom.

The therapist needs to consider the following questions:

- Do familiar people alter their conversational style with a deaf child? Is this more marked when a fluctuating hearing loss becomes more severe?
- If there are alterations to conversational style, what are they? What effect are they having on conversations?
- Are conversational partners aware of their own modifications?
- What strategies are being used in communication between a deaf child and others? If children are not understood, what can they or their conversational partners do to change this?

Input

In addition to initial information-seeking about the languages used in a child's environment, the therapist needs to consider the nature of the input of language. This will involve observing interactions at home and at school, and noting the type and quality of language being offered to the child. It is not uncommon for people to reduce the overall amount of input to deaf children, to restrict their vocabulary and to limit their use of complex structures; and while these features may be helpful in the short term, they may constrain overall linguistic development (Wood *et al.* 1986; Harris 2000). In addition, people often over-articulate and speak too loudly, or may miscue topics or joint-referencing.

Data gathering at this stage will help decisions concerning how much indirect work to do with people in the child's environment. Such an approach would provide the child with wider linguistic experiences of meaning, structure or speech perception.

Questions that need to be asked at this stage in the process:

- What is the nature of the input in the environment in general, and does this differ from the input given to the child? If so how? Why?
- How much is the child spoken to? How much signed to?
- Is the vocabulary in use limited and/or context-bound to avoid communication breakdown?
- Are sentences kept short and simple to prevent loss of understanding?
- Is volume increased? Are lip patterns overemphasised in an attempt to help speech perception?
- How can the therapist change the nature of input from family, teachers, and peers?

Comprehension and speech perception

Published assessments cannot capture the full range and complexity of processes that a deaf child might have to use to understand an utterance. It is best to acknowledge the difficulty of the task and use the knowledge of people close to the child, and the child's views, in addition to speech and language therapy assessment. A continuous exploratory teaching approach will enable constant additions to be made to the data.

When making decisions when working with deaf children, therapists must be clear whether they are commenting on perception or comprehension difficulties. For example, it might be background noise, dim lighting, a speaker with a high-pitched voice, or a poor hearing-aid battery that prevents a child from understanding an utterance, rather than a lack of comprehension. Or, such difficulties might be due to inexperience with a new listening device such as a cochlear implant.

Questions that need to be asked at this stage in the process:

- Does the child understand more in one language than in others?
- Are there native speakers/signers acting as co-workers to aid assessment in other languages?
- Are there some speakers whom the child finds easier to understand? If so, why?
- What are the child's receptive skills a) in quiet/noisy conditions? b) with/without visual cues?
- What are the child's listening skills like in relation to the perception of speech cues, such as vowel, consonant or intonation contrasts?

Output

A therapist has a number of tools to examine this area, especially in grammar and intelligibility (Parker 1999; Crystal 1992), but needs to decide which are appropriate for a deaf child. Where a child's preferred language is not spoken English, the therapist needs to decide whether tools designed for monocultural speakers are relevant to bilingual users, including those using different modalities such as sign language (Woll and Herman 1999).

Many deaf children develop a variety of strategies to aid their intelligibility, such as pointing, gesturing, writing and drawing. The effectiveness of these techniques also needs to be explored.

With most deaf children, there will be numerous targets identified for therapy. Exploration at this stage should assist in prioritising a few targets that will have the greatest impact on the child's communication.

Questions that need to be asked at this stage in the process are:

- Is the child able to make him/herself understood to familiar listeners? To strangers? To deaf people? To hearing people?
- Does the child use a strategy or a hierarchy of strategies to make him/herself understood?
- How are the child's lexical and structural semantic systems developing? In spoken language? In signed language?
- Is grammatical development immature rather than exhibiting unusual patterns?
- Is phonology immature, with normal non-segmental features developing as for hearing speakers? Or is it showing 'non-English' type patterns?

Other influences

A therapist may wish to explore other areas that are influencing the communication process. For example, social skills (Beazley 1992), self-identity and motivation (Van Gurp 2001) because this might influence decisions about the style and focus of therapy. It needs to be established whether the child knows about the role of the speech and language therapist with deaf people and how the child views him/herself in relation to 'hearing' and 'deaf' worlds. It is important to establish, as in any therapy, what are the child's expectations of speech and language therapy, and what is his/her motivation.

Summary

Decision-making is complex for a speech and language therapist working with deaf children. The models described in this chapter are set in the context of the social model of disability. Readers need to think about the disabling and enabling process surrounding deaf children and their families in their struggle for equal access to information and education through the successful and easy development of communication.

CHAPTER 16

Multicultural issues in assessment and management

Carolyn Letts

Learning outcomes

By the end of this chapter, the reader should be aware of the following:

- Different cultural attitudes towards language development, communication impairment, and accessing healthcare and education.
- The normal and abnormal speech and language acquisition that may take place in the context of more than one language.
- Management procedures need to be adapted to the cultural background of children and their families.
- The limitations of standardised assessments when assessing a child from a multilingual background.
- Issues related to working with interpreters and bilingual co-workers.

Introduction: why are multicultural issues important?

All major cities in the UK have sizeable multi-ethnic populations, many now into third or fourth generations. The extent to which the distinct languages and cultures of these populations has been preserved will vary from group to group and of course from individual to individual. It is also important to be aware that different groups will originally have arrived in the UK at different times and for differing reasons – for example, as refugees or as the result of seeking employment and other opportunities.

Whatever might have motivated migrating populations originally, there now exists a considerable proportion of UK citizens (and others who may remain in the UK for several years, such as Japanese visitors who migrate with their companies) with distinct and unique cultural mixes in their background. All have the same rights of access to services as other UK citizens, but this can be problematic for services such as speech and language therapy where language and culture play an important role.

As an example of linguistic variation, data were collected between 1979 and 1983 (Linguistic Minorities Project 1985) with the aim of profiling the history and background of South Asian, East Asian, Italian, Portuguese, Greek, Turkish and Eastern European linguistic minorities within the UK. Each of these groups is made up of speakers of a number of different languages and dialects. Pattanayak (1991), in the foreword to an edited volume on multilingualism in the UK, states that 'it was found in the Language Census of 1987 that there were 172 different languages spoken by children in Inner London Education Authority Schools' (p. vii). It is also important not to forget the indigenous languages and cultures of the UK, namely the Welsh- and Gaelic-speaking communities, who are trying hard to preserve their unique identities.

Most speech and language therapists will, therefore, encounter clients at some point in their career who speak languages other than English, and whose social, religious and family lives reflect their wider cultural origins. As will become clear, such bilingual/bicultural situations pose unique and highly complex challenges to the therapist. In addition, the privileged position of speech and language therapists in terms of understanding language and language processing leaves them with the responsibility of helping other professionals to work with such clients in an optimal way.

Cultural attitudes

Before thinking about how to assess and manage children from differing cultural backgrounds, it is worth giving some consideration to how a speech and language therapy service might be viewed and interpreted by potential clients and their families. Groups more recently arrived in the UK may be unfamiliar with such a service and somewhat baffled as to its purpose. Linked to this are the attitudes to speech and language development and the importance that is attached to such development in a child – something given high priority by most typically 'Western' communities. Families fleeing war and poverty, moreover, will be primarily concerned with the mental and physical well-being of their children. Educational achievement is also likely to be valued, but this may be viewed in terms of developing good literacy and numeracy skills, without the link being apparent between these skills and adequate language development (see Chapter 18).

Attitudes to disability, child rearing and perceptions of how children learn and develop will also vary. Reporting on an earlier study, which found differences in service delivery of the Portage scheme (Cameron and White 1987) when comparing delivery to Asian and monolingual English families, Roberts and Gibbs state that 'these differences were thought to be due, perhaps, to the effect of differences in child-rearing practices, differing attitudes towards and opportunities for play within the home and differing reactions to handicap among the Asian families' (1989: 158). For example, reactions to handicapping conditions might be ones of shame and unwillingness to involve outsiders, or the feeling that there is no point in trying to improve the child's abilities.

The practicalities of accessing services may also pose differences and possible problems. Obvious factors are the language in which items such as appointment letters and information sheets are written, availability of transport to attend clinics, and the possibility of finding suitable adults within a child's environment with whom to work when planning intervention. It is a common experience with the monolingual English community, that someone who normally devotes a good deal of their time to looking after a child accompanies that child to any clinical session and fulfils this role. Often – but of course not always – this is the child's mother. However, in some Moslem societies (for example), it will be a male member of the family who will accompany the child, and contact with the child's main caregiver might not be possible.

Therapists need to be aware that they might need to make modifications to their usual practice – for example, by ensuring that appointment letters are translated into the appropriate language. It is important also to avoid stereotyping; each group will be different, and may well differ in attitude from that of the original 'home' country, as each generation is influenced by British culture. Also, individuals from within the same cultural group will differ. It will be important to take advice from bilingual co-workers on service-delivery issues and for clinical practice to be adapted accordingly. For example, it will need to be established whether it is best to see a child in the clinic, home or school, and how to ensure home practice is carried out effectively. Chapters by Ara and Thompson, Roberts and Gibbs, and Duncan and Gibbs, in Duncan (1989) illustrate some of these adaptations with different client groups.

Speech and language acquisition in a multilingual context

One of the immediate problems facing professionals wishing to assess a child who comes from a different ethnic background from their own is likely to be that of language. Many such children will have a language (or languages) other than English, and one of those other languages may well be the more dominant: in other words, the children will not respond well to any English-based assessment procedure because English is their weaker language. For the speech and language therapist, a common and basic aim of assessment at this point is to establish whether any speech or language disorder in fact exists, or whether the children's apparent communication difficulties are the direct result of being in an environment where they are unable to make use of the language skills they have. This means that a primary requirement is that some assessment is carried out in all the child's languages. The sections in this chapter about assessment and about the use of bilingual co-workers will suggest how this daunting task might be achieved.

With monolingual children, the established method for ascertaining the presence and severity of a speech and language disorder is to make a comparison between a child's performance and the norm for speech and language development for a child of that age. This is done either by formal tests, or by sampling spontaneous speech and comparing this with what is known to be expected of children of different ages. If a formal test is used that is also standardised, comparison with the norm is explicit and robust, provided that the standardisation sample is large and representative. Conveniently for UK therapists, there is a large pool of literature on English first-language acquisition and many English-based test materials. In contrast, resources available for other languages are often severely limited, and the therapist must rely on general principles of language acquisition to make assessment judgements.

Garman (1999) suggests some broad stages that all pre-school children will go through when acquiring a language and relates these to difficulties that might face children acquiring English as a second language. While such broad stages based on English acquisition research are of use, there are still problems, particularly in dealing with language features that do not occur in English. When, for example, does a child acquire complex case, number and gender inflections such as exist in many European languages? The research so far suggests that such acquisitions occur at an early stage (Meisel 1990). Or when might an unusual feature, such as the mutation system in Welsh, be acquired? Nevertheless, until research on acquisition patterns in a wide range of languages is available, therapists will need to use their awareness of general norms of linguistic development and behavioural cues that may suggest a communication disorder is present.

A further issue is that children encountered by therapists will be likely to be living in dual- or multilingual environments, and thus be acquiring more than one language at the same time. Although the term 'bilingual' (or multilingual) is used to cover all instances of this kind, it obscures the fact that there is enormous variation in the bilingual population regarding the balance of the languages and the time of initial exposure to each. The term 'balanced bilingual' can be used for the individuals who use their languages more or less equally, and are more or less equally competent in both.

However, native-like competence in two or more languages is likely to be rare. More often, the adult who is bilingual uses different languages competently for different purposes, rather like a monolingual speaker uses different socio-linguistic varieties of their one language. For further discussion and a critique of the term 'balanced bilingual', see Romaine (1995).

This means that children cannot be expected to show the same degree of development in all of their languages as native-speaker monolingual children would show at any particular stage; rather, there should be an overall degree of competence that allows children to communicate adequately in all situations.

There is extensive research literature on how bilingual language acquisition takes place. One of the major issues is whether the two languages may have a fused form in the early stages of acquisition, or whether they are strictly separate almost immediately. Volterra and Taeschner (1978), for example, suggested that separate language systems evolve gradually, while more recent work suggests otherwise (de Houwer 1990; Schelletter and Sinka

1998). Much of this work applies only to children exposed to two languages from birth or very early childhood – 'simultaneous bilingualism' – rather than the 'sequential bilingualism' that will be the experience of children who acquire one language in the home in the early years and are then exposed to a second language when they attend playgroup or nursery school.

Thus, professionals must be extremely cautious in applying 'monolingual norms' to bilingual children. In particular, the normative sample for any standardised monolingual test is not valid for a bilingual child, and so age norms and standardised scores must not be used to help with diagnosis. This is not to say that such tests should not be used for somewhat different purposes – for example, identifying areas of weakness in one language, or estimating how a child might be able to cope in certain language contexts.

The author has used tests of language comprehension, standardised on monolingual English-speaking children, as part of an English-language assessment for two Japanese–English bilingual children. In each case, the children were not able to demonstrate understanding of English structures to the same level as monolingual English-speaking children of the same age. This might suggest that they would have some difficulty understanding fully what was said in an English classroom where they were working alongside their English peers.

However, the underlying cause of this difficulty was different in each case. In one instance a five-year-old girl was able to perform much better on a Japanese assessment. It was felt that she did not have a language disorder but needed more exposure and practice with English to enable her to cope better at her English school. The other case, a nine-year-old boy, displayed similar difficulties in Japanese, and in addition displayed pragmatic problems in both languages. It was concluded that he had a general communication disorder, related to learning difficulties. In this instance, a programme aimed at improving his communication skills generally would be required, preferably using both languages for intervention.

Every bilingual child's 'history' of exposure to different languages is different, and careful account needs to be kept of when exposure to each language began, the amount of exposure to each language on an ongoing basis, and the situations in which each language is used. This information should be sought when the case history is taken. It should be possible to build up a picture of expected competence in each language on the basis of this. However, research to date does not provide therapists with adequate information about the course of bilingual acquisition in a variety of situations. As has already been indicated, most research has focused on the simultaneous bilingual child who has been exposed to two languages from birth.

It should also be borne in mind that if exposure to a language ceases during the acquisition period, it will be quickly forgotten by the child, and that this process of language attrition is perfectly normal. The reader is referred to Seliger and Vago (1991) for studies of language attrition.

In summary, every attempt needs to be made to establish a child's pattern of language use and exposure, in order to decide whether there is a general language disorder present. Where children's skills do not match up to what might be expected in any of their languages, then there is good reason to suspect a language disorder. Of course, all the usual factors that are routinely taken into account when assessing children must be considered with the bilingual child. These include medical and educational history, general development and non-linguistic skills, as well as environmental factors.

Bilingual co-workers

The need to assess children in languages other than English poses obvious problems for most therapists, who will rarely feel competent to carry out assessments even if they have some knowledge of the relevant languages. One extreme solution is that assessment and therapy is only offered where the therapist is fluent in the required languages, and there are numbers of specialist therapists who fulfil this role. Resources are such, however, that there will be many situations where bilingual therapists are not available. The use of interpreters is, therefore, largely unavoidable even though it is fraught with potential pitfalls.

Any interpreter needs to have some awareness of what the speech and language therapist is trying to find out and what are the important variables to look for in any assessment situation. If the interpreters are asked to provide translations of test material, they must be aware of how the linguistic demands of the material may be changed by the translation. Different functions may be expressed formally in different ways, so that, for example, something expressed through a prepositional phrase in one language might be expressed through noun inflections in another. When commenting on a child's communication, the interpreters need some knowledge of basic principles regarding such aspects of language as the complexity of grammatical structure, or phonological characteristics – a tall order when such knowledge might not be available for that particular language, even to the therapist.

Even relatively straightforward aspects of the assessment, such as collecting case-history information, are sometimes not easy. It cannot be assumed that, because the interpreters speak the same language as the clients, they will be acceptable and trusted by those clients. Parents might be unwilling to divulge confidential information in these circumstances, or unwilling to accept the interpreter in any capacity.

The author has had the experience of arranging for an interpreter to help with the assessment of an Arabic-speaking child. The interpreter was ideal from the therapist's point of view, being a research student within a university linguistics department and therefore linguistically aware and highly knowledgeable about his own language. However, in this instance he was unacceptable to the child's family, who did not wish details of the child's communication difficulties to go outside the immediate family.

While there is little that can be done in situations like that outlined above, some of the potential pitfalls can be avoided by briefing any interpreter thoroughly and discussing issues likely to arise. Even so, it is better to be able to draw on people from the relevant cultural and linguistic background who have training specific to the speech and language therapy setting. They will then be able to participate in both assessment and treatment. Bilingual co-workers are employed for this purpose in many cities in the UK, usually on the same basis as speech and language therapy assistants. The video entitled *My Language is Yours* (SIG Bilingualism) features examples of the work of bilingual co-workers, presented by the co-workers themselves.

Assessment and management processes

Assessment and management processes with children from multicultural backgrounds are essentially the same as for all children, with two important additions. First, aspects of the child's cultural background must be taken into account, especially when interacting and liaising with members of the child's family. Secondly, the child's individual linguistic background must also be considered when making diagnostic decisions, and when making decisions about management that are based on diagnosis.

Minimally, assessment should include a case history, a picture of the child's exposure to the languages and the use of the languages within his/her environment, measures of the child's ability in all languages and an assessment of how the child's communication problems could be affecting him/her in different environments. Each of these aspects is discussed below.

Case history

A full case history should be taken so that all the usual factors that are important in diagnosis are considered. These include hearing loss, developmental history, and potential genetic and medical factors (see Chapter 1). This ensures that all possible aetiological factors have been taken into consideration. It is important not to miss any factors that may be masked by the child's presentation as a bilingual child or a child for whom English is an additional language. For example, problems should not be attributed entirely to poor English when in fact the child has a hearing loss.

Exposure to language

A picture needs to be built of the child's exposure to languages and the child's use of languages within his/her environment. This needs to include information about who uses which language, for how long, and in what setting. It is also important to consider the child's exposure to English TV and video. This will give an idea of what level of competence might be expected of the child in each language, and what linguistic demands are made on the child.

Measures of the child's ability in all languages

Measures need to be taken of the child's ability in all languages. These measures need to be both informal and formal wherever possible. This will give an indication of how the child compares with norms, as well as enabling a differential diagnosis to be made between an underlying language problem or a lack of exposure and opportunity to learn one of the required languages.

Affects of the communication problem

The affect of the child's communication problems at home, at play and at school needs to be assessed. This will give an indication of the impact of the child's difficulties on his or her ability to function within different settings.

Testing and observation

Some of the problems associated with formal tests have already been discussed. Informal observation is often a good way of commencing the assessment process, and helps the therapist to decide whether a communication problem is present or not. Some of the techniques from conversational analysis are useful here, and it may be possible to apply these with only minimal knowledge of the language being used. Further information on using conversation analysis in assessment can be found in McTear and Conti-Ramsden (1992) and in Leinonen *et al.* (2000).

The following are some of the questions that could be asked while observing a child in a variety of settings:

- Does the child participate in ongoing interaction?
- Is the child able to respond to initiations from others, and are his or her responses listened to and accepted? If responses are ignored or rejected, this may suggest either a less-than-optimal interactive approach from the adults around the child, or that the child's responses pose real difficulties of interpretation for fellow-interlocutors.
- Does the child attempt to gain the attention of other participants?
- Does the child initiate interactions, and how successful is this?

Lack of appropriate interaction skills may give the therapist some idea of whether the child has problems of a pragmatic nature. Such a hypothesis would need to be followed up with more systematic linguistic testing in order to exclude the possibility of a severe but specific speech or language impairment. Observation needs to take place in situations where each of the child's languages is used. More interaction with one language than the other might be an indication of limited second-language ability. Limited verbal interaction in all languages, perhaps replaced by attempts to communicate non-verbally, would indicate a possible language delay or disorder. More information on using a 'communicative competence' approach to observing children in a bilingual context can be found in Rivera (1983).

Formal tests of speech and language can be useful to pinpoint specific areas of difficulty and will also give an indication of severity. For example, a child's response to items on the Reynell Developmental Language Scales III (Edwards *et al.* 1997) might indicate problems understanding prepositions in English, or problems constructing sentences with four clause-level elements. The child's responses to items on the South Tyneside Assessment of Phonology (Armstrong and Ainley 1988) might indicate problems with producing fricative sounds in English. It should be noted, however, that in most instances, because of a paucity of other-language testing materials, such details are unlikely to be available for all the child's languages. Specific probing to investigate for similar problems might be of use here. For example, is a problem with fricatives apparent when appropriate responses are elicited in the other language?

As indicated above, when using standardised tests, standardisation and age-equivalent scores cannot be used unless the test is standardised on the bilingual population of which the child is a part. The Sandwell Bilingual Screening Assessment Scales (Duncan *et al.* 1988) is an example of an assessment that has been standardised on bilingual Punjabi- and English-speaking children in the UK. Such tests are comparatively rare, however. In other instances, formal tests can only be used to identify areas of difficulty.

Management

Essentially, the decision-making process for children from multilingual environments should be no different from that for other children. Decisions regarding whether to intervene and how to deliver intervention should be made according to the same principles. However, one aspect that is different concerns the management of the two, or more, languages that the child is using or to which the child is exposed.

Currently, there is no research evidence to suggest that it is helpful to restrict the child to one language, i.e. the language through which the child will be educated (usually English), although this is a common misapprehension among many professionals. There are, however, indications that such a restriction might work against the child's interests in many instances. Children's home language is their means of accessing the home culture, including, for example, being able to communicate and learn from older members of the family who may not have learned English. It enables them to participate in family celebrations and religious festivals. The psychological damage caused by restricting such access may be great. Wong-Fillmore (1991) describes how the children of Chinese migrants and visitors to the USA are often able to develop English very quickly, and are highly motivated to do so; but at the same time they begin to lose their home language skills, much to the distress of their families.

Of equal concern is whether an artificial restriction to one language is in the child's best interests developmentally and educationally. If parents are encouraged to communicate with their child in a language with which they do not feel wholly comfortable and in which they may have limited proficiency, the natural flow of parent–child interaction is likely to be hampered, thus depriving the child of the social and communication benefits of this interaction (see Chapter 5).

At school level, it has been pointed out that some children may be at risk because they are required to develop academic skills – especially literacy – through a language in which they are not competent. At the same time they cannot rely on the competence they have in their home language, because this is not used in school. This is sometimes called 'subtractive bilingualism' (see Cummins and Swain 1986). This is the rationale behind 'mother-tongue teaching', which is offered in some schools. If a child has the opportunity to learn school skills in a language for which the child has a firm grounding, then these skills will transfer at a later date to the new language.

The conclusion to be drawn here is that not only is it not helpful for a bilingual child to be restricted to input from one language but also, ideally, speech and language therapy intervention should address both languages. Without bilingual co-workers, this may well be difficult. However, the therapist should try, wherever possible, to enlist the support and understanding of appropriate members of the child's family, so that they are able to carry out activities in the home language that mirror those carried out by the therapist or class-room assistant in the clinical or school setting. Ideally, an activity can be modelled in English, followed by discussion as to whether this would be appropriate in the home language. For example, with a specific grammatical structure, or set of vocabulary items, two particular questions need to be asked: 'Is there a relatively straightforward translation between the two?' and 'Are they a problem for the child in both languages?' A family member can then experiment with the activity, with the therapist present, before trying it out at home.

To date, it is unclear whether progress in one language results in carry-over to the other language. However, where a child has, for example, a language delay, and benefits from general stimulation and rewarding communication in one language, it would seem likely that she or he would then feel confident to start experimenting with greater communication in the other language.

In summary, there are several procedures that therapists need to follow when a child from a multicultural background is referred for speech and language therapy:

- Find out whether the child is exposed to languages other than English, and what these are.
- Locate suitable help in the form of bilingual co-workers or interpreters.
- Brief untrained interpreters fully, and discuss any difficulties that are likely to arise.
- Take a full case-history, including aspects of language use and exposure.
- Conduct observations of the child in a variety of linguistic and social environments.

- Carry out more formal assessments in order to pinpoint the nature of the difficulty and formulate targets for intervention.
- Decide the mode of intervention delivery.
- Formulate plans for carrying over intervention into the other language(s).

Further information on the assessment and treatment of bilingual children can be found in the volumes edited by Duncan (1989), Miller (1988) and Abudarham (1987).

Measuring efficacy

Measurement of efficacy of intervention should also follow the same principles as with monolingual children. Questions such as the amount of carry-over into a non-treated language, and the degree to which family members can successfully help with the home language, need to be answered by means of efficacy studies.

Any such measurement of efficacy should be considered against a background where it is accepted that working with bilingual children tends to take at least twice the amount of time when compared to similar work with monolingual children. Nevertheless, if services to such children are going to begin to approach the level of those offered to the monolingual population, appropriate resources, combined with efficient procedures, must be found and implemented.

Summary

Within this chapter different cultural attitudes towards children with communication problems have been considered and difficulties in accessing healthcare and education have been highlighted. The importance of adapting management procedures when working with children from different cultural backgrounds has been stressed, including working with bilingual co-workers and adapting therapy materials.

Acknowledgements

The assessments of Japanese–English students, as described on page 181, were carried out jointly with Dr Asako Yamamoto of the University of Reading. I am grateful to her for agreeing to allow me to quote them here as examples.

I am also grateful to Nick Miller for his comments on an earlier draft of this chapter.

CHAPTER 17

Children with communication problems and additional emotional/behavioural problems

Alison Wintgens

Learning outcomes

By the end of this chapter, the reader should:

- be aware of current trends in defining and classifying emotional/behavioural difficulties and be able to understand their relationship with disorders of communication;
- have knowledge of features of certain relevant emotional/behavioural/psychiatric disorders;
- have knowledge of ways in which a speech and language therapist might manage children with emotional/behavioural difficulties; how they might be assessed, and the decisions affecting styles of therapy.

Introduction

When children have difficulty understanding what others say, or have difficulty in expressing themselves, this often affects their confidence and behaviour. This is more likely to occur if they have a significant impairment of speech and/or language. Anxiety, depression and even excessive anger also affects communication, and disorders of communication and emotional/behavioural problems are closely linked. Consequently, speech and language therapists need to recognise emotional/behavioural problems in their clients. They need skills in managing these behaviours and information about available mental health services.

Definitions of emotional and behavioural difficulties

For descriptive purposes, the majority of children with emotional/behavioural problems who are referred to child psychiatry, or child mental health, departments can be divided into two broad diagnostic groupings: emotional disorders and disruptive behaviour disorders. Each may be further defined by their severity and also by their characteristics. These latter two aspects are discussed next, after which a description of the main diagnostic groupings is given.

Classification by severity

It is important to recognise the point at which mild or ordinary displays of emotions and behaviours – moodiness, shyness, liveliness, or difficulties in relationships – become disorders that need the help of mental-health professionals. When children show emotional reactions or behaviours that are more severe or extensive than might be expected, these are problems that can be referred to as 'clinically significant'. It is appropriate to apply this term when these reactions interfere with the children's development and everyday lives, or cause them or their families considerable suffering.

Classification by characteristic

Classifications of emotional and behavioural problems are complex and constantly changing as child psychiatrists have used various criteria over the years to define and classify such problems in children and adolescents. Some key points regarding classification are discussed below.

Two main classifications are currently in use. They give clinical descriptions and diagnostic guidelines designed to provide a more uniform use of terminology across different centres and different countries. The tenth revision of the International Classification of Diseases (ICD-10) covers adult and child mental and behavioural disorders and is produced by the World Health Organisation (WHO 1993). A different system has been devised by the American Psychiatric Association (1994); this is its *Diagnostic and Statistical Manual*, which is now in its fourth version (DSM-IV).

Historical and geographical factors dictate which classification is used within any one country. DSM-IV is used in the USA, whereas ICD-10 tends to be preferred in the UK and other parts of Europe. Currently, there are slight differences in some of the clinical descriptions in each of these systems, and this can lead to debates between professionals over how conditions may be identified in individual children. However, the two systems are gradually converging as international communication improves and this should make for greater clarity in the diagnosis of child mental health disorders in the future.

Main diagnostic groupings

Emotional disorders are sometimes described as 'internalised', resulting from stresses that are turned inwards. This group of disorders includes anxiety disorders, depression, phobias and obsessive-compulsive disorder.

Disruptive behaviour disorders are said to be 'externalised', with the stresses turned outwards into behaviours that impinge on others. These disorders include conduct disorder, oppositional defiant disorder, and hyperactivity.

Child psychiatrists are also concerned with children with symptoms that fall outside these two main diagnostic groupings: children with developmental disorders such as autistic disorder; eneuresis and encopresis; general learning disabilities; and specific learning difficulties involving speech, language or reading problems. They might also become involved with children or adolescents who have feeding and eating disorders, or disorders more commonly associated with adults, such as schizophrenia.

Child and adolescent mental health service (CAMHS)

In many CAMHSs, patients are registered under one dominant diagnostic category, and this may cause difficulties as discussed below. CAMHS encompasses the old community child guidance clinics and hospitals' child psychiatry departments. Generally, the service is split into multidisciplinary teams based in hospital or community settings. The range of disciplines from which the team members are drawn varies according to the size of the team, its location and the extent to which it provides a general or specialised service (see Chapter 11). Most teams have a psychiatrist, clinical psychologist, social worker, psychotherapist and nurse. Some may have a family therapist, occupational therapist, speech and language therapist, paediatrician, educational psychologist, educational therapist or arts therapist. For more details, see Wintgens (2000).

Multi-axial classification

When children are registered under one dominant diagnostic category, this may be expedient from the point of view of data entry but, for several reasons, this has its limitations.

First, since 'pure' diagnoses are rare, there is debate about whether a single diagnostic label is adequate to describe any child's symptoms. Many children could qualify for two or even three diagnoses, both within and across different groupings. For example, one child may have hyperactivity and speech and language difficulties; another might have autistic disorders, learning disabilities and depression. Choosing just one diagnostic label in these cases does not give the full picture of the child, and such data are insufficient either as a clinical indicator or for research purposes.

Secondly, in some cases a child will not fit into any of these diagnostic categories. For example, some children with emotional, behavioural and family problems do not have a formal psychiatric disorder. Thirdly, it is questionable whether developmental disorders such as reading or speech and/or language difficulties should in themselves ever be labelled as 'psychiatric disorders', especially if only one diagnostic label is to be used. Lastly, it might be important to include other medical, social and psycho-social factors, such as epilepsy or abuse, to complete the diagnostic picture.

To overcome this problem in classification, some CAMHSs may choose to register patients using what is called a multi-axial approach. For example, a special version of ICD-10 offers six axes: psychiatric, developmental, intellectual, medical, social and psycho-social disability (or adaptive functioning). An optional part of DSM-IV, with five axes, is similar.

It is hard to construct an ideal classification system. However, while the practical and conceptual difficulties in the various classification systems are still being debated, it is important for therapists to understand the meaning behind any diagnostic label that is used about a child who is referred for therapy. Therapists need to know the features of the diagnosis and how they might affect or relate to the speech and language function; and they need to understand the implications of these features in relation to speech and language therapy management, assessment and treatment.

Case example

Jane is ten years old. She has mild learning disabilities and severely impaired language, Tourette's syndrome (a tic disorder) and hyperkinetic disorder (hyperactivity). There is a history of emotional abuse within the family, and parental separation, divorce and remarriage. In addition, there are psycho-social factors; for within the family the girl is scapegoated, being blamed for all the family's problems.

Shown below is how significant information would be recorded using the ICD-10 multi-axial classification system.

Axis 1:	Psychiatric:	Tourette's syndrome
		Hyperkinetic disorder
Axis 2:	Developmental:	Language disorder
Axis 3:	Intellectual:	Mild learning disability
Axis 4:	Medical:	None
Axis 5:	Social:	Problems related to upbringing
		Problems related to primary support group
Axis 6:	Psycho-social disability:	(Rated as level 3)

Making a formulation

No matter how information is recorded, the diagnostic process should involve two aspects: the gathering of a wide range of information about the child, and the putting together of a formulation – a hypothesis based on all the data from the assessment. This includes incorporation of all the significant diagnostic features and possible explanations of the relevance of any predisposing, precipitating and perpetuating factors that might be contributing to how the child presents, as well as affecting the choice and effectiveness of interventions (see Wintgens 1996).

The relationship between emotional/behavioural problems and communication problems

There is evidence of a strong link between significant emotional/behavioural problems and communication disorders; most figures indicate co-occurrence rates of 40–67 per cent (Giddan *et al.* 1996). There is some evidence that, in special schools for children with emotional and behavioural disorders (EBD), the figures are higher (Camarata *et al.* 1988; Burgess and Bransby 1990), possibly because these schools have a predominance of children with disruptive behaviour disorders.

The author's experience in a CAMHS in London bears out several of the findings above. An informal study by the author within a local child-psychiatric day unit revealed that 40–60 per cent of under-fives in that unit had speech/language delay, and many were known to the community speech and language therapy service. The author also found that 19 out of 20 children in the local primary-level EBD school had moderate to severe problems with speech, language and social interaction skills, requiring the attention of a speech and language therapist.

The data collected from the caseload of the speech and language therapists in the author's department revealed that, in practice, the children seen by the therapists fall mainly into the diagnostic categories shown in Table 17.1. The communication disorders seen in most of the children involve some form of language impairment. This includes difficulties in receptive and expressive language, affecting syntax, semantics and pragmatics. A few children have problems with speech or fluency, or have dysphonia.

Table 17.1 Diagnostic categories for a sample caseload

Emotional Disorders	Behaviour Disorders	Developmental Disorders
Anxiety – including selective mutism and other social anxiety problems	Conduct disorders – including aggression and defiance	Autistic spectrum disorders
	Attention deficit hyperactivity disorder (ADHD) – which can include additional conduct problems	Learning disabilities

The content of Table 17.1 again highlights the limitations of the classification system. The referred children all have disorders of communication – which would be listed by some as a separate developmental disorder. Some children might have learning disabilities and conduct disorders; others might have anxiety and conduct disorders.

It is known that communication disorders and emotional/behavioural problems co-exist in conditions such as autism and learning disabilities, where impairment of both language and behaviour are always found (see Chapter 13). What is less certain is the nature of this link and how communication disorders and emotional/behavioural problems are interrelated. The same can be said of hyperactivity, where behaviour and pragmatic language impairment are difficult to separate.

In other conditions, the relationship is equally unclear. For example, children with developmental language difficulties can become frustrated, withdrawn and have low self-esteem. Such behaviour may affect the parent–child relationship. Conversely, environmental factors such as when children are abused and neglected can affect their communication. Children might become withdrawn, speaking less, so that they develop fewer conversational skills. They might also be unwilling to volunteer information, and their vocabulary may remain limited.

There is a risk that disorders of communication might remain undiagnosed or untreated in children with emotional/behavioural problems. In addition, there is evidence (Cohen and Lipsett 1991) that children with previously undiagnosed language impairment show more delinquent behaviour when compared with children with known language impairment or normal language development. The implication of these findings is that behavioural problems may become less severe if the children's communication disorders are recognised and handled appropriately. See Donahue *et al.* (1999) for recent studies on interactions between oral language and emotional/behavioural disorders.

Characteristic features of specific disorders

The features that are most commonly encountered by speech and language therapists will be described below. See Goodman and Scott (1997) for an introductory reference and Rogers-Adkinson and Griffith (1999) for the DSM-IV diagnostic criteria for many child psychiatric disorders.

Disruptive behaviour problems: conduct and oppositional-defiant disorders

In its mildest form, this group of problems includes those where children argue, lose their temper, blame and/or annoy others. Often with younger children there is a pattern of negative, hostile and defiant behaviour. The more severe features of disruptive behavioural problems include aggression towards people and animals, such as bullying, threatening and fighting; destruction of property; deceitfulness, and severe violation of social rules.

Hyperactivity

Children with attention deficit disorder (ADD) or with ADHD are inattentive, restless and impulsive. The inattention includes: being easily distracted; finding difficulty in persisting with any one task; having difficulty in organising and sequencing tasks; and in following long instructions. These children have great difficulty controlling their activity when required and may often be seen to be fidgeting in their seats, getting up and shifting position or wandering around and fiddling with objects. They seem to be constantly 'on the go' and this can include talking excessively. These children may be impulsive, interrupting others, blurting out answer (sometimes before the end of the question), failing to take turns and generally acting without sufficient reflection.

Emotional disorders: including anxiety, depression, mutism and reactions to loss and stress

Children with such emotional disorders may have severe tantrums or be extremely tearful if they are anxious that they will be separated from their parent. They may cling excessively to the parent in a particular manner, constantly seeking an extreme amount of physical contact. If their anxiety is more general, they might be extremely tense and self-conscious and appear to be unusually shy. Their excessive anxiety may sometimes affect their sleep, and this can lead to children being very tired. Depressed children and adolescents may be particularly tearful, irritable or withdrawn. Their concentration may be significantly reduced, and they are likely to have extremely low self-esteem. They may demonstrate a lack interest in their surroundings and in activities.

It is important to recognise that many of the symptoms described above may be manifest by children who do not have mental health problems. However, if the symptoms appear to be extreme, they should be investigated as they may be clinically significant.

Autistic disorders

The diagnosis of autistic spectrum disorders is usually made following consideration of the triad of impairments (see Chapter 13). However, it is helpful for therapists to know the criteria used by whichever of their colleagues are normally in a position to diagnose that condition. These children usually have social impairment, as well as a communication impairment, and restricted and repetitive activities and interests. They usually show resistance to change, and lack reciprocity, appearing aloof and disinterested in other people.

Managing the children

It is not uncommon for any of the children on a speech and language therapist's caseload to have emotional and behavioural problems, although not all of these problems will be clinically significant. For example, there may be children who do not comply with assessments or other tasks, and some who are reluctant to sit down. There will be those who have poor concentration and some who do not speak. Although not necessarily clinically significant, any of these behaviours might interfere with the effectiveness of treatment.

These difficulties may range in severity and they may manifest themselves at various stages in the course of therapy. Therapists will need to consider how significant they are and how best to manage them. In particular, they should undertake the following:

- Check that the behaviour has not arisen because the task set is too hard or too long.
- Try to be flexible, so as to alleviate distress and, where possible, to avoid confrontation.
- Use general behavioural-management methods to shape difficult behaviours – for example, give praise, ignore undesirable behaviour and encourage appropriate behaviour.
- Observe and record the behaviour. The ABC approach is a useful framework, noting what happens just before the behaviour (**A**ntecedents), the **B**ehaviour itself, and what happens immediately afterwards (**C**onsequences) See Wintgens (1996) for further details of this approach.
- Share any concerns with others. Discussion with colleagues and parents can increase understanding of a child's emotional/behavioural problems. This may enable suitable strategies for management to be planned.

Children with specific emotional/behavioural/psychiatric disorders

In order to make management decisions, it may be helpful to know in advance whether a child referred for a speech and language assessment has any known specific emotional/behavioural problems. In some cases, it might be more appropriate to pass the referral to a specialist therapist, or wait till the child has been seen by the CAMHS or a psychologist or psychiatrist. However, if there is concern about the child's communication skills, the therapist may wish to see the child more urgently for assessment and to give support and guidance to the parents and teachers.

Therapists need to be aware of the specific characteristics of the individual emotional/behavioural/psychiatric disorders, as described above, in order to make decisions about designing effective management strategies. They need to decide whom to invite to the first appointment and whether to see the child and family separately or together. For example, a 'demanding' child may initially need the therapist's attention and may not be able to play alone while a case history is taken from the parent. If a child is highly disruptive or anxious, or has been referred because of concern about possible selective mutism, time will be required to take a full case history and to discuss the child's problem in depth. In this situation it may be best to see the parents alone.

Children with conduct and oppositional-defiant disorders

Therapists working with children who have disruptive behaviour problems including conduct and oppositional defiant disorders need to be aware of behavioural principles, such as staying calm and not rewarding negative behaviour. Children with such difficulties require consistency in the way in which they are managed. They need clear rules for what is acceptable behaviour and an understanding of the consequences of unacceptable behaviour. They need a high level of reinforcement – for example, stickers, stars or other rewards may be offered for participation, engagement and sometimes even to help coax them into the therapy room.

It is important for therapists to seek support from colleagues and to ensure consistency by working within the policies for managing disruptive or aggressive behaviour that are already in use within the team. Speech and language therapists might need additional training in techniques and strategies for managing extreme situations such as when a child runs out of the therapy room, is destructive to property or physically attacks the therapist.

Children with hyperactivity (ADD, ADHD)

When seeing a child who is said to be 'hyperactive' – another disruptive behaviour problem – it is important to establish whether this is an observation, a suspicion, or whether the condition has been diagnosed and treated. If medication has been prescribed (usually Ritalin), the therapist needs to know the dosage, frequency and timing of the medication. Therapists need to have knowledge of possible side-effects as well as the symptoms of over-medication. It may be best initially to see the child after medication has been taken.

In the preparation of the room to work with a child whose behaviour is hyperactive, it is important that it should be kept as free as possible from distractions. Only one piece of equipment should be visible at a time, and tasks should be of short duration.

Children with emotional disorders

Children with emotional disorders including anxiety, depression, mutism and reactions to loss and stress, need a lot of reassurance, praise and encouragement. It is also important to realise the close link between anxiety and behavioural problems. Anxious or mute children may come across as stubborn or controlling, and their behaviour is often mistakenly judged to be deliberate and provocative.

Children with autistic disorder

Speech and language therapists need skills in managing the stereotyped behaviours, echolalia and resistance to change that are characteristic of children with autistic disorder. Flexibility is an asset when engaging with these children so that the specific needs of the child are met – for example, a supply of unusual objects might help to distract the child while talking to the parents.

Engaging the parents

Therapists need always to be open, non-judgmental and sensitive to parental concerns when working with children and their families. However, when working with the client group of those with emotional and behavioural difficulties, therapists need to be particularly empathic. Parents will have two major concerns: the child's speech and the child's behaviour. It is, of course, important to establish a good rapport with parents – although this can be more difficult with parents who may be feeling more than usually stressed, guilty, vulnerable, anxious or embarrassed.

As with all parents with whom therapists work, some may have had unhelpful experiences themselves with authority figures. They will see the therapist as another authority figure and may transfer their negative feelings to the therapist. They may come across as angry or uncooperative, making it more difficult for the therapist to work in partnership with them. This can be a particular difficulty when working with the parents of children with emotional/behavioural disorders. The therapist needs to have an awareness and understanding of the underlying issues. It is important to be sensitive to the parents' concerns, to be empathic, non-judgmental and not to apportion blame (see Chapter 9).

Assessment

Children with communication problems and emotional/behavioural problems are more likely to be erratic in their performance in an assessment situation, so making results unreliable. They may not cope with formal assessments, especially if their anxiety leads to mutism or non-compliance. The therapist will be required to give a wider diagnostic opinion, commenting on aspects of the child's behaviour. There are several areas that need to be considered in order that assessment may be carried out effectively.

Gathering information

Information needs to be gathered from a range of sources to provide the fullest picture of a child's communication skills across different settings (see Chapter 2). Information should be obtained from school, either through a school visit or through telephone contact with the class teacher or SENCO. A school report may describe not only the child's speech and language in school but also social interaction skills, play and cognitive skills, and any concerns the teachers may have. There may be a need for a more detailed parental interview than a case-history discussion. This may be needed at the initial stage of contact, or later if the child is not making progress. It is also important for the parents' and the child's view of the communication difficulty to be taken into account. This will not only help to provide a more holistic profile of the child but may also suggest approaches for remediation, such as the need to work with the parents or through the school rather than directly with the child.

Questionnaires or checklists may also be used to gather information. With children who are on the autistic spectrum, the Children's Communication Checklist (Bishop 1998) might be helpful in evaluating the quality of the child's interactions.

Formal assessment

Children with emotional/behavioural problems are likely to find standardised assessments particularly difficult, and therapists may be tempted to avoid them. However, since they can give us the most objective measurement of the child's skills, it may be worth persisting. Therapists should focus on counteracting children's suspicions and fears, which may arise from feeling a lack of control and a dread of failure. A reassuring, open and matter-of-fact approach is recommended, helping the child to understand the usefulness of the assessments. It may be helpful to explain that assessments range from easy to hard, encouraging the child at least to try.

Breaks and variety can be built into the assessment process, as appropriate, and rewards for maintaining attention may be offered. If the child is lacking in confidence or is mute, receptive assessments could be used first as these require minimal – and non-verbal – responses. Assessments of expressive abilities could then be used. If children are erratic in their responses, perhaps because they are easily distracted or sense failure and lack persistence, it is permissible to 'test to the limits'. For example, it may be useful to continue testing beyond the ceiling item on a test, or to repeat a stimulus to see whether this evokes the desired response. Any deviation from the instructions given in the manual of a standardised test will invalidate the standardised score, but it is important to obtain as much information about the children and how they behave during the assessment. With such children, information about their approach to the test – what they do, how they do it and what they do not do – are as important in deciding on remediation as the raw or standardised scores.

When assessing children with hyperactivity who are on medication, their language potential should be assessed after they have taken their medication, provided that this is the optimum dosage. If medication has been prescribed but not taken prior to the assessment, this needs to be recorded with the test results because the performance may vary with the medication cycle. More knowledge is needed about this complex area. In the meantime, therapists should record the timing of medication in relation to their assessment, and liaise closely with relevant professionals.

Observation and informal assessment

From the moment that a therapist meets a newly referred child, observations about the child's social interaction skills and behaviour at the various stages of the encounter will all contribute to an assessment and evaluation. With the particular client group being considered in this chapter, such details are especially important.

If formal assessments cannot be completed, the therapist will need to tap the different aspects of the child's language and communication skills, perhaps through a variety of informal tasks and also through conversation and play. With a child who is autistic, mute or non-compliant, for example, observations and informal assessments may solely form the basis of the therapist's report.

Observation of parent–child interaction can give indications both of contributing and remediation factors. Such observation might point to the need, for example, for parent training.

Deciding on service delivery

Usually the results of a full assessment indicate the best way to approach therapy with a child. However, additional decisions need to be made with children with emotional/behavioural problems as well as communication difficulties. Therapists might need to evaluate the effectiveness of the therapy more frequently. They also need to be flexible enough to switch to another style of delivery in order to be more effective, although it may not be helpful for too many changes to be made too quickly. Decisions about service delivery options are discussed below (see also Chapter 4).

Individual therapy

Children who are disruptive, anxious or vulnerable will often do better in individual- rather than group-therapy sessions: in an individual setting with one-to-one attention, they do not have to compete with other children and so they might respond better. The tasks and activities need to be at the right level and broken into small, structured, achievable targets. The children will usually benefit from having a choice of activities as well as from receiving much praise and rewards.

There may be some children who are unable to cope with individual therapy. This may be for several reasons. First, sessions may prove difficult if the tasks are too complex. Secondly, there may be something that has occurred outside the session that is worrying or upsetting the child; it is important to check this with the child and/or family. Finally, it may be that the style of therapy is too direct and therefore threatening. A block of sessions that are more child-centred and based around play may be more suitable. These sessions might still include specific targets for aspects of syntax or phonology, or they may include social communication or more general language-enrichment activities. A speech and language therapy assistant could carry out language enrichment sessions, under supervision. The aim might be to enable the child to have fun while talking and playing. The assistant would follow the child's lead within clearly set boundaries.

Group therapy

Small-group sessions may well be appropriate for some disruptive, anxious or vulnerable children where they need to practise social interaction skills with other children, even if they have mastered these skills with adults. If their attention span is short, they may benefit from turn-taking activities with 'rest' periods while others are having their turns. Some children may be able to learn from others when working in a small group. The rest of the group may provide good role-models, or it may be that it is easier to accept constructive criticism from peers rather than adults.

However, group therapy for children with behavioural problems can be very demanding for the therapist. Many such children are disenchanted with their experience of life; they may be under-achieving and have often been socially excluded. Close attention must be paid to the content, style and relevance of the therapy. Therapy cannot just focus on speech and language targets; attention must be paid to these children's emotional/behavioural needs, and the therapy must incorporate behaviour management as well as including ways to improve self-esteem. In addition, the importance of a high and consistent staff ratio is emphasised by Sivyer (1999), who gives a helpful account of effective group therapy with children excluded from schools.

Evaluating effectiveness

Speech and language therapists working with children with additional emotional and/or behavioural problems can use the same evaluation methods as are used with other children. Aims for this client group more often reflect the importance of functional communication or social-interaction skills, such as attention and listening, turn-taking and topic maintenance. Questionnaires and rating scales such as the Talkabout Self-assessment (Kelly 1996) are frequently used for measuring outcome in CAMHSs, because standardised tests or more direct measures are less useful.

Summary

By now it will be clear that, in their caseload, all therapists will come across children who not only have communication problems but also emotional and/or behavioural problems to varying degrees. Information about mental-health services, details about the diagnosis of specific disorders and the relevance of the presenting features will help therapists to make appropriate decisions for such children.

CHAPTER 18

Working with children with written language difficulties

Sarah Simpson

Learning outcomes

By the end of this chapter, the reader should:

- be aware of the processes involved in the normal development of written language;
- be familiar with current theory regarding the cause and nature of developmental dyslexia;
- have an understanding of the relationship between spoken and written language;
- be able to recognise which children are at risk for written language difficulties;
- have a working knowledge of procedures used in the assessment of children with specific literacy difficulties.

Introduction

In English, written symbols represent spoken sounds. Learning to read and write in an alphabetic script such as English makes heavy demands on a number of cognitive processes. It is now generally recognised, however, that the greatest demands are on language skills (Catts 1996).

When children begin to learn to read and write, their spoken language is usually sufficiently robust to support the acquisition of written language. The speed with which they learn the names and sounds of the letters of the alphabet, and the ease with which they learn to read and spell single words, can be related to the integrity of their speech-processing skills and to their phonological awareness – an awareness that language has a sound structure that is separate from its meaning. Speech processing involves the ability to transform linguistic information, which has been received as an acoustic signal, into abstract lexical representations. It also involves planning and executing the movements required to produce these representations as speech.

The level of children's reading comprehension and their ability to express their ideas in writing will reflect their semantic, syntactic and pragmatic skills (Nation and Snowling 1997). It follows that the child whose spoken language is failing to develop normally will be disadvantaged when learning and using written language.

In this chapter, reference will be made to the assessment and management of children with broad-based spoken and written language difficulties. Attention will be focused on children with more specific literacy difficulties, namely those with specific learning difficulties or dyslexia – two terms that are often used interchangeably. There will be a review of the normal development of written language and the part played by phonological skills in this process. The decision-making process when working with children with written language difficulties will then be discussed.

Overview of the normal development of written language

Learning to read and write is neither a natural nor a simple process. Before a child can be considered literate, a number of skills must be taught, acquired and integrated. In an alphabetic script there is a systematic relationship between letters (graphemes) and sounds (phonemes), as well as between letter strings (orthographic units) and units of meaning (morphemes). It is not enough for children to learn to recognise whole words by sight, or to write them from memory. To access the meaning of written words, children must learn to translate letters into sounds and to synthesise these into words. Similarly, they must learn to represent the spoken word by segmenting the speech stream into sound units and translating these into letters.

Children must also develop the manual dexterity to produce legible handwriting. At sentence and text level, they must be able to read for meaning and be able to express themselves through writing. There is no one theory that can adequately explain the process by which, in a relatively short time, children learn all these skills and become literate. But models that detail the stages to be passed through, and the skills required, help to cast light on the subject.

Frith (1985) describes three strategies – logographic, alphabetic and orthographic – as integral to the process of learning to read and spell single words. She suggests that reading and spelling develop alongside, but out of step with, one another; and her six-step model details the process by which children acquire and integrate these crucial strategies.

According to this model, the first step relates to reading and involves the application of visually based logographic strategies, which allow the child to recognise words by making a connection between their dominant visual features, or context, and their meaning. For example, the word 'yellow' is recognised on the basis of the centrally placed and distinctive feature of the doubled letter, and the word 'stop' on the basis of its location.

At step two, the logographic strategies that have been developed for and through reading are applied to spelling. However, these strategies are less useful for spelling. At this point the child's writing is limited to attempts at reproducing the obvious visual features of a word, or well-practised words such as familiar names. As children recognise a greater number of words, they begin to appreciate patterns in the correspondence between the letters and sounds of words. This awareness, the growing desire to write, and phonics teaching – the explicit teaching of the relationships between sounds and symbols – pave the way for the development and application of sound-based alphabetic strategies.

At steps one and two of Frith's model, reading is the pacemaker for spelling, but at steps three and four the pattern is reversed. At step three, alphabetic strategies are applied in rudimentary spelling attempts – for example, 'elephant' written as <elft>. At step four, as the alphabetic strategies become more secure, they are applied to reading and attempts are made at sounding out words. These alphabetic strategies do not supplant logographic strategies, however; they supplement them. Sight vocabulary will continue to grow, but it is now possible for children to encode (write) and decode (read) unfamiliar words by mapping between sounds and symbols.

As children's reading experiences increase, links are made between familiar strings of letters and 'chunks' of sound. For example, the orthographic unit <-ight> is associated with the common sound pattern in 'light', 'night', 'fight'. In this way, according to Frith's model, a child develops the orthographic strategies that allow sound and meaning to be accessed simultaneously, and moves on, at step five, to a stage where these strategies are applied to reading. Orthographic strategies will gradually become better-specified with reading experience. However, it is through explicit teaching that they become even further refined and so become useful for spelling as the child moves on to the sixth step of Frith's model. At this point, although errors will still be made, children can now be described as having the skills needed for reading and spelling at the level of the single word.

Using stage models, development is viewed as taking place in a series of steps or stages. At each new stage, new skills develop and merge with old skills. Stage models, however, do not explain the skills that children bring to the process of learning to read and spell, nor do they explain how children acquire the strategies they need if they are to move from one stage to the next. Furthermore, these models are not necessarily applicable across languages. They do not always account for the data from children who are failing to develop normally; nor do they take account of the effect of learning experiences.

Goswami and Bryant's (1990) theory of reading and spelling development addresses some of these issues. They draw particular attention to the interaction between children's developing phonological skills and their acquisition of literacy. They point out that pre-literate children who show an appreciation of rhyme (such as 'string', 'ring', 'king') and alliteration (such as 'big', 'bad', 'beast') demonstrate phonological awareness at the level of the linguistic units of 'onset' and 'rime'. The onset is any consonant or consonant cluster that precedes a vowel nucleus (as for the 'str' in string); the rime is a vowel plus any following consonants (as for 'east' in beast).

Goswami and Bryant (1990) suggest that children use this awareness to make associations between onsets and rimes and letter strings. They may also use it to draw analogies between familiar words and unknown words; that is, they will use a known word (for example, 'look') as a basis for reading or spelling an unfamiliar word (such as 'book').

Studies by Muter *et al.* (1998) and Hatcher and Hulme (1999) have questioned the importance of rhyme awareness, and suggested that phoneme segmentation skills may be more crucial to the development of reading and spelling. It has also been suggested that the relationship between phonological skills and literacy may change with teaching and a child's continuing development. Different aspects of phonological awareness may also be important at different points in children's reading and spelling development. Equally, it has been proposed that there may be an important distinction between phonological awareness at an implicit level, such as that involved in the detection of rhyme or alliteration, and awareness at a more explicit level, such as in the generation of rhyme or alliteration (Stackhouse and Wells 1997).

Additionally, it has been suggested (Goswami 1999) that it may be the quality and distinctiveness of children's phonological representations that is instrumental in their development of literacy skills. It may also be that the central role afforded to phonological skills in the process of literacy acquisition has, to some extent, been overstressed, leading to other factors being overlooked. For this reason, there has been a growing interest in connectionist models.

Connectionist models

Connectionist models, otherwise known as parallel distributed processing models, suggest that learning to read should be viewed as a continuous process. In these models, phonological, orthographic and semantic representations are conceptualised as interacting with one another, with the rate of learning dependent on learning experience and opportunities. In short, they suggest that word reading involves mapping between orthography and the most likely pronunciation (Snowling 1998). Connectionist models reflect real-life learning in that they recognise the interaction between the skills that children bring to the task and those acquired through experience. They are also able to accommodate the suggestion that literacy acquisition is not determined by linguistic factors and learning experiences alone, and they allow for the fact that children's individual profiles of cognitive strengths and weaknesses, their personality, emotional well-being and motivation will have an impact on the development of their written language.

Although the relationship between phonological skills and literacy acquisition may change over time, children's phonological skills are crucial to literacy development. It is also known that phonological skills can be trained (Troia 1999) and that this has an effect on literacy acquisition. Furthermore, it has been shown that individual differences in phonological skills correlate with variations in reading skills (Brady and Shankweiler 1991). Indeed, so great is the empirical evidence to suggest that phonological skills are causally related to written language development that dyslexia has been described as 'a phonological-core deficit' (Stanovich 1988). That is, it is hypothesised that at the root of the difficulty some children face in the development of word-level literacy skills lies a problem with phonological processing.

Reviewing the research and defining the terms

In medicine and cognitive psychology, the term 'dyslexia' is generally used for children who have difficulties acquiring literacy skills, despite its lack of a precise scientific definition. In an educational setting, 'specific learning difficulty' is often considered more descriptive and less controversial. One source of confusion between the terms is whether they are to be viewed as equivalent or as hierarchically related. The Code of Practice (DfEE 1994) makes suggestions for identifying children with a specific learning difficulty, based on a range of behavioural signs and symptoms.

Identification on the basis of either the presence of behavioural signs, or a discrepancy between ability and attainment, can lead to inconsistency in diagnosis, identification by exclusion, and, ultimately, inequality in provision. More importantly, however, such approaches to diagnosis fail to reflect current understanding of the cognitive deficit underlying the difficulty experienced by many children in the development of written language. For all of these reasons, the term 'specific learning difficulty' needs to be viewed with caution, and should not necessarily be interpreted as being synonymous with 'dyslexia'. For further discussion, see Frith (1997).

The evidence suggesting that dyslexia is a developmental disorder with a biological basis is mounting (DeFries *et al.* 1997; Beaton 1997; Hogben 1997). Frith (1999) points out that the co-occurrence of biological or cognitive deficits is not uncommon in developmental disorders and that a deficit in one cognitive skill may have implications for the development of others. She observes that 'the consensus is emerging that dyslexia is a neuro-developmental disorder with a biological origin, which impacts on speech processing with a range of clinical manifestations' (1999: 214).

The British Psychological Society has proposed the following definition (BPS 1999: 18):

Dyslexia is evident when accurate and fluent word reading and/or spelling develops very incompletely or with great difficulty. This focuses on literacy learning at the 'word level' and implies that the problem is severe and persistent despite appropriate learning opportunities. It provides the basis for a staged process of assessment through teaching.

This definition describes the behavioural signs of dyslexia rather than offering a causal explanation. However, it provides a starting point for generating and testing hypotheses about the underlying cause of some children's written language difficulties, and it accommodates the contribution made by a range of factors. If it is to be useful to practitioners, it needs to be viewed in the light of the normal acquisition of literacy skills and the reciprocal relationship between spoken and written language.

Learning to be literate makes different demands on children's speech and language over time. Therefore, the relationship between spoken and written language difficulties is complex and needs to be explored from a developmental perspective (Stackhouse and Wells 1997).

The relationship between spoken and written language difficulties

Early literacy development and decoding at the single-word level makes heavy demands on phonological processing and lower-level language skills such as speech perception, speech production, word finding, rapid naming and verbal working memory. Children who experience problems at this level of spoken language must be considered at risk for early reading difficulties, and they may have persisting difficulty in spelling and reading accuracy.

Later-developing literacy skills are dependent on semantic and syntactic knowledge, together with higher-level skills such as the ability to make predictions and deductions. Pragmatic awareness is also important if children are to appreciate stylistic differences, to look beyond literal meaning, drawing inferences and monitoring their own performance. Children who have difficulty with any of these aspects of language may experience associated difficulty in reading comprehension and written expression (see De Montfort Supple 1998).

When higher-level language impairments occur in the presence of well-developed lower-level language skills, children may read fluently but without understanding – hyperlexia.

Well-developed higher-level language skills allow many dyslexic children who have difficulty in decoding to use context for support, and many rely heavily on it. For this reason, the better developed their higher-level language skills, the more these can be used to compensate for lower-level difficulties, so that dyslexic children may eventually become relatively competent, if inaccurate, readers. Higher-level skills, however, are more important for reading than spelling and do not support children in the development of their spelling. Invariably, such children have intractable spelling difficulties.

Nevertheless, not all children who have difficulty in the development of spoken language have associated difficulties in the development of phonological awareness and, as a consequence, with written language. When considering which children are at risk for dyslexia, the most significant factors would seem to be the severity, pervasiveness and persistence of their spoken language difficulties. Children who have difficulties in both speech and language development, and have deficits in both input and output speech processing, have been shown to be the most at risk, especially if these difficulties persist beyond the age of five years (Stackhouse *et al.* 1999).

It is also important to note that not all children with written language difficulties have a history of spoken language difficulties. Many children may show little or no overt signs of a spoken language impairment, and it is only through well-targeted assessment that a subtle, underlying phonological-processing deficit may be uncovered. Such a deficit may have a relatively minor impact on the spoken language; however, it may have a more significant effect on the fluency and accuracy of single-word context-free reading and spelling.

Assessing children with written language difficulties

An important decision to be made by a therapist when assessing a child with literacy difficulties is whether this is related to a spoken language difficulty or is due to some other barrier to learning such as lack of opportunity to learn, dyspraxia, or emotional/behavioural difficulties (see Chapter 17). Each child's written language levels must be viewed in relation to their spoken language levels, and for this reason some broad-based language assessment will be needed (Catts 1996; see also Chapter 14).

Although there may be an overlap between speech difficulties and language difficulties, once a child's overall language level has been determined a more focused assessment of phonological skills will be required. In addition, it will be necessary to consider short-term auditory memory – working memory – and word finding as they place considerable demands on a child's phonological system. Assessment results cannot, however, be interpreted without reference to the wider context. Thus, before a therapist can decide which assessment tasks will be most useful in building a profile of a child's strengths and weaknesses, it will be necessary to consider that child's learning experiences and opportunities in order to identify the factors that may be exacerbating or ameliorating their difficulties.

Careful attention to case history, and school liaison, will provide information about children's learning experiences; but underlying non-verbal ability and literacy skills should be tested by an appropriately trained professional. Results from Key Stage 1 or 2 Statutory Tests (QCA 1998) may be available, or schools can be asked to provide information about progress across the curriculum. In addition, where literacy test results are available, these can be analysed quantitatively and qualitatively (Goulandris 1996). The therapist can assess a child's phonological awareness.

Stackhouse and Wells (1997 and 2001) suggest a psycholinguistic approach. This allows hypotheses to be formulated and systematically tested about the nature of the breakdown within the speech processing system, which in turn will lead to more accurately targeted intervention. For example, it will allow a child whose weakness in auditory discrimination is due to a peripheral hearing loss to be distinguished from a child whose problems are associated with imprecise phonological representations. A child whose faulty speech output is due to a breakdown at the level of motor execution may be differentiated from one in whom the underlying cause is a deficit in motor programming or in motor planning.

The decision-making process for selecting appropriate assessments

Assessing phonological skills

Phonological assessment tasks vary in the load they place on the child's memory, in the cognitive demands of their instructions, and in their use of pictorial support. As a result, a child's age and stage of development will be important considerations when deciding which tests to use, as will the child's ability to cope with the demands of the task.

When interpreting the results, therapists must remember that children will differ in the degree to which they make use of their orthographic or semantic knowledge in their responses, and they may trade accuracy for speed, or speed for accuracy. In deciding how to relate a child's performance on one task to that on another, or to that of a peer, it will be important to consider the particular demands of the tasks and to make cross-task comparisons of a child's performance (Stackhouse and Wells 1997; Vance 1996).

A number of formal and informal assessments of phonological processing are available (see Table 18.1), and these can be used in conjunction with tasks such as those suggested by Stackhouse and Wells (1997). There are some areas of overlap between the phonological processing assessments in Table 18.1, but they cannot be compared directly with one another as each has its own theoretical rationale, makes different demands, and tests different aspects of a child's phonological skills. Choices will need to be made regarding assessment tasks, and the subtests selected from a range of assessment procedures will depend on a therapist's initial hypotheses about the nature of a child's difficulty. The choice will also be influenced by the need to profile input and output processing at different levels of linguistic analysis, such as syllable, onset/rime or phoneme.

The Phonological Abilities Test (PAT; Muter *et al.* 1997) and the Phonological Assessment Battery (PhAB; Frederickson *et al.* 1997) are tests standardised for use with different age groups, and they can each be used to compare children's performances with that of their normally developing peers. In both, however, floor effects, seen when children fall just within the age range for the test, can sometimes mask their emerging difficulties. These tests comprise a number of subtests and make demands on both input and output processing.

When deciding which tests or subtests to select, research findings that highlight predictors or markers for dyslexia need to be borne in mind. In the pre-school child, letter-name knowledge and phoneme deletion skills have been shown to be closely associated with

Assessment	Age Range	Details	Comments
Phonological Abilities Test (PAT) Muter et al. (1997)	4–7 years	Rhyme Detection & Production; Word Completion; Phoneme Deletion; Speech Rate; Letter Knowledge.	Standardised in UK
Phonological Assessment Battery (PhAB) Frederickson et al. (1997)	6–14.11 years	Rhyme & Alliteration Detection; Rhyme, Alliteration & Semantic Fluency; Naming Speed; Spoonerisms; Non-word reading.	Standardised in UK
Graded Nonword Reading Test Snowling et al. (1996)	5–11 years	20 non-words of increasing difficulty; 10 single syllable words with consonant clusters, 10 two syllable words.	Standardised in UK
Clinical Evaluation of Language Fundamentals –3uk (CELF) Rapid Automatic Naming Semel et al. (2000)	5–15.11 years	Three speeded naming trials – colour naming, shape naming, and a combination of colours and shapes to explore the interference effect.	This subtest is criterion referenced (in UK) rather than standardised
The Auditory Discrimination and Attention Test Morgan-Barry (1989)	3.6–12 years	A picture-based test of attention and auditory discrimination.	Raw score converts to an age equivalent
The Dyslexia Early Screening Test (DES) Nicholson and Fawcett (1996); Dyslexia Screening Test (DST) Fawcett and Nicholson (1998)	4.6–6.6; 6.6–16.6 years	Both assess naming speed, phonological skill, memory, motor skill, balance, temporal processing; DES tests letter and digit knowledge and shape copying; DST has attainment tests for reading, writing and spelling fluency; verbal/semantic fluency.	A standardised screening test to identify children at risk
Cognitive Profiling System (CoPS) Singleton et al. (1995)	4–8 years	Visual/Verbal Sequential Memory for Colours and Symbols; Visual Sequential Memory; Visual/Verbal Associative Memory; Auditory/Verbal Associative and Sequential Memory; Phonological Awareness; Auditory Discrimination.	A standardised screening test to identify children at risk
Test of Auditory Organisation Bradley (1984)	No errors by 8 years	Assesses detection of rhyme and alliteration.	Age guidelines only
Sound Linkage Hatcher (1994)	7 years +	An integrated programme for overcoming reading difficulties which includes a screening to gauge where to start the programme.	Not standardised; test highlights areas of difficulty
Phonological Awareness Assessment North et al. (1993)	No age range suggested	Attention Skills; Syllable Clapping; Auditory Discrimination; Identification of Onset & Coda; Sound Blending; Rhyme Matching.	Not standardised, and no developmental norms given
Phonological Awareness Procedure Gorrie et al. (1995)	8 years to adult	19 subtests looking at all levels of phonological awareness and involving appreciation and manipulation of phonological information. Teaching ideas and games included.	Not standardised, and no developmental norms given

Table 18.1 Assessments of phonological skills developed in the UK

later success in literacy acquisition; the PAT offers particularly useful subtests of these skills. Difficulty with rapid naming has also been identified as an early and enduring deficit in children with literacy difficulties. Both the PhAB and CELF – 3[UK] (Semel *et al.* 2000) have tests to measure naming speed, while the PAT contains a measure of speech rate, which is important not only in naming speed but also in phonological recoding and working memory.

As literacy acquisition affects phonological awareness, older or more literate children may rely on what orthographic knowledge they have to support their test performance. It can then be difficult to assess the real level of a child's underlying phonological awareness. For the older age group, the PhAB includes a useful spoonerism subtest. Although orthographic knowledge can be called upon to complete this task, this might slow the process down; time taken to complete such a task is, therefore, an important consideration in the interpretation of test results.

Persisting difficulty in fluent and accurate single word reading is a well-attested marker for dyslexia. In real word reading, children's semantic knowledge can be an important source of support. In non-word reading, however, more demands are made on phonological processing. The PhAB contains a non-word reading test that is suitable once children have acquired some literacy skills, although the Graded Non-word Reading Test (Snowling *et al.* 1996) may be preferred because the non-words are presented separately and acceptable pronunciations for responses are provided. Results from either test can be considered both quantitatively and qualitatively, and can be compared with a child's real word reading level.

Assessments such as the Cognitive Profiling System (Singleton *et al.* 1995) and the Dyslexia Early Screening Test (Nicolson and Fawcett 1996) are more appropriate for use in a statutory baseline assessment, routinely carried out in children's first year in school (QCA 1998). The remaining assessments in Table 18.1 can be used for screening purposes or for testing preliminary hypotheses about the nature of a child's difficulties. However, as developmental norms are not always offered, care needs to be taken when interpreting and comparing performances on these tests.

Children with written language difficulties may or may not have noticeable difficulty with speech output. For some children, a full assessment of this aspect may be considered necessary to complete the phonological processing assessment. For others it will be sufficient to observe their ability to use a full range of speech sounds (especially th, r, w, l, y) and to note any difficulty they may have with complex sound and syllable combinations and less-familiar vocabulary. In particular, attention should be paid to connected speech, where unstressed syllables may be omitted or difficulties at word boundaries may be evident. If speech output difficulties are observed, once again further psycholinguistic assessment will be needed to test hypotheses about the level at which these may have arisen.

Assessing short-term auditory memory

Difficulty with short-term auditory memory is frequently reported in children with dyslexia, and it is an important area to explore at the word or sentence level when reaching decisions about the nature of a child's literacy difficulties (see Table 18.2).

Table 18.2 Assessments for language-related sills

Assessment	Age Range	Details	Comments
The Aston Index – Auditory Sequential Memory	5–10 years	A digit span test (two conditions: forward recall and reverse recall)	Raw score related to age norms
Clinical Evaluation of Language Fundamentals –3^{uk} (CELF –3^{uk}), Recalling Sentences	5–16 years	This subtest involves recalling orally presented sentences of increasing length and grammatical complexity. It makes demands on auditory memory and expressive language.	This version standardised in UK (CELF–R^{uk} standardised in US)
Children's Test of Non-word Repetition (CNRep)	4–8 years	Described as a test of short-term auditory memory, but makes demands on several levels of speech processing, and so provides diagnostic information when results are compared to those on other tasks	Standardised in UK
Renfrew Word Finding Test	3–9 years	Picture Naming Task	Developed in UK Raw score related to an age range
National College of Education Test of Word Finding (TWF)	6–12.11 years	Picture naming: Nouns; Sentence completion naming; Description naming; Picture naming: Verbs; Picture naming: Categories	Standardised in US Separate measures for speed and accuracy

A digit span test, such as that in the Aston Index (Newton and Thompson 1982), taps short-term auditory memory at the word level, and the use of digits rather than semantically richer vocabulary reduces the contribution of long-term memory. It is quick to administer, but the instructions for the rate of delivery need to be followed exactly; otherwise the results will be invalidated. The forward recall condition requires storage and retrieval; the reverse condition requires storage, processing and retrieval; and children with dyslexia may have particular difficulty with this condition.

The Children's Test of Non-word Repetition (Baddeley and Gathercole 1996) requires the child to repeat a series of non-words. Therapists may decide that this offers a suitably sensitive short-term memory test as the use of non-words separates phonological processing from semantic processing. However, inevitably there is a 'word like' effect, and children may be supported in this test by their stored vocabulary knowledge. In addition, such a task makes demands on all levels of speech processing, and cross-task comparisons will be needed to decide whether a child's difficulties are due to a breakdown in input processing, output processing, or short-term memory.

The 'Recalling Sentences' subtest from the CELF – 3^{UK} (Semel *et al.* 2000) provides a sentence level probe for auditory memory but, as it also makes demands on a child's expressive language, interpreting a child's errors can be difficult. Many children with dyslexia will recall the meaning of a sentence without the exact detail, while children with more general language difficulties are likely to focus on some of the details and may fail to grasp the meaning of the sentence as a whole.

Assessing word finding

When concerns are expressed about a child's word finding, one of the decisions to be made is whether the child also has a receptive vocabulary difficulty. It is important that expressive vocabulary is compared with receptive vocabulary, and that results from tests of word finding are analysed qualitatively as well as quantitatively. At word and sentence level, observation of a child's use of strategies such as circumlocution, substitutions, false starts, fillers and non-specific vocabulary will also be relevant. In order to make well-founded hypotheses about the source of a child's word finding difficulties, errors will need to be analysed and comparisons made of performance across a range of speech processing tasks.

Hypotheses could be formulated either about the quality of the information stored in the child's phonological representation and motor programme, or about the links between semantic representations and motor programmes if a high number of a child's responses:

- bear a phonological relationship to the target (e.g. 'ankle' for 'ANCHOR');
- are not real words;
- are produced after some groping.

Alternatively, if many of the errors are semantically related to the target (e.g. 'nail' for 'SCREW', hypotheses about the child's level of vocabulary development might be better founded.

A confrontation naming task such as the Renfrew Word Finding Test (Renfrew 1997) is a useful starting point. It is quick to administer and the number of pictures correctly named can be converted into an age-equivalent score.

The advantage of the Test of Word Finding (German 1989) lies in its scope for comparing a child's performance in tasks making different linguistic demands, for measuring speed of response and for recording self-cueing strategies. However, it is a longer test, is standardised in the USA, and some of the pictures and vocabulary might not be familiar to children in the UK.

The management of children with written language difficulties

The responsibility for meeting the needs of children with written language difficulties does not rest with speech and language therapy services alone but will involve collaboration with a number of statutory and voluntary services.

The role of the therapist will be determined by factors related to the individual, as well as to service-delivery policies. In line with a growing understanding of the links between language and literacy has come an increased expectation of the contribution that a therapist can make towards meeting the needs of children with written language difficulties. However, clear policies about case management are needed. A distinction might need to be made between the management of children whose written language difficulties are associated with marked difficulties with spoken language, and those whose spoken-language skills fall within the average range.

As with all children with communication disorders, important factors to be considered in case management will include the child's age, the nature and severity of the underlying language disorder, and any causal or maintaining factors (Bray *et al.* 1999). With regard to the age of the child and the nature of the deficit, a therapist is in a position to recognise the pre-school at-risk child before the negative consequences of struggling and failing with literacy are experienced. Furthermore, if action can be taken at this early stage to remediate the core phonological deficit, the prognosis for the at-risk child will be improved: research has shown how effective phonological training can be with the younger child (Troia 1999). At this stage, intervention may involve direct therapy, but the balance between this and the indirect approach of working in partnership with parents and pre-school service providers will be dictated by the extent and severity of a child's difficulties, and consideration of factors that may affect the process of change.

Under the terms of the Code of Practice (DfEE 1994), once children are in school then responsibility rests with the LEA for meeting the needs of those who experience difficulty with written language. The therapist could still have an important contribution to make, however; and at this stage a collaborative approach might be more appropriate than direct therapy (see Chapter 11).

Not all children with written language difficulties will require the services of a speech and language therapist, because the needs of many children can be equally well identified and met by an educational psychologist or a teacher with a specialist qualification in this area. However, where children's spoken language skills are also of concern, an in-depth investigation into the nature of their difficulties can usefully complement any school-based assessment. Collaboration of this sort, coupled with consultation with the child and parents concerned, will result in well-founded targets for an IEP and more appropriate suggestions for differentiation of the National Curriculum.

For a child whose written language difficulties are associated with higher-level language problems, the advice that a therapist offers may relate to subjects across the curriculum; for the child with a breakdown in the speech-processing system and dyslexia, any advice given may be more closely linked to meeting the objectives in the National Literacy Strategy (DfEE 1998b). Research has shown the mutual benefits of integrating phonological awareness training with work on literacy and, therefore, the advice the therapist can offer, and the techniques that can be demonstrated, have a proven efficacy.

For the younger child, advice may focus on teaching techniques aimed at remediating the underlying speech-processing deficit; whereas for the older child – where research is more equivocal about the efficacy of phonological training – the advice may be more concerned with facilitating the development of compensatory strategies and teaching metacognitive skills (Broomfield and Combley 1997; Snowling and Stackhouse 1996). At all ages, however, it will be important that lower-level skills are not emphasised at the expense of higher-level skills, and that children are encouraged to appreciate the communicative value of written language.

Summary

In this chapter the complexity of the relationship between spoken and written language has been discussed, as well as the relationship between dyslexia and a number of language-related skills. The role and responsibilities of a speech and language therapist in the management of children with written language difficulties has been considered, and the need for a collaborative approach emphasised.

CHAPTER 19

Cleft palate and velopharyngeal anomalies

Anne Harding and Debbie Sell

Learning outcomes

By the end of this chapter, the reader should understand about:

- different types of cleft palate, their aetiology and prevalence;
- roles and responsibilities of the members of the cleft team at different stages in the care pathway;
- the management of cleft palate and velopharyngeal anomalies;
- the effect of a cleft palate on pre-speech and speech development;
- aetiological, diagnostic and treatment considerations in managing 'nasal' speech in relation to velopharyngeal function.

Introduction

Cleft lip and palate is the most common congenital craniofacial abnormality, occurring in approximately 1 in 700 live births in the UK. Its management is not a simple, cosmetic problem solved by surgery in early infancy; it is a complex process that continues until facial growth is complete around 18 years of age, often requiring multiple surgical procedures. Treatment needs to be led and coordinated by specialist interdisciplinary teams in order to address feeding, facial growth, dental aspects, cosmetic aspects, speech, hearing and the emotional consequences.

Different types of cleft palate: prevalence and aetiology

There is considerable variation in the presentation of clefts of the lip and palate. Cleft lip alone, occurring in 25 per cent of cases, may be complete or incomplete, resulting in a notched lip only, and may be unilateral or bilateral. When cleft lip occurs in association with cleft palate, a unilateral cleft lip and palate (UCLP; see Figure 19.1a) or a bilateral cleft lip and palate (BCLP; see Figure 19.1b) may result. The incidence of UCLP is 40 per cent and that of BCLP is 10 per cent. Clefts, too, may be complete or incomplete. The incidence of cleft palate without a cleft lip is 25 per cent. The extent of the cleft is variable as shown in Figure 19.1c, and Figure 19.1d where the oral mucosa is intact as the cleft only affects the muscle layer.

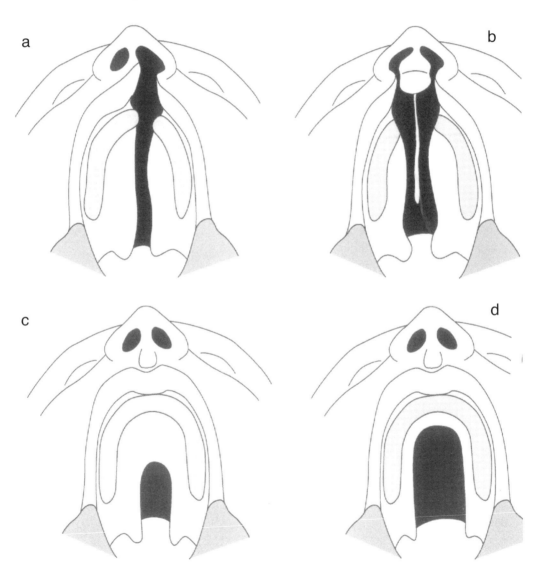

Figure 19.1 Examples of cleft lip/palate

Cleft lip and palate with no other anomalies or associated syndrome has a multifactorial aetiology involving environmental and genetic factors. Current thinking is that there are multiple genes involved, which may interact not only with each other but also with environmental factors such as certain drugs, alcohol, pesticides, and maternal smoking. A family history is present in about a quarter of cases. The chances of a sibling also being affected is around 30 to 40 times greater than of children who do not have a cleft lip/palate (Lees 2001). In the majority of cases the cleft will be the only defect, but clefts may also be found in association with other congenital anomalies, or they may occur as part of a syndrome. More than 400 syndromes include cleft lip and/or palate (Winter and Baraitser 1998) – most commonly Stickler and Velocardiofacial syndrome, which can be associated with the Pierre Robin Complex.

Roles and responsibilities of a cleft lip and palate team

Team members

Team members include the cleft surgeon; orthodontist; specialist speech and language therapist; specialist nurse; cleft team coordinator; paediatrician; ENT surgeon; audiologist; psychologist; social worker; geneticist; paediatric dentist; and restorative dentist. Wherever possible, the surgeon visits on the maternity unit a new-born infant with a cleft. Centralisation of services may mean that a local team-member such as the specialist nurse or the specialist speech and language therapist will make initial contact.

Initial contact with the team is made prior to primary surgery, when parents bring their children to an interdisciplinary clinic. The team's protocol for surgical management is explained and parents' questions are addressed. Subsequent attendances are offered at specific intervals – usually until the child reaches his or her late teens. In Table 19.1 is an example of such a 'care pathway'.

For the antenatal period and then for each of the stages shown in Table 19.1, the timings of surgical treatment, specific difficulties that may be encountered, and the team members involved in the nature of the rehabilitation are each described below.

Antenatal diagnosis

When a cleft lip is diagnosed antenatally, the parents are referred to the cleft team for further counselling (Bradbury and Bannister 2001). Antenatal diagnosis of cleft lip *in utero* is now possible by ultrascan, from about 17 weeks. Such diagnosis, however, is not simple. Only around 40 per cent of clefts of the lip and palate are detected in the absence of other gross foetal abnormalities (Chitty and Griffin 2001). Cleft palate only is rarely detected through an antenatal scan.

Many parents benefit from an antenatal diagnosis because they can prepare themselves, their relatives and friends. They can meet the cleft team and gather information about

Table 19.1 Example of a cleft lip and palate 'care pathway'

Age	Timings of Surgical Treatment	Nature of Rehabilitation
0		+/- Orthodontic appliances; feeding support from specialist nurse.
0 or 3 months	Cleft lip repair	
6 months	Cleft palate repair +/- Insertion of grommets	Speech and language therapy monitoring and advice; ENT monitoring; genetic counselling
18 months		ENT/Audiology; speech and language therapy assessment/early intervention
3.6 to 5–6 years	Management of velopharyngeal dysfunction (VPD)	Speech and language therapy review/treatment
4 to 6 years	Lip and/or nose revision	
9 to 12 years	Repair to alveolar fistula Alveolar bone grafting	Pre- and post-operative orthodontic treatment
16 to 20 years	Maxillary osteotomy; rhinoplasty; final lip revision	

approaches to feeding and about surgery. Many parents are put in contact with their local Cleft Lip and Palate Association (CLAPA) groups (Davies 2001).

Birth

Many clefts are diagnosed at birth and an immediate referral is made to a cleft surgeon, although an isolated cleft palate is not always diagnosed before discharge from the maternity unit. Problems with nasal regurgitation of milk and/or failure to gain weight may lead a midwife or health visitor to consider the possibility of a structural defect.

0–18 months

Feeding: the specialist nurse

Since all babies with a cleft palate establish their feeding pattern with an unrepaired palate, feeding difficulties are not uncommon and decisions need to be made about the advice to be given to parents. Although feeding advice has been provided by speech and language therapists, specialist nurses are increasingly responsible for this. Advice focuses on exploration of breast feeding versus bottle feeding, appropriate bottles and teats, feeding positions, and managing problems such as wind. Particular care is taken in monitoring nutrition and weight gain and in offering both practical assistance and emotional support to the parents (Bannister 2001). In some centres, feeding plates are fitted until the time of palate repair.

To ensure appropriate management of feeding problems, parents need direct access to their cleft team's feeding advisor. Where oral feeding cannot be achieved, consultation with a specialist dysphagia speech and language therapist is advisable.

Primary lip and/or palate surgery: the cleft surgeon

The cleft surgeon is usually a plastic surgeon or oral-maxillofacial surgeon. The optimum timing and technique of primary lip and palate surgery remains controversial. In most centres in the UK, lip repair is undertaken at 3 months and palate repair between 6 and 12 months. The relative success of primary surgery largely determines the extent to which further surgery, remedial orthodontic treatment, and speech and language therapy become necessary. However, the final outcome also depends on the severity of the cleft, on the availability of specialist treatments, and on each family's motivation and resources.

Hearing: the ENT consultant/consultant audiologist

Hearing is monitored closely from birth because children with a cleft palate are at increased risk of middle-ear effusions. The attachments of the levator palati muscle around the entrance to the eustachian tube are abnormal, which affects aeration of the eustachian tube and drainage of the middle ear. Grommet insertion is frequently recommended. Regular review by the ENT surgeon and audiologist aims to prevent the adverse consequences of otitis media, particularly intermittent conductive hearing loss and chronic ear disease.

3–6 years

Surgical revision of lip and nose

Results of primary surgery may look excellent at the time of repair, but subsequent growth of the face can result in adverse changes in appearance. Soft-tissue modifications to the shape of the nostrils or the lip can be carried out at this stage, but bony changes are delayed until more growth has occurred (9–12 years).

Fistula repair

Sometimes following surgery, a hole (or fistula) might remain in the palate. It is likely to diminish gradually with time, but further surgery may be considered if there are persistent feeding difficulties and/or specific speech problems that are directly attributable to the fistula.

Velopharyngeal investigations/surgery

If excessive hypernasality and nasal emission are identified, velopharyngeal investigations, and even surgery, are often undertaken. See the section below on velopharyngeal dysfunction (VPD) for further information.

9–12 years

Orthodontic treatment

Facial growth and dentition alignment are monitored by the orthodontist and, where necessary, modified in order to achieve a pleasing appearance by maturity. Young people with UCLP or BCLP are treated with an appliance to expand the maxillary arch after the eruption of the second dentition. This creates space for insertion of a bone graft. Following this, final alignment of the teeth often involves fixed appliance therapy in much the same way as in children who do not have a cleft.

Alveolar bone grafting (ABG) and fistula repair are performed by an oral-maxillofacial surgeon, optimally at the same time. This involves grafting bone from the hip into the alveolar cleft defect, providing a structure for subsequent orthodontic treatment. Introduction of this procedure has minimised the need for prosthetic replacement of teeth, permanent bridges and dentures in later life. Where necessary, these would be fitted by a restorative dentist. In addition to the orthodontic benefits, the facial symmetry achieved by an ABG markedly improves appearance.

16–20 years

Maxillary osteotomy

Distorted mid-face growth is commonly found in teenage patients. Surgical advancement of the maxilla is the well-established treatment for mid-face retrusion. This is usually delayed until facial growth is complete. Unfortunately, this timing means that young people have to go through their vulnerable adolescent years with a deteriorating facial appearance. Gradually, each individual takes more responsibility for decision-making about his or her management. Furthermore, since maxillary osteotomy can result in increased nasal resonance, pre- and post-operative assessments of speech and velopharyngeal function are also essential.

Rhinoplasty, an exclusively cosmetic procedure, is the final surgical procedure in the care pathway and is aimed at improving the appearance of the nose.

Other team members

Psychologist

In recent years, psychologists have revealed the complexity of psychological effects of cleft lip and/or palate on family dynamics. Parents frequently suffer guilt and grief, which can lead to depression, mental illness and marital breakdown. The affected child may suffer emotional difficulties, which commonly become evident in middle childhood. Poor self-esteem and impaired social relationships can lead to depression in adolescence. While peer acceptance and positive parent–child relationships are the best protection for these children, professional help may be necessary. Workshops for facially disfigured teenagers are available at Changing Faces, based in London.

It is essential that all families have access to a specialist clinical psychologist for support, counselling and treatment.

Clinical geneticist

Parents usually want to know the genetic risks of having further affected children. The clinical geneticist has a role in the diagnosis, management and counselling of children with clefts, and their families. In addition the geneticist would be involved in investigating any suspected associated syndromes. A referral is made when there are dysmorphic features, additional anomalies, or concerns regarding development.

Paediatrician

The paediatrician is the team member who takes a holistic view of the child (Habel 2001). The paediatrician may act as advisor to the team on the timing of surgery, particularly in the case of a failure to thrive; may identify a need to screen for underlying defects such as congenital heart disease; usually monitors growth and development; and oversees appropriate referral to the clinical geneticist. The paediatrician liaises with local paediatricians and the social, educational and community health services to ensure there is appropriate provision for the child and family. The paediatrician has a pivotal role in investigating concerns raised by abnormal behaviour, bullying, impaired concentration and suspected seizures. She or he should have an understanding of how personal and family functioning is affected by the occurrence of the cleft.

Social worker

A social worker may be involved in the team to support families with practical and financial difficulties related to hospital attendances, disability allowance and housing issues.

Developments in management

In the late 1990s, there was a national investigation by the Clinical Standards Advisory Group that showed services for cleft lip and/or palate patients had developed in an ad-hoc manner across the UK (CSAG 1998). Many of the smaller units with small numbers of cases were found to produce less than satisfactory results and, hence, the key recommendation was to centralise services into major centres. Institution of rigorous audit protocols would ensure that results could be closely monitored.

The role of speech and language therapists

As new centres of excellence are established, teams of 'hub and spoke' speech and language therapists are developing. Although each centre will vary in its methods of service delivery, the following description of speech and language therapy care reflects the recommendations made by RCSLT to the Clinical Standards Advisory Group.

Ideally, a child's pre-speech and speech and language development is monitored by a member of the cleft lip and palate speech and language therapy team from birth to maturity. The centre is the base for interdisciplinary team management; specialist speech assessments; differential diagnoses; therapy provision for some complex cases; clinical advice; investigations of velopharyngeal function; audit; research, teaching, and networking with the relevant speech and language therapy departments. Much of the advisory therapy is necessarily provided more locally by a trained cleft specialist. Where regular therapy is required, a speech and language therapist from the cleft team should be available to liaise with the community therapist.

0–9 months prior to palate closure

At the first meeting with the family, key objectives are to admire the baby, and to counsel, inform and advise the parents. Explanations about the function of the palate for babble and speech can be supported with leaflets and CLAPA literature.

9–18 months after palate closure: monitoring babble and early speech

Evidence of any oral-pressure consonants [p, b, t, d, k, g] followed by a vowel usually suggests that there is potential for velopharyngeal closure. Following palate repair, each child varies in the speed at which babble changes. Some centres offer a specialist service to monitor and influence babble development in order to minimise the effect of the cleft on speech development. Participative babble techniques (Albery and Russell 1984) encourage discovery of new consonants and maximise articulatory potential. Increased parent interaction in babble-play also aims to prevent subsequent language delay, which is a risk in children who have a cleft palate.

Frequent use of any two plosive consonants by 18 months of age gives an indication that velopharyngeal closure can be achieved for at least some speech sounds. Velopharyngeal closure is essential for the successful production of [b] (Grunwell and Sell 2001). Continued monitoring throughout speech development is recommended because the cleft may affect later-developing fricative and affricate consonants and/or consonant clusters. The most difficult consonants to produce with a cleft palate are /b d s/, and so their presence in babble and early speech is a strong indicator for normal speech development (Harding and Grunwell 1996).

18–30 months

Speech acquisition needs to be closely monitored in relation to oral/nasal structures and nasal airway. Since there is an increased incidence of middle-ear infections and associated fluctuating hearing loss in the cleft palate population, close monitoring of hearing status is important. The combination of poor hearing and a history of a cleft palate puts speech and language development very much at risk. Advice can be given to minimise the effect of possible hearing loss on speech and language development.

Early intervention aims to modify emerging, atypical phonological processes before they become fully stabilised. An indirect therapy programme can be formulated whenever any cleft-related influences are identified. Therapy that is non-directive and non-corrective and that focuses attention on listening to, watching and feeling sounds can often engage very young children for extended periods (Harding and Grunwell 1998).

Decisions about the selection of therapy targets need to be based on phonological analysis and understanding of the normal versus 'cleft-type' developmental processes. Harding and Grunwell (1998) state that 'cleft-type' phonological development is characterised as follows:

- voiceless plosives and fricatives /p t k f s ʃ/ emerge before voiced counterparts /b d g v z/;
- fricatives may emerge before plosives;
- /ʃ/ may emerge before /s/ because /ʃ/ requires slightly less articulatory precision than /s/;
- word final consonants appearing before word initial because less intra-oral pressure is required for word final consonants;
- back consonants emerge before front consonants.

Early speech that is hypernasal (i.e. has excessive nasal resonance) needs careful monitoring. Specialist assessment and management advice is particularly important if hypernasality coexists with a restricted consonant range [m n ŋ w l j h], or prevalent glottal, pharyngeal [ħ ʔ] and/or nasal fricative [ñ̥] consonant realisations.

30 months onward

Approximately 80 per cent of children with a cleft palate will have received at least some input from speech and language therapists prior to age five. Therapy in the UK aims for maximum speech progress by school entry (CSAG 1998). However, approximately 20 per cent of children with a cleft palate still have speech difficulties when five years and over.

The GOS.SP.ASS (Sell *et al.* 1999), a recommended screening assessment, provides a systematic framework in which to assess and record the speech parameters most affected by a cleft lip and/or palate or velopharyngeal dysfunction.

Characteristics of 'cleft palate speech'

The term 'cleft palate speech' encompasses possible disturbances of resonance, airflow, consonant production and voice. Such disturbances can be categorised as follows:

- *Nasality and nasal airflow.* Abnormal nasal resonance includes hypernasality – particularly noticeable on vowels and glides/approximant [ã ũ w̃ j̃] Sell *et al.* 1999) – and hyponasality (inadequate nasal resonance) – observable on target nasal consonants [m n ŋ]. It also includes mixed nasality when nasality and hyponasality co-occur.
- *Nasal emission* involves excessive airflow through the nose during the production of pressure consonants [p t k f s ʃ tʃ].
- *Nasal turbulence* is a distracting nasal 'noise' which accompanies consonant production. It occurs when air is pushed through a constricted gap in the nasopharynx.
- *Nasal or facial grimace* occurs when a speaker with a cleft palate attempts to inhibit excessive nasal airflow by constricting the nares and sometimes other facial muscles.
- *Hoarseness and reduced volume of the voice* can co-occur with cleft palate and can confound resonance judgements.
- *Consonant production.* Incorrect consonant realisations are transcribed as precisely as possible; if the transcription is not known, then descriptions are required. For describing speech patterns and for inter-centre comparison of results, the following broad categories can now be used:

  – anterior-oral cleft-type characteristics;
  – posterior-oral cleft-type characteristics;
  – non-oral cleft-type characteristics;
  – passive cleft-type characteristics

(Harding *et al.* 1997).

Anterior-oral cleft-type characteristics

Dentalisation and interdentalisation frequently occur with a dental malocclusion. Lateralisation and palatalisation [l̪s l̪z t̪ʲ t̪ʲ d̪ʲ] and lateral/palatal realisations /s z / => [ɫ ʒ ʝ] are commonly found in association with abnormal dentition, malocclusion and collapsed arches. Double articulation may be a therapy effect or may be an articulatory adaptation to a fistula.

Posterior-oral cleft-type characteristics

Backed articulation /n t d s l/ =>[ŋ k ɡ x j] can occur.

Non-oral cleft-type characteristics

Glottal and pharyngeal articulation, and active nasal fricatives – often called a 'nasal snort' – are all non-oral consonant realisations. An active nasal fricative requires therapy to modify the nasally directed airstream. Since active nasal fricatives are often specific to one or two phonemes, this error is frequently called Phoneme-Specific VPD. Holding the nose during attempted [s] reveals whether the nasal fricative is active or passive as defined by Harding and Grunwell (1998).

Passive cleft-type characteristics

Passive errors occur when the production of sounds are planned correctly but a structural abnormality precipitates errors. This produces weak, or nasal, realisation of pressure consonants, for instance / b / => [m], /s / => [n̥]. It is usual for hypernasal resonance to coexist with passive errors. Passive errors can be changed by modification of the structure, i.e. surgery; but active errors require therapy to modify the existing motor programme.

With *absent pressure consonants*, the consonant range is restricted to nasals and approximants. If hypernasal resonance is also present, velopharyngeal investigations are usually required (Sell and Ma 1996).

The gliding of fricatives/affricates, which can be /ʃ/ or / tʃ/ => [j], in the context of a cleft palate/velopharyngeal anomaly is considered to be a consequence of the structural defect.

Aetiological factors

Influences on speech production are frequently multifactorial and may be difficult to determine. Possible factors are listed in GOS.SP.ASS. (Sell *et al.* 1999). In order to make decisions that will maximise speech potential, it is important to identify those factors that can be modified and the order in which this may be done (LeBlanc 1996).

Structural anomalies, such as dental problems and difficulties with occlusion, oronasal fistulae, velopharyngeal insufficiency and impaired hearing, are likely to constrain the phonetic repertoire. Advice might be needed on the management of nasal airway obstruction with its associated open-mouth posture, on hyponasal resonance, and on any possible impact on appetite and sleep patterns. In addition, social and psychological factors, the nature and timing of primary palate surgery, and speech and language therapy support may be contributing factors that need to be taken into account.

When palatal problems co-occur with a distinctive appearance or a complex medical history, a syndrome may be present. Consultation with the cleft team may lead to referral to a geneticist. Children born with a cleft palate are also subject to the same influences on speech and language development as the non-cleft population. Assessment of 'cleft speech' should not ignore neurological, cognitive, developmental, environmental and emotional factors, which might require further assessment from speech and language therapists.

Differential diagnosis

Irrespective of a medical diagnosis, a specific speech diagnosis is necessary. When making decisions about differential diagnosis, speech findings are analysed and the evidence is considered in the context of aetiological factors. The most likely speech diagnostic categories are listed here (see also Chapter 12) as follows:

- *resonance disorder* associated with diagnosed/suspected VPD or fistula, or nasal obstruction;
- *articulation disorder related to structural constraints*, such as a fistula, or possible VPD, does not affect phonological contrasts and the target sound cannot be produced in either speech or non-speech activity;
- *articulation disorder with phonological consequences*, an articulation disorder related to structural constraints, which affects a group or class of consonants with a loss of meaningful contrast, for example /b d g/ => [g];
- *phonological disorder*, where it is possible to stimulate consonant targets in isolation, often as non-speech sounds, e.g. a leaky balloon noise [ffff], but where these cannot be produced in a linguistic context (e.g. 'f' in 'four' is [m̥̃]);
- *developmental speech delay or disorder*, occurring with or without a cleft-related speech disorder;
- *developmental verbal dyspraxia*, which is common in children with Velocardiofacial syndrome;
- *dysarthria*, which is a likely diagnostic category in hypernasality associated with myotonia dystrophia or hypotonia;
- *dysphonia*;

- *speech disorder related to hearing impairment;*
- *developmental language delay/disorder* (Scherer and D'Antonio 1995).

Two or more diagnostic categories can be appropriately included in the diagnosis. A period of diagnostic therapy or a second opinion from a specialist therapist may be necessary to aid the decision-making process.

Therapy

Although the primary diagnosis may be an articulation disorder, with or without phonological consequences, a structural problem does not necessarily cause a speech disorder and, equally, a speech disorder may not be structurally based. Indeed, often a structural problem is not a limiting factor and therapy can proceed in its presence.

Some cleft-type characteristics are affected by surgery but can be eliminated with appropriate therapy (Harding and Grunwell 1998). For example, an alveolar fistula makes production of [t d] impossible but many children can produce a softly articulated inter-dental [t̪] by flattening the blade of the tongue into the fistula. Throughout babble development, adult modelling of fronted alveolars [n̪ t̪ d̪ l̪] encourages anterior contacts and prevents preference for velar contacts with a subsequent 'backing' phonological process / n t d l / => [k g ŋ j]. Furthermore, softly articulated models discourage the excessive articulatory effort that might precipitate glottal or pharyngeal articulation instead of the oral target.

Video and audio tapes of therapy activities provide repeated exposure to the precise input mode that stimulates motor programming and possibly silent rehearsal. While listening to therapy in privacy through headphones, children can practise without fear of failure.

Velopharyngeal dysfunction (VPD)

Normal velopharyngeal closure occurs through movements of the soft palate, the right and left pharyngeal walls and the posterior pharyngeal wall. VPD exists when the palate does not separate the mouth from the nose effectively during speech and there is inappropriate coupling of the oropharynx and nasopharynx during non-nasal consonants and vowels. This is often associated with hypernasality, nasal emission, nasal turbulence and certain consonant error types, such as passive and non-oral errors.

Aetiology of VPD

The prevalence of velopharyngeal insufficiency following primary palate repair varies across studies from 5 to 40 per cent (McWilliams *et al.* 1990). This range of outcomes is influenced by the effectiveness of different surgical techniques, and differences in methodology and assessment techniques.

Cleft teams are responsible for the management of VPD in children who have no history of overt cleft palate (Sell and Ma 1996). Indeed, up to 50 per cent of children assessed for nasal speech in cleft centres will have no history of overt cleft palate (Watson *et al.* 2001).

Submucous cleft palate (SMCP)

This is the mildest form of cleft palate, in which the oral mucosa is intact but the underlying muscles are abnormally inserted into the posterior margin of the hard palate, with resulting impaired palate function. This form occurs in 40 per cent of VPD cases.

An SMCP varies in presentation and may only be confirmed at surgery. It is particularly important for therapists to be aware of SMCP as its initial presentation is often in the form of abnormal speech. There is often a history of nasal regurgitation of milk in infancy, recurrent ear infections and possible grommet insertion.

Post-adenoidectomy

The removal of the adenoid pad on the posterior pharyngeal wall can lead to velopharyngeal insufficiency, in some cases uncovering an undiagnosed SMCP.

Neurological factors

Children with neurological difficulties are a heterogeneous group. They may include children with speech dyspraxia and/or dysarthria. Historically, the view has been that surgery and prosthetics are rarely appropriate for these children. However, with improved diagnostic investigations, these interventions are worth considering, especially if the dominant speech symptoms are hypernasality and/or nasal air escape.

Phoneme Specific VPD

Where active nasal fricatives exist, and there is no hypernasal resonance, the likely diagnosis is Phoneme Specific VPD. The velopharyngeal sphincter closes for most oral pressure consonants but does not close for specific consonant targets. This indicates mislearned patterns. Such a speaker is oral on most consonants and vowels – for instance, the plosives /p b t d k g/ – but habitually 'speaks through the nose' on certain consonants such as / s z / and sometimes /ʃ tʃ d /. These active nasal fricatives are nevertheless frequently produced by children who have no identifiable velopharyngeal insufficiency or oral structural defect.

Congenital VPD and palatopharyngeal disproportion

These terms describes an overlarge nasopharynx, preventing appropriate closure of the velopharyngeal mechanism during speech.

Assessment of VPD

In addition to perceptual assessment, instrumentation has been developed to provide acoustic and aerodynamic objective measurements of nasal tone and nasal airflow. The preferred method for measuring nasal resonance is known as nasometry (Dalston and Seaver 1992); for measuring nasal airflow, the most sophisticated system is the PERCI SARS (Warren *et al.*1985).

Velopharyngeal investigations of the vocal tract

A cleft surgeon and specialist speech and language therapist should investigate anatomical and functional characteristics of the velopharyngeal mechanism with multiview videofluoroscopy and nasendoscopy. The latter involves passing a flexible fibre-optic tube, with a small camera attached to one end, through the nose to a position above the velopharyngeal mechanism. The size, shape and location of the gap may then be observed during speech.

Treatment of VPD

When a velopharyngeal gap is identified, treatment is usually surgical (Sell and Ma 1996). Surgery may reposition the muscles in the palate or conduct a pharyngoplasty, narrowing or blocking the nasopharyngeal space. The nature of surgery is usually determined by the findings of nasendoscopy and videofluoroscopy.

Other treatment options include prosthetic appliances such as a palatal lift or speech bulb obturator. An obturator consists of a dental retainer with an 'extension' that is designed to occlude the residual velopharyngeal gap that occurs during speech; it is particularly effective for cases where there is severe pathology and surgery is contra-indicated (Sell and Grunwell 2001). Palatal lift is often used for neurological aetiologies when surgery is judged to be inappropriate.

Sometimes speech therapy for hypernasality, nasal emission or nasal turbulence may be appropriate, particularly where there is inconsistency in the pattern of movements. Articulation therapy, or visual biofeedback therapy using endoscopy or PERCI SARS may have a place. Indeed, there are times when it is recommended that articulation should be changed in the presence of velopharyngeal insufficiency, so as to permit a valid assessment of velopharyngeal function. Furthermore, post-operatively it cannot be assumed that the patient now has an adequate velopharyngeal mechanism that he or she will automatically learn to use effectively (Witt and D'Antonio 1993); conversely, not all children necessarily require post-operative therapy.

It is recommended that the specialist speech and language therapist in the team should lead decisions about techniques for pre- and post-operative therapy. Many clinicians assert that speech therapy for hypernasality, nasal air emission and nasal turbulence *per se* are inappropriate; however, if consonant production is affected, therapy that targets this aspect of speech can sometimes increase velopharyngeal activity. Specialist-led therapy can often elicit weak realisations of voiceless pressure consonants, whereas voiced pressure consonants may require articulatory adaptations.

Velocardiofacial syndrome

Children with velocardiofacial syndrome present in early childhood with severe hypernasality and often have pervasive glottal/pharyngeal articulation or a predominance of nasals and approximants. This syndrome has an extensive list of associated features: velopharyngeal insufficiency; language and pragmatic difficulties; mild learning disabilities; poor attention and concentration; and feeding problems in infancy (Thomas and Graham 1997). Imaginative thinking tends to be slow to develop and, hence, children tend to be rigid thinkers. In addition to the velopharyngeal anomalies, these children may present with congenital heart disease, facial dysmorphism, variable degrees of immunodeficiency, hypocalcaemia and endocrine abnormalities. Complex psychological and social problems may also occur, particularly in adolescence.

Comprehensive, long-term interdisciplinary management is required for this condition, ideally led by the cleft team's paediatrician.

Summary

This chapter has presented an overview of the care pathway for children with cleft lip and palate. The roles of the multidisciplinary cleft team, the likely presenting symptoms and the long-term management programme facing children with this abnormality have been outlined. Distinctions have been highlighted between cleft-related and non-cleft speech problems.

CHAPTER 20

Children who stammer

Louise Wright

Learning outcomes

By the end of this chapter, the reader should know how to:

- identify children who are at risk of persistent stammering;
- carry out appropriate assessment;
- plan therapy to suit individual needs;
- recognise when discharge is appropriate.

Introduction

Stammering (which may also be called stuttering or dysfluency) is the abnormal disruption of speech fluency. It is recognised by frequent repetitions of words, syllables or sounds; by the prolongations of sounds; or by 'blocks' that interrupt the airflow or voicing in speech. Severe stammering can be tense and effortful, and children might well feel embarrassed and anxious about their speech. They may try to cope with the physical and emotional experience of stammering in many ways, such as changing words, avoiding situations, or trying different ways of speaking – for example, whispering.

All young children who are developing language show some hesitancies that are normal. Non-fluency describes the normal hesitancies that all speakers experience, particularly if tired, rushed or uncertain. Non-fluency includes pausing, repeating whole words or phrases, and saying 'er' or 'um'.

What is known about stammering?

Stammering is a developmental disorder that can begin as young as 18 months, but most commonly begins between 2 and 5 years of age. As with other speech and language difficulties, more boys stammer than girls. It is estimated that at any time 1 per cent of the adult population stammer, although around 5 per cent report having stammered at some time (Bloodstein 1995). These figures indicate that many children recover from stammering, and a longitudinal study by Yairi and Ambrose (1999) indicates that at least 74 per cent of young children experience spontaneous recovery.

Speech and language therapists in the UK generally agree that the development of stammering involves a complex interaction between a number of factors (Rustin *et al.* 1996). These factors include a possible neurophysiological predisposition to stammer, which may be inherited. The stammer may then be precipitated or maintained by a variety of factors.

The Demand Capacity (DC) model (Starkweather and Gottwald 1990) describes how fluency breaks down when environmental demands, and/or demands imposed by the children themselves, exceed their cognitive, linguistic, motoric (physical) or emotional capacities. For example, a child might have low linguistic capacities in the face of average demands; have average or even high capacities but face higher demands; or be unable to cope with the balance of demands and capacities at a particular time in development. The DC model can be useful in helping parents and teachers to understand the complexities of stammering in children (Turnbull and Stewart 1996).

The introduction of the Lidcombe Programme to the UK has challenged some previously held assumptions (Onslow *et al.* 1997). The Lidcombe Programme, developed in Australia, contrasts with the DC model in that it advocates that early stammering is a motor speech disorder and can be eliminated using operant procedures (Lincoln and Harrison 1999). Although growing numbers of speech and language therapists in the UK are trained in the use of the Lidcombe Programme, many are still reluctant to adopt a purely motor explanation of stammering until further evidence is available.

This chapter is based on the most commonly held view in the UK, that stammering is multicausal. The chapter includes the Lidcombe Programme as one way of working directly on children's speech.

Implications for assessment and therapy

The effective management of children who stammer depends on:

• identification of children who are a priority for therapy because they are at risk of not recovering spontaneously;
• thorough assessment of all the possible contributory factors in terms of capacities and demands;

- identification of the combination of factors that need to be addressed in therapy;
- deciding on the order in which these will be addressed;
- an agreed outcome of therapy that will enable discharge.

In this chapter the assessment and management of children from 18 months to the teenage years will be considered. Stammering may present differently at different ages. Below are descriptions of three boys of different ages who all stammer.

Case examples

Alex is 3. He has been slow to start talking and his phonology is delayed. He started to repeat and prolong sounds about six months ago. The amount of stammering varies but, when frequent, he sometimes gives up on what he is saying. His mother stammers. She is very worried that Alex will not grow out of it. His father believes it is just a normal phase of development.

Ben is 8 and has stammered for three years. Although of average ability, Ben is not enjoying school. He talks freely, despite stammering in most situations. Mostly he repeats and prolongs sounds, but he sometimes blocks and blinks when stammering. He is good at football and has many friends.

Carl is 14 and has experienced some teasing about his stammer while at secondary school. He mostly blocks when he stammers and he avoids answering questions in class. He has some close friends who do not notice his stammer. He is thinking about what subjects he should choose at school and what kind of job he might like to do.

Now read the above descriptions again as if they describe the *same boy* at different ages.

This exercise illustrates not only the individual nature of stammering and how it might develop over time, but also the wide range of stammering problems that can be encountered by a therapist working with children who stammer.

Referral

Speech and language therapists recommend referral as soon as possible after the onset of stammering. However, health visitors and GPs often delay referral in the belief that the child will grow out of it (Christie 2000). A child as described in any one of the case examples above might therefore be referred at any of the three ages.

Ben, at 8 and Carl at 14 years, might both have had therapy before; and previous therapy may have ended for a variety of reasons. Therapy might have resulted in increased fluency but stammering later worsened due to changing demands; they might have been discharged because they were comfortable with their level of stammering; they might have failed to attend because their speech was not a priority at that time; or they might have left therapy because they did not feel it was helping.

Referrals are usually made because the parents are concerned. A referral may be directly from the parents or via other professionals. Parents may have been seeking referral for some time. The child may or may not be concerned about stammering. It is important to find out why and how referral was made, and to gather information about any previous therapy because this will effect the decision-making process in the management of the case (see Chapter 1).

Initial contact

It is necessary to make contact with the family of a child referred for stammering before the first appointment in order to explain the assessment process. In contrast to other speech and language therapy cases, it is strongly recommended that both parents attend assessment and therapy (Rustin *et al.* 1996) because they may have differing perceptions and management of the problem. In one-parent families, different appointments may be arranged for separated parents, depending on their wishes and their relationship with the child. Alternatively, therapy may only involve the primary carer. The therapist needs to explain why it is preferable that both parents attend and to agree an appointment time that is mutually convenient.

Assessment

In order to carry out a thorough assessment of possible factors contributing to the stammer, it is recommended that the therapist employs all of the assessment tools described below.

Observation of parent–child interaction

It is suggested that this is the first assessment carried out while parents are unchanged by discussion with the therapist and in order that the therapist can see examples of the child's stammering before interviewing the parents.

The therapist observes the child's stammer, the interaction (verbal and non-verbal) between parents and child, and their reactions to any stammering. This can be done formally or informally – for example in the waiting area, in the clinic room while the therapist is seemingly engaged in another activity, or through a one-way mirror. Ideally, the interaction should be videotaped, although audiotaping or note-taking may be the only option if a video recorder is not available. Checklists can be used to structure observation of parent–child interaction (Rustin *et al.* 1996; see also Chapter 5).

Parental interview

A comprehensive interview is required with the parents of any child or teenager who is stammering. It may also be advisable to interview any other significant people in the child's life, such as grandparents or others involved in childcare. See Guitar (1998) for a suggested content for the interview.

The initial interview serves a number of purposes. Primarily it is used to gather information about: the child and his or her family; any family history of stammering or other speech and language problems; the history of the child and the stammer; how the stammer presents, and how the child and parents react to and manage the stammer. Cultural and linguistic factors will be explored for children from linguistic minority communities (see Chapter 16). In addition, the therapist will provide the parents with information on stammering and speech and language therapy, and will begin to build a collaborative working relationship with them (see Chapter 9).

Child–clinician interaction

The aim of this part of the assessment is to collect samples of stammering, to investigate the child's awareness of stammering, and to screen their language and general development.

Collecting samples of stammering

Stammering varies in different situations, which makes collecting a representative sample problematic. The most useful sample of stammering is obtained by creating a variety of conditions during assessment.

The therapist begins by playing with the younger child, using age-appropriate toys or engaging a teenager in general conversation. Initially, the therapist interacts in a relaxed manner that facilitates fluency. Demand is then increased – for example, by increasing the rate of speech, or by asking questions and interrupting – in order to assess the effects of such demands. This may be particularly useful if the child is fluent in clinic although the parents report stammering in other situations. Parents can also supplement the data gathered with taped samples from home.

The therapist should also assess whether the stammering is modifiable by decreasing demands, modelling a slower rate of speech or showing the child how to modify their speech – for instance by slowing down until fluency is achieved. Experimenting in this way allows the therapist to test hypotheses as to how best to increase the child's fluency.

There are formal fluency assessments such as Riley's Stuttering Prediction Instrument (1981) or Pindzola's Protocol for Differentiating the Incipient Stutterer in the Stuttering Intervention Program (1987). However, these assessments are not recommended because of their limited sampling of stammering and because they predate the latest research results on risk factors for developing persistent stammering (Yairi and Ambrose 1999).

Investigating the child's awareness

Once rapport has been established with the child, the therapist can talk to the child about his or her stammer. This is now recommended with all children, however young (Rustin *et al.* 1996). It is important to establish how aware such children are of their stammer, whether they are distressed, to reassure them that it can be talked about openly, and that help is available.

The therapist should have asked the parents beforehand whether they think the child is aware, and the therapist should also have gathered evidence during observations of the child as to the possible level of the child's awareness. Initially, questions like 'Do you know why you have come to see me today?' are used to initiate the topic and can be followed by more exploratory questions if the child shows any level of awareness. The therapist takes care to use language that is appropriate to the cognitive and linguistic level of the child, based on informal observation and formal assessment, and uses the child's words for stammering – for example, 'getting stuck' or 'trouble talking'.

If the child appears unaware, the therapist can introduce normal non-fluencies into her/his own speech, commenting that she or he sometimes has trouble talking, and can then ask whether that ever happens to the child. This gives the child further opportunity to discuss his or her stammering – or it may confirm that the child is unaware of stammering or is unwilling to discuss it.

Language and other development

Finally, the therapist should carry out a general assessment of the child, including language and motor skills. This is done in the usual manner (see Chapters 12, 13 and 14) using initial observations followed by a more detailed formal assessment as necessary.

School contact

If the child attends school or nursery, it is important to gather information from teachers by visiting, telephoning or using a checklist/questionnaire (Cooper and Cooper 1985). If a school visit is possible, it can also be helpful to observe the child interacting in the classroom (Stewart and Turnbull 1995).

Time spent on assessment

Carrying out all of the above assessments generally takes two to three hours, but longer if formal language assessments are needed. The therapist can choose whether to carry out all of the assessments in one session or spread them over two or three shorter sessions. Alternatively she or he can work with a colleague, one interviewing the parents while the other simultaneously assesses the child. Both therapists then share their findings with the family at the end of the session.

It cannot be stressed enough that trying to save time on assessment will lead to difficulties planning the appropriate therapy; it is also likely to waste valuable therapy time later (Conture and Melnick 1999). Therapists can, therefore, justify the time employed on grounds of both efficacy and efficiency. During the assessment process, the therapist is also building a working relationship with the parents and demonstrating her/his commitment to the case. Parents are generally only too pleased to be offered a thorough assessment.

Once the assessment has been completed, various decisions need to be made to decide what further action should be taken. These decisions are described next.

Is the child stammering?

The first decision to be made following assessment is to establish whether the child is stammering or is normally non-fluent. This decision will be based on analysis of the child's speech behaviours and by consensus (Packman and Onslow 1999). A behavioural diagnosis can be reached by counting the percentage of stammered words and using checklists of types of dysfluencies.

Gregory and Hill's Continuum of Disfluent Speech Behaviour (1993) can be used to identify which dysfluencies are judged to be normal non-fluency and which are typical of stammering. In terms of frequency, stammering may be diagnosed if more then 2 per cent of words spoken are judged to be stammering behaviours. In most cases, stammering is easily diagnosed by consensus between the therapist, parents and other significant people in the child's life.

What is the risk of persistent stammering?

The second decision to be made concerns the level of risk of the child developing persistent stammering. Yairi and Ambrose (1999) suggest that children are at greater risk of persistent stammering if:

- they are male;
- they have been stammering for more than two years;
- they have family members who have not recovered from stammering;
- they have delayed phonological development.

The role of language development in relation to stammering is not as yet clear and, surprisingly, severe early stammering is not a predictor of persistent stammering. Parents and therapists should therefore be reassured that, even if a child is stammering very severely, he or she might not persist in stammering. However, the aforementioned risk

actors for persistent stammering must be borne in mind when deciding whether to prioritise a child for intervention.

Management of children who are not stammering

If the child is not stammering his or her normal non-fluencies may have been perceived as
stammering by the parents. Parents should be reassured and given information about non-
fluency, stammering and normal language development to create more realistic expectations.

Alternatively, parents' reports may indicate that the child was stammering but has
returned to normal non-fluency prior to the assessment. Parents of children who are
judged to be at low risk of the stammer recurring need to be given information about
stammering, and reassured that they can contact the therapist in the future if they have
any concerns. If the child is judged to be at high risk of persistent stammering, the therapist may choose to monitor progress using telephone contact.

Management of children who are stammering

Therapy is appropriate if any one of the following is present:

- the child is at high risk of persistent stammering;
- the child has developed negative reactions to the stammer;
- the parents are requesting therapy.

Therapy may address any of the following elements that contribute to the stammering
problem. The purpose of this section is to guide the reader through the decision-making
process of planning, implementing and evaluating therapy.

Parental concern

Most parents enter therapy feeling guilty that they are responsible in some way for their
child's stammer. Others are highly anxious about the stammer and about the possible
educational, vocational and social effects should it persist. Speech and language therapists
have basic counselling skills that are usually adequate in dealing with such parental anxiety.
By listening to parents' fears, by providing them with information and skills to help their
child, and by challenging negative stereotypes about stammering, most parents can be
supported effectively while their child is in therapy. In some cases, parents benefit from
referral to another professional for specific counselling in order to deal with their own
reactions to their child's stammer.

Some children who are particularly at risk of persistent stammering have a parent who
stammers. This issue should be addressed sensitively but directly, and time may be

required alone with the parent who stammers. The needs of such parents must be considered if their child is to be helped effectively in therapy. Referral to, or support from, a therapist who specialises in adult stammering therapy might be required.

Contributory/maintaining factors in the environment

Therapy aimed at decreasing the demands on a stammering child from the environment may be the only intervention that is needed to increase capacity for fluency and return the child to normal fluency levels. It is generally the first therapy option in cases where risk of persistence is low, where stammering is mild, and where the child is unaware or unconcerned about his or her stammer. Alternatively, reducing demands can also complement direct fluency techniques, the aim being to create an environment in which the child has the best chance of using his or her new fluency skills.

Environmental demands might include behaviours by the parents, siblings or other family members, the general family lifestyle or school issues (Starkweather 1997). Children's capacities to cope with demands vary, and each demand must be treated as a hypothesis to be tested in therapy. Parents should therefore never be given standardised, general advice.

Care must be taken not to overload families with too many changes or to increase their guilt at having contributed to the development of the stammer. Therapists and parents should begin by changing one factor that they think will make the biggest difference and that they have the best chance of changing successfully. Therapists should not underestimate how difficult it is to change some of the identified behaviours. Indeed, parents may need the therapist to model the relevant behaviours, which they may then practise inside and outside the clinic. For example, a family might be asked to watch the video of their parent–child interaction and choose to pause more frequently while talking with their child. They might need to be taught how to pause more, gradually introducing this into short play situations, while acknowledging that they are unable to use pauses consistently during everyday speaking situations.

Continual evaluation of changes by the therapist and the parents allows the management of the child to evolve in response to the child's changing capacities as well as the changing environmental and self-imposed demands. Collaborative working with the therapist also empowers parents to manage their child's fluency levels themselves.

Stammering

Management of the child's stammering behaviours will be determined by the severity of the stammer and the child's reaction to the stammering.

If stammering is mild, or moderate but the child is unaware, modelling slow and easy speech without drawing attention to stammering may be sufficient to increase fluency

(Heinze and Johnson 1985). If stammering is severe, with struggle and avoidance behaviours, the child is usually aware and therefore stammering should be addressed openly in therapy. If the child has minimal awareness, it may be helpful to increase the child's awareness in a supportive and non-punitive manner. This can increase the child's understanding of stammering and help with self-monitoring.

Therapy dealing directly with stammering behaviours can be approached in three ways:

- The Lidcombe Programme employs operant strategies to increase fluency, to praise stammer-free speech, and to apply gentle correction of stammering behaviours. This approach may be useful for early stammering, where child and parents are suited to a behavioural approach.
- A fluency technique can be taught where the overall speech rate is reduced and words flow smoothly together with gentle articulation. This technique is helpful for children who have frequent or severe stammering, rapid speech and little natural fluency.
- Children who experience greater natural fluency, interspersed with occasional tense stammers, can be taught how to stammer more easily. They are taught to monitor the stammers and relax the articulators before or during the stammer. This helps the child to say each difficult word more smoothly – or even to say the word fluently. Learning how to stammer in a relaxed manner is useful for older children and teenagers, who are less likely to regain complete fluency and should therefore benefit from a way of managing their stammer in the long term.

Various therapy programmes have been published (Cooper and Cooper 1985; Pindzola 1987; Heinze and Johnson 1987; Meyers and Woodford 1992). These provide structured therapy activities to help children identify and monitor stammering behaviours; learn strategies to increase their fluency; establish fluency skills in clinic; transfer fluency into everyday speech; and cope with demanding situations. It is recommended that therapists attend a training course before using the Lidcombe Programme.

It might seem confusing to less experienced therapists that so many therapy approaches and programmes have been published. Initially, they might find it useful to select one published programme and follow it in its entirety. However, as their experience grows and they become familiar with different therapy techniques, they will be able to select elements from different programmes to suit individual clients and their own preferred therapy style.

Possible contributory/maintaining factors within the child

General assessment of a stammering child may reveal deficits in the child's development that lower the capacity for fluency or that create demands. For example, speech and language difficulties, such as delayed language, disordered phonology, poor oral motor performance or word-finding difficulties, may impede a child's capacity for fluency; other difficulties, such as dyspraxia, long-sightedness or asthma, might create stressful demands for the child. Children's own responses to events may create demands – for example, a low tolerance to frustration or general high self-demands.

Therapists will need to address such issues in therapy. If felt to be primary contributory factors, they may be addressed before attempting direct therapy on the stammering behaviours. Alternatively, they can be worked on simultaneously with direct therapy on fluency. For example, some language therapy can be incorporated into fluency technique exercises. Therapists need to use their judgement as to whether working on other issues may increase or decrease demands for the child. If it is not possible to make such a judgement with available information, trial therapy may be needed.

Children's reactions to their stammer

Children can react to their stammering with such emotions as embarrassment, frustration, anger, or helplessness. They may try to help themselves by forceful articulation, hitting themselves or avoiding words or speaking situations. Direct therapy on fluency is indicated if any such negative reactions are observed or reported. Therapy programmes such as Winning in Speech (Waugh 1991) can be helpful in dealing with the emotions and attitudes related to stammering. Therapy can help children to deal more positively with their stammer, setting it in the context of their other personal qualities.

In the teenage years, therapy will need to help the client come to terms with the increased likelihood of a persistent stammer. Teaching easier ways of stammering contributes to this, but work on positive attitudes towards communication, good social skills and the ability to make life choices – independent of the stammer – all minimise the restrictions that might result from persistent stammering. Many of these issues can be addressed most effectively through therapy delivered in a group setting (Rustin *et al.* 1995; see also Chapter 4).

Possible outcomes of therapy

Therapy can be judged to be successful by different criteria depending on the age of the child, the type of stammer, the circumstances of therapy and the resources available. Discharge following successful therapy will not be judged on fluency alone.

For example, for a young child, referred early with low-risk factors and committed parents, therapy should end when the child achieves normal fluency for at least six months. The case example of Alex, in the three quoted in the Introduction to this chapter, is one where the child has been referred relatively early after onset of stammering. However, Alex is at high risk of persistent stammering because he is male, his mother has a persistent stammer and he has delayed phonology. His recovery may therefore be slow and therapy must allow for this – it is possible that, despite early intervention, his stammer will persist and therapy aims will need to be revised accordingly.

Ben (another of the three case examples) is less likely to recover spontaneously as he is male and has been stammering for three years. The aim of therapy, therefore, could be successful use of a fluency technique. Therapy should aim to build a positive attitude to communication in Ben, and his parents should be equipped with skills to manage variations in fluency. He may require long-term review appointments and blocks of therapy until he reaches a level of fluency with which he and his parents are comfortable. Although he is at high risk of persistent stammering, the possibility of recovery cannot be ruled out.

By the teenage years, it is highly unlikely that Carl (the third of the case examples) will achieve complete fluency. A positive outcome of therapy would be if he successfully used a combination of a fluency technique and easy stammering. He could be discharged when his confidence, communication and social skills were sufficiently good to enable him to manage speaking situations without avoidance. His attitude to himself and his stammer should also be sufficiently positive to enable him to make decisions about education and employment based on factors other than his stammer.

Efficacy and efficiency

Outcome measurement for child stammering therapy is still in the process of development (Ingham and Riley 1998). Measures need to include reliable descriptions of stammering behaviours within and outside clinic, consideration of reactions to stammering, functional communication, and satisfaction of the child and parents as to their communicative abilities.

Determining which therapy is most effective is problematical because most intervention involves a number of different procedures, thus making it difficult to know which contributed to a successful outcome. In addition, high levels of spontaneous recovery make it impossible to know whether treatment alone was responsible.

Evidence of spontaneous recovery also influences decisions as to when therapy should begin. There is still debate as to whether therapists should monitor children at low risk of persistent stammering, or begin therapy early (Attanasio 1999). Given present knowledge, and if resources are available, there is consensus that early intervention is advisable. It is ethically preferable to treat some children unnecessarily than to fail to treat children who would benefit from early intervention, particularly as therapy does not harm a child (Starkweather 1997).

If, however, therapists are obliged to prioritise cases for therapy because they are working with limited resources, they could justifiably monitor children between the ages of 2 and 5 who have been stammering for less than 18 months, have no negative reactions to their stammering, and whose parents are not requesting therapy.

Summary

The highly individual nature of stammering and the changing needs of children as they develop into teenagers require a therapist to demonstrate flexibility and perseverance. Therapists who approach their work with commitment and enthusiasm will be rewarded by seeing some children achieve normal fluency and others develop into well-adjusted young adults for whom stammering is not the problem that it would have been without therapy.

CHAPTER 21

Children with severe learning disabilities

Gaye Powell

Learning outcomes

On completion of this chapter, the reader should have an awareness of:
- the terminology applied to children with severe learning disabilities (SLD);
- the basis of some classification systems;
- theoretical frameworks underpinning assessment and management;
- issues in decision-making in the assessment and management of children with SLD.

Introduction

It would seem appropriate to begin with a simple definition of severe learning disabilities to enable discrete differentiation of this client group from others in terms of their clinical presentation and subsequent communication profile and therapeutic needs. However, this is not easy to do when taking into consideration all the domains that might be encompassed – not least the interrelationship of language, cognition and social interaction (National Joint Committee on Learning Disability 1991; Pinker 1993). It is further complicated by the existence of differing terminology and classification systems.

Terminology

Reading through the literature, a variety of terms describing individuals with SLD will be encountered that differ not only within the UK but also across the world. Preconceptions, expectations and definitions have changed radically over the past 50 years or so as a result of changes in social and educational policies, which now seek to integrate individuals with learning disabilities into society rather than segregate them in long-stay institutions (DfEE 1994; DES 1981). Research into the effects of social and educational contexts, aetiologies, and clinical practice upon cognitive and language development have increased understanding of the diversity and potential that exists among this population (Buckley *et al.* 1996; Le Provost 1993; Rondal and Edwards 1997).

In the UK, the terms 'learning disabilities', 'learning difficulties' and 'intellectual and cognitive impairments' tend to prevail (Fawcus 1997; Grove and Dockrell 1999; RCSLT 1996), while in the USA and the rest of Europe 'mental retardation' and 'mental handicap' are more common, preceded by the descriptors 'mild', 'moderate' or 'severe'. In the latter contexts, 'learning difficulties' is reserved for individuals with normal or above-average intelligence who experience specific difficulties in learning to read, write and perform age-appropriate mathematical calculations. This diversity in terminology can be misleading when studies report apparently high levels of attainment and progress in programmes of intervention, and it needs to be borne in mind when reading literature and when selecting keywords for a literature search.

Classification systems

Historically, measures of IQ based upon performance on standardised assessments of intelligence have provided diagnostic boundaries for SLD and profound learning disabilities, namely scores of 20–35 and less than 20 respectively (Grossman 1983). However, from a practitioner's point of view, a quantitative score provides little information about an individual's communicative performance – or communicative need – upon which to base a programme of intervention (see Grove and Dockrell 1999 for a discussion of a clinical classification of IQ).

An alternative form of classification is the medical, or cause-and-effect, model, which is based upon underlying aetiology. The presumption here is that a linear relationship exists between the underlying cause and the symptoms that manifest themselves as a direct result, and vice versa (Kamhi 1995). A good example of this might be Down's Syndrome, where a diagnosis is made at, or close to, birth based on a number of physical characteristics. As a result of this diagnosis and an accumulated knowledge of commonly co-occurring organic features that impact upon the sensory systems, predictions can be made about future developmental patterns. This will include poor motor coordination, delayed onset of speech, poor speech intelligibility, auditory processing difficulties and delayed language (Pueschel and Sustrova 1996).

Alternatively, it may be deduced that a child has severe learning disabilities because of a combination of presenting symptoms that are not syndrome-specific: delayed motor milestones, limited communication and social skills, poor attention and discrimination, and restricted play development. This approach is more informative than an IQ score and can alert practitioners to potential areas that might require syndrome-specific intervention

(Rondal and Edwards 1997). However, it is inadequate in reflecting individual and environmental differences that are known to have considerable influence upon development (Simonoff *et al.* 1996).

Another feature of this cause-and-effect approach is a tendency to focus on areas of inability or weakness, rather than strengths that can be built upon during the therapeutic process. In view of this, while aetiological information can be useful, caution needs to be exercised in terms of overreliance upon syndrome-specific characteristics that could compromise developmental expectations (Simon *et al.* 1995). See De Montfort Supple (1995) for issues in the classification of communication disorders, and Rondal and Edwards (1997) for a review of IQ and syndrome-specific features.

These last two approaches may have proved useful for the purposes for which they were devised: identifying individuals who were considered to be atypical and in need of social and educational provision that was different from the norm. However, the needs of therapists are quite different. In general, speech and language therapists seek to promote development, which is defined by Bray *et al.* (1999: 19) as: 'The lifelong, continuing and chronologically related process of physical, perceptual, cognitive, personality and social change. Intervention actively aims for the person to enhance and maximally attain his or her potential for development.'

A working definition

The definition of SLD that is proposed for this text is based upon the notion that children with SLD, even though displaying areas of strength, experience persistent difficulty in acquiring, processing, manipulating and retaining information necessary to enable them to function socially and educationally in line with their typically developing peers.

It is also recognised that not all areas of development will necessarily be affected equally. For example, gross motor skills may be within normal limits whereas speech may be very delayed. This may also change across time as different skills develop either spontaneously as a result of the maturational process or as a direct result of intervention, such as the introduction of a hearing aid or form of AAC. The effects of underlying neurological and sensory impairments can also be increased or decreased depending upon the context. For example, within the family setting, compensatory strategies may lessen the effect of an expressive language difficulty, which may appear more severe in a day-nursery setting with less familiar others.

This definition is based upon an essentially transactional model (Kamhi 1995) and supports a dynamic approach to intervention encompassing the interaction of internal and external variables in the developmental process. A number of factors are highlighted that will affect the learning process and that require consideration when working with children and their carers.

Theoretical considerations

Underpinning any approach to decision-making in assessment and management are a number of theoretical beliefs or philosophies, whether they are implicit or explicit (Stengelhofen 1993). In working with children with SLD, it is considered helpful to make some of these theoretical frameworks explicit as this will affect how the therapist will:

- view developmental potential;
- select assessment frameworks;
- devise programmes of intervention;
- select goals that are timely and appropriate for individual needs;
- select learning opportunities/strategies to facilitate the success of agreed goals.

Delay or deviance?

Discussion has been ongoing for many years as to whether the development, including speech and language, of children with SLD is delayed – i.e. occurs in the same sequence as typically developing children – or is deviant (Kamhi and Masterson 1989; Grove and Dockrell 1999). See Rondal and Edwards (1997) for a review.

Research into the speech and language development of children with SLD has historically rendered a number of differing views on the delay/deviance question, particularly in comparative studies. Children with SLD have been variously matched with typically developing children for mental age, chronological age, or language age – but with inconsistent conclusions (Conti-Ramsden 1997; Fowler 1990). While there are some syndrome-specific exceptions – for example, William's syndrome where relatively developed levels of language coexist with lower cognitive abilities (Bellugi *et al.* 1988) – current opinion on balance supports the view that the sequence of language development is in line with accepted developmental norms. However, the rate of acquisition differs in that speech and language onset is later, its progress is slower, and the ceiling is lower both quantitatively, in terms of vocabulary size, and qualitatively, in terms of complexity of syntax and range of functions. Theoretically, this supports a sequential, 'staged' approach to language development. See Bohannon and Bonvillian (1997) for an overview of theoretical approaches to language acquisition.

The practical implications of this for the therapist and parents are that the majority of children can be seen within a framework of typical development. This is helpful, particularly when profiling development and planning programmes of intervention. For example, it would be unrealistic to expect a child to produce utterances containing two information-carrying words when there is limited comprehension at the one information-carrying word level (Knowles and Masidlover 1982); such a goal might take a number of years to achieve, or may be inappropriate. In such cases, a more beneficial long-term goal might be to broaden the functions available at the one-word level. Likewise, play sequences and associated language would only be promoted when the child has passed through the stage of self-pretend play.

Theoretical frameworks

The working definition supplied earlier indicates that children with SLD do not learn as effectively as their peers for a number of potential reasons. These may be internal, such as intermittent hearing loss, or external, for example, over-directive parental language, or lack of developmentally appropriate play equipment. They may also be permanent, for example, sensory blindness, or temporary, as in intermittent hearing loss. Whatever the reasons, an SLD child will be failing to develop through incidental learning and exposure to the same, or similar, experiences to his/her peers.

In light of this, programmes of intervention will necessarily involve the creation of more overt or explicit learning opportunities employing different theoretical approaches. This may include those based within a naturalistic framework – relying on natural contexts and interactions in which the child is seen as an active participant – and those in a behaviourist framework where the child's role is more passive and desired behaviours are directed, prompted, modelled and reinforced by the adult. In reality, an eclectic approach is likely to be the most successful, as different techniques may be required at different points in the therapeutic process to facilitate optimum learning.

Assessment and management

Assessment is an ongoing process inextricably linked to intervention through the constant hypothesis-testing (see Chapter 2) that occurs not only during the initial assessment period but also throughout therapy and particularly in the re-evaluation of progress toward set goals. For therapists working with individuals with SLD, the RCSLT states (1996, p. 134) that the profession '… recognises the importance of good functional communication and eating and drinking skills in the pursuit of independence in ordinary life'. In addition, it states (1996, p. 134) that 'carryover of intervention is frequently difficult for this client group and therefore the actual locations and situations themselves should be used wherever possible'.

The keywords in the above, in terms of theoretical frameworks, are 'functional communication' and 'actual locations and situations'. There is an implication that assessment and management need to be based on an individual's needs and that a naturalistic context for intervention would be the most beneficial to help them to generalise their skills. This has been shown historically in many studies where children with SLD have demonstrated acquisition of communication skills in a clinical setting but failed to transfer this to other contexts (Calculator 1988).

The assessment process within the overall case management would follow the guide-lines of good practice outlined in *Communicating Quality 2* (RCSLT 1996) and Bray *et al.* (1999). However, some of the issues that are particularly significant for therapists working with children with SLD and their families are highlighted below.

Timing of first contact

The timing of the first contact with a family will be critical for all concerned and will affect decisions in the assessment process and the nature of the programme of intervention. Some of the critical questions at this stage of the decision-making process are:

- *Who made the referral?*
- *Who else is actively involved?*
- *What information is currently available from other sources prior to contacting the family?*

If the child is of pre-school age, there may already be involvement of a Portage Service (Sturmey and Crisp 1986) and other therapies. The speech and language therapist's role would be working jointly with the parents, other therapists and the Portage worker in planning and implementing a programme.

If the child is in school, the functional demands for both comprehension and use of language in an educational context, which is curriculum-based, will be different from those within a home setting. Assessment and goal planning for IEPs should be carried out jointly with the teaching staff and, where possible, with parents in order to promote effec-tive collaborative practice and the achievement of jointly agreed goals (Martin and Miller 1996; see also Chapter 11).

The next question in the decision-making process is: *How old is the child?*

If the involvement of the speech and language therapist is fairly soon after birth, as might be the case for a baby with Down's Syndrome, it is important to ask what information the family has been given. The clinician's role at this stage is likely to be one of support and counselling, and advising on feeding. Engagement with the family will need to be sensitively handled. The lead will need to be taken from them, particularly while they are adjusting to the new baby, and grieving for the baby they were expecting and whom they may now feel is lost (Kubler-Ross 1997). There is no finite period within which this process may occur, and therapists need to be respectful of the needs of individual families and their constituent members. It may be some time before family members feel ready to be actively involved in the therapeutic process, although in some families this can happen almost immediately.

The decision about how quickly to proceed with an assessment will have to be respon-sive to individual need. The focus is likely to be on patterns of interaction (see Chapter 5) and, in certain cases, this may involve introducing the idea of AAC (see below and, more fully, Chapter 23).

The next question in the decision-making process is: *Do the family already have a medical diagnosis of SLD from a paediatrician?*

If the therapist's involvement is part of the diagnostic process, liaison and information-sharing with all parties concerned is essential in making a differential diagnosis. The role of the therapist may, again, be one of support in the early stages and may be based on naturalistic observation and formal assessment procedures.

If the family already have a medical diagnosis, it may be possible to embark on more overt methods of assessment, particularly stressing strengths and working towards joint planning of goals.

The final question at this stage of the process is: *Have sensory abilities been assessed?*

If current results of visual or audiometric screening are not available, it may be difficult to draw any firm conclusions about the presenting communicative abilities and contributory factors. An onward referral to the appropriate agency is essential, because sensory impairments are known to be more prevalent in children with SLD and will adversely affect their learning processes.

Formal versus informal assessment

There is strong evidence to support the use of standardised assessments (Bishop and Mogford 1988) in order to establish a communication profile. Many such assessments involve an essentially behavioural procedure involving a verbal description (stimulus) where the child is required to point to the appropriate picture (response) in order to demonstrate understanding. While recognising this as a way of information gathering, it is proposed that a more pragmatic and context-based approach is adopted for children with SLD that is commensurate with the goal of enhancing 'functional communication skills' appropriate to their daily life.

For assessment to provide an ecologically valid database, it needs to occur in the social contexts pertinent to the child's daily life. This would include carers and significant others (Gallagher 1991; Lund and Duchan 1993). This naturalistic assessment recognises the developmental importance of interaction in different social contexts (Bronfenbrenner 1986). This approach also views the child as an active rather than passive participant in the developmental process.

Assessment within the theoretical framework above is essentially qualitative and descriptive. Information gathering will usually involve a number of methodologies, including analysis of videoed interactions and comparisons of styles of interaction between the child and different conversational partners (Bray *et al.* 1999). Formal developmental assessments are also useful, although the nature of the test materials may disadvantage children with difficulties with fine motor coordination and visual perception. In addition, because of the frequent association of motor coordination and physical disabilities with SLD, the development of eating and drinking skills are often also part of the therapist's overall assessment and management (Winstock 1994; see also Chapter 24).

Several published assessments/profiles have been found to be particularly useful. The Pre-verbal Communication Schedule (Kiernan and Reid 1987) provides a detailed profile of early skills, whereas the Pragmatics Profile of Early Communication Skills (Dewart and Summers 1995) is useful for assessing functional skills. The Pre-school Language Scale – 3 (UK) (PLS–3^{UK}) (Boucher and Lewis 1997) starts from the age of six months and allows observation of interactions. The principles of the Derbyshire Language Scheme (Knowles and Masidlover 1982) can be adapted for individual children in both home and educational settings.

During the assessment process, it is also helpful to note whether a child appears to be more responsive to one type of learning style than another. Some children may not respond to a direct, behaviourist type of approach and may withdraw, while others may thrive on the stimulus–response–reward process.

Maintaining factors

Having built up a profile of the child's communicative abilities, it is necessary to re-examine the information and to identify any factors that might be maintaining the current level of development and constraining progress. This needs to be constantly reviewed.

For example, a child will not be able to progress with finger feeding if unable to sit independently, and an onward referral to the occupational therapist and physiotherapist will be required before this can be effectively addressed. Similarly, a young child with little or no intelligible speech will be unable to progress in terms of expressive and, potentially, receptive language if he or she does not have access to an AAC (see Chapter 23). Without AAC, balanced conversational exchanges, in which the child plays an active contributory role, initiating and responding meaningfully, will be impossible.

Management

The aim of a programme of intervention for children with SLD is usually to optimise the development of functional communication abilities in context (Owens 1995). In order to achieve this aim effectively, the therapist will need to devise optimum learning opportunities in collaboration with significant others in a child's life, and to evaluate the outcome(s). Several of the issues that arise when planning programmes are outlined below.

Style of intervention

How a programme of intervention is implemented may be dictated by a number of factors that are common across client groups. These include: available resources, such as the number of therapists and assistants; size of caseload; local policy and practice; and the child's current and future context(s) – home/pre-school or school.

Given the difficulties in learning and generalisation experienced by children with SLD, they need as much exposure to optimal learning opportunities as possible. This necessarily implies that those who have most contact with the child should be skilled in creating such opportunities. The approach to intervention is, therefore, mostly indirect: working through others, training others, and passing on skills required to support a planned programme (see Chapter 10).

AAC

Over the past twenty years, there has been a revolution in the therapeutic approach for children with SLD and others at risk of failing to develop spoken language. There has been a shift away from speech-based programmes to those that introduce keyword signs and/or graphic symbols alongside the spoken word. The function of this for children with SLD is to support comprehension of the spoken word and to provide them with an alternative or augmentative means of expression (Martinsen and von Tetzchner 1996). The overriding evidence currently supports this as an effective method of promoting language alongside social and cognitive skills, particularly for children with Down's Syndrome (Launonen 1996 and 1998).

The introduction of the concept of AAC to a family needs to be handled carefully. The perception of such a system for the parents of a school-aged child who has failed to acquire meaningful spoken expression may be different from that of the parents of a baby who has yet to reach that developmental stage. The fear that introducing AAC will inhibit speech development, while not uncommon, is unsupported. Available evidence suggests that in fact it enhances vocal output (Clarke *et al.* 1986; Sisson and Barrett 1984).

Principles to facilitate learning opportunities

The following principles are based on a functional context-based approach to intervention (Owens 1995). They are essentially child-centred and seek to enhance existing abilities. Opportunities for learning should include the principles listed below.:

Utilise areas of strength

The assessment process should highlight areas of strength, and programmes of intervention should build on these and widen their potential use. Focusing on areas of inability where prerequisite skills might not yet be in place will lead to a less effective programme in terms of rates of progress and levels of motivation.

Allow a child to express available meanings

When selecting vocabulary for AAC, children have been found to acquire keyword signs and/or symbols more rapidly for currently available receptive vocabulary. So, it would be helpful to establish the current lexicon and base the initial introduction of vocabulary on this before progressing to new vocabulary.

Allow a child to work within a zone of proximal development

A child has a zone of proximal development (Vygotsky 1978) within which success can be achieved so long as support is given. For example, semi-independent drinking from a cup may be possible if an adult steadies both of a child's forearms. The adults' actions are said to be 'scaffolding' the activity and helping the child to achieve. By working from existing abilities and strengths, the adult can 'scaffold' activities and support the child in experiencing new and more complex skills that might eventually be mastered independently.

This strategy for learning occurs in typical development when children experiment with emerging skills in play situations before they are integrated into their independent repertoire. To assist in this process, a therapist must have an in-depth knowledge of typical development and be creative in guiding parents and others in how to facilitate new skills. For example, it might be necessary to use the behavioural techniques of physical prompting and modelling to help a child towards independent self-pretend play.

Promote use of available language for a variety of functions

It is important to broaden the functional use of language at any one level – for example, at a one-word/sign/symbol level. Opportunities need to be created to allow a child to request, refuse, comment, question, label and initiate in order to increase success in interaction and exploit a limited lexicon.

Facilitate a child to obtain motivating materials

Planning strategies to achieve goals must include consideration of what is motivating for an individual child. Learning to sign to pictures and receiving verbal praise from a therapist is likely to be less motivating than being able to ask for – and get – a favourite toy, cake or activity. This is an important factor when deciding on vocabulary selection and will influence the rate of vocabulary acquisition and use.

Recognise a child's preferred learning style

At the beginning of a programme of intervention, it will be important to work with a child in his or her preferred learning style. For example, a child might be unable to take the initiative in play if an over-directive, behavioural style has been used at home or in a nursery setting. It might be necessary to be directive initially in order to engage the child.

Verbal cues may then gradually be withdrawn, while non-verbal cues are maintained. Eventually, all cues are withdrawn until independent play is established. However, it is usually necessary to use both naturalistic and behavioural approaches to optimise learning within a child's zone of proximal development as outlined above.

Allow a child to be directive rather than passive

As a result of delayed patterns of early interaction, many children with SLD tend to take a passive role in interactions, while parental language tends to be more directive. It is important for the development of communication that children learn how to be active participants. An approach using video analysis can promote this change by identifying how and when an adult can follow a child's lead in play and in conversations. The Hanen Early Language Parent Programme (Girolametto *et al.* 1986) is based on this transactional approach. However, any approach that involves advice on changing an already established parental style of interaction must be sensitively handled in view of both the emotions involved and any differing cultural perspectives. (See also Chapters 5 and 16.)

Supply an environment that supports a child's communication style

An ongoing issue in the use of keyword signs and/or symbols is the low level of spontaneous use. There are a number of potential reasons for this, but one of them is how often children observe others using the same communication style as themselves. The typical pattern is that of speech as the primary input/receptive mode and manual signs or graphic symbols as the primary output/expressive mode (Grove and Smith 1997). When children and adults with SLD are in environments where the staff and others around them are using AAC, their own use increases (Powell 1999).

In terms of social learning theory (Bandura 1977), if children are unable to observe others using language as they do, this learning opportunity is denied and may constrain development and maintain the current developmental level. For therapists, this has implications for training others and is an important part of the role of creating optimum communication environments.

Critical periods for optimal language learning

The concept of critical periods for optimal language learning is supported by a nativist approach that rests on there being biologically determined periods that are particularly sensitive for development. A number of critical periods have been proposed for language acquisition, which may affect prioritisation of intervention (Rondal and Edwards 1997).

While vocabulary and pragmatic skills may be acquired well beyond adolescence, this does not appear to be the case for syntax in either spoken or sign languages, which are optimally acquired before the age of 8. A decline in the plasticity for phonological learning – the ability of the brain to establish optimal neural connections – after the age of 7 has also been suggested. This might indicate that intervention in this area should occur early if the best outcomes are to be attained.

As children with SLD often have poor speech and minimal expressive language skills at the end of the critical period for first language learning (Fowler 1990), there are implications for the timeliness of programmes addressing different aspects of language development.

Summary

The content of this chapter has attempted to highlight some of the issues that might influence the decision-making process in the assessment and management of children with SLD where this might differ from other client groups.

CHAPTER 22

Children with acquired speech and language problems

Janet Lees

Learning outcomes

By the end of this chapter, the reader should understand:
- the distinction between developmental and acquired speech and language problems (ASLP) in childhood;
- some of the models relevant to managing children with ASLP;
- the main causes of ASLP in childhood;
- how to select assessment tools appropriate for children with ASLP;
- the main issues facing the speech and language therapist working with children with ASLP.

Introduction

This chapter is about speech and language problems that are secondary to cerebral dysfunction, arising in childhood after a period of normal development. They are called acquired speech and language problems (ASLP).

Normal development proceeds as a result of cerebral maturation, and developmental disorders are a result of a delay or disorder in that maturation, the causes of which have been shown to be environmental or biological in origin. Acquired speech and language disorders, most commonly encountered when working with adult clients, are typically the result of an interruption to normal cerebral functioning. Thus, children, irrespective of age, will be said to have an acquired disorder if normal cerebral functioning is interrupted after it has been established, however briefly.

There has traditionally been a split in the way in which professionals work with people with communication disorders. Developmental disorders have always been seen as the domain of the paediatric speech and language therapist, and acquired disorders are the concern of those therapists working with adults. Children with ASLP, or acquired aphasia (loss of language) have been the concern mainly of those working in specialist locations and those who have developed specialist skills in the area.

Developmental disorders may persist throughout a life span, and acquired disorders may occur at any stage. It is important to understand how and why developmental and acquired disorders differ, particularly for different age groups.

Epidemiology

Developmental problems dominate the speech and language therapist's work with children. Each child is born with a certain developmental potential. It is the development of this potential that is the focus of attention during childhood. Acquired problems are rare in the first 20 years of life. However, more recently there has been a general increase in the chances of having an acquired basis for a communication problem during the second decade, where head injury is the commonest cause of acquired problems for those under 20. There are no epidemiological data concerning developmental versus acquired communication problems in childhood. The only UK figures, by Robinson (1991), suggests that acquired aphasias accounts for less than 10 per cent of the language problems presenting in childhood.

These figures also point to a 'grey area' somewhere between developmental and acquired problems. Indeed, clinically it can be difficult to answer the question 'When is a problem an acquired problem?' For example, the origin of the language problem was uncertain for approximately 7 per cent of Robinson's (1991) sample. Included in the sample were children who had an incident within either the first or second year of life, which was later thought to have contributed to their communication problem. It also included children who clearly had delayed development but who later lost some of their skills gradually or suddenly. This 'greyness' in diagnosis contributes to the complexity of managing children with ASLP.

Furthermore, epidemiology of ASLP is a changing field. There has been a fall in some types of cerebral infections, as a result of effective immunisation programmes in the UK that have led to changes in morbidity and mortality in some 'at risk' groups. In other parts of the world, a different pathogenesis occurs, such as the role of cerebral malaria as a cause of ASLP in Kenya.

Models

There are a number of different models that can be used to understand the effects on a child of an ASLP. When planning services for children who have ASLP and their families, it is preferable to work in a way that draws on all of these models in order to get a holistic picture of the child.

In this chapter, the following three models will be used interactively:

- A *medical model* emphasises the malfunctioning of a particular body system and the nature of the impairment that results. The model enables a therapist to appreciate the causes of impairments and the types of cerebral dysfunction that usually underlie these.
- A *psycholinguistic model* emphasises what had gone wrong in the linguistic process (Stackhouse and Wells 1997) and enables the development of working hypotheses, which can be tested clinically. This model can be used to demonstrate ways in which speech and language processing difficulties can be assessed and managed.
- A *social model,* in which children are viewed within context in order to understand the effect of the communication impairment on their functioning. Each child's context is fundamental to the rehabilitation process, and this model enables discussion of important contextual questions in the management of children with acquired aphasias.

Causes of acquired aphasia in childhood

The brain is the vital organ in the processing of language, speech and communication. It is particularly vulnerable during childhood. It used to be thought that children were relatively resistant to long-term speech and language difficulties after early brain injury, but more recent evidence has led to different conclusions. It is now thought that significant brain injury is likely to have long-term consequences for a child at any age. The severity and duration of these consequences are dependent on several factors, which cannot yet be mapped precisely to outcome.

Furthermore, there are a number of different disease processes that can affect the brain during childhood and lead to an acquired aphasia. These do not necessarily result in the same types of speech and language problems, or problems that have the same duration or prognosis. This is because the disease processes themselves affect the brain tissue in different ways and also because the brain will have reached a different level of maturation depending roughly on age.

There is a distinction between a condition that has an acute onset and one that has a chronic onset. In the first, the child presents with symptoms straight away, or very quickly; in the second, the symptoms are slower to emerge, perhaps being preceded by a period of developmental regression or loss of skills over several weeks or months. The main causes of acquired aphasias in childhood and some of the ensuing problems and prognoses have been summarised in Table 22.1; see also Lees and Urwin (1997), Lees (1993a).

Table 22.1 Causes, problems and prognoses of acquired aphasias

Cause	Damage	Problems	Prognosis
Head injury open/closed	Diffuse and bilateral. May be combined with additional focal damage.	May include motor, cognitive and sensory deficits. Epilepsy may be a sequela.	Poor if initial aphasia very severe and persists for 6+ months. Acquisition of written language may be impaired.
Unilateral cerebrovascular lesions	Usually focal.	Visual field defects; hemiplegia may also occur. Epilepsy may be a sequela.	Good, if there is a return to within 2 std deviations for a verbal comprehension score within 6 months of onset.
Cerebral infections: meningitis, encephalitis, cerebral abscess	Ranges from diffuse to focal depending on aetiology and response to treatment.	Additional motor, cognitive and sensory deficits are common in severe cases.	Where damage is cortical, the aphasia is usually moderate to mild.
Cerebral tumour	Usually focal; disruption of wider cerebral function possible if tumour extends or after the effects of some treatment.	An initial delayed period of mutism is common after surgery for some posterior fossa tumours. Epilepsy may be a sequela.	Additional treatments (radiotherapy /chemotherapy) can affect the prognosis for speech and language abilities.
Epileptic aphasia	Aphasia may occur as a consequence of convulsive status.	Learning problems may occur, particularly after long and repeated convulsive status.	Language disturbance is variable.
Landau–Kleffner syndrome	May be preceded or followed by epilepsy.	Severe receptive aphasia.	Variable: see Lees 1993a.
Retts syndrome	Developmental disorder: motor and cognitive skills lost between 6 and 12 months. All known cases are girls.	Inappropriate social interaction, slowing of head growth, severe communication difficulties, abnormal oral movements.	No known recovery.

Focal versus diffuse injury

The damage to brain tissue can be described as 'focal' or 'diffuse', and each of these terms is used in Table 22.1 to describe the likely damage occurring from specified causes. As is clear from the table, whether damage is focal or diffuse will depend on the sort of injury a child has received. Focal injury is localised and usually lateralised, involving only one cerebral hemisphere. Diffuse injury is more widespread and can be bilateral. Subsequent injury might arise from oedema (swelling), from neurosurgery undertaken to help stabilise the condition, or from seizure activity that is secondary to the injury.

Focal brain injury is likely to have different consequences from diffuse injury. After focal injury, specific impairments are likely as a result of underlying damage. For example, a kick by a horse to the left side of the head of a 14-year-old girl above the ear is reported to have led to non-fluent aphasia with severe word-finding difficulties. A non-fluent aphasia is characterised by telegrammatic sentences, where small function words and unstressed morphemes may be omitted and where the style is hesitant. In fluent aphasia there is a larger volume of words in the flow of speech, although sentences may not be completely grammatical or semantically correct.

Diffuse injury is more likely to result in non-specific difficulties in speech and in the amount of information that can be processed and recalled. Alternatively, it may lead to high-level deficits of metalinguistic skills, resulting in misunderstanding or misuse of prosodic features such as stress to mark grammatical differences between sentences. For example, a 16-year-old boy, three years after a severe head injury, seemed to have made a good recovery except for a continuing difficulty in distinguishing between question and exclamatory forms of similar sentences.

Prognosis

There are many factors that affect prognosis and consequently that will affect the decisions made about management. These include:

- age at injury;
- extent/severity of injury;
- developmental level/status before injury;
- profile and severity of initial communication deficit;
- extent of initial recovery;
- access to services/resources for rehabilitation.

It was thought that the younger a person was when he or she had a brain injury, the better this was for prognosis. This view has been seriously challenged and it is now clear that 'younger is not better'. Rose and Johnson (1996) state: 'The inherent vulnerability of the brain is greatest during its first 16 years or so of development, with the frontal lobes of the brain not maturing until adolescence.' Once there has been brain injury, the brain has indeed been damaged even though it does appear to have remarkable capacities to recover and reorganise.

Children who sustained a brain injury when they were very young may appear to do better in some domains of function but lose out in others, such as the acquisition of more complex, highly integrated and flexible functioning. Furthermore, Rose and Johnson add that 'recent studies have suggested that not all professionals concerned with brain injury are aware of, or guided by, the available scientific information regarding age and vulnerability' (1996: 186). It is important to measure the extent or severity of injury and to try to establish the level of functioning prior to the injury. However, this may be difficult to establish – although school records, family videos and discussion with appropriate relatives and friends may help.

Profiling the severity of initial communication difficulty can only be partial, and a comprehensive profile will need to be built up during the course of recovery. A multidimensional scoring system such as that used in the Paediatric Oral Skills Package (POSP; Brindley *et al.* 1996) will show how a child functions and where progress is occurring. Even so, most children with an ASLP go through a short burst of initial recovery that, for some at least, will take them back to functioning within the normal range. When this happens it does not mean that the child's recovery will be trouble-free or that later problems may not become apparent, especially where more complex learning is concerned.

However, the most contentious and under-researched aspect of recovery from ASLP is the contribution of rehabilitation or therapy. There are only a few single case studies available worldwide; moreover, access to specialist rehabilitation centres is often difficult to gain, and these are not spread uniformly across the UK. A number of voluntary support networks have sprung up to provide information in what, for most families, often prove to be difficult circumstances. The most well-known are Afasic, CHIT (Children's Head Injury Trust) and FOLKS (Friends of Landau–Kleffner Syndrome).

When considering prognosis, it is important to remember that significant residual problems may persist for at least two years for children who are between 2 and 15 years of age at the time of onset of the aphasia. Even mild residual deficits can cause significant problems – often quite specific ones, particularly those affecting the speed and amount of processing or recall. For example, a 13-year-old girl is known to have made an excellent recovery in terms of formal language test scores but continued to have auditory processing difficulties three years after her stroke; this made classroom learning difficult for her (Lees 1997).

The extent to which a difficulty is of significance to a child – and therefore influences management decisions – depends on a variety of factors, such as the presence of linked residual deficits. These include epilepsy, behavioural problems and other learning difficulties. In an unpublished study by Kirkham *et al.* 1990 of 34 children surviving coma, it was found that linked residual deficits were more commonly encountered in children who went on to have special educational needs. The coping characteristics of the individual and family and the rehabilitation resources available are also important factors. It is, therefore, important to describe in detail children's communication skills, including their strengths and weaknesses, rather than using labels that might not adequately summarise the difficulties.

Assessment and management

According to Coombes (1987), there are four questions that each therapist thinks about at the beginning of a consultation:

* How do you know what to do?
* What do you do?
* When do you do it?
* When do you stop?

Each of these is considered in more depth in this section.

How do you know what to do?

On referral, all children need to be assessed in order to establish the areas of difficulties and each child's strengths, from which intervention may be planned. However, before beginning an assessment, the speech and language therapist needs to know about the nature and characteristics of acquired communication problems in children and the type of progress that can be expected. The therapist also needs to know about the strengths and weaknesses of different assessment approaches (see Lees 1993c) and a wide range of assessment materials. Assessment is normally ongoing throughout the therapist's involvement with a child because it also includes information about the child's progress with treatment, whether the child's problems have been resolved, and whether new problems can be identified.

Acquired communication difficulties arising from a disruption in cerebral function can be divided into three main groups:

* language disorders;
* speech disorders;
* social communication disorders.

Assessment approaches may be formal or informal. The strengths and weaknesses of these two approaches are reviewed by Lees (1993c) and a wide range of assessment materials have been reviewed by Lees and Urwin (1997). For children with acquired aphasias it is generally true that, in the very early stages of the disorder, informal methods may be more useful than formal.

There are few formal assessments designed for use with children with acquired problems. An assessment with a multidimensional scoring system (POSP) is probably more use in long-term management than one with a plus/minus scoring system such as the Reynell Developmental Language Scales III (Edwards *et al.* 1997), which involves only one level of scoring. In the RDLS, the number of correct responses forms the raw score, which is related to normal data that have been collected from the general population to show how the child compares.

Most other speech and language assessments for children use such a plus/minus scoring system. It may be possible to determine from the pattern of errors which sections of the test cause the child most difficulty and thereby which aspects of speech and language are most affected. However, such a system does little to help the assessor understand what other problems may be contributing to low scores – problems such as poor attention, motor difficulties, or slow response time.

The main advocate for multidimensional scoring was Porch. In his Porch Index of Communicative Ability in Children (1972), the 16-point multidimensional scoring system provided a systematic way of analysing a child's response style. This gives further insight into why the child gets an item wrong.

In some assessments, the importance of understanding what makes children fail the test is recognised. Bishop (1989) provides a vocabulary checklist in the Test for Reception of Grammar (TROG) to ensure that children are not seen as having grammatical problems when it is the vocabulary content of the sentences that is causing the difficulty. Bishop also identifies two other types of responses for which it is important not to penalise children: the slow response, and a child's need for an item to be repeated.

Lees and Urwin (1997) describe a simple qualitative scoring system that can be used alongside tests to note when responses are delayed but accurate, or accurate after requested repetition, or self-corrected. Furthermore, German (1989) includes information about patterns of response in her Test of Word Finding, recognising that patterns of cueing and delay are important in understanding children's lexical recall problems and developing a treatment hypothesis. Again, a correct or incorrect response will only provide so much information about a child's naming problems. Naming difficulties may include different kinds of paraphasia (naming errors) such as those related semantically or phonemically to the target item as well as unrelated strings of phonemes (neologisms). Naming may be helped with gestural self-cueing or, for example, when phonemic cues are provided. This can help to generate treatment hypotheses based on suggestions about how a child's lexicon is organised and accessed. Knowing how a response relates to the target response is, therefore, as important as knowing whether the response is correct or not.

Language problems (aphasias)

Children with ASLP display a range of language difficulties, described below. For a more detailed review of the subtypes of language difficulty, see Lees (1993b). The difficulties can manifest themselves thus:

- both nonfluent and fluent aphasias occur in children with acquired disorders, although the former is more common;
- paraphasias, lexical organisation and naming problems can be persistent;
- comprehension and auditory processing problems occur in the majority of children with ASLP;
- written language problems are a more likely consequence of cerebral damage occurring before age five years.

When carrying out an initial assessment of language problems in the acute stage, it is important for a speech and language therapist to establish which skills have been affected and how. The Children's Aphasia Screening Test (Whurr and Evans 1995) or the Derbyshire Language Scheme (Knowles and Masidlover 1982) can form the basis of such a 'bedside' assessment of communication skills in the early stages of recovery. As with any child, it is important to establish how other skills such as play and non-verbal communication are affected.

Following the acute stage, during each of the stages of recovery the clinician will need to decide which tests to use to establish a profile of language skills. Some may use a battery that covers many subskills, such as CELF – 3UK (Semel *et al.* 2000) or the preschool version (Wiig *et al.* 2000). Others may prefer individual tests that tap particular skills, as described by Lees (1993a and 1993c). Some may prefer the TROG (Bishop 1989) and the Test of Word Finding (German 1989). Psycholinguistic profiling techniques (Stackhouse and Wells 1997) may also be used.

Speech problems (dysarthrias)

It should be noted that:

- dysarthrias arise in some conditions more often than in others (for example, when injury or dysfunction of the cerebellum is indicated, after surgery to remove tumours in the fourth ventricle, or after a head injury at the base of the back of the skull);
- they can co-occur with aphasias or other cognitive deficits;
- they can co-occur with swallowing problems (dysphagia; see Chapter 24).

Most approaches to motor speech problems in children are informal, and a structured approach as outlined in POSP (Brindley *et al.* 1996) might be useful.

Objective assessment may be difficult with children who have acquired motor speech problems because compliance can be difficult. Nasoendoscopy may be available for viewing palatal movement (see Chapter 19); and for those who have associated dysphagia difficulties, videofluoroscopy has become invaluable.

Social communication disorders or autism

Acquired autistic symptoms have been reported as resulting from a range of neurological diseases after three years of age, including a 14-year-old girl who had herpes simplex encephalitis (Gillberg and Coleman 1992).

A scale is being developed by the Epilepsy Research Team at Great Ormond Street Hospital London, UK, in order to compare developmental levels with the extent of interference by social communication deficit in the treatment of children with epileptic aphasias. This includes early-onset Landau–Kleffner Syndrome. The scale has demonstrated improvement in 52 per cent of a group of 20 such children treated with antiepileptic drugs, including steroids.

A number of more formalised scales can be used to assess social communication, including The Checklist of Everyday Communication Skills by Dewart and Summers (1995).

What do you do?

Few specific intervention techniques have been reported for children with ASLP, although single case studies such as Vance (1991 and 1997) provide useful information. In summary:

* AAC (see Chapter 23), which involves sign and symbol languages, pictures, objects and communication aids, and which may develop into a total communication approach where all modes of communication are used in a 24-hour programme (Vance 1991);
* a psycholinguistic framework for speech, reading and spelling difficulties (Vance 1997);
* structured grammatical training: the John Lea Colour Scheme (Lea 1970) and Language Through Reading (see Vance 1991).

As with other client groups, parents and professionals need to work in partnership. Therapists working with children who have acquired problems must be prepared to listen, to explain their philosophy, and to modify their approach. The three issues that are most commonly raised during the rehabilitation of a child with an ASLP are:

* the use of non-verbal communication which may or may not lead on to more formalised AAC therapy;
* the benefits of individual versus group therapy (see Chapter 4);
* the variation in methods used by different speech and language therapists.

Some families see the introduction of AAC as a sign that verbal language will not be regained or may not be seriously pursued as a therapy option. There is often a social stigma attached to the use of such methods of communication. Therapists need to explain the benefits that children may derive from the use of such communicative methods.

Equally, the different benefits to be gained from group or individual therapy need to be explained. Communication is a social activity, and spending therapy time in groups of different sizes might be a more natural way of developing aspects of communication.

It can be confusing for both child and family when changes in personnel mean that therapy also changes for no apparent reason. Different methods of managing particular speech and language difficulties should be acknowledged and discussed with everyone involved, so that informed decisions can be made.

When do you do it?

Lees and Urwin (1997) recommend that, for the speech and language therapy given to children with ASLP:

- it should begin early;
- it should be intensive;
- it should be specific to the child's needs;
- it should be structured rather than just involving general language-stimulation principles;
- it should be consistent;
- it should be built on the child's success.

Some professionals advocate that a child with ASLP does not need structured intervention until the period of rapid recovery is over and the situation has stabilised, so that residual deficits are more apparent. Yet loss of communication skills can be seen to be catastrophic to a child and to the family. Reactions to this loss can vary, and those observed have included selective mutism. Early intervention by a speech and language therapist should aim to support the child and the family in relation to the communication loss. The exploration of modes and methods of communication which are functional for the child and family are important in this phase, even if they are used as a temporary measure. Part of the therapist's role is to raise the awareness of communication skills and strategies of all those involved in working with the child.

Dysphagia

Where dysphagia presents as part of the initial problem, a specialist paediatric dysphagia therapist needs to be involved. Such a specialist can help in establishing the extent and severity of the problem and advising about management – for example, the type of feeding and the type of food. Most specialist dysphagia therapists work as part of a dysphagia team, which will also include other specialists such as a dietician and psychologist (see Chapter 24).

When do you stop?

A child's need for therapy will change and develop as a result of:

- the course of recovery;
- changes due to drug treatment or surgery;
- changes due to developmental progress;
- changes due to social situation.

There are three phases in recovery from an acquired aphasia in childhood: acute, steady progress, and plateau (see also Lees 1993a). The length of each phase will vary depending on the child, the cause of the aphasia and its severity, and so it is not possible to say how long each phase will last. The two main variables are the speed at which the child's communication skills change and how quickly goals are reached. The main decision-making issues at each phase need to be based on comprehensive observation and discussion with the parents and the child.

There is no age limit regarding such children's need for therapy, which may persist into the transition to adulthood. The problems specific to those whose communication problems began in childhood need to be understood by those who provide services to adult clients.

Summary

By now it will be clear that ASLPs pose particular difficulties to the child, the family and those professionals involved in the rehabilitation. Some progress has been made in managing this client group but it is a rapidly changing field in which the practitioner needs to keep abreast of current research. The less common nature of these problems for most therapists makes them challenging and means teamwork is particularly important.

CHAPTER 23

Augmentative and alternative communication

Mike Clarke, Katie Price and Nicola Jolleff

Learning outcomes

By the end of this chapter, the reader should:

- have a basic understanding of different types of augmentative and alternative communication (AAC) systems;
- understand who can benefit from AAC;
- have an understanding of historical perspectives in assessment in AAC;
- be able to identify factors to consider in assessment of children and their environment.

Introduction

Terry is an Arsenal fan. He is nine years old and has dystonic cerebral palsy, which affects his whole body. He uses an attendant-propelled wheelchair to move around. His speech is severely affected by his motor difficulties: he is only intelligible to people who know him well, and when he is speaking on a known topic. He uses gesture and facial expression to support his speech. He has a chart of printed symbols and pictures, and has recently had access to a voice output communication aid (VOCA). He is unable to use his VOCA effectively with his hands, and so he operates it through switches mounted in the headrest of his wheelchair.

Sian is 7. She loves pop music. She has mild four-limb cerebral palsy. Her muscles for speech and feeding are severely affected. She can produce a range of vowel sounds, but has extreme difficulty generating any other speech sounds. She can walk independently. She communicates using a combination of speech, Makaton manual signs, facial expression, and a book of graphic symbols and pictures. The book is fairly large now, and Sian complains that it is too heavy to carry around school.

What is augmentative and alternative communication?

The children in the previous two example cases use AAC systems to support their natural communication skills. AAC is a generic term used to describe any mode or channel of communication that replaces or supports speech and/or writing. Traditionally, AAC is broadly categorised in terms of signs and symbols. Signs refer to manual signs such as those used in sign languages by deaf speakers. The term 'symbol' is usually used to refer to a graphic representation of meaning other than the written word. These symbols may be pictorial or iconic, such as the symbols used in everyday situations to show 'No Smoking', 'Fire exit this way' or 'One Way'. AAC, then, is fundamentally concerned with symbolic representation of meaning by modes other than speech and may be used in support of speech and/or writing.

In this chapter, issues will be considered concerning the introduction of AAC systems for children, as well as approaches to the assessment of children already using AAC systems. Current viewpoints on assessment and management are considered in the light of changing theoretical perspectives. The chapter is principally concerned with the introduction and use of symbols and pictures, rather than manual signs and objects, although these will be referred to where appropriate. For discussion of manual signs, readers are referred to Kyle (1987); similarly, for discussion of tangible signs (objects), see Park (1995).

Symbols

Symbols tend to fall into two categories, symbol sets and symbol systems (McNaughton 1985; Johnson 1992; Clark 1981; Walker *et al.* 1985; Baker 1982).

A symbol set is a vocabulary or lexicon of symbols. Published symbol sets used commonly with children in the UK include Picture Communication Symbols (PCS) or Mayer-Johnson Symbols, Rebus symbols and Makaton symbols. Symbol sets tend to be pictographic – see Figure 23.1 for an example.

Figure 23.1: PCS symbols 'Do you know what's on TV tonight?'

Symbol systems such as Blisssymbols (McNaughton 1985) go some way to representing language. The symbol system has its own 'phonology' and 'grammar', since symbol elements are repeated with consistent meaning in different combinations. For example, the three-element Blissymbol shown in Figure 23.2 comprises 'to lead, a person, to knowledge'. Its summary meaning is understood as 'to introduce'.

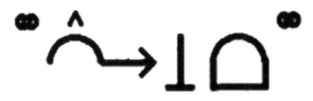

Figure 23.2 Blissymbol for 'to introduce'

Types of communication aid

Communication aids are conventionally categorised as high-tech and low-tech systems. High-tech systems are electronic communication devices, speech synthesisers or VOCAs. They may use digitised voice, which has been recorded onto the device by an adult or friend and stored digitally, or a synthesised artificially-created voice. Low-tech systems are paper systems – that is, books and charts of symbols and pictures. Children using VOCAs will almost invariably also require a low-tech system, not least because machines can go wrong.

Who can benefit from AAC?

Clinical consensus suggests that significant numbers of children with motor impairments affecting oro-motor musculature, such as cerebral palsy or severe dyspraxia, are likely to experience difficulties developing functional intelligibility. This can often be true, even after positive changes to speech through therapy and changes resulting from maturation. Consequently, AAC has been most strongly associated with children with physical impairments – either developmental or acquired – and a poor prognosis for speech.

However, there is growing evidence that AAC strategies also have a place in supporting language development. This includes verbal understanding (Weitz *et al.* 1997), as well as the development of literacy skills (see *Topics in Language Disorders* 1993) and supporting communication for children with autism (Peterson *et al.* 1995).

AAC is, therefore, no longer considered the 'last chance' for children with chronic speech impairments. In addition, the work of McConachie *et al.* (1998) has dispelled the myth that AAC systems suppress the development of speech and has highlighted AAC as an option for many children who are not traditionally associated with forms of alternative communication. Essentially, AAC systems offer support to children who experience a discrepancy between their understanding of language and their ability to express themselves.

Historical perspectives

Assessment theory

Case example
Jeremy has a girlfriend. He says she asked him out, but she says Jeremy asked first. At school he is learning to use a symbol chart in class. He points to symbols to ask questions and contribute to group discussions, and his LSA relays his words to the group. He is also learning to use a VOCA and he enjoys using it to tell jokes. He says he does not need symbols to chat to his girlfriend; he says he does that best with speech and gestures. He also says he does not use symbols much at break. He only wants to play wheelchair football then. At home, Jeremy's mother understands his speech and so they do not use symbols, but he does use his VOCA to play 'Battleships' with his father.

The field of AAC is relatively new. Developments in assessment theory mirror changes observed in the approach to assessment and management of communication difficulties in children generally. Essentially, perspectives on assessment have shifted from a reductionist approach to an approach based on an holistic view of the children and their environment. Assessment theory has moved away from an insistence on developmental criteria as prerequisites to AAC options, to employing a developmental perspective as a guideline for introducing AAC options at an appropriate level. It has also moved away from considering the child as an impaired individual, to viewing the child as an active co-participant in interaction.

The developmental model

Historically, decision making concerning AAC options was founded on a detailed understanding of the child's developmental status. Agreed developmental criteria were used as the staging posts for the introduction of AAC systems. For instance, children who had not yet developed an understanding of cause and effect – a skill seen as essential for effective use of symbols – would undergo training in this before an AAC system was to be introduced. Critics of the developmental perspective of impairment viewed it as an unwarranted gate-keeping approach to AAC systems and functional communication. Instead, they believed that AAC systems should be employed as tools in the development of cognitive, communicative and physical skills. This approach would reflect more accurately the communication learning patterns of typically developing children.

Thus, by using communication, children can develop an understanding of their effect on the environment. This shift in approach is summarised in the description of the Communication Needs Model: 'In time, the concept of prerequisite skills was abandoned and interventions were organised to match the individual's needs and capabilities for today while building future capabilities for tomorrow' (Beukelman and Mirenda 1992: 100). Indeed, clinicians now employ a developmental perspective as a guideline for introducing AAC options at an appropriate level for the child's skills and interests at the time of assessment, rather than excluding discussion of AAC options if certain developmental criteria are not met.

From impaired individual to active co-participant

Historically, assessment concentrated on the individual child as the focal point of intervention. However, speech and language develops within naturally occurring interactions. For children with physical disability, the communication messages imparted often have to be co-constructed, so that the listener has as much responsibility for establishing successful communication as does the non-speaking child.

Research concerning interaction between adults and children with physical impairments using symbol systems has revealed distinctive patterns of interaction. For instance, speaking adults are inclined to take more turns, control and maintain a topic, ask yes/no questions, and fill the gaps in a conversation; and adults are often concerned with a particular conversational goal. Conversely, physically impaired children often take passive roles, rarely initiating interaction, often communicating single items of information and rarely requesting clarification in conversation (Pennington and McConachie 1999; Light *et al.* 1985a, 1985b and 1985c). For children using AAC systems, it is apparent that the characteristics of interaction differ from those observed between natural speakers. Assessment has consequently evolved to include an understanding of the child in context and his or her communication partners.

Assessment

Assessment objective

Assessment can aim to achieve several different objectives, including: an appraisal of strengths/needs; finding out what a child might want to talk about; changing the way a child communicates; testing language comprehension; identifying goals; finding out what the teacher needs; and choosing the right VOCA.

Assessment is a complex, diverse and continual process. The next subsection looks at this process in terms of gathering information, observation, testing and decision making, speech and language assessment, and implications for decision making. The speech and language therapist's role is often to draw all this information together.

Assessment as the collation of information

For some children, particularly those with more severe physical involvement and complex needs, it is necessary to gather appropriate information from anyone with an interest in the child's communication strengths and needs. These are likely to include the child, their friends and family, school staff, community medical teams and information from specialist services. A team approach is valuable when working with such children, and the team may comprise an occupational therapist, a paediatrician, a rehabilitation engineer and a psychologist as well as a speech and language therapist. The assessment may take place at the child's school and/or home, although it may not be possible to assemble all the team together at any one time.

The child in context

Assessment must include an understanding of children in their context. This includes identifying all those involved. In Jeremy's case, for instance, they might have varied ideas about his needs. His teacher might want him to be able to access the National Curriculum more effectively by answering questions on the science topic for the term, covering batteries, axles and engines. His LSA might want to know how to programme his VOCA. His speech and language therapist might feel that he would benefit from some training in managing extended turns in conversation. Jeremy's mother does not use symbols at home and his father might like him to be working on accessing the spelling facility on his VOCA. Jeremy, however, wants to tell jokes and play football.

A speech and language therapist is likely to have a coordinating role in assessment and treatment. This coordination may involve the use of negotiation strategies (Dale 1996), negotiating effective partnerships with the family and professionals to gain consensus in relation to assessment of developing skills and changing priorities for therapy. The therapist may find that the consultative model is a powerful one in working towards effective use of AAC equipment and strategies (see Chapter 11). It allows the child's own role in decision-making to be acknowledged, the necessity and value of which has been recognised by government departments (DoH 1991).

General health issues

Success in assessment and, ultimately, in the use of AAC systems will be influenced by a child's level of general health and well-being. It is not easy to study and work when you feel unwell or are in pain, and children with physical disability are vulnerable to a number of conditions that can give rise to discomfort and pain. For example, the incidence of gastro-oesophageal reflux, a painful and often chronic condition whereby the acid contents of the stomach pass back up into the oesophagus, has been observed in as many as 75 per cent of children with central nervous system damage (Sondheimer and Morris 1979).

It will be important to consider general medical issues in partnership with a child's GP, community paediatrician or school doctor; moreover, in particular, speech and language therapists will be aware of the significance of any feeding difficulties (see Chapter 24). Below are some observations that may be made by a therapist which may contribute to the identification of conditions that can restrict a child's progress with communication and learning.

Questions a therapist might wish to ask

- Does this child look well nourished? What is the child's current nutritional status? Does the child have a history of aspiration – the passage of food and/or liquid into the lungs?
- Does the child have a history of gastro-oesophageal reflux? What is their current status? Difficulties might be indicated by crying without obvious cause, repeated periods of coughing, not necessarily at meal times, and poor sleeping patterns.
- Does the child have constipation? Dehydration can be a serious problem for many children with physical disabilities. Dehydration leads to many complications, including constipation and subsequent pain.
- Does the child have a history of epilepsy? What is their current status?

Sensory impairments

Many of the systems and approaches used in AAC are based on visual skills. It will therefore be important to make a careful appraisal of a child's visual abilities, with reference particularly to his or her near vision, and scanning skills. Again, this assessment is likely to involve input from several sources and necessitate the collation of information by the speech and language therapist to ensure that a full picture of the child's visual skills is available to all team members.

The argument for the assessment of hearing is similarly important, as is the importance and value of an accurate understanding of the child's general intellectual or cognitive abilities. Such an assessment will involve staff with skills, knowledge and experience of this group of children. A general sense of the child's level of intellectual ability can be gleaned through discussion with parents and school staff. What are his or her interests? What do they enjoy playing with? What do they enjoy watching most on television? How is he or she coping with school work?

If the child is of school age, and has a Statement, the annual review document will prove an excellent source for this type of information. In addition, the local educational psychology services may hold a record of the child's achievement in assessments of intellectual functioning.

Decision making based on assessment

The following is a guide to assessment and decision making (adapted from Jones *et al.* 1990) concerning sensory impairments, physical abilities and accessing skills.

Decisions on sensory impairments

See Tables 23.1–3 for details of the decisions likely to be made in relation to vision, oculomotor abilities and hearing.

Table 23.1 Decisions on vision

Status		Decision
Normal vision	→	No amendments to standard symbol systems/sets required
Restricted visual field	→	Position assessment materials and symbols within known visual field
Poor visual acuity	→	(a) Position assessment materials and symbols for best light access
	→	(b) Consider clarity of visual presentation, e.g. black/white contrast rather than colour
	→	(c) Position symbols and materials on an angled board

Table 23.2 Decisions on oculo-motor abilities

Status		Decision
Scans in all directions	→	No amendments to standard symbol systems/sets required
Scans most reliably horizontally or vertically	→	(a) Consider the design of a symbol layout (b) Set the scanning mode on a VOCA to match child's strength
Difficulty scanning in any direction	→	Consider the speed of scanning on an automatic communication aid, ensure those working with the child are aware of this difficulty and employ strategies to compensate

Table 23.3 Decisions on hearing

Status		Decision
Normal hearing	→	No amendments to standard symbol systems/sets required
Partial hearing loss	→	Consider the use of symbols in aiding comprehension of language
Severe hearing loss	→	(a) In the absence of marked physical difficulties, consider using a signing system (b) If using VOCA, consider the use of visual feedback

Decisions on physical skills

Children need to be in a stable, comfortable and relaxed seating position, in order for them to maximise their function and reduce their chances of developing structural deformity. Tables setting out possible decisions in relation to mobility and posture appear as Tables 23.4 and 23.5 respectively.

Table 23.4 Decisions on mobility

Status		Decision
Walking independently	→	Any symbol system/set must be light and easy to carry
Aided walking	→	Consider the portability of the VOCA. Can it be attached to a walking aid?
Wheelchair user (pushed by another)	→	(a) Consider how the VOCA will be mounted on the chair (b) Consider visual acuity, oculo-motor skills and postural seating with respect to mounting the VOCA
Powered wheelchair	→	Think about an integrated system to control a VOCA, with environmental user-control and mobility via one accessing device (e.g. joystick, 4-switch scanning)

Table 23.5 Decisions on posture

Status		Decision
Sits independently	→	Ensure the child's resting position is stable and relaxed
Sits with support	→	(a) Ensure the child is aligned and supported appropriately b) VOCA must be positioned to take account of resting/seating position

Decisions on accessing symbol systems

Clearly, children need to be able to access their symbol systems to use them. Methods of accessing communication aids can be classified as 'direct' or 'indirect'.

Direct access means:

- pointing with eyes, a finger, or a fist to a symbol on a chart;
- pressing a symbol on a touch screen VOCA;
- using a light-pointer – which may, for example, be mounted on a headband – so as to activate symbols on a VOCA or point to a chart.

For children with more involved physical difficulties, any reliable and repeatable physical movement may be used to access one or more switches. This is indirect access to equipment, and is usually a much slower option for access. Switches are used to access VOCAs and other assistive technology.

Set out in Table 23.6 are the decisions likely to be considered in relation to accessing skills.

Table 23.6 Decisions on accessing skills

Status		Decision
Good hand function	→	(a) Direct access to keyboard-operated services such as computers, VOCAs, writing and writing aids (b) Index finger pointing to symbols (c) Use of sign systems/gesture
Limited hand function	→	(a) Use of switches to access VOCAs, computers and writing aids (b) Direct selection of symbols by fist pointing (c) Limited use of approximated gestures and signs
No reliable hand function. Other consistent reliable response present, e.g. foot movement	→	(a) Use of switches to access VOCAs, computers and writing aids b) Direct selection of symbols by eye pointing

Speech and language assessment

Assessment for children with complex physical disabilities, will take a considerable amount of time, and the therapist will need to show imagination, flexibility and invention. There are a range of issues that will need to be considered in assessing children who may benefit from using graphic symbol-based communication aids, or those who already use such systems and whose progress is being evaluated.

For some children, their physical difficulties will make consistent and readable responses difficult. It will be important to determine reliable and consistent access to assessment materials in discussion with each child's occupational therapist. For children with no speech and a restricted range of physical movements, it is essential to establish a consistent 'yes/no' response before starting the assessment. This might be a conventional nod and shake of the head, or an idiosyncratic use of gesture such as looking up for 'yes' and down for 'no'.

Children's 'performance' can also be affected by all the other factors discussed above, such as epilepsy control, the general state of health, or attention, because these might all fluctuate and confound the results of an assessment session. A child's parents will be anxious to be sure that he or she 'performs' at the best level possible, and again it will be important to incorporate interview data with results from more formal testing.

In order to establish comprehension levels of the children, therapists can use many of their familiar assessments, although adaptations would need to be noted when reporting the results as these would affect the standardised scoring. It must be emphasised that findings from norm-referenced assessment should be considered in the light of other formal assessment findings, informal assessment, and observations.

Published assessments that would typically be used in the UK include: Test for Reception of Grammar (Bishop 1989), British Picture Vocabulary Test (Dunn *et al.* 1997), CELF – 3^{UK} (Semel *et al.* 2000) and Derbyshire Language Scheme (Knowles and Masidlover 1982). Such assessments might have to be adapted for children who have oculo-motor difficulties and who therefore cannot easily scan picture array. If the standard four-picture array is cut up and arranged on a table-top, or presented on an eye-transfer frame, a child with this impairment might be able to scan more easily.

Symbolic understanding and comprehension of spoken language

A fundamental principle underpinning consideration of symbol options is the idea that symbol sets/systems should be 'maximally accessible for the cognitive abilities and style of the user' (Arvidson *et al.* 1999: 178).

The guide to assessment and decision making (adapted from Jones *et al.* 1990) that is given in Table 23.7 concerns the level of symbolic representation most appropriate for a child's level of understanding. Readers should note that children do not necessarily pass from one level/system to another as they develop.

Table 23.7 Decisions on symbolic understanding

Status		Decision
Appropriate comprehension level and good reading and spelling skills (to 8–9-year equivalent)	→	Consider the written word as an augmentative system, which would include opportunities for spelling (letter-based VOCA or alphabet chart)
Comprehension equating with a 5-year level and small sight vocabulary	→	The child is likely to be able to deal with a complex/abstract symbol system/set such as 'MinSpeak'
Comprehension equating with a 3–4-year level	→	Consider the possibility of using a complex/abstract symbol system/set
Comprehension equating with a 2½ – 3 year level	→	Consider using a more iconic symbol system (such as PCS/Rebus)
Comprehension 12–18-month level	→	Use of low-tech symbols such as pictures and photos on a chart or in a book
Comprehension below 12 months	→	Explore the use of 'objects of reference' (Park 1995) in familiar everyday routines

Expressive communication skills

Few published assessments are designed to assess expressive skills for children using symbols at a functional level. However, the Renfrew Action Picture Test (1997) is one example of a standardised assessment that can provide repeatable measures. In an initial appraisal of a child's communication skills, the therapist would need to combine results from such an assessment with informal assessment and observations. All aspects of the child's speech would need to be considered, including: the range of sounds and sound system used; the complexity of the child's utterances; the range of vocabulary available; and the pragmatic deployment of the utterances. With children with complex needs, the value of natural observation cannot be overstated. Observation has strong ecological validity, and it has been shown that therapists are able to recognise communication needs within functional settings (Remmington and Clarke 1998).

Implications for decision making

Currently, therapists and researchers working with children using AAC lack theoretical models of language acquisition to support guidelines for decision making (Von Tetchner *et al.* 1996). Here is another example: Amie-Belle is a six-year-old girl with four-limb cerebral palsy who is consistently combining two symbols, and who gestures and uses some speech when retelling a familiar story. It would not be clear from a theoretical base what might be the next stage of language development for her. Therapists try to overcome this lack by documenting an accurate baseline of observed communication modes, such as symbol use, speech, vocalisation, gesture, and signing across different settings and in different communicative contexts.

Decisions about the pattern of intervention will depend on the significance of the following for each individual child:

- Intervention might reflect spoken language development. For instance, intervention might focus on developing syntactic skills in symbol use, such as combining symbols or using grammatical markers. Alternatively, it might focus on semantic skills, improving the use of a wider range of word classes. Or it might focus on developing pragmatic skills, increasing the range of language functions used (McConachie and Ciccognani 1995).

- Intervention might focus on the barriers to the opportunities to communicate. Research has demonstrated atypical patterns in interaction between children using AAC systems and adults. This information has focused therapists' attention on the communicative environments and the need to develop this in order to facilitate AAC users' inclusion in interaction and shared participation in learning. Thus, therapists might choose to spend time training significant adults in facilitative strategies (see Chapter 10).

- Information gathered through observations might lead the therapist to decide to make amendments to the child's symbol vocabulary, redesigning and adding additional content to symbol charts and books. For example, it would be important to add words relating to a child's hobbies or interests, and to things that the child wants to talk about. Symbol pages might be organised as topics – for example, there might be a Scouts page, and a pop music page, arranged according to syntax where all the verbs are together and all the nouns are together; or it may be organised semantically, grouping professions, animals or sports (for example).

- It might be appropriate to focus on accessing the National Curriculum. Decision making will be shaped by educational needs, guided by curriculum requirements. However, it may not reflect interactional communication needs.

- Therapists working with children using AAC systems may be influenced in their decision-making by the theoretical model of communicative competence proposed by Light (1989). Light has developed four categories of core skills essential for the development of communicative competence in AAC systems. The first is linguistic skills: syntactic and referential aspects of communication, including learning the meanings of pictures and symbols. The second is operational skills: technical skills required to operate the communication system, such as learning the layout of symbols and symbol-accessing techniques. The third category is social skills: knowledge, judgement and skills in the social rules of communication. The fourth is strategic skills: compensatory skills and strategies to allow effective communication when the limitations of the communication system restrict the user.

It should be noted that although the teaching of functional communication is usually performed within a functional setting such as the classroom, interviews conducted with children and young people using communication aids reveal a strong preference for one-to-one therapy taking place outside the classroom (Clarke and Price 1998).

Summary

AAC is concerned with symbolic representation of meaning in support of speech and/or writing, and systems are considered for any children with a discrepancy between their understanding of language and their ability to express themselves. The process of assessment is continual and should be revisited with the changing needs and demands of each child and his or her environment.

CHAPTER 24

Children with feeding difficulties

Carolyn Anderson

Learning outcomes

By the end of this chapter, the reader should:

- understand some of the main aspects that need to be considered when making decisions about children with feeding problems;
- be aware of the importance of taking a holistic approach to a child's overall needs;
- be aware of the importance of a team approach to assessment and intervention;
- recognise the factors that need to be taken into account when assessing a child with dysphagia.

Introduction

This chapter addresses some of the main issues in management for children with eating problems and provides a structure for understanding the processes of assessment and intervention. The chapter begins with identifying what is meant by feeding difficulties, with a brief discussion of terminology. The organisation of a service to address identified problems and service-delivery issues are outlined. Composition of the multidisciplinary team is discussed as well as the speech and language therapist's roles and responsibilities within that team. The chapter then follows the therapeutic sequence, starting from referral, moving to assessment procedures and on to intervention, planning and management, and ending with discharge.

Therapists also need to consider the ethical issues involved, which may present a challenge as these types of decisions arise less often in communication fields. Although this chapter does not deal with specific issues for neonate feeding problems and patterns with degenerative diseases, similar principles will apply to management in these areas.

Defining the problem

Eating and drinking are normally pleasurable experiences. But children with physical and developmental disability or severe to complex learning disabilities are more likely to have eating problems, which might make mealtimes distressing or compromise their health.

Pitcher and Crandall (1997) note that a satisfactory definition to encompass feeding problems in children has not been agreed. Their definition includes a refusal to eat orally, or an inability to sustain oral feeding sufficient to maintain adequate calorie intake. In her work with adults, Logemann (1983) states that the term 'feeding' refers to only the first two stages of swallowing and argues that swallowing, or deglutition, is more descriptive of the entire process. Dysphagia can be defined as any disorder of swallowing. In this chapter, the terms 'eating difficulties', 'feeding problems' and 'dysphagia' will be used interchangeably.

Feeding problems will be observable by such clinical signs as failure to thrive, poor oral feeding skills, possible aspiration of food or liquid into the lungs (often indicated by choking and coughing), or problems in changing from non-oral to oral feeding (Pitcher and Crandall 1997). Other indicators that should also be considered are discomfort or upset during mealtimes, refusing food, and a failure to develop more mature eating patterns (Rosenthal *et al.* 1995). Weight loss and the time taken to feed (if this is excessive for the child or is judged to be excessive by the carers) should also be considered. Causes can be due to neuro-developmental factors such as cerebral palsy, cleft palate or prematurity related to learning disabilities or through learned behaviour (Lachenmeyer 1995).

For children with feeding difficulties, eating becomes an important part of their education and care. Not only is it vital for nutrition and health, but also it provides an opportunity to establish early bonding and develop social communication. Intervention aims are to treat children while taking their overall needs into account, so as to ensure safe nutrition, to develop eating skills, to improve the quality of mealtimes and to encourage social communication (Winstock 1994).

The first decision: service delivery issues

Prioritisation of services is often the first decision in the management of eating difficulties. The policy decisions of the unit or health trust will define the working practice.

Communicating Quality 2 (RCSLT 1996) remains the definitive source of information on professional conduct. The speech and language therapist would have a role designated by contract, with sessions assigned for carrying out this role that are based on an audit of patient needs. Time must be specified for working in this area, in order to prevent therapists having to make a decision about whether to allocate resources to either a communication or a dysphagia caseload. Priority criteria would include (RCSLT 1996): possible effects on a child's health, the level of child/parent anxiety, the time elapsed since onset of the problem, the child's or parents' ability to cope with intervention, the optimum time for intervention, the potential for change, the expected outcome, and the availability of trained staff.

A dysphagia service

A dysphagia service ideally should have a defined role within the speech and language therapy community and acute services, or in an educational setting. This service would also have a base where equipment could be kept and administrative support provided for the therapist. Some therapists may take responsibility for supervising and training less experienced therapists if they have had advanced training and/or sufficient experience in the field.

Working within a recognised speech and language therapy team would promote liaison and collaboration among colleagues, allow for peer review and audit of the service, and encourage continuing professional development. Management structures are necessary to evaluate service delivery, and a designated budget should facilitate decision-making based on resource allocation.

Roles and responsibilities

Policies and procedures are essential guidelines for therapists, and professional standards endorse monitoring and evaluation of the service. Guidelines for paediatric dysphagia and the current position on pre-registration and postgraduate recommendations are available from RCSLT. Local policies on dysphagia management must be comprehensive so as to clarify the service's aims and allow evaluation of practice (RCSLT 1996). The issues of legal responsibility, clinical accountability, competence, insurance and knowledge of the relevant NHS acts of (the UK) Parliament are outlined in *Communicating Quality 2* (RCSLT 1996).

Therapists need to be aware of their duties of care for liaison, consent, delegation, discharge and knowledge of emergency procedures (RCSLT 1996). Risk management, including health and safety issues, is the responsibility of local health trusts and other employers, and therapists should be aware of local policies and procedures.

The multidisciplinary team

A multidisciplinary team is essential in managing eating difficulties in children. The composition of the team might include the parents, as well as such people as doctors, nurses, educational staff, dieticians, physiotherapists, occupational therapists, dental surgeons, psychologists, social workers, audiologists, ENT specialists and radiologists (Winstock 1994). If a team does not exist, the speech and language therapist should liaise with any of these professionals as required during the course of assessment and intervention.

The speech and language therapist has a key role to play in the team, and to do this effectively the therapist's remit within the team must be identified (see Chapter 11). The therapist may be required to provide the intervention programme directly for the child or to offer training in order to enable others to carry out this function. The therapist may have a role that is defined as one of assessment and consultation or, alternatively, one of coordinating the assessment by the team (Bray *et al.* 1999).

Accessing the service: referrals

Referrals require consent from a parent and follow, in the UK, the 'consent to treatment guidelines' in the Children Act 1989, as recommended by RCSLT (1996). A speech and language therapy department should provide a referral form to ensure that standard and relevant background information is received prior to an initial appointment. *Communicating Quality 2* (RCSLT 1996) recommends that in-patients are seen within two working days and outpatients within two weeks of initial referral. By means of a collation of referrals through a central base, cases can be allocated within the system by clinical experience wherever possible; for example, neonatal work might be considered a specialism and referrals might therefore be allocated to a therapist with experience in this area.

Once a referral is accepted, the child becomes the speech and language therapist's responsibility. The child's needs are considered along with available resources to meet those needs. Decisions about prioritising for assessment can be taken, depending on a child's age and condition, and the available support from the parents, the school and other agencies. Direct intervention is not always indicated, as support and guidance for family and carers may be an alternative.

Assessment

In common with speech and language areas, assessment for eating involves collecting information from a number of sources. This information forms the basis for describing the problem and deciding on appropriate management aims. Assessment begins with background information gathered from an initial referral letter, case history taking and parent interview(s) (see Chapter 2). The child is then assessed using guidelines to direct the observation of his or her eating patterns.

This process may take place in different settings, such as home and school, and it might be continued over a number of sessions in order to build a detailed profile of the child's abilities and difficulties. Depending on the outcome, further assessment might be required through referral to other agencies – for example, physiotherapy and occupational therapy. Other team members might be involved in assessment depending on the type of problem that presents. Alternatively, the speech and language therapist might assess initially and request further evaluation from other team members as required.

Joint assessment is preferable, but as a full team assessment may not always be possible at any one time, video evidence may be useful. Parental involvement is essential in the assessment, not only for case history taking but also for observations of eating routines at home.

Background information

Some information should be gathered before a child is observed. Initially, the therapist will have information from the referral. If the child has had previous contact with speech and language therapy or medical services, case notes containing a history of the child's development might also be available. This information forms the basis of a parent interview prior to the child being assessed in feeding situations. Suggestions for case history questions are provided by Arvedson and Rogers (1997).

The aim of gathering background information is to identify the probable nature of the eating difficulty in order to focus the assessment observations on factors that influence the problem, and should include the following areas:

- the eating problem, as indicated by the referring agent and by the child's parents;
- the child's medical history, including any medical diagnosis and any available information about the child's birth and developmental history, the pattern of weight gain, medications, hospitalisation, surgical interventions or investigations (such as videofluoroscopy), the child's general health, and a history of chest infections, food allergies and bowel habits;
- details of the child's feeding history, covering previous feeding experiences and methods of eating (including oral or tube feeding), associated difficulties (including reflux or vomiting), dietary preferences, any nutritional supplements taken, and any previous feeding interventions;
- information about present eating patterns, outlining the time taken for meals; the child's and family's daily eating timetable; the amount eaten; food preferences in texture, temperature and tastes; utensils used; variations in seating and positioning; identification of the people involved in feeding the child; and factors that appear to make the child's eating more difficult (such as catarrh).

Speech and language therapists also need to find out which other professionals are involved, and to identify any safety issues. The therapist should be aware of the aetiologies of dysphagia, and the physical and neurological implications of different conditions and syndromes (for an overview, see Arvedson and Rogers 1997).

Eating observations

Following the case history taking and parental interview, it is common practice to observe the child's eating using a checklist. Assessment checklists provide structure for observations of eating in infants (Wolf and Glass 1992) and older children (Winstock 1994; Helm 1990). The main areas are listed to demonstrate considerations that may affect management.

There is consensus that the position of a child when eating is the most important factor to consider in assessment (Finnie 1997; Levitt 1995; Winstock 1994). Assessment should include head control and the effect of this on eating skills; muscle tone; patterns of flexion and/or extension; and the presence of primitive reflexes and their relation to the child's developmental level. Restraints and methods of release also need to be noted, as well as the relative heights of the tables and chairs, and the position of the feeder. If speech and language therapists do not have extensive experience in assessing physical development, collaboration with a physiotherapist and/or occupational therapist is essential. Levitt (1995) and Finnie (1997) detail physical development and handling skills used with children with physical disabilities, principally cerebral palsy.

A detailed oro-motor assessment of the child is recommended. This should include the appearance and function of the oral area in order to note facial symmetry; any oral reflexes that may interfere with development of any new eating skills; the movement of the jaw, lips and tongue during eating; palatal movement; the teeth and dental hygiene; and breathing patterns (Morris and Klein 1987).

Knowledge of oral anatomy and physiology, neurophysiology and the neurology of swallowing in children is used by therapists as a reference point from which to evaluate structure and function (Tuchman and Walter 1994). An understanding of the coordination of breathing and swallowing is also necessary in assessing the risks that may be involved in choking, aspirating and coughing (Brodsky and Volk 1993).

Eating and drinking skills such as sucking, swallowing, biting and chewing need to be evaluated as part of the assessment process. It is also important to note the influence of reflexes on these patterns, any sensory aspects such as tolerance of touch, hypersensitivity and hyposensitivity as well as whether the child is able to self-feed and how he or she copes with different food textures. Morris and Klein (1987) and Winstock (1994) detail normal and abnormal patterns for these aspects of eating. A useful rating scale for guiding the observations of oral feeding patterns is provided by Helm (1990), and this can be used as a baseline measure for noting changes over time.

Other areas of concern in assessment are the interaction between the child and parent; methods of communication; environmental factors; behaviour; and the organisation of the child's eating programme (Morris and Klein 1987). Eating should be evaluated in different settings if the child is fed at school as well as at home, and the results from these settings should be compared for any differences in the process or feeding methods used. Assessment may also involve experimenting with different positions for eating or testing different textures to determine which facilitate the child's eating skills.

Extending the assessment

Further investigations, such as instrumental assessments, might be required to check the child's feeding status. For example, if aspiration is suspected, the assessment team will need to determine whether oral feeding presents a risk to the child and it may request instrumental investigations. Guidelines on invasive procedures are available from RCSLT (1999). These outline the use in assessment of a fibre-optic endoscopic evaluation of swallowing (FEES) and of the vocal tract; and radiological imaging, commonly known as videofluoroscopy. Logemann (1986) describes the procedure in videofluoroscopy and the variations required in examining swallowing in children.

Following any such investigations, referral to other agencies may be necessary. For example, referral to a clinical psychologist may be appropriate if a child who has no mechanical eating difficulties nevertheless has behavioural problems that interfere with mealtimes.

Disseminating the assessment results

Following assessment by the team, the nature of the problem should be summarised and distributed to all those involved in the assessment. The speech and language therapist is responsible for presenting case history information and assessment results to the team. The planning of most appropriate intervention should be determined by the team, based on a summary of the child's abilities and problem areas.

Intervention

Intervention must be negotiated with the child and the parents in order that realistic short-term goals and long-term aims are formulated. The agreed intervention plan should outline aims with time references, and it should be written and distributed to all involved in the intervention. Although it has been noted that the efficacy of specific interventions has rarely been proven in the literature (Pitcher and Crandall 1997), it is hoped that future research will provide new evidence.

Principles of intervention

Arvedson (1993) describes the differences between feeding therapy, where the main aim is oral feeding, and an integrated oral-motor management programme aimed at developing coordinated movements of the mouth with respiration and phonation. By focusing on motor skills, improvements should be noted not only in developing feeding skills but also in oral communication. Most of the texts cited in this chapter on management take this combined and multifactorial approach to intervention. However, as Arvedson (1993) comments, researchers have not yet explored whether the link between improving motor movement and these areas is causal.

Developing aims for intervention

The main issues addressed at this stage of the management of the child are medical, nutritional, therapeutic and social. Deciding on management aims with multiple factors is often a complex process, and so team decisions are vital. Thus:

- *Medical issues* relate to health and risks for the child in feeding. If medical management was identified as a need during assessment, this would then become a priority aim. This is discussed further below under the heading of non-oral feeding.
- *Nutrition* is increasingly recognised as vital not only for health, development and growth but also for a child's daily state of alertness and well-being (Young 1993). For this reason, nutritional aims are often a second priority in planning intervention.
- *Therapeutic aims* may range from developing independence and reaching a child's developmental potential to improving the quality of life. Or they may range from working toward parents' acceptance of their child's eating difficulties to adjusting to the changing effects of a degenerating condition.
- *Social goals* include, for example, creating communication opportunities during meals, signalling choices, attempting a reduction in drooling, or enabling a child to cope with distractions during feeding.

Further considerations for intervention

Intervention is based on normal development. Knowledge of oral-motor development and the acquisition of feeding skills is used to plan intervention. The assessed developmental level in eating is compared to the child's chronological age and to the expectations of parents in order to identify goals. The child's medical condition, physical abilities, learning disabilities and behavioural influences may all have an effect on recommendations for intervention.

Intervention strategies can include direct therapy for improving oral-motor skills, and Mueller (1997) and Arvedson (1993) offer practical intervention suggestions. Compensatory techniques in positioning, changing food textures and altering feeding procedures may also be used (RCSLT 1996). Changes in position are used to reduce immature motor patterns, which may be preventing the child from developing more mature eating skills (Finnie 1997). While Arvedson and Rogers (1997) outline major features in skill development, Winstock (1994) and Morris and Klein (1987) provide comprehensive intervention advice based on developmental considerations. Published material such as parent handouts are useful for general advice in working with children with special needs (Klein and Delaney 1994).

Non-oral feeding

Non-oral feeding is often the management choice for children with neurological impairments who have poor nutrition due to persistently inadequate oral intake or where aspiration presents a serious health risk. Surgical options include percutaneous endoscopic gastrostomy (PEG), which has become more accepted as an intervention treatment (Khattack *et al.* 1998). Winstock (1994) compares gastrostomy with feeding by nasogastric tube and recommends PEG as the preferred option for longer-term intervention. Morris and Klein (1987) offer practical management for the transition from tube to oral feeding. The decision between oral and non-oral feeding options must be accepted as the joint responsibility of the team.

Team involvement in the decision-making process is illustrated by the following case example.

Case example

Ben is a ten-year-old boy who has always been orally fed. He has severe athetosis and epilepsy. He has a history of slow eating and poor weight-gain. His paediatrician is concerned because his weight has been falling for the last 6 to 12 months. She raises the possibility of PEG with Ben's speech and language therapist and his parents. The therapist reports that Ben has made minimal progress in his feeding programme. He has been able to take puréed food without regurgitation for some time, but attempts to change textures have been unsuccessful.

Ben's parents are positive in their attitude to PEG as some of the other children in Ben's school have had the operation with good results. However, they are concerned that Ben continues to have some oral feeding so that he can join the family at meal times. The options for this flexible programme are discussed with the dietician and the school before the operation is performed.

Family involvement

Many texts recognise the importance of involving parents and carers as key team members (Winstock 1994; Morris and Klein 1987). Awareness of different attitudes to food and eating practices must be considered in recommending changes to feeding patterns. This understanding is essential with different cultures, which may have different customs and issues relating to aspects concerned with feeding. For example, some cultures place less importance on developmental progress than others; furthermore, some families with specific religious beliefs may find it difficult to accept surgical intervention in feeding.

Implementing the intervention plan

Following formulation of an intervention plan, the speech and language therapist is responsible for ensuring that personnel involved in implementing the plan understand their role and use the recommended strategies. Depending on the therapist's role within this plan, she or he may be providing a consultation service or may be involved in direct training and supervision.

Recognition of a wider training role and the need for liaison with different services will require extra time allocated for these responsibilities (see Chapter 10). It may be possible to extend the service to provide a preventive role, which may prove effective in early intervention, possibly reducing some dysphagia problems – although further research is required to establish the efficacy of such an approach.

Balancing needs

A holistic approach to any child with eating problems is essential because these are often part of a larger picture that includes educational, social and emotional needs. Within this wider context, a feeding programme might not necessarily be the primary focus of intervention. Flexibility is also required in planning, in order to be able to respond to a child's changing needs and abilities. The implementation of planned aims might need modification, depending on factors such as available resources, parental attitudes or school policies. Intervention might not always be a preferred course of action – for example, in safe feeding where there is little prospect of change, where there is limited support from carers, or when the child uses good compensatory techniques with no risks to health.

Case example

Some of the difficulties of balancing needs are shown in the case of Ruth who started nursery school at the age of 3 and who had complex problems including feeding difficulties. She was fed on her mother's lap with nutritional supplements from a bottle.

The school team, involving Ruth's teacher, a speech and language therapist, a physiotherapist and an occupational therapist, recognised that Ruth's needs for nutrition were being met. However, they wanted to see how she might progress with different seating positions and food textures. Ruth's mother had been resistant to any suggestions for changes in how she fed Ruth in the past, and the team respected her need to cope with Ruth's difficulties in this way. She nevertheless accepted the school policy that individual feeding programmes were part of curriculum planning. The team hoped that by introducing an intervention programme at school, Ruth's mother might come to accept changes at home.

Although Ruth made some progress over the next two years, her mother continued to feed Ruth in the same way at home as she had always done. Without an integrated approach, the team felt that more progress was unlikely and a maintenance programme replaced the intervention plan.

Ethical issues

Ethical issues are moral issues. It is important to identify whether issues are service-based, such as lack of resources, or whether they are client-related, perhaps when the service is withdrawn for a child if parents disagree with the speech and language therapist's intervention.

Case example

Consider the ethical decisions that professionals are making in the following example. A five-year-old child is dying from a progressive degenerative metabolic disease. The therapist knows that the child is aspirating and wants the doctor to agree to tube feeding. The doctor expects that the child's frequent chest infections will precipitate death. He says he does not want to start tube feeding because of the child's poor quality of life. The parents do not know about this conflict and, if asked, would prefer their child to live as long as possible but not to suffer.

In applying ethics to decision making, the first step is to identify the issues, because key elements might differ for the people involved. This process will define the issues by discussion from different viewpoints, to arrive at a description of the problem that is then communicated to all. The issues can be dealt with as a team effort working toward consensus and resolution. Issues should not have to be resolved in isolation, as support mechanisms should be in place to deal with these routinely. Seedhouse (1988) discusses ethical decision-making for healthcare professionals in more detail.

Discharge

Terminating therapy involves a team decision, with agreement on reasons for discharge contained in written documentation. Discharge policy should be specifically designed for the needs of the eating difficulties team.

Summary

A holistic approach is essential in oral feeding problems. Eating problems may be of short duration or long term, requiring consideration of changes due to maturation and a growing child's needs. As feeding problems are usually linked with physical, cognitive or behavioural difficulties, the influence of multiple factors makes decision-making a complex process.

References

Abba, L., Ayub, S. and Selwyn Barnett, V. (1999) *Total Phonology*. Bicester: Winslow Press.

Abudarham, S. (ed.) (1987) *Bilingualism and the Bilingual*. Windsor: NFER-Nelson.

Adams, C., Byers-Brown, B. and Edwards, M. (1997) *Developmental Disorders of Language*. London: Whurr Publishers Ltd.

Albery, E. and Russell, J. (1984) *Cleft Palate Sourcebook*. Bicester: Winslow Press.

American Psychiatric Association (1994) *Diagnostic and Statistical Manual of Mental Disorders*, 4th edn (DSM IV). Washington, DC: American Psychiatric Association.

Anderson-Wood, L. and Smith, B. (1997) *Working with Pragmatics*. Bicester: Winslow Press.

Armstrong, S. and Ainley, M. (1988) *South Tyneside Assessment of Phonology (STAP)*. Bicester: Winslow Press.

Arvedson, J. (1993) 'Management of Swallowing Problems', in Arvedson, J. and Brodsky, L. (eds) *Pediatric Swallowing and Feeding – Assessment and Management*, 327–88. London: Whurr Publishers Ltd.

Arvedson, J. and Rogers, B. (1997) 'Swallowing and Feeding in the Pediatric Patient', in Perlman, A. and Schulze-Delrieu, K. (eds) *Deglutition and its Disorders*. 419–48, London: Singular Publishing Ltd.

Arvidson, H. H., McNaughton, S., Nelms, G., Loncke, F. T. and Lloyd, L. L (1999) 'Graphic symbols: Clinical issues', in Loncke, F. T., Clibbens, J., Arvidson, H. H. and Lloyd, L. L (eds) *Augmentative and Alternative Communication: New Directions in Research and Practice*. London: Whurr Publishers Ltd.

Attanasio, J. (1999) 'Treatment of Early Stuttering: Some Reflections', in Onslow, M. and Packman, A. (eds) *The Handbook of Early Stuttering Intervention*. 189–203. London: Singular Publishing Ltd.

Baddeley, A. and Gathercole, S. (1996) *Children's Test of Nonword Repetitions*. London: The Psychological Corporation.

Baker, B. (1982) 'Minspeak: A semantic compaction system that makes self-expression easier for communicatively disabled individuals', *Byte* **7,** 186–202.

Bandura, A. (1969) *Principles of Behaviour Modification*. New York: Holt, Rinehart and Whiston.

Bandura, A. (1977) *Social Learning Theory*. Engelwood Cliffs, NJ: Prentice Hall.

Bannister, P. (2001) 'Early feeding management', in Watson, A. C. H., Grunwell, P. and Sell, D. (eds) *Management of Cleft Lip and Palate*, 139–49. London: Whurr Publishers Ltd.

Bantock, A. (2000) *Child Health Surveillance Programme*. Camden and Islington NHS Trust and Royal Free Hampstead NHS Trust.

Barker, P. (1998) *Basic Family Therapy*, 4th edn. Oxford: Blackwell Publishers Ltd.

Barnes, C. (1990) *Cabbage Syndrome: the Social Construction of Dependence*. Basingstoke: Falmer Press.

Baron-Cohen, S. (1995) *Mindblindness: An Essay on Autism and Theory of Mind*. London: MIT Press.

Beaton, A. A. (1997) 'The relation of planum temporale asymmetry and morphology of the corpus callosum to handedness, gender, and dyslexia: a review of the evidence', *Brain and Language* **60**, 255–322.

Beazley, S. (1992) 'Social Skills Group Work with Deaf People', in Fawcus, M. (ed.) *Group Encounters in Speech and Language Therapy*. London: Whurr Publishers Ltd.

Beazley, S. (2000) 'Accessing The Views Of Children Who Do Not Use the Majority Language', in Moore, M. (ed.) *Insider Perspectives: Unit 3, MEd Special and Inclusive Education*. Sheffield University Publication.

Beazley, S. and Moore, M. (1995) *Deaf Children, Their Families and Professionals*. London: David Fulton Publishers.

Beck, A. T. (1976) *Cognitive Therapy and Emotional Disorders*. New York: International University Press.

Bellugi, U., Marks, S., Bihrle, A. and Sabo, H. (1988) 'Dissociation between language and cognitive functions in William's syndrome', in Bishop, D. and Mogford, K. (eds) *Language Development in Exceptional Circumstances,* 177–89. London: Livingston Churchill.

Bergman, B. (1994) 'Signed Languages', in Ahlgren, I. and Hytlenstam, K. (eds) *Bilingualism in Deaf Education*. Hamburg: Signum-Verl.

Beukleman, D. R. and Mirenda, P. (1992) *Augmentative and Alternative Communication: Management of Severe Communication Disorders in Adults and Children*. Baltimore: Brooks.

Bines, H. and Watson, D. (1992) *Developing Professional Education*. Buckingham: Society for Research into Higher Education and Open University Press.

Bishop, D. V. M. (1985) 'Age of onset and outcome in acquired aphasia with convulsive disorder (Landau–Kleffner syndrome)', *Developmental Medicine and Child Neurology* **27**, 705–12.

Bishop, D. V. M. (1989) *Test for Reception of Grammar*, 2nd edn. Manchester: University of Manchester.

Bishop, D. V. M. (1997) *Uncommon Understanding*. Hove, Sussex: Psychology Press.

Bishop, D. V. M. (1998) 'Development of the Children's Communication Checklist: a method of assessing qualitative aspects of communicative impairment in children', *Journal of Child Psychology and Psychiatry* **39**, 879–92.

Bishop, D. V. M. (2000) 'Pragmatic language impairment: a correlate of SLI, a distinct subgroup or part of the autistic continuum?', in Bishop, D. V. M and Leonard, L. B. (eds) *Speech and Language Impairments in Children*. Hove: Psychology Press Ltd.

Bishop, D. and Mogford, K. (eds) (1988) *Language Development in Exceptional Circumstances*. London: Churchill Livingstone.

Bishop, D. V. M. and Rosenbloom, L. (1987) 'Classification of childhood language disorders', in Yule, W. and Rutter, M. (eds) *Language Development and Disorders*. London: MacKeith Press.

Bloodstein, O. (1995) *A Handbook on Stuttering*, 5th edn. London: Chapman and Hall.

Bloom, L. and Lahey, M. (1978) *Language Development and Language Disorders*. New York: John Wiley and Sons.

Boehm, B. (2000) *Boehm Test of Basic Concepts,* 3rd edn. London: The Psychological Corporation.

Boehm, B. (2001) *Boehm – 3 Preschool.* London: The Psychological Corporation.

Bohannon, J. N. and Bonvillian, J. D. (1997) 'Theoretical approaches to language acquisition', in Berko Gleason, J. (ed.) *The Development of Language,* 4th edn, 259–316. Needham Heights, MA: Allyn & Bacon.

Boucher, J. and Lewis, V. (1997) *Preschool Language Scale – 3* (PLS–3[UK]). London: The Psychological Corporation.

Bowen, C. and Cupples, L. (1999) 'Parents and children together (PACT): a collaborative approach to phonological therapy', *International Journal of Language and Communication Disorders* **34**, 35–54.

Boyle, J. and McLellan, E. (1998) *Early Language Skills Checklist: Observation Based Language Assessment for Early Education.* London: Hodder and Stoughton.

Bracken, B. A. (1998) *Bracken Basic Concept Scale – Revised.* London: The Psychological Corporation.

Bradbury, E. and Bannister, P. (2001) 'Prenatal, perinatal and postnatal counselling', in Watson, A. C. H., Grunwell, P. and Sell, D. (eds) *Management of Cleft Lip and Palate,* 119–24. London: Whurr Publishers Ltd.

Bradley, L. (1984) 'Test of auditory organization', in Assessing Reading Difficulties: A diagnostic and remedial approach. London: Macmillan.

Brady, S. A. and Shankweiler, D. P. (eds) (1991) *Phonological Processes in Literacy.* Hillsdale, NJ: Erlbaum.

Bray, M., Ross, A. and Todd, C. (1999) *Speech and Language Clinical Process and Practice.* London: Whurr Publishers Ltd.

Brindley, C., Cave, D., Crane, S., Lees, J. and Moffat, V. (1996) *Paediatric Oral Skills Package (POSP).* London: Whurr Publishers Ltd.

Brodsky, L. and Volk, M. (1993) 'The airway and swallowing', in Arvedson, J. and Brodsky, L. (eds) *Pediatric Swallowing and Feeding – Assessment and Management,* 93–122. London: Whurr Publishers Ltd.

Bronfenbrenner, U. (1986) 'Ecology of the family as a context for human development', *Developmental Psychology* **22**, 723–42.

Broomfield, H. and Combley, M. (1997) *Overcoming Dyslexia: A Practical Handbook for the Classroom.* London: Whurr Publishers Ltd.

Buckley, S., Bird, G. and Burn, A. (1996). The practical and theoretical significance of teaching literacy skills to children with Down's syndrome, in Rondal, J., Perera, J., Nadel, L. and Comblain, A. (eds) *Down's syndrome: psychological, psychobiological and socio-educational perspectives,* 119–28. London: Whurr Publishers Ltd.

Burgess, J. and Bransby, G. (1999) 'An evaluation of the speech and language skills of children with emotional and behavioural problems', *RCSLT Bulletin* **453**, 2–3.

Burnard, P. (1992) *Effective Communication Skills for Health Professionals.* London: Chapman and Hall.

Burns, K. (1999) 'Focusing on Success: Brief Therapy in Practice', *RCSLT Bulletin,* 10–22 Nov.

Bzoch, K. and League, R. (1971) *Receptive-Expressive Emergent Language Scale: 2nd edn.* Windsor: NFER-Nelson.

Calculator, S. (1988). 'Promoting the acquisition and generalisation of conversational skills by individuals with severe disabilities', *Augmentative and Alternative Communication* **4**, 94–103.

Camarata, S. M., Hughes, C. A. and Ruhl, K. L. (1988) 'Mild/moderate behaviourally disordered students: a population at risk for language disorders', *Language, Speech and Hearing Services* **19**, 191–200.

Cameron, R.. and White, M. (1987) *The Portage Early Education Programme.* Windsor: NFER Nelson

Carrow-Woolfolk, E. (1998) *Test for Auditory Comprehension of Language*, 3rd edn. Windsor: NFER-Nelson.

Catts, H. W. (1996) 'Defining dyslexia as a developmental language disorder: an expanded view', *Topics in Language Disorders* **16**(2), 14–29.

Chitty, L. and Griffin, D. (2001) 'Abnormalities of the fetal lip and palate: sonographic diagnosis', in Grunwell, P., Sell, D. and Watson, A. C. H. (eds) *Management of Cleft Lip and Palate*, 119–24. London: Whurr Publishers Ltd.

Christie, E. (2000) *The Primary Healthcare Workers Project: A four-year investigation into changing referral patterns to ensure the early identification and referral of dysfluent preschoolers in the UK.* London: The British Stammering Association.

Clark, C. R. (1981) 'Learning words using traditional orthography and the symbols of Rebus, Bliss, and Carrier', *Journal of Speech and Hearing Disorders* **46**, 191–6.

Clarke, M. T. and Price, K. (1998) 'Back to the broom cupboard? Some findings from discussion with AAC users', *Communication Matters UK* (International Society for Augmentative and Alternative Communication) **12**, 13–16.

Clarke, S., Remmington, B. and Light, P. (1986) 'An evaluation of the relationship between receptive speech skills and expressive signing', *Journal of Applied Behaviour Analysis* **19**, 231–9.

Clinical Standards Advisory Group (CSAG) (1998) *Cleft Lip and Palate*. London: HMSO.

Cohen, N. J. and Lipsett, L. (1991) 'Recognised and unrecognised language impairment in psychologically disturbed children: prevalence and language and behavioural characteristics', *Canadian Journal of Behavioural Science* **23**(3), 376–89.

Collard, R. (1993) *Total Quality: Success Through People*, 2nd edn. London: Institute of Personnel Management.

Conti-Ramsden, G. (1997) 'Parent–child interaction in mental handicap: a commentary', in Beveridge, M., Conti-Ramsden, G. and Leudar, I. (eds) *Language and Communication in People with Learning Disabilities*, 218–25, London: Routledge.

Conti-Ramsden, G. and Botting, N. (1999) 'Characteristics of children attending language units in England: a national study of 7-year-olds', *International Journal of Language and Communication Disorders* **34**(4), 359–66.

Conti-Ramsden, G., Crutchley, A. and Botting, N. (1997) 'The extent to which psychometric tests differentiate subgroups of children with specific language impairment', *Journal of Speech, Language and Hearing Research* **40**, 765–77.

Conture, E. and Melnick, K. (1999) 'Parent–child group approach to stuttering in preschool children', in Onslow, M. and Packman, A. (eds), *The Handbook of Early Stuttering Intervention*, 17–51. London: Singular Publishing Ltd.

Coombes, K. (1987) 'Speech therapy', in Yule, W. and Rutter, M. (eds) *Language Development and Disorders*. Oxford: McKeith Press.

Cooper, E. B. and Cooper C. S. (1985) *Cooper Personalised Fluency Control Therapy (Revised)*. Allen, Texas: DLM Teaching Resources.

Cooper, M., Pettit, E. and Jones, P. (1994) 'Parentwise: A collaborative project to promote effective parenting', *CSLT Bulletin*.

Corey, G. (1996) *Theory and Practice of Counselling and Psychotherapy*, 5th edn. Pacific Grove, CA: Brooks/Cole.

Corker, M. (1998) *Deaf and Disabled or Deaf Disabled*. Buckingham: Open University Press.

Corker, M and French, S. (1999) *Disability Discourse*. London: Open University Press.

CPLOL (1998) *1988–1998: Ten Years of Activities*. L'ortho-edition Isbergues, France.

Crystal, D. (1992) *Profiling Linguistic Disability*. London: Whurr Publishers Ltd.

Crystal, D. and Varley, R. (1998) *Introduction to Speech Pathology*, 4th edn. London: Whurr Publishers Ltd.

Cummins, J. (1984) *Bilingualism and Special Education: Issues in Assessment and Pedagogy*. Clevedon: Multilingual Matters.

Cummins, J. and Swain, M. (1986) *Bilingualism in Education: Aspects of Theory, Research and Practice*. London: Longman.

Cummins, K. and Hulme, S. (1997) 'Video a reflective tool', *Speech and Language Therapy in Practice*, 4–7.

Cunningham, C. and Davis, H. (1985) *Working with Parents: Framework for Collaboration*. Milton Keynes: Open University Press.

Curtiss, S., Katz, W. and Tallal, P. (1992) 'Delay versus deviance in language acquisition of language impaired children', *Journal of Speech, Language and Hearing Research* **35**, 373–83.

Dale, M. and Bell J. (1999) *Informal Learning in the Workplace*. DfEE Research Briefs: Research Report No 134.

Dale, N. (1996) *Working with Families of Children with Special Needs*. London: Routledge.

Dalston, R. M. and Seaver, E. J. (1992) 'Relative values of various standardised passages in the nasometric assessment of patients with velopharyngeal impairment', *Cleft Palate Craniofacial Journal* **29**, 17–21.

Davies G. (2001) 'Role of Parent Support Groups', in Watson, A. C. H., Grunwell, P. and Sell, D. (eds) *Management of Cleft Lip and Palate*, 388–94. London: Whurr Publishers Ltd.

Davis, K. (1993) 'The Crafting of Good Clients', in Swain, J., Finkelstein, V., French, S. and Oliver, M. (eds) *Disabling Barriers – Enabling Environments*. London: Sage.

DeFries, J. C., Alarcon, M. and Olson, R. K. (1997) 'Genetic aetiologies of reading and spelling deficits: developmental differences', in Hulme, C. and Snowling, M. (eds) *Dyslexia: Biology, Cognition and Intervention*, 20–37. London: Whurr Publishers Ltd.

de Houwer, A. (1990) *The Acquisition of Two Languages from Birth: A Case Study*. Cambridge: Cambridge University Press.

De Montfort Supple, M. (1995) 'Classification of Communication Disorders', in Leahy, M. (ed.) *Disorders of Communication: the science of intervention*, 14–29. London: Whurr Publishers Ltd.

De Montfort Supple, M. (1998) 'The relationship between oral and written language', *Folia Phoniatrica et Logopaedicia* **50**, 243–55.

Department for Education and Employment (DfEE) (1994) *Code of Practice on the Identification and Assessment of Special Educational Needs*. London: HMSO.

DfEE (1996) *Education Act*. London: HMSO.

DfEE (1997) *Excellence for all children: meeting special educational needs*. London: The Stationery Office.

DfEE (1998a) *Meeting Special Educational Needs – a programme for action*. London: The Stationery Office.

DfEE (1998b) *National Literacy Strategy: Framework for Teaching*. London: The Stationery Office.

DfEE (1999a) *The Management, Role and Training of Learning Support Assistants*. London: The Stationery Office.

DfEE (1999b) *National Numeracy Strategy: Framework for teaching mathematics*. London: The Stationery Office.

DfEE (1999c) *The SEN Code of Practice and Associated Legislation – Proposed Changes and Areas for Revision*. London: The Stationery Office.

DfEE (1999d) *Sure Start: Making a difference for children and families*. London: The Stationery Office.

DfEE (2000a) *Provision of Speech and Language Therapy Services to Children with Special Educational Needs. (England)*. Report of the Working Group, London: The Stationery Office.

DfEE (2000b) *Draft Revised Code of Practice for Special Educational Needs*. London: The Stationary Office.

Department of Education and Science (DES) (1981) *Education Act*. London: HMSO.

DES (1988) *Education Reform Act*, London: HMSO.

Department of Health (DoH) (1991) *The Children Act 1989 Guidance and Regulations*, vols 1–9. London: HMSO.

Department of Health (1998) *National Health Service White Paper: A First Class Service*. London: The Stationery Office.

De Shazer, S. (1985) *Keys to Solution in Brief Therapy*. London: Norton.

Dewart, H. and Summers, S. (1995) *The Pragmatics Profile of Everyday Communication Skills in Pre-school and School-aged Children*. Windsor: NFER-Nelson.

Dollaghan, C. and Kaston, N. (1986) 'A comprehension monitoring programme for language impaired children', *Journal of Speech and Hearing Disorders* **51**, 264–71.

Donahue, M. L., Hartas, D. and Cole, D. (1999) 'Research on Interactions among Oral Language and Emotional/Behavioural Disorders', in Rogers-Adkinson, D. and Griffith, P. (eds) *Communication Disorders and Children with Psychiatric and Behavioural Disorders*. London: Singular Publishing Ltd.

Duncan, D. M. (ed.) (1989) *Working with Bilingual Language Disability*. London: Chapman and Hall.

Duncan, D., Gibbs, D., Noor, N. and Whittaker, H. (1988) *Sandwell Bilingual Screening Assessment Scales for Expressive Panjabi and English*, Windsor: NFER-Nelson.

Dunn, L. M., Wetton, C. and Burley, J. (1997) *The British Picture Vocabulary Scale II*. Windsor: NFER-Nelson.

Dysphagia Working Group (Education & Training) (1999) *Recommendations for Pre and Post-registration Dysphagia Education and Training*. London: RCSLT.

Eastwood, J. and Whitehouse, J. (1993) 'Practical Work Experience: A review of the literature', in Stengelhofen, J. (ed.) *Teaching Students in Clinical Settings*, London: Chapman and Hall.

Edwards, S., Fletcher, P., Garman, M., Hughes, A., Letts, C. and Sinka, I. (1997) *Reynell Developmental Language Scales III*. Windsor: NFER-Nelson.

Einzig, B. (1996) 'Parenting education and support', in Bayne, R., Horton, I. and Bimrose, J. (eds) *New Directions in Counselling*. London: Routledge.

Ellis Weismer, S. (2000) 'Intervention for children with developmental language delay', in Bishop, D. V. M. and Leonard, L. B. (eds) *Speech and Language Impairments in Children*. Hove: Psychology Press Ltd.

Emery, S (1978) *Actualizations*. Garden City, NY: Dolphin Books.

Enderby, P. and John, A. (1997) *Therapy Outcome Measures (TOM): Speech and Language Therapy*. London: Singular Publishing Ltd.

Eraut, M. (1994) *Developing Professional Knowledge and Competence*. London: The Falmer Press.

Evans, J. L. and Macwhinney, B. (1999) 'Sentence processing strategies in children with expressive and expressive-receptive specific language impairments', *International Journal of Language and Communication Disorders* **34**(2), 117–34.

Fawcett, N. and Nicholas, R. (1996) *Dyslexia Screening Test (DST)*. London: The Psychological Corporation.

Fawcus, M. (1992) *Group Encounters in Speech and Language Therapy*. Kibworth: Far Communications Ltd.

Fawcus, M. (ed.) (1997) *Children with Learning Difficulties*, London: Whurr Publishers Ltd.

Fenson, L., Dale, P. S., Reznick, J. S., Thal, D., Bates, E., Hartung, J. P., Pethick, S. and Reilly, J. S. (1993) *MacArthur Communicative Development Inventories*. California: Singular Publishing Ltd.

Fey, M. E. (1986) *Language Intervention with Young Children*. San Diego: College Hill Press.

Fey, M. E., Cleave, P. L., Long, S. E., Hughes, D. (1993) 'Two approaches to the facilitation of grammar in children with language impairment: an experimental evaluation', *Journal of Speech, Language and Hearing Research* **36**, 141–57.

Fey, M. E., Long, S. E., Cleave, P. L., (1994) 'Reconsideration of IQ criteria in the definition of specific language impairment', in Watkins, R. and Rice, M. (eds) *Specific language impairments in children*. Baltimore, MD: Paul H. Brookes.

Finnie, N. (1997) *Handling the Young Cerebral Palsied Child at Home*, 3rd edn. London: William Heinemann.

Flynn, L. and Lancaster, G. (1996) *Children's Phonology Sourcebook*. Bicester: Winslow Press.

Forster, M. (2000) *Get Everything Done and Still Have Time to Play*. London: Hodder and Stoughton.

Fowler, A. (1990) 'Language abilities in children with Down syndrome: evidence from a specific syntactic delay', in Ciccetti, D. and Beeghly, M. (eds) *Children with Down syndrome. A developmental perspective*, 302–28. New York: Cambridge University Press.

Frederickson, N., Frith, U. and Reason, R. (1997) *Phonological Assessment Battery (PhAB)*. Windsor: NFER–Nelson.

Frith, U. (1985) 'Beneath the surface of developmental dyslexia', in Patterson, K. Marshall, J. and Coltheart, M. (eds) *Surface Dyslexia*, 301–30. London: Routledge and Kegan Paul.

Frith, U. (1997) 'Brain, mind and behaviour in dyslexia', in Hulme, C. and Snowling. M. (eds) *Dyslexia: Biology, Cognition and Intervention*, 1–19. London: Whurr Publishers Ltd.

Frith, U. (1999) 'Paradoxes in the definition of dyslexia', *Dyslexia* **5**, 192–214.

Furnham, A (1997) *The Psychology of Behaviour at Work*. London: Psychology Press.

Gallagher, T. (1991) (ed.) *Pragmatics of language: Clinical practice issues*. London: Chapman and Hall.

Gallaway C. and Woll, B. (1994) 'Interaction and childhood deafness', in Gallaway, C. and Richards, B. (eds) *Input and Interaction in Language Acquisition*. Cambridge: Cambridge University Press.

Garman, M. (1999) 'The acquisition of English by British children', in Yamada Yamamoto, A. and Richards, B. R. (eds) *Japanese Children Abroad*. Clevedon: Multilingual Matters.

George, E., Iveson, C. and Ratner, H. (1990) *Problem to Solution: Brief Therapy with Individuals and Families*. London: Brief Therapy Press.

Gerard, K. A. and Carson, E. R. (1990) 'The decision making process in child language assessment', *British Journal of Disorders of Communication* **25**(1), 61–75.

German, D. J. (1989) *National College of Education Test of Word Finding (TWF)*. Allen, Tex: DLM Teaching Resources.

German, D. J. (1992) 'Word-finding intervention for children and adolescents', *Topics in Language Disorders* **13**(1), 33–50.

Gibbard, D. (1998) *Parent-Bases Intervention Programme: A group approach for language-delayed children*. Bicester: Winslow Press.

Giddan, J. J., Milling, L. and Campbell, N. B. (1996) 'Unrecognized language and speech deficits in preadolescent psychiatric inpatients', *American Journal of Orthopsychiatry* **66**(1).

Gillberg, C. and Coleman, M. (1992) *The Biology of the Autistic Syndromes*, 2nd edn. Clinics in Developmental Medicine No. 126, Oxford: MacKeith Press/Blackwell Scientific Publications Ltd.

Girolametto, L., Greenberg, J. and Manolson, H. (1986) 'Developing Dialogue Skills: The Hanen Early Language Parent Program', *Seminars in Speech and Language,* **7,** 367–82.

Girolametto, L., Weitzman, E., Wiig E. H. and Steig-Pearce, S (1999) 'The relationship between maternal language Measures and language development in Toddlers with Expressive Vocabulary delays', *American Journal of Speech-language Pathology* **8**, 364–74.

Glogowska, M. and Campbell, R. (2000) 'Getting in, getting on and getting there: investigating parental views of involvement in pre-school speech and language therapy', *International Journal of Language and Communication Disorders* **35**.

Goldberg, S. (1997) *Clinical Skills for Speech and Language Pathologists*. San Diego: Singular Publishing Ltd.

Goodman, R. and Scott, S. (1997) *Child Psychiatry*. Oxford: Blackwell Science.

Gorrie, B. and Parkinson, E. (1995) *Phonological Awareness Procedure*. Northumberland: STASS Publications.

Goswami, U. (1999) 'Causal connections in beginning reading: the importance of rhyme', *Journal of Research in Reading* **22**(3), 217–40.

Goswami, U. and Bryant, P. (1990) *Phonological Skills and Learning to Read*. Hove, Sussex: Erlbaum.

Goulandris, N. (1996) 'Assessing reading and spelling skills', in Snowling, M. and Stackhouse, J. (eds) *Dyslexia Speech and Language: A Practitioner's Handbook*, 77–107. London: Whurr Publishers Ltd.

Graham, J. (1995) *Interprofessional Collaboration in the Special School*. Unpublished Phd thesis. London: Institute of Education.

Green, R. (1995) 'Non-managerial supervision as a statutory requirement for the speech and language therapy profession', *Caring to Communicate*, Proceedings of the Golden Jubilee Conference, London: RCSLT.

Gregory, H. and Hill, D. (1993) 'Differential evaluation – differential therapy for stuttering children'. in Curlee,R. (ed.) *Stuttering and Related Disorders of Fluency*, 23–44. New York: Thieme Medical Publishers, Inc.

Gregory, S., Knight, P., McCracken, W., Powers, S. and Watson, L. (eds) (1998) *Issues in Deaf Education*. London: David Fulton Publishers.

Grossman, H. (1983) (ed.) *Classification in Mental Retardation*. Washington, DC: American Association on Mental Deficiency.

Grove, N. and Dockrell, J. (1999) 'Growing and learning with cognitive impairments', in Messer, D. and Millar, S. (eds) *Exploring Developmental Psychology*, 220–42. London: Arnold.

Grove, N. and Smith, M. (1997) 'Input/output asymmetries: language development in AAC', *ISAAC Bulletin* **50**.

Grundy, K. (ed.) (1995) *Linguistics In Clinical Practice*. London: Whurr Publishers Ltd.

Grundy, K. and Harding, A. (1995) 'Developmental speech impairments', in Grundy, K. (ed.) *Linguistics In Clinical Practice*. London: Whurr Publishers Ltd.

Grunwell, P. (1982) *Clinical Phonology*. Windsor: NFER–Nelson.

Grunwell, P. and Harding, A. (1995) *PACSTOYS*. London: NFER-Nelson.

Grunwell, P. and Sell, D. (2001) 'Speech and cleft palate/velopharyngeal anomalies', in Grunwell, P., Sell, D. and Watson, A. C. H. (eds) *Management of Cleft Lip and Palate,* 68–86. London: Whurr Publishers Ltd.

Guitar, B. (1998) *Stuttering: An Integrated Approach to its Nature and Treatment.* London: Williams and Wilkins.

Habel, A. (2001) 'The role of the paediatrician', in Grunwell, P., Sell, D. and Watson, A. C. H. (eds) *Management of Cleft Lip and Palate,* 125–38, London: Whurr Publishers Ltd.

Hall, D. M. B. (1996) (ed.) *Health for all children,* 3rd edn. Oxford: Oxford University Press.

Hamrouge, S. (1998) 'An audit of personal logs 1997', *International Journal of Language and Communication Disorders* 33, supplement 50–2.

Harding, A. and Grunwell, P. (1996) 'Cleft Palate speech characteristics: a literature review', *European Journal of Disorders of Communication* 31, 331–58.

Harding, A. and Grunwell, P. (1998) 'Active versus passive cleft-type speech characteristics: implications for surgery and therapy', *International Journal of Language and Communication Disorders* 33, 329–52.

Harding, A., Harland, K. and Razzell R. (1997) *Cleft Audit Protocol for Speech.* British Craniofacial Society.

Hargie, O., Saunders, C. and Dickson, D. (1994) *Social Skills in Interpersonal Communication,* 3rd edn. London: Routledge.

Harris, M. (2000) 'Social Interaction and early language development in deaf children', *Deafness and Education International* 2(1).

Hatcher, P. (1994) *Sound Linkage.* London: Whurr Publishers.

Hatcher, P. J. and Hulme, C. (1999) 'Phonemes, rhymes, and intelligence as predictors of children's responsiveness to remedial reading instruction: Evidence from a longitudinal intervention study', *Journal of Experimental Child Psychology* 72, 130–53.

Hegde, M. N. and Davis, D. (1992) *Clinical Methods and Practicum in Speech–Language Pathology,* London: Chapman and Hall.

Heinze, B. A. and Johnson, K. L. (1985) *Easy Does it 1.* East Moline: Lingui Systems Inc.

Heinze, B. A. and Johnson, K. L. (1987) *Easy Does it 2.* East Moline: Lingui Systems Inc.

Helm, J. (1990) *Oral-Motor Feeding Rating Scale.* London: The Psychological Corporation.

Hoddell, S. (1995) 'Building confidence and communication', *CSLT Bulletin* 514, 13–15.

Hogben, J. (1997) 'How does a visual transient deficit affect reading?', in Hulme, C. and Snowling, M. (eds) *Dyslexia: Biology, Cognition and Intervention,* 59–71. London: Whurr Publishers Ltd.

Howlin, P., Baron-Cohen, S. and Hadwin, J. (1999) *Teaching Children with Autism to Mind-Read.* Chichester: John Wiley and Sons Ltd.

Iacono, T. A., Chan, J. B. and Waring, R. E. (1998) 'Efficacy of a parent-implemented early language intervention based on collaborative consultation', *International Journal of Language and Communication Disorders* 33, 281–304.

Idol, L. and West, J. F. (1991) 'Educational collaboration: a catalyst for effective schooling', *Intervention in School and Clinic* 27, 70–8.

Ingham, J. and Riley, G. (1998) 'Guidelines for Documentation of Treatment Efficacy for Young Children who Stutter', *Journal of Speech, Language and Hearing Research* 41, 753–770.

Jeffers, S. (1987) *Feel the Fear and Do It Anyway.* London: Arrow Books.

Johnson, R. (1992) *Picture Communication Symbols – Book III.* Solona Beach CA: Mayer-Johnson.

Jones, S. Jolleff, N., McConachie, H and Wisbeach. A. (1990) 'A model for assessment of children for augmentative communication systems', *Child Language Teaching and Therapy* **6**, 305–21.

Kamhi, A. G. (1995) 'Childhood language' in Leahy, M. (ed.) *Disorders of Communication; the science of intervention.* 61–95. London: Whurr Publishers Ltd.

Kamhi, A.G. and Masterson, J. (1989) 'Language and cognition in mentally handicapped people: last rites for the difference delay controversy', in Beveridge, M., Conti-Ramsden, G. and Leudar, I. (eds) *Language and Communication in People with Learning Disabilities*, 83–111. London: Routledge.

Kanner, L. (1943) 'Autistic disturbances of affective contact', *Nervous Child* **2**, 217–50.

Kaplan, H., Balley, S. and Garretson, C. (1987) *Speech-Reading: A Way to Improve Understanding.* University of Gallaudet.

Katz, J. (1994) *Handbook of Clinical Audiology.* London: Williams & Wilkins.

Kelly, A. (1996) *Talkabout.* Bicester: Winslow Press.

Kelman E. and Schneider, C. (1994) 'Parent–Child interaction: an alternative to the management of children's language difficulties', *Child Language Teaching and Therapy* **10**, 81–95.

Kersner, M. and Wright, J. A. (1996) 'Collaboration between speech and language therapists and teachers working with children with severe learning disabilities (SLD): implications for professional development', *British Journal of Learning Disabilities* **24**(1), 33–7.

Khattack, L., Kimber, C., Kiely, E., and Spitz, L. (1998) 'Percutaneous endoscopic gastrostomy in paediatric practice: complications and outcome', *Journal of Pediatric Surgery* **33**(1), 67–72.

Kiernan, C. and Reid, B. (1987) *Pre-verbal Communication Schedule.* Windsor: NFER-Nelson.

Kirkham, F., Edwards, M. and Lees, J. (1990) *Recovery of cognitive and language skills after prolonged coma in childhood.* Paper presented at the IV International Aphasia Rehabilitation Congress, 4–6 September 1990, Edinburgh.

Klein, M. and Delaney, T. (1994) *Feeding and Nutrition for the Child with Special Needs: Handouts for Parents.* London: The Psychological Corporation.

Knowles, W. and Masidlover, M. (1982) *The Derbyshire Language Scheme.* Ripley: Derbyshire Education Office.

Kolb, D. (1984) *Experiential Learning.* Englewood Cliffs, NJ: Prentice Hall.

Kubler-Ross, E. (1997) *On Death and Dying.* London: Collier Books.

Kyle, J. (1987) *Sign and Symbol in School.* Avon: Multilingual Matters.

Lacey, P. and Lomas, J. (1993) *Support Services and the Curriculum.* London: David Fulton Publishers.

Lachenmeyer, J. (1995) 'Behaviour aspects of feeding disorders', in Rosenthal, S. *et al.*, (eds) *Dysphagia and the Child with Developmental Disabilities*, 143–52. London: Singular Publishing Ltd.

Ladefoged, P. (1974) *Elements of Acoustic Phonetics.* University of Chicago.

Lancaster, G. and Pope, L. (1989) *Working with Children's Phonology.* Bicester: Winslow Press.

Lane, H. (1994) 'The cochlear implant controversy', *Laserbeam* **23**, Winter, 27–33.

Lane, H. (1995) 'Constructions of deafness', *Disability and Society* **10**(2), 171–90.

Launonen, K. (1996) 'Enhancing communication skills of children with Down's syndrome: Early use of manual signs', in von Tetzchner, S. and Jensen, M.H. (eds) *Augmentative and Alternative Communication: European Perspectives*, 213–30. London: Whurr Publishers Ltd.

Launonen, K. (1998) 'Early manual sign intervention: Eight year follow-up of children with Down's syndrome', *ISAAC Dublin 1998: UCD, Dublin, Ireland*, Conference Proceedings, 371–2. Dublin: Ashfield Publications.

Law, J. (1999) 'Does Speech and Language Therapy Work?', *RCSLT Bulletin* **571**, 14–15.

Law, J., Boyle, J., Harris, F., Harkness, A. and Nye, C. (1998) 'Screening for speech and language delay: a systematic review of the literature', *Health Technology Assessment* **2**(9).

Law, J., Lindsay, G., Peacey, N., Gascoigne, M., Soloff N., Radford, J. and Band, S. (2000) *Provision for Children with Speech and Language Difficulties in England and Wales: Facilitating communication between education and health.* London: The Stationery Office.

Lea, J. (1970) *The colour pattern scheme: a method of remedial language teaching.* Oxted, Surrey: Moor House School.

Le Blanc, E. M.(1996) 'Fundamental Principles in the Speech Management of Cleft Lip and Palate', in *Cleft Lip and Palate with an introduction to other craniofacial anomalies,* Perspectives in Management, 75-84. London: Singular Publishing Ltd.

Lees, J. (1993a) *Children with Acquired Aphasias.* London: Whurr Publishers Ltd.

Lees, J. (1993b)'Differentiating language disorder subtypes in acquired childhood aphasia', *Aphasiology* **7**, 481–8.

Lees, J. (1993c) 'Assessment of Receptive Language', in Beech, J. R., Harding, L. M., Hilton-Jones, D. (eds) *Assessment in Speech and Language Therapy.* London: Routledge.

Lees, J. (1997) 'Long-term effects of acquired language disorders in childhood', *Pediatric Rehabilitation* **1**, 45–9.

Lees, J. and Urwin, S. (1997) *Children with Language Disorders,* 2nd edn. London: Whurr Publishers Ltd.

Lees, M. (2001) 'Genetics of cleft lip and palate', in Grunwell, P., Sell, D. and Watson, A. C. H. (eds) *Management of Cleft Lip and Palate,* 87–104. London: Whurr Publishers Ltd.

Leinonen, E. and Kerbel, D. (1999) 'Relevance theory and pragmatic impairment', *International Journal of Language and Communication Disorders* **34** (4), 367–90.

Leinonen, E., Letts, C. and Smith, B. R. (2000) *Children's Pragmatic Communication Difficulties.* London: Whurr Publishers Ltd.

Le May, M. (1999) 'Six Tips for Success', *RCSLT Bulletin* **564**.

Leonard, L. B. (1998) *Children with Specific Language Disorders.* London: MIT Press.

Lennox, N. and Watkins, K. (1998) 'Teaching and learning together', *RCSLT Bulletin* **551**, 13–15.

Le Provost, P. (1993) 'The use of signing to encourage first words', in Buckley, S., Emslie, M., Haslegrave, G. and Le Provost, P. (eds) *The development of language and reading skills in children with Down's syndrome.* Portsmouth: University of Portsmouth Press.

Lewis, V. and Boucher, J. (1997) *Test of Pretend Play (ToPP).* London: The Psychological Corporation.

Levitt, S. (1995) *Treatment of Cerebral Palsy and Motor Delay,* 3rd edn. Oxford: Blackwell Science.

Light, J. (1989) 'Toward a definition of communicative competence for individuals using augmentative and alternative communication systems', *Augmentative and Alternative Communication* **5**, 137–44.

Light, J., Collier, B. and Parnes, P. (1985a) 'Communicative interaction between young nonspeaking physically disabled children and their primary caregivers: Part I – discourse patterns', *Augmentative and Alternative Communication* **1**, 74–83.

Light, J., Collier, B. and Parnes, P. (1985b) 'Communicative interaction between young nonspeaking physically disabled children and their primary caregivers: Part II – communicative function', *Augmentative and Alternative Communication* **1**, 98–107.

Light, J., Collier, B. and Parnes, P. (1985c) 'Communicative interaction between young nonspeaking physically disabled children and their primary caregivers: Part III – modes of communication', *Augmentative and Alternative Communication* **1**, 125–33.

Lincoln, M. and Harrison, E. (1999) 'The Lidcombe Program', in Onslow, M. and Packman, A. (eds) *The Handbook of Early Stuttering Intervention*, 103–17. London: Singular Publishing Ltd.

Linguistic Minorities Project (1985) *The Other Languages of England*. London: Routledge and Kegan Paul.

Locke, A. and Beech, M. (1991) *Teaching Talking: a screening and intervention programme for children with speech and language difficulties*. Windsor: NFER-Nelson.

Logemann, J. (1983) *Evaluation and Treatment of Swallowing Disorders*. London: College Hill Press.

Logemann, J. (1986) *Manual for the Videofluorographic Study of Swallowing*, 2nd edn. Austin, Tex: PRO-ED.

Lund, N. and Duchan, J. (1993) *Assessing Children's Language in Naturalistic Contexts*, 3rd edn. Engelwood Cliffs, NJ: Prentice-Hall.

Luscombe, M. and Shaw, L. (1996) 'Agreeing priorities for a school service', *RCSLT Bulletin* **536**, 8–9.

Lynas, W. (1994) *Communication Options in the Education of Deaf Children*. London: Whurr Publishers Ltd.

McAnally, P. L., Rose, S. and Quigley, S. P. (1987), *Language Learning Practices with Deaf Children*. Boston: College Hill Press.

McCartney, E. (1999a) 'Barriers to collaboration: an analysis of systemic barriers to collaboration between teachers and speech and language therapists', *International Journal of Language and Communication Disorders* **34**, 431–40.

McCartney, E. (1999b) *Speech/Language Therapists and Teachers working Together: A systems based approach to collaboration*, London: Whurr Publishers Ltd.

McConachie, H. R. and Ciccognani, A. (1995) 'What's in the box?' Assessing physically disabled children's communication skills', *Child Language Teaching and Therapy* **11**, 253–63.

McConachie, H. R., Clarke, M. T., Wood, P., Price, K. and Grove, N. (1998) *Evaluation of speech and language therapy for children using communication aids*, report to the NHS Executive Programme for People with Physical and Complex Needs.

McCormick, B., Archbold, S. and Sheppard, S. (eds) (1994) *Cochlear Implants for Young Children*. London: Whurr Publishers Ltd.

McNaughton, S. (1985) *Communicating with Blissymbols*. Ontario: The Blissymbols Communication Institute.

McTear, M. F. and Conti-Ramsden, G. (1992) *Pragmatic Disability in Children*. London: Whurr Publishers Ltd.

McWilliams, B. J., Morris, H. L. and Shelton, R. L. (1990) *Cleft Palate Speech*. San Diego, C.V. Mosby Company.

Makin, T. (1995) 'The social model of disability', *Counselling: The Journal of the BAC* **6**, 274.

Martin, D. and Miller, C. (1996) *Speech and Language Difficulties in the Classroom*. London: David Fulton Publishers.

Martinsen, H. and von Tetzchner, S. (1996) 'Situating augmentative and alternative communication intervention', in von Tetzchner, S. and Hygum Jensen, M. (eds) *Augmentative and Alternative Communication: European perspectives*, 37–48. London: Whurr Publishers Ltd.

Matthews, S., Williams R. and Pring, T. (1997) 'Parent–child interaction therapy and dysfluency: a single case study', *European Journal of Disorders of Communication* **32**(3), 346–57.

Meisel, J. M. (ed.) (1990) *Two First Languages*. Dordrecht: Foris Publications.

Metaphon Clinical Forum (1995) *Clinical linguistics and phonetics* **9**(1), 1–58.

Meyers Fosnot, S. and Woodford, L. L. (1992) *The Fluency Development System for Young Children*. Buffalo: United Educational Services.

Miller, C. (1991) 'The needs of teachers with children with speech and language disorders', *Child Language Teaching and Therapy* **7**(2), 179–91.

Miller, C. and Roux, J. (1997) 'Working with 11–16 year old pupils with language and communication difficulties in the mainstream school', *Child Language Teaching and Therapy* **13**(3).

Miller, N. (ed.) (1988) *Bilingualism and Language Disability*. London: Croom Helm.

Milloy, N. (1991) *Breakdown of Speech*. London: Chapman and Hall.

Milloy, N. and Morgan-Barry, R. (1990) 'Developmental neurological disorders', in Grunwell, P. (ed.) *Developmental Speech Disorders*. London: Churchill Livingstone.

Mogford-Bevan, K. and Sadler, J. (1993) *Child Language Disability: Volume III*. Clevedon: Multilingual Matters.

Moon-Meyer, S. (1998) *Survival Guide for the Beginning Speech–Language Clinician*. Gaithersburg, Maryland: Aspen Publishers.

Moorey, M. and Mahon, M. (1996) 'Recognising Hearing Problems', in Kersner, M. and Wright, J. A. (eds) *Managing Communication Problems in Young Children*. London: David Fulton Publishers.

Morgan-Barry, R. (1989) *The Auditory Discrimination Test*. Windsor: NFER-Nelson.

Morris, S. and Klein, M. (1987) *Pre-Feeding Skills*. Tuscon, Arizona: Therapy Skill Builders.

Mueller, H. (1997) 'Feeding', in Finnie, N. *Handling the Young Child with Cerebral Palsy at Home*, 3rd edn. 209–21. Oxford: Butterworth-Heinemann.

Murray, S. and O'Neill, J. (2000) 'Four assistants and an NVQ', *RCLST Bulletin* **573**, 11–12.

Muter, V., Hulme, C., Snowling, M. and Taylor, S. (1998) 'Segmentation, not rhyming, predicts early progress in learning to read', *Journal of Experimental Child Psychology* **71**, 3–27.

Muter, V., Hulme, C. and Snowling, M. (1997) *Phonological Abilities Test (PAT)*. London: The Psychological Corporation.

Nation, K. and Snowling, M. (1997) 'Assessing reading difficulties: the validity and utility of current measures of reading skill', *British Journal of Educational Psychology* **67**, 359–70.

National Joint Committee on Learning Disability (1991) 'Learning disabilities: issues on definition', *ASHA* **35**, 18–20.

Nelson, K. E., Camarata, S., Welsh, J., Butkovsky, L. and Camarata, M. (1996) 'Effects of imitative and conversational recasting treatment on the acquisition of grammar in children with SLI and younger language-normal children', *Journal of Speech, Language and Hearing Research* **39**, 850–59.

New, E. (1998) 'An effective model for a speech and language therapy service in mainstream schools', *International Journal of Language and Communication Disorders* **33** (Supplement), 602–7

Newton, A. and Thompson, M (1982) *The Aston Index*. Wisbech, Cambridgeshire: LDA.

Nicolson, R. and Fawcett, A. (1990) 'Automaticity: A new framework for dyslexia research?', *Cognition* **30**, 159–82.

Nicolson, R. and Fawcett, N. (1996) *The Dyslexia Early Screening Test (DES)*. London: The Psychological Corporation.

North, C. and Parker, M. (1993) *Phonological Awareness Assessment*. Althorne Essex.

Northern, J. and Downs, M. (1991) *Hearing in Children*. London: Williams & Wilkins.

Norwich, B. (1997) *A trend towards inclusion Statistics on Special School Placements and Pupils with Statements in Ordinary Schools in England 1992–1996*. Centre for the Study of Inclusive Education.

Oliver, M. (1990) *The Politics of Disablement*. London: Macmillan.

Oliver, M. (1996) *Understanding Disability: From Theory to Practice*. London: Macmillan.

Olswang, L. B., Rodriguez, B. Timler, G. (1998) 'Recommending intervention for toddlers with specific language learning difficulties: We may not have all the answers but we know a lot', *American Journal of Speech–Language Pathology* **7**, 23–32.

Onslow, M., O'Brien, S. and Harrison, E. (1997) 'Clinical Forum: The Lidcombe Programme', *European Journal of Disorders of Communication* **32**, 231–66.

Owens, R. (1995) *Language Disorders: a functional approach to assessment and intervention*, 2nd edn. London: Allyn and Bacon.

Ozanne, A. (1995) 'The search for developmental verbal dyspraxia', in Dodd, B. (ed.) *Differential Diagnosis and Treatment of Children with Speech Disorder*. London: Whurr Publishers Ltd.

Packman, A. and Onslow, M. (1999) 'Issues in the treatment of early stuttering'. in Onslow, M. and Packman, A. (eds) *The Handbook of Early Stuttering Intervention,* 1–16. London: Singular Publishing Ltd.

PACT clinical forum (1999) *International Journal of Language and Communication Disorders* **34**(1), 35–83.

Park, K. (1995) 'Using objects of reference: A review of the literature' *European Journal of Special Needs Education* **10**, 40–46.

Parker, A. (1999) *PETAL: Phonological Evaluation and Transcription of Audio-Visual Language*. Bicester: Winslow Press.

Parker, A. and Cummins, K. (1998) 'Group placements in Under Fives Centres', *Speech and Language Therapy in Practice*, 13–15.

Parker, A. and Kersner, M. (1997) 'How you look is what you find: observing the phonology of deaf speakers', *Journal of Clinical Speech and Language Studies*, 1–15.

Parker, A. and Kersner, M. (1998) 'New approaches to learning on clinical placement', *International Journal of Language and Communication Disorders* **33** (Supplement), 255–60.

Parker, A. and Wirz, S. (1986) 'Towards a Better Understanding', *Speech Therapy in Practice*.

Passey, J. (1990a) *Cued Articulation*. Ponteland, Northumberland: STASS Publications.

Passey, J. (1990b) *Cued Vowels*. Ponteland, Northumberland: STASS Publications.

Pattanayak, D. P. (1991) 'Foreword', in Alladina, S. and Edwards, V. (eds) *Multilingualism in the British Isles*. London: Longman.

Pennington, L. and McConachie, H. R. (1999) 'Mother-child interaction revisited: Communication with severely physically disabled children', *International Journal of Language and Communication Disorders* **34**, 391–416.

Peterson, S. L., Bondy, A. S., Vincent, V. and Finnegan, C. S. (1995) 'Effects of altering communicative input for students with autism and no speech: two case studies', *Augmentative and Alternative Communication* **11**, 93–100.

Pickersgill, M. and Gregory, S. (1998) *Sign Bilingualism: A Model*. LASER.

Pickstone, C. (1997) 'Weighting not waiting', *Human Communication* Febuary/March 23.

Pindzola, R., (1987) *Stuttering Intervention Program.* Tulsa: Modern Education Corporation.

Pitcher, J. and Crandall, M. (1997) 'Pediatric Feeding Assessment', in Leonard, R. and Kendall, K. (eds) *Dysphagia Assessment and Treatment Planning: a team approach.* London: Singular Publishing Ltd.

Plomin, R. and Dale, P. S. (2000) 'Genetics and Early Language Development: A UK study of twins', in Bishop, D. V. M and Leonard, L. B. (eds) *Speech and Language Impairments in Children.* Hove: Psychology Press Ltd.

Popple, J. and Wellington, W. (2001) ' Working together: The psycholinguistic approach within a school setting', in Stackhouse J. and Wells, B. (eds) *Speech and Literacy difficulties 2: Identification and intervention.* London: Whurr Publishers Ltd.

Popple, J. and Wellington, W. (1996) 'Collaborative working within a psycholinguistic framework', *Child Language Teaching and Therapy* **12**(1), 60–70.

Porch, B. (1972). *The Porch Index of Communicative Ability in Children.* Palo Alto: Consulting Psychologists Press.

Powell, G. (1999) 'Current research finding to support the use of signs with adults and children who have intellectual and communication difficulties'. Makaton Vocabulary Development Project.

Prochaska, J. and Di Clemente, C. (1986) 'Towards a comprehensive model of change', in Miller, W. and Heather, N. (eds) *Treating Addictive Behaviours.* New York: Plenum Press.

Pueschel, S. M. and Sustrova, M. (1996) 'Visual and auditory perception in children with Down's syndrome', in Rondal, J., Perera, J., Nadel, L. and Comblain, A. (eds) *Down's syndrome: psychological, psychobiological and socio-educational perspective,* 53–64. London: Whurr Publishers Ltd.

Pugach, M. C. and Johnson, L. J. (1995) *Collaborative practitioners collaborative schools.* Colorado: Love Publishing Company.

Qualifications and Curriculum Authority (1998) *The National Framework for Baseline Assessment.* London: QCA Publications.

Qualifications and Curriculum Authority (1999) *The Revised National Curriculum for 2000: What has changed?* London: QCA Publications.

Rapin, I. and Allen, D. (1983) 'Developmental language disorders: Nosologic considerations', in Kirk, U. (ed.) *Neuropsychology of language, reading and spelling.* New York: Academic Press.

Raven, J. C. (1986) *Coloured Progressive Matrices.* London: H. K. Lewis.

RCSLT (1996) *Communicating Quality 2,* 2nd edn. London: RCSLT.

RCSLT (1998) *Clinical Guidelines by Consensus for Speech and Language Therapists.* London: RCSLT.

Reid, J., Millar, S., Tait, L., Donaldson, M. L., Dean, E. C., Thomas, G. O. B. and Grieve, R. (1996) *The Role of Speech and Language Therapists in the Education of Pupils with Special Educational Needs.* Edinburgh: Centre for Research in Child Development

Remmington, B. and Clarke, S. (1998) *Alternative and augmentative systems of communication for children with Down's Syndrome.* http//www.soton.ac.uk/rondal.html

Renfrew, C. (1988) *The Word Finding Vocabulary Test.* Bicester: Winslow.

Renfrew, C. (1997) *The Action Picture Test.* Bicester: Winslow.

Rescorla, L. (1989) 'The Language development survey: A screening tool for delayed language in Toddlers', *Journal of Speech and Hearing Disorders* **54**(4), 587–99.

Richards, K. (1999) 'Understanding and Ownership', *Speech and Language Therapy in Practice* Spring, 26.

Richards, P. (1993) 'Helping Students Develop Insights and Skills in Management', in Stengelhofen, J. (1993) *Teaching students in clinical settings*, Therapy in Practice 37. London: Chapman and Hall.

Riley, G. D. (1981) *Stuttering Prediction Instrument for Young Children*. Austin: PRO-ED.

Rinaldi, W. (1992) *Social Use of Language Programme*. Windsor: NFER-Nelson.

Rinaldi, W. (1996) *Understanding Ambiguity*. Windsor: NFER-Nelson.

Rivera, C. (1983) *An Ethnographic/Sociolinguistic, Approach to Language Proficiency Assessment*. Clevedon: Multilingual Matters.

Roberts, A. and Gibbs, D. (1989) 'The bilingual child with special education needs,' in Duncan, D. M. (ed.) *Working with Bilingual Language Disability*. London: Chapman and Hall.

Robinson, R. J. (1991) 'Causes and associations of severe and persistent specific speech and language disorders in children', *Developmental Medicine and Child Neurology* **33**, 943–62.

Rogers, C. (1951) *Client-Centered Therapy*. Boston: Houghton Mifflin Company

Rogers-Adkinson, D. and Griffith, P. L. (1999) *Communication Disorders and Children with Psychiatric and Behavioural Disorders*. London: Singular Publishing Ltd.

Romaine, S. (1995) *Bilingualism*, 2nd edn. Oxford: Blackwell.

Rondal, J. and Edwards, S. (1997) *Language in Mental Retardation*. London: Whurr Publishers Ltd.

Rose, F. D. and Johnson, D. A. (1996) *Brain Injury and After: Towards Improved Outcome*. London: Wiley.

Rosenthal, S., Sheppard, J. and Lotze, M. (1995) *Dysphagia and the Child with Developmental Disabilities*. London: Singular Publishing Ltd.

Roulstone, S. (1997) 'What's driving you? A template which underpins the assessment of preschool children by speech and language therapists', *European Journal of Disorders of Communication* **32**(3), 299–315.

Roux, J, (1996) 'Working collaboratively with teachers: supporting the newly qualified speech and language therapist in a mainstream school', *Child Language Teaching and Therapy* **12**(1) 48–59.

Rustin, L., Botterill, W. and Kelman, E. (1996) *Assessment and Therapy for Young Dysfluent Children*. London: Whurr Publishers Ltd.

Rustin, L., Cook, F. and Spence, R. (1995) *The Management of Stuttering in Adolescence: A Communication Skills Approach*. London: Whurr Publishers Ltd.

Rustin, L. and Kuhr, A. (1999) *Social Skills and the Speech Impaired*, 2nd edn. London: Whurr Publishers Ltd.

Schelletter, C. and Sinka, I. (1998) 'Morpho-syntactic development in bilingual children', *International Journal of Bilingualism* **2**, 301–26.

Scherer, N. J. and D'Antonio, L. L. (1995) 'Parent questionnaire for screening early language development in children with cleft palate'. *Cleft Palate-Craniofacial*.

Schon, D. A. (1987) *Educating the Reflective Practitioner*. San Fransisco: Jossey-Bass.

Seedhouse, D. (1988) *Ethics: The Heart of Health Care*. Chichester: John Wiley and Sons.

Seliger, H. W. and Vago, R. M. (eds) (1991) *First Language Attrition*. Cambridge: Cambridge University Press.

Sell, D. and Grunwell, P. (2001) 'Speech assessment and therapy', in Grunwell, P., Sell, D. and Watson, A. C. H. (eds) *Management of Cleft Lip and Palate,* 231–62. London: Whurr Publishers Ltd.

Sell, D., Harding, A. and Grunwell, P. (1999) 'Revised GOS.SP.ASS (98): Speech assessment for children with cleft palate and/or velopharyngeal dysfunction', *International Journal of Disorders of Communication* **34**(1), 17–33.

Sell, D. and Ma, L. (1996) 'A model of practice for the management of velopharyngeal dysfunction', *British Journal of Oral and Maxillofacial Surgery* **34**, 357–63.

Semel, E., Wiig, E. H. and Secord, W. (2000) *Clinical Evaluation of Language Fundamentals – 3rd Edition^UK (CELF)*. London: The Psychological Corporation.

Sheridan, J. (1999) 'Children need a Sure Start', *RCSLT Bulletin*.

Shields, J., Varley, R., Broks, P. and Simpson, A. (1996) 'Social cognition in developmental language disorders and high-level autism', *Developmental Medicine and Child Neurology* **38,** 487–95.

Simon, E. W., Rappaport, D. A., Papka, M., and Woodruffpak, D. S. (1995) 'Fragile X and Down's syndrome – are there syndrome specific cognitive profiles at low IQ scores?', *Journal of Intellectual Disability Research* **39**, 326–30.

Simonoff, E., Bolton, P., and Rutter, M. (1996) 'Mental retardation: genetic findings, clinical implications and research agenda', *Journal of Child Psychology and Psychiatry* **37**, 259–80.

Simmons, K. (1998) 'Rights at Risk', *British Journal of Special Education* **25**, 9–12.

Singleton, C., Thomas, K., Leedale, R. and Beverley, E (1995) *Cognitive Profiling System (CoPS)*. Yorks: Lucid Research.

Sisson, L. and Barrett, R. (1984) 'An alternative treatments comparison of oral and total communication training with minimally verbal retarded children', *Journal of Applied Behaviour Analysis* **17**, 559–66.

Sivyer, S. (1999) 'Listening and quietness and making new friends', *RCSLT Bulletin* **570**, 13–15.

Smith, L. (1998) 'Predicitng communicative competence at 2 and 3 years from pragmatic skills at 10 months', *International Journal of Language and Communication Disorders* **33**(2) 127–48.

Smith, A. and Inder, P. (1993) 'Social interaction in same and cross gender pre-school peer groups: A participant observation study', *Educational Psychology* **13**, 29–42.

Snow, C. (1994) 'Beginning from Baby Talk: twenty years of research on input in interaction', in Gallaway, C. and Richards, B. (eds) *Input and Interaction in Language Acquisition*. Cambridge: Cambridge University Press.

Snowling, M. (1998) 'Reading development and its difficulties' *Educational and Child Psychology* **15**(2), 44–58.

Snowling, M. and Stackhouse, J. (1996) (eds) *Dyslexia Speech and Language: A Practitioner's Handbook*. London: Whurr Publishers Ltd.

Snowling, M., Stothard, S. and McClean, J. (1996) *Graded Nonword Reading Test*. Thames Valley Test Company.

Sokolov, J. and Snow, C. (1994) 'The changing role of negative evidence in theories of language development', in Gallaway, C. and Richards, B. (eds) *Input and Interaction in Language Acquisition*. Cambridge: Cambridge University Press

Sondheimer, J. M. and Morris, B. A. (1979) 'Gastroesophageal reflux among severely retarded children', *Journal of Paediatrics* **94**, 710–14.

Sperber, D. and Wilson, D. (1995) *Relevance: Communication and Cognition*, 2nd edn. Oxford: Blackwell.

Stackhouse, J. and Wells, B. (1997) *Children's Speech and Literacy Problems: A Psycholinguistic Framework*. London: Whurr Publishers Ltd.

Stackhouse, J. and Wells, B. (2001) (eds) *Children's speech and literacy difficulties 2: identification and intervention*. London: Whurr Publishers Ltd.

Stackhouse, J., Nathan, L. and Goulandris, N. (1999) 'Speech processing, language and emerging literacy skills in 4 year old children with specific speech difficulties', *Journal of Clinical Speech and Language Studies*, 11–14.

Stanovich, K. E. (1988) 'Explaining the differences between the dyslexic and the garden variety poor reader: the phonological-core variable-difference model', *Journal of Learning Disabilities* **21**, 590–612.

Starkweather, C. W. (1997) 'Therapy for younger children', in Curlee, R. and Siegal, G. (eds) *Nature and Treatment of Stuttering: New Directions*, 2nd edn. 257–79. Boston: Allyn & Bacon.

Starkweather, C. W., and Gottwald, S. R. (1990) 'The demands and capacities model: II. Clinical implications', *Journal of Fluency Disorders* **15**, 143–57.

Stengelhofen, J. (1993) *Teaching students in clinical settings*, Therapy in Practice 37. London: Chapman and Hall.

Stewart, S. (1998) 'The Place of Portfolios within Continuing Professional Development', *British Journal of Therapy and Rehabilitation* **5**, 266–9.

Stewart, T. and Turnbull, J. (1995) *Working with Dysfluent Children*. Bicester: Winslow Press.

Stone, E. and Priestly, M. (1996) 'Parasites, pawns and partners: disability research and the role of non-disabled researchers', *British Journal of Sociology* **47**(4) 609–716.

Stothard, S. E., Snowling, M. J., Bishop, D. V. M., Chipchase, B. B. and Kaplan, C. A. (1998) 'Language impaired preschoolers: a follow up into adolescence', *Journal of Speech, Language and Hearing Research* **41,** 407–18.

Sturmey, P. and Crisp, A. G. (1986) 'Portage guide to early education: a review of research', *Educational Psychology* **6**, 139–57.

Tait, M. E., Nikolopoulos T. P., Lutman, M. E., Wilson, D. and Wells, P. (2001) 'Video analysis of preverbal communication behaviours: use and reliability', *Deafness and Education International* **3**(1). London: Whurr Publishers Ltd.

Thomas, J. A. and Graham, J. M. (1997) 'Chromosome 22q11 deletion syndrome: an update and review for the primary paediatrician', *Clinical Paediatrics*.

Tomblin, J. B. and Buckwalter, P. (1994) 'Studies of genetics of specific language impairment', in Watkins, R. and Rice, M. (eds) *Specific language impairments in children*. Baltimore: Paul H. Brookes.

Topics in Language Disorders (1993) **13**(2).

Topping, C., Gascoigne, M. and Cook, M. (1998) 'Excellence for all children – a redefinition of the role of the speech and language therapist', *International Journal of Language and Communication Disorders* **33** (Supplement), 608–13.

Troia, G. A. (1999) 'Phonological awareness intervention research: A critical review of the experimental methodology', *Reading Research Quarterly* **34**(1), 28–52.

Tuchman, D. and Walter, R. (1994) *Disorders of Feeding and Swallowing in Infants and Children*. London: Singular Publishing Ltd.

Tuckman, B. (1965) 'Developmental sequence in small groups', *Psychological Bulletin* **63**, 384–99.

Turnbull, J. and Stewart, T. (1996) *Helping Children Cope with Stammering*. London: Sheldon Press.

UNESCO (1994) *The Salamanca Statement and Framework For Action on Special Needs Education*. UNESCO.

Urwin, S. (1992) 'Working with groups of children in the community clinic', in Fawcus, M. (ed.) *Group Encounters in Speech and Language Therapy*. Kibworth: Far Communications Ltd.

van der Gaag, A., McCartan, P., McDade, A., Reid, D. and Roulstone, S. (1999) *The Early Communication Audit Manual*. London: RCSLT.

Van der Klift, E. and Kunc, N. (1994) 'Hell-bent on helping: benevolence, friendship and the politics of help', in Thousand, J., Villa, R. and Nevin, A. (eds) *Creativity and Collaborative Learning: a Practical Guide to Empowering Students and Teachers*. Baltimore: Brooks.

Van Gurp, S. (2001) 'Self-concept of Deaf Secondary School Students in Different Educational Settings', *Journal of Deaf Studies and Deaf Education* 6(1), 54–69.

Van Riper, C. (1973) *The Treatment of Stuttering*. Engelwood Cliffs, NJ: Prentice-Hall.

Vance, M. (1991) 'Educational and therapeutic approaches used with a child with acquired aphasia with convulsive disorder (Landau-Kleffner Syndrome)', *Child Language Teaching and Therapy* 7, 41–60.

Vance, M. (1996) 'Assessing speech processing skills', in Snowling, M. and Stackhouse, J. (eds) *Dyslexia Speech and Language: A Practitioner's Handbook*, 45–61. London: Whurr Publishers Ltd.

Vance, M. (1997) 'Christopher Lumpship: developing phonological representations in a child with an auditory processing deficit', in Chiat, S., Law, J. and Marshall, J. (eds) *Language Disorders in Children and Adults*. London: Whurr Publishers Ltd.

Vlachou, A. (1997) *Struggles for Inclusive Education*. Buckingham: Open University Press.

Volterra, V. and Taeschner, T. (1978) 'The acquisition and development of language by bilingual children', *Journal of Child Language* 5, 311–26.

Von Tetchner, S., Grove, N., Loncke, F., Barnett, S., Woll, B. and Clibbens, J. (1996) 'Preliminaries to a comprehensive model of augmentative and alternative communication', in Von Tetchner, S. and Jensen, M.H. (eds) *Augmentative and Alternative Communication: European Perspectives*. London: Whurr Publishers Ltd.

Vygotsky, L. S. (1978). *Mind and Society*. Cambridge: Harvard University Press.

Walker, M., Parson, P., Cousins, S., Carpenter, B. and Park, K. (1985) *Symbols for Makaton*. Black Hill: Earo, The Resource Centre.

Ward, S. (1992) 'The predictive validity and accuracy of a screening test for language delay and auditory perceptual disorder', *European Journal of Disorders of Communication* 27, 55–72.

Warren, D. W., Dalston, R., Trier, W. C. and Holder, M. B., (1985) 'A Pressure Flow technique for quantifying temporal patterns of palatopharyngeal closure', *Cleft Palate Journal* 22, 11–19.

Watson, A. C. H., Sell, D. A. and Grunwell, P. (eds) (2001) *Management of Cleft Lip and Palate*. London: Whurr Publishers Ltd.

Watson, S. (1990) 'Pre-school Project: an evaluation of group therapy', *Child Language Teaching and Therapy* 6(3), 270–8.

Waugh, M. G. (1991) *Winning in Speech*. Vero Beach, Florida: The Speech Bin, Inc.

Weiss, C., Gordon, M. and Lillywhite, H. (1987) *Clinical Management of Articulatory and Phonological Disorders*. Baltimore: Williams and Wilkins.

Weitz, C. R., Dexter, M. E., and Moore, J. R. (1997) 'AAC and children with developmental disabilities', in Glennen, S. L. and DeCoste D. C. (eds) *Handbook of Augmentative and Alternative Communication*. San Diego: Singular Publishing Ltd.

Whitehead, S. (1999) 'The First Post : Are Students Ready?', *RCSLT Bulletin*, 14–16.

Whitehurst, G. J. and Fischel, J. E. (1994) 'Practitioner review: Early developmental language delay:

What, if anything, should the clinician do about it?', *Journal of Child Psychology and Psychiatry* **35**(4), 613–48.

Whurr, R. and Evans, S. (1995*) The Children's Aphasia Screening Test*, 2nd edn. London: Whurr Publishers Ltd.

Wiig, E. H., Secord, W. and Semel E. (2000) *CELF-Preschool* [UK]. London: The Psychological Corporation.

Wills, C. (1999) 'Learning to be a parent', *RCSLT Bulletin* 13–14.

Winstock, A. (1994) *The Practical Management of Eating and Drinking Difficulties in Children*. Bicester: Winslow Press.

Winter, R. and Baraitser, M. (1998) *London Dismorphology Database*. Oxford: Oxford University Press.

Wintgens, A. (1996) 'Links between emotional/behavioural problems and communication difficulties', in Kersner, M. and Wright, J. A (eds) *How To Manage Communication Problems In Young Children*, 2nd edn. London: David Fulton Publishers.

Wintgens, A. (2000) 'Child Psychiatry', in Kramer, S. and France, J. *Communication and Mental Health*. London: Jessica Kingsley.

Withers, P. (1993) 'Making children a priority', *CSLT Bulletin*,12–13

Witt P. D. and D'Antonio L. L. (1993) 'Velopharyngeal insufficiency and secondary palatal management. A new look at an old problem', *Clinics in Plastic Surgery* **20**(4), 707–21.

Wolf, L. and Glass, R. (1992) *Feeding and Swallowing Disorders in Infancy: assessment and management*. London: The Psychological Corporation.

Woll, B. (1998) 'Development of signed and spoken languages', in Gregory, S., Knight, P., McCracken, W., Powers, S. and Watson, L. (eds) *Issues in Deaf Education*. London: David Fulton Publishers.

Woll, B. and Herman, R. (1999) *BSL Pack*. Clevedon: Multilingual Matters.

Wong-Fillmore, L. (1991) 'When learning a second language means losing the first', *Early Childhood Research Quarterly* **6**, 323–46.

Wood, D., Wood, H., Griffiths, A. and Howarth, I. (1986) *Teaching and Talking to Deaf Children*. Chichester: Wiley.

Wood, J. (1998) 'Styles of interaction used by learning assistants: the effectiveness of Training', *International Journal of Language and Communication Disorders* **33** (Supplement), 614–19.

Wood, J., Wright, J. A. and Stackhouse, J. (2000) *Language and Literacy: Joining together. An Early Years training package*. Reading: British Dyslexia Association.

World Health Organisation (1980) *ICIDH – International Classification of Impairment, Disability and Handicap*. Geneva: WHO.

World Health Organisation (1993) *The ICD-10 classification for mental and behavioural disorders: Diagnostic criteria for research*. Geneva: WHO.

Wright, J. A. (1996) 'Teachers and therapists: the evolution of a partnership', *Child Language Teaching and Therapy* **12**(1), 3–17.

Wright, J. A. and Kersner, M. (1998) *Supporting children with communication problems: Sharing the workload*. London: David Fulton Publishers.

Yairi, E. and Ambrose, N. G. (1999) 'Early childhood stuttering I: Persistency and recovery rates', *Journal of Speech, Language, and Hearing Research* **42**, 1097–112.

Yoder, D. E. and Kent, R. D. (1988) *Decision making in speech-language pathology*. B. C. Decker Inc.

Young, C. (1993) 'Nutrition', in Arvedson, J. and Brodsky, L. (eds) *Pediatric Swallowing and Feeding – Assessment and Management*, 157–208. London: Whurr Publishers Ltd.

Videos

GOS.SP.ASS (1998) Training Videos are available from the Department of Medical Illustration, Great Ormond Street Hospital NHS Trust, Great Ormond Street WC1N 3JH.

These videos cover:

• Speech assessment profile for children with cleft palate and/or velopharyngeal dysfunction.
• Speech assessment profile for children with cleft palate and/or velopharyngeal dysfunction. Principles and techniques of speech therapy treatment.

Video of the SIG Bilingualism, *My Language is Yours: Bilingual Co-Workers in Speech Therapy* available from RCSLT.

Index